*Before All Memory Is Lost*

# THE AZRIELI SERIES OF HOLOCAUST SURVIVOR MEMOIRS: PUBLISHED TITLES

## ENGLISH TITLES

*Across the Rivers of Memory* by Felicia Carmelly
*Album of My Life* by Ann Szedlecki
*Alone in the Storm* by Leslie Vertes
*As the Lilacs Bloomed* by Anna Molnár Hegedűs
*Bits and Pieces* by Henia Reinhartz
*A Drastic Turn of Destiny* by Fred Mann
*E/96: Fate Undecided* by Paul-Henri Rips
*Fleeing from the Hunter* by Marian Domanski
*From Generation to Generation* by Agnes Tomasov
*Gatehouse to Hell* by Felix Opatowski
*Getting Out Alive* by Tommy Dick
*The Hidden Package* by Claire Baum
*Hope's Reprise* by David Newman
*If, By Miracle* by Michael Kutz
*If Home Is Not Here* by Max Bornstein
*If Only It Were Fiction* by Elsa Thon
*In Fragile Moments* by Zsuzsanna Fischer Spiro/ *The Last Time* by Eva Shainblum
*In Hiding* by Marguerite Élias Quddus
*Inside the Walls* by Eddie Klein
*Joy Runs Deeper* by Bronia and Joseph Beker
*Knocking on Every Door* by Anka Voticky
*Little Girl Lost* by Betty Rich
*Memories from the Abyss* by William Tannenzapf/ *But I Had a Happy Childhood*
   by Renate Krakauer
*My Heart Is At Ease* by Gerta Solan
*A Name Unbroken* by Michael Mason
*Never Far Apart* by Kitty Salsberg and Ellen Foster
*The Shadows Behind Me* by Willie Sterner
*Spring's End* by John Freund
*Stronger Together* by Ibolya Grossman and Andy Réti
*Suddenly the Shadow Fell* by Leslie Meisels with Eva Meisels
*Survival Kit* by Zuzana Sermer
*Tenuous Threads* by Judy Abrams/ *One of the Lucky Ones* by Eva Felsenburg Marx
*Traces of What Was* by Steve Rotschild
*Under the Yellow and Red Stars* by Alex Levin
*Vanished Boyhood* by George Stern
*The Violin* by Rachel Shtibel/ *A Child's Testimony* by Adam Shtibel
*W Hour* by Arthur Ney
*We Sang in Hushed Voices* by Helena Jockel
*The Weight of Freedom* by Nate Leipciger
*Where Courage Lives* by Muguette Myers

# Before All Memory Is Lost:
# Women's Voices from the Holocaust

EDITED BY MYRNA GOLDENBERG

THE AZRIELI FOUNDATION
www.azrielifoundation.org

Cover and book design by Mark Goldstein
Cover image courtesy of Yad Vashem
Endpaper maps by Martin Gilbert
Map on page xx–xxi by François Blanc

Irena Peritz's original diary image on page 8 appears courtesy of USHMM, with permission from the author. Translation of Irene Zoberman's memoir on pages 215–258 by Marek W. Stobnicki. Translation of Catherine Matyas's diary excerpts on pages 283–290 by Marietta Morry and Lynda Muir. Translation of Svetlana Kogan-Rabinovich's memoir on pages 453–475 by Irina Sadovina. Translation of Koine Schacter Rogel's memoir on pages 499–534 by R. and V. Shaffir.

LIBRARY AND ARCHIVES CANADA CATALOGUING IN PUBLICATION

Before all memory is lost : women's voices from the Holocaust / edited by Myrna Goldenberg.

(The Azrieli series of Holocaust survivor memoirs. Series VIII)
Includes bibliographical references and index.
ISBN 978-1-988065-11-3 (softcover)

1. Holocaust, Jewish (1939-1945) — Personal narratives. 2. Jewish women in the Holocaust. 3. Holocaust survivors. 4. Holocaust survivors — Canada — Biography. 5. Jewish women — Canada — Biography. 6. Jews — Canada — Biography. I. Goldenberg, Myrna, editor II. Series: Azrieli series of Holocaust survivor memoirs. Series VIII

D804.195.B45 2017      940.53'1809252      C2017-900256-2

PRINTED IN CANADA

# The Azrieli Series of Holocaust Survivor Memoirs

Naomi Azrieli, Publisher

Jody Spiegel, Program Director
Arielle Berger, Managing Editor
Farla Klaiman, Editor
Matt Carrington, Editor
Elizabeth Lasserre, Senior Editor, French-Language Editions
Elin Beaumont, Senior Education Outreach and Program Facilitator
Catherine Person, Educational Outreach and Events Coordinator,
    Quebec and French Canada
Marc-Olivier Cloutier, Educational Outreach and Events Assistant,
    Quebec and French Canada
Tim MacKay, Digital Platform Manager
Elizabeth Banks, Digital Asset Curator and Archivist
Susan Roitman, Office Manager (Toronto)
Mary Mellas, Executive Assistant and Human Resources (Montreal)

Mark Goldstein, Art Director
François Blanc, Cartographer
Bruno Paradis, Layout, French-Language Editions

# Contents

# Series Preface:
# In their own words...

*In telling these stories, the writers have liberated themselves. For so many years we did not speak about it, even when we became free people living in a free society. Now, when at last we are writing about what happened to us in this dark period of history, knowing that our stories will be read and live on, it is possible for us to feel truly free. These unique historical documents put a face on what was lost, and allow readers to grasp the enormity of what happened to six million Jews — one story at a time.*

David J. Azrieli, C.M., C.Q., M.Arch
Holocaust survivor and founder, The Azrieli Foundation

Since the end of World War II, over 30,000 Jewish Holocaust survivors have immigrated to Canada. Who they are, where they came from, what they experienced and how they built new lives for themselves and their families are important parts of our Canadian heritage. The Azrieli Foundation's Holocaust Survivor Memoirs Program was established to preserve and share the memoirs written by those who survived the twentieth-century Nazi genocide of the Jews of Europe and later made their way to Canada. The program is guided by the conviction that each survivor of the Holocaust has a remarkable story to tell, and that such stories play an important role in education about tolerance and diversity.

Millions of individual stories are lost to us forever. By preserving the stories written by survivors and making them widely available to a broad audience, the Azrieli Foundation's Holocaust Survivor Memoirs Program seeks to sustain the memory of all those who perished at the hands of hatred, abetted by indifference and apathy. The personal accounts of those who survived against all odds are as different as the people who wrote them, but all demonstrate the courage, strength, wit and luck that it took to prevail and survive in such terrible adversity. The memoirs are also moving tributes to people — strangers and friends — who risked their lives to help others, and who, through acts of kindness and decency in the darkest of moments, frequently helped the persecuted maintain faith in humanity and courage to endure. These accounts offer inspiration to all, as does the survivors' desire to share their experiences so that new generations can learn from them.

The Holocaust Survivor Memoirs Program collects, archives and publishes these distinctive records and the print editions are available free of charge to educational institutions and Holocaust-education programs across Canada. They are also available for sale to the general public at bookstores. All revenues to the Azrieli Foundation from the sales of the Azrieli Series of Holocaust Survivor Memoirs go toward the publishing and educational work of the memoirs program.

～

The Azrieli Foundation would like to express appreciation to the following people for their invaluable efforts in producing this book: Doris Bergen, Sherry Dodson (Maracle Press), Dana Francoeur, Barbara Kamieński, Therese Parent, Allegra Robinson, Irina Sadovina, and Margie Wolfe & Emma Rodgers of Second Story Press.

# About the Footnotes and Glossary

The following memoirs contain a number of terms, concepts and historical references that may be unfamiliar to the reader. Each anthology piece contains footnotes relevant to the memoir; where works are not cited, the explanations of terms were generated from the Azrieli Foundation's extensive glossary. For general information on major organizations; significant historical events and people; geographical locations; religious and cultural terms; and foreign-language words and expressions that will help give context and background to the events described in each text, please see the glossary beginning on page 541.

# Introduction

The voices of Jewish women in this anthology reflect the diversity of life in rural and urban settings before and during the Nazi occupation and the attempt to annihilate European Jewry. These women came from pre-war poverty and wealth, religious and secular communities and professional and working-class families; they range from being well-educated to poorly educated. In short, they demonstrate the presence of an active and widely varied Jewish life in central and eastern Europe. Through centuries, European Jewish communities experienced expulsion, exclusion and antisemitic pogroms; sometimes, they responded by immigrating to western Europe, Palestine or America. However, those who didn't leave — or couldn't, due to increasingly restrictive immigration policies — shared the fate of being Jewish at a time when to be Jewish was an automatic death sentence. Hitler's Final Solution created an environment that was constructed to facilitate their deaths and obliterate an ancient, and active, culture and religion. That Jews survived at all is testimony to the human spirit and the persistence of a moral force for good and for liberty.

More than thirty thousand Holocaust survivors immigrated to Canada in the ten years after their brutal experiences at the hands of the Nazis. They had endured the dehumanization, physical violence, hunger and thirst, and the psychological terrors of living in a system that was organized to murder them. They had survived in various

xvi  BEFORE ALL MEMORY IS LOST

states of weakened health — both physical and mental. They needed to find new and nurturing homes. For some, Canada was not their first choice, but other doors were closed, immigration quotas restricted, and Palestine a great unknown for those who were not necessarily ardent Zionists. More often than not, Canada was their only choice. Yet they encountered hostility, for Canada had "exhibited the poorest humanitarian record in the Western world" in terms of granting asylum to Jews needing refuge between 1933 and 1947.[1] As was true in the United States, Canadian humanitarian efforts met opposition from xenophobes and racists. Moral fortitude triumphed, however, and, gradually, Canada's immigration laws softened. In May 1947, the nation's immigration policy became more liberal and attitudes toward immigrants changed, as demonstrated by the passing of the Canadian Citizenship Act, effective January 1947.

It was another few years before Canadian authorities and social service groups, such as the Canadian Jewish Congress (CJC) and the Jewish Immigration Aid Society (JIAS), were able to begin to provide for this population. Most survivors persisted in spite of obstacles and struggled to learn the language and to re-engage in meaningful work. Because traditional gender roles prevailed, men received more help in getting work than women did. However, men who had been professionals had to prepare for exams and/or licensing in English. If they were fortunate, they re-entered their fields or found jobs that allowed them to support their families. All too often, they did not and found themselves "dethroned breadwinners,"[2] dependent upon their wives. Women who expected to stay home and raise children were surprised when they, too, were required to work in order to receive even a modicum of government help to sustain the family.

---

1   Adara Goldberg, *Holocaust Survivors in Canada: Exclusion, Inclusion, Transformation, 1947–1955* (Winnipeg: University of Manitoba, 2015), pp. 234–240. This book, and particularly this chapter, is the source of immigration data with regard to Jewish survivors seeking refuge in Canada.

2   Ibid, 228.

All in all, survivors faced poverty and, when women found work and their husbands did not, they also faced an unwelcome shift in the balance of power in the family. The reversal of traditional gender roles, however temporary, was also a cause for concern among Canadian social service agencies and survivor families who worried that such reversals would influence the children and upset the balance of power in the home.[3] Moreover, Canadian social workers complained that these young immigrant mothers did not have appropriate parenting skills, although it was a few years before social service agencies and organizations provided the necessary training and support to remedy the situation. To complicate matters, the absence of extended families created problems for women with children who wanted to learn new skills. There were exceptions, of course, most famously Chava Rosenfarb. Her skill as a Yiddish poet and novelist was recognized and appreciated. Most mothers, however, faced either leaving their children in whatever daycare facilities were eventually organized or staying at home, where they had to fight the agencies that required them to go to work in order to receive any support. Once these women relinquished their roles as breadwinners, they were usually relegated to subservient positions in the home and the workplace.

Nevertheless, their memoirs reflect hardships and bitterness less often than they express gratitude toward Canada for giving them the opportunity to renew and build their lives. Whether they feared the consequences of complaining about the government that gave them refuge or whether they truly felt more gratitude than bitterness remains unknown.[4] What is clear is that their expressions of

---

3  Ibid, 229. This social change was similar to the post–World War II Rosie the Riveter imbalance in that survivor women who enjoyed being the breadwinner or contributing substantially to the family's finances were expected to quit their jobs once their husbands began earning enough to support the family.

4  Many of the memoirs in this collection were written in the 1990s and beyond, when women had the opportunity to reflect on their lives. It is possible that the passage of time, combined with resilience and pride in rebuilding lives and families, superseded reminiscences of earlier struggles in Canada.

gratitude obscure the difficulties they had in adjusting to the distress inherent in making a new life without the comfort of an extended family or a supportive social circle. Most women settled for the satisfaction of raising children who were able to integrate themselves into society, primarily through education and opportunities that enabled them to become financially independent enough to have children of their own.

The women whose memoirs comprise this anthology must be viewed in their particularity. Yet, although they are divided into four groups according to where and how they spent the war years — hidden, passing as gentiles, in the camps or in the USSR — their experiences overlap. For example, before deportation, they may have lived for a time in hiding or in passing. Each, however, speaks of experiences particular to her specific circumstance. The survivors who came from Lodz lived under different conditions than those who experienced unrelenting cold and hunger in remote sections of the USSR. Imprisonment in the Gulag spoke to isolation born of unfathomable and trumped-up political guilt while the Jews in ghettos, whose only so-called crime was being Jewish, were still part of a community. Did "community" make surviving more bearable than the isolation of the Gulag?

What ties all these recollections of memories together? I call them memoirs, but, in essence, they are more like collections of memories. Seldom are they structured like a polished memoir; rather, they are glimpses into a painful past where themes of family and fear dominate. Unlike most memoirs, which normally begin in pre-war times and follow the inevitable route to the ghetto and then to labour or concentration camps and eventual liberation, several of these memoirs follow no particular structure. They are episodic, shreds of particular painful experiences that linger and become sources of "accidental" personal victory over extreme adversity. "Accidental" because they contain few overt declarations of the will to survive. For the most part, they are unselfconscious narratives of survival. The "I" is often submerged into the circumstance, and the circumstances are frightening, violent, unforeseen and without reason.

The voices in these narratives are seldom analytical. They are instead descriptive. The major preoccupation of these women survivors during the Holocaust was the concern for family members and friends; they relied on family and social connections. In fact, some of these narratives are replete with details of family genealogy, which situate the narrator within a community or family. These women are reluctant to relinquish past identities and refuse to forget the past, but at the same time they knew they had to move on; however, moving on was a hesitant, challenging process, because very few had families or connections that could welcome them into their adopted communities. Some hold onto pre-war expectations and hopes even though they are aware of the impossibility of re-creating or restoring the past. They share experiences that are beyond the reader's ability to know, simply because even in the telling they are unimaginable, knowable only to a sister survivor. Paradoxically, they convey the power of Nazi dominance and survivor helplessness and, at the same time, celebrate the power of the human to overcome or, at least, endure the horror that was the Holocaust.

*Myrna Goldenberg*
2016

North
Sea

SWEDEN

DENMARK

Baltic

Sea

Stutthof

Bergen-Belsen

BERLIN

GERMANY

WARSAW

Lodz

Piotrków
Trybunalski

Theresienstadt

Częstochowa

PRAGUE

Auschwitz-
Birkenau

Krakow

Bodzanów

CZECHOSLOVAKIA

Sečovce

VIENNA

Kisvárda

BUDAPEST

Debrecen

HUNGARY

LEGEND

Borders 1921-1938

Borders 1939-1944

0        250        500km

N

ESTONIA

LATVIA

Šiaulai •

LITHUANIA

MOSCOW •

U S S R

• Baranovicze

POLAND

• Sandomierz

• Lwów

Borysław •

• Kiev

• Skvyra

• Kharkov

• Pechora

Tulchin

Rachov • Ciudin

ROMANIA

'Twas not storks that gave birth to us,
We had a father, a mother, and
in the blink of an eye, we lost them.
That was the destiny.

Even the zaidehs and the bubehs were put to death
as though they had never existed.
No name remained.
No one to lead the children to the chuppah.

Wanderers for two thousand years,
with a pack on the back,
from generation to generation,
from shtetl to the village market.

The human nature of God's blessing;
from the root, let a branch remain.
Let the family line continue.
Record it for history.

Wandering through many wars,
switching languages,

looking for a place of rest,
for a future in freedom.
To speak and learn languages,
working at all kinds of trades,
to raise children in the future;
to continue the chain of life,
our ancestors' traditions.

Lives were cut short
because of pogroms and false accusations.
Who now speaks about the Destruction in Europe,
where no one wanted to spare us?

Let someone record
for the remaining children.
Let the future know
all the trials of yesterday.

Let there be a name in memory of papa and zaideh
Of mama and bubeh.
Let their memory live forever.

*Ifa Demon*
Translated from Yiddish by Miriam Beckerman

1

2

1 Ifa Demon, 1945.
2 Ifa Demon, 1972.

Hiding

# Foreword

In her short story "The Key Game,"[1] barely two and a half pages, Ida Fink narrates the rehearsal of a three-year-old tasked with hiding his father from the Gestapo, who are ringing their doorbell. The point of the game was simply to create a delay so that the father had time to hide in a predetermined place — a bathroom wall of the apartment. The little boy feigns looking for the key that would open the door. He opens and closes drawers loudly. He noisily drags a chair to a high chest and searches the top shelf. The game is played over and over again, but each time the father needs just a little more time to hide.

Hiding was indeed a challenging process — for both the hidden and for the brave people who hid them. Hiding a Jew during the Holocaust put the family of the person who offered the hiding place, or the rescuer(s), in a highly precarious position. Yad Vashem, the Holocaust memorial museum in Israel, cites such rescuers as Righteous Gentiles, most of whom were still alive when so designated. A garden of hundreds of trees is devoted to their memory. There are scores, though, of rescuers who go unnamed and, therefore, unacknowledged, who gave their lives to do the right thing. One example serves

---

1 Ida Fink, "The Key Game," in *Women and the Holocaust*, eds. Dalia Ofer and Lenore J. Weitzman (New Haven: Yale University Press, 1998), pp.120–22.

to remind us of the heroism of rescuers who were murdered along with the Jews they tried to hide. In a village not far from Warsaw, the Kowalski family hid two Jewish girls in a cellar purposely built as a hiding place. A suspicious neighbour notified the local SS, who found the seven Kowalskis in the house as well as the two Jewish girls and burned them all alive in the backyard barn of their home.[2] Obviously, most stories about failed attempts to hide Jews died with their rescuers, who became as victimized as the Jews they hid.

The risks that non-Jewish rescuers took cannot be overstated. Neither can the effects of being hidden on the children and young adults who are the subjects of this section. Their childhoods were stolen; they lived quietly and invisibly, as the situation required. Those who were older when they were hidden understood the necessity of trusting their rescuers, but these children were required to grow old before their time, to be quiet, to be accepting of the restrictions placed on them, to be what no child should have to be — a displaced, orphaned, silenced victim. However, they are often told that they were lucky — they lived. Yes, but they paid a heavy price. Most hidden children were separated from the rest of their family; most could not seek safety from bombings for fear of being seen if they went to a shelter; most were confined to a tiny space and didn't see daylight for weeks, months or even years; most were shifted from hiding place to hiding place; many were exploited or abused; some were baptized and some remained in the monasteries or convents in which they were hidden. Sickness, for most hidden children or adults, was particularly difficult. For example, Felicia Graber cites a case of a young child who had tonsillitis and was hidden by nuns. Calling a doctor would have put the whole convent in danger, so a nun cut the diseased tonsils out

---

2   Shiryn Ghermezian, "Holocaust Hiding Place for Jewish Sisters Revealed for First Time Intact in Home of Polish Christian Family." *The Algemeiner*, August 22, 2014. www.algemeiner.com. Accessed on March 2, 2016.

with garden pliers that were usually used to cut grapes from bushes.[3]

No one involved in hiding a Jew remained unscarred. Fear shadowed their lives. And they had reason to fear. Theirs was a time when fear of the "other" played a major role — fear of being discovered as a Jew in hiding, fear of being discovered as a rescuer, fear of being blackmailed, fear of every action that was not in their control. Indeed, for Jews in hiding, every action was out of their control. Perhaps less so for the rescuer, but for all involved, fear was the dominant and natural emotion.

In this section, we meet hidden Jewish women and their rescuers who range from genuinely kind, highly moral people to people who feared what they were doing but hid Jews anyway to those who were paid to hide Jews. Some in the last category betrayed the Jews they hid and were thus collaborators.

Irena Peritz and her family left Warsaw for Lwów almost immediately after the Nazis invaded Poland. Travelling by foot, train, and horse and buggy, it took about a month to reach what they expected to be safety. Eight days after the Nazis broke the Molotov-Ribbentrop Pact with the Soviets, the pogroms began — mayhem and hiding place after hiding place followed. Four years "on the run… with no end in sight" and then four months in hiding are the subjects of Irena's memoir and diary. Sixteen years old, Irena cries to her diary, "I would like to live and live it up. I would like to drink my glass of wine to the last drop." Her landlord is a drunk who was paid to hide the family; her landlady is moody and scornful. Irena can't help but feel that her safety is compromised. One close call after another frays her nerves and leads to hopelessness. Finally, on August 8, 1944, the Soviets liberated her area and it was safe to come out of hiding. In 1949, she and her family left for Canada.

---

3   "Hidden Child," Holocaust Museum Learning Center, St. Louis, MO. www.mlc.org. Accessed on March 2, 2016.

Eva Kuper attributes her survival to miracles. An infant at the onset of the war, she and her family were forced into the Warsaw ghetto and then into hiding. Eva writes, "My father always carried two cyanide pills…determined to kill both of us rather than be taken alive by the Nazis." A trip through the Warsaw sewers led them to temporary safety. Soon, Eva's hiding place was in a convent, where she learned Catholic prayers and rituals; after the war, at the age of six, she had her first communion. Only after leaving Europe on the ship to Canada did her father tell her she was Jewish, and at first she was horrified. It took years, she said, to learn to be proud of her heritage. Decades later, she returned to the Franciscan Sisters convent to see Sister Klara Jaroszyńska, the nun who protected and loved her when she needed it most.

Magda Neuman Sebastian recalls how her happy childhood in Slovakia was interrupted when she was twelve years old and had to hide in the mountains with her family. After several near-escapes, they "settled" in a village under a non-Jewish family name and attended church, eventually converting to keep their cover. They hid in plain sight for the next three years until liberation. Because Magda could speak German, she interacted with some of the soldiers when necessary; for example, to take her mother to a doctor or bluff her way out of a chance visit from SS officers looking for partisans. Some encounters were humorous; all were tense. Even in mature adulthood, she is saddened by the war and how it affected her life as a child and a teenager.

Bianka Kraszewski's memoir closes this section. Her memoir, she writes, is the grave of her parents and brother, their "stone, their memorial." And, in keeping with her aim, she divides her memoir into three sections, one for each member of her beloved family. She remembers that her aunt's non-Jewish housekeeper found hiding places for them, how Nazi oppression robbed her father of his place in the family and community and how her mother, with "Aryan" good looks, could still walk freely on the streets of Warsaw. Bianka's keen memory takes us to the pre-Nazi years when the whole family enjoyed being together on vacations, learning and sharing various entertainments. Hers was a "normal" middle-class life, not only cut short by the Nazis but, more accurately, eliminated by them. Her recollections of the Warsaw Ghetto Uprising add personal detail to this historical account, especially of the hunger and overcrowding everyone endured.

Here are four accounts of childhoods that should have been happy and healthy, but were brutally interrupted by the Nazis.

A page from Irena Peritz's diary. March 27, 1944.

# Each Day Could Be Our Last: Irena's Wartime Diary
# Irena Peritz

*For my children and grandchildren.*

The evil that men do lives after them;
the good is oft interred with their bones.

William Shakespeare, *Julius Caesar*, Act 3, Scene 2

*To my parents, Rozalia and Józef Koretz, whose love and devotion helped me to survive. To my mother, a gentle person, whose courage and strength maintained our sense of family through the most difficult times. To my father, whose authority and self-assurance protected us from harm. His motto was, "We either live together or die together." We lived — the only family among the survivors in Borysław that stayed intact. And to our non-Jewish friends, whose unwavering convictions and great courage sustained us in our time of need. Without them all, we would not have survived. Luck played its part; many others who perished were equally brave and wise. To have survived at all was a miracle. This story is to keep alive the memory of the millions for whom there were no miracles and who are silenced forever.*

IN GRATITUDE

Ferri Meszaros, Feliks Druszkiewicz and Ewa Fedorow and her family
were gentile friends of ours and members of the Polish Underground.
These exceptional people courageously helped us and many others.
They gave us moral, emotional and financial support, as well as essential information and practical help. Their selfless and heroic actions contributed to our miraculous survival, and they will never be
forgotten.

AUTHOR'S PREFACE

On September 1, 1939, Germany invaded Poland and World War II
began. The city of Warsaw, where I lived with my family, was seized
with panic and confusion. We carried gas masks in preparation for
air raids and stocked up on food. From our home, we could hear
explosions in the distance. Events beyond my capacity to understand
were unfolding around me. In the uncertainty, fear took hold of my
young imagination.

   My father, an officer in the Polish army, decided that our family
should leave Warsaw. On September 6, my parents, my sister, Olga,
and I took whatever belongings we could carry and began our odyssey into the unknown. I left my childhood and most of my possessions behind. The chapter of my life in a comfortable and peaceful home at 49 Mokotowska Street ended abruptly. By the time we
returned to Warsaw for a visit six years later, we found most of our
home reduced to rubble.

   When the journey began, I was eleven years old. We headed east-
ward in order to escape the German army, which was closing in from
the west. Passing through burning villages and bombed-out cities,
we joined the massive flow of disoriented refugees seeking a road to
safety. We travelled on foot, by train and by horse and buggy. Chaos
and confusion were all around.

By October, we had arrived in Lwów, where my mother's family offered to shelter us. Through an agreement worked out between Germany and the Soviet Union, Poland was divided between the two countries[1] and in Lwów we were under Soviet occupation. My new daily reality was one of food shortages, curfews and soldiers in the streets. The winter of 1939 was severe. Lack of fuel and warm clothing added to our hardship. No one seemed to know what to do next. The uncertainty was overwhelming.

In the spring of 1940, my father found a job in nearby Borysław with a branch of his Warsaw plumbing supplies firm. We followed him soon after. Borysław was my birthplace, where we had lived for a short while before moving to Warsaw. Our return was almost like a homecoming. My parents rekindled old friendships with people whose children became my friends. Among them was the Kessler family, who rented us a room in their house.

The Teichers lived next door. Their comfortable house became my second home. Daughters Janka and Niuta, as well as Ewa Kessler and Romek Engelberg, became my closest friends. We went to the same grade school and spent time together after classes. We shared secrets and laughter, played in the park and celebrated birthdays. We were inseparable. Despite the difficulties of being away from our home in Warsaw, life seemed almost normal. In this brief period of innocence, unaware of what was to come, I was happy.

It all came to a sudden end on June 22, 1941, when war broke out between the Soviet Union and Germany. On July 1, the German army marched into Borysław. Four days later, the first pogrom began. The Germans stood by and gave the local population a free hand for twenty-four hours, letting them settle old scores. The twenty-four hours

---

1   The Hitler-Stalin Pact, also known as the Molotov-Ribbentrop Pact and the German-Soviet Non-Aggression Pact, was forged in August 1939 and breached in 1941 when Germany invaded the Soviet Union.

stretched into three days of mayhem. Approximately three hundred and fifty people were murdered. The shrieks and spilled blood have never left my memory.

It was during this pogrom that my mother's beloved youngest sister, Stefa, and her husband, Stefan, were brutally murdered in the streets of the nearby town of Schodnica. Stefa was the first member of our family to lose her life so tragically. My mother was inconsolable. She wept for days. We were overwhelmed with horror and disbelief at what was happening.[2]

The restrictions and regulations of the German occupation took over our lives. We wore armbands with a Jewish star. We were forced to abandon our home and move to a restricted area, the first of many moves. There were sporadic deportations and executions. Food was scarce and hunger was widespread.

By January 1942, the Nazis' Final Solution to annihilate European Jewry had officially begun.[3] By August, rumours about impending deportation from the local ghetto reached Borysław. Hunted like animals, people scattered in search of a place to hide.

At the time, my father and Olga were working for a German oil company that was supplying fuel essential for the war effort. My father felt that the work gave him and my sister some protection, which

---

2   Seventy-five per cent of Borysław's Jews were murdered from July 1941 to July 1944. The census of 1941 indicates that there were 17,000 Jews out of a population of about 50,000. http://kehilalinks.jewishgen.org/drohobycz/shtetls/shtetls_hist-boryslaw.asp.

3   The Wannsee Conference on January 20, 1942, a meeting only eighty-five minutes long, was the moment when fifteen middle- and high-level Nazi officials were told of the Final Solution — the plan to murder Europe's Jewish populations. The meeting was called by *Reichsprotektor* and RSHA Chief Reinhard Heydrich and the minutes were taken by Colonel Adolf Eichmann. On Eichmann's orders, all copies of the minutes were to be destroyed. One copy was found after the war was over.

my mother and I did not have. He suggested that we hide and asked Olga to take us to the Fedorows, the parents of her friend Ewa, who lived on a farm on the outskirts of town. Risking our lives by removing our armbands, we walked to their place. This good family knew why we had come — the pleading looks on our faces said it all. They also knew the potentially deadly consequences for hiding us, but with no questions asked they led us to their barn.[4] Olga turned back to join Daddy in the ghetto.

My mother and I climbed a short ladder into the hayloft. We crawled to the far end under the sloping roof and buried ourselves beneath loose piles of hay. We lay motionless. Moments later we heard voices in German shouting "Wo sind die Juden?" (Where are the Jews?) We froze in terror. My mother covered me with her body. We held our breaths. We heard one of the men stomp halfway up the ladder and fling open the trapdoor. Leaning in, he jabbed violently around in the straw with his bayonet. The tip was only inches away from us. I felt my life slipping away. Suddenly, he stopped. Shouting in anger that there was no one up there, he descended in fury to the barn. Cursing the terrified Fedorow family, the men left. As their voices faded away, my mother's whisper broke the agonizing silence, "Irusiu, we are alive." How fine is the line between life and death! Later we found out that a passerby who had seen us walking to the farm had denounced us.

We remained in our hiding place for three days and nights. Not knowing where Olga and my father were was unbearable. We learned later that they had found some protection from the authorities in the office of their workplace. We returned to the ghetto. It was a scene of devastation with empty streets, abandoned homes and scattered be-

---

4  The Fedorow family was recognized as Righteous Among the Nations in 2013. For more information, see the Yad Vashem database at http://db.yadvashem.org/righteous/family.html?language=en&itemId=10307122

longings. While we had taken refuge in our hiding place, 5,000 people had been rounded up in three days and sent to the Bełżec death camp. Among them were Romek and his mother.

News from Tarnów reached us soon after about the fate of my mother's other two sisters, my cousins and my paternal grandmother. They had all perished. My parents were numb. This was the first and only time I saw my father cry.

We managed to avoid a number of other roundups and massacres, and in the spring and early summer of 1943, the Germans shut down the ghetto and forced the remaining Jews into the city's labour camp. We were among them. Spread over several blocks, the camp was surrounded by watchtowers and barbed wire. Families bunked together in overcrowded, rundown army barracks. Food was rationed. Fortunately for our family, we had a room to ourselves with a shared kitchen. We were free to move around the camp after work, but forbidden to step outside the boundaries. It was a *Zwangsarbeitslager*, a slave labour camp. The camp provided labour for the same German oil company for which my father and Olga worked. We were marched to work outside the camp every day under the watchful eyes of guards and dogs.

The terror continued unabated. Roundups and deportations occurred daily. Inside the camp, despite the conditions, or perhaps because of them, we lived intensely, as if each day could be our last. We formed strong friendships and built brief but intense relationships. We shared almost every aspect of our daily lives, including the struggle to survive. We laughed and we loved, and we talked of the day when we would be free.

In the spring of 1944, rumours of the approaching Soviet offensive from the east gave us a ray of hope. One day we were rounded up in the camp's courtyard and told by Friedrich Hildebrand, SS commander of the camp, that we were to be deported farther west, away from the advancing troops. We knew that we had to defy the order. We had to find a hiding place where we could await the moment of liberation. I had already been on the run with my family for four years, but there was still no end in sight. Driven by hope and fear, we prepared our next move.

I was sixteen years old.

~

MY DIARY: MARCH 26 TO AUGUST 8, 1944

Sunday, March 26
The Russians are approaching fast. We have to make a decision about our next move. Everybody is scattering to go into hiding. We will be leaving the camp any day now. Daddy has found a hiding place. I am frightened. I am young; life is ahead of me. I would like to live to see better times with all my loved ones. Everything is in God's hands. Keep us in your care. I know that I cannot escape my fate. Whatever must happen will happen.

Monday, March 27
My diary! My only friend! We are leaving any day now to go into hiding. I don't know if what we are doing is right or wrong. Some kind of psychosis has gripped people. I don't know where to turn. Life is long and I am so young! I am only sixteen. I would like to live and live it up. I would like to drink my glass of wine to the last drop.

There is panic everywhere. People are leaving, saving themselves any way they can. They escape to the forest, or bunkers, anywhere they can hide. That is all everyone talks about. We live in agony. To suffer for four years and die at the end! There is tremendous panic. I walk around feeling crazy. But one cannot give up. My friend Dozia is sick. I spent the day with her. Wuna and Dolek came to visit in the evening. The camp seems deserted.

Tuesday, March 28
The panic doesn't let up. The German army came to the gates of the

camp. Thank God, it turned out to be a false alarm. Julek left to go into hiding. We said goodbye.

Wednesday, March 29
Dozia is still sick. The atmosphere is depressing. I don't feel strong enough to carry on. I just want to live through it all! We are supposed to be leaving soon. The evening was beautiful, the sky full of stars and the moon looking down at us. Zygo, Wuna and I walked around. All we talked about was who was leaving and when. Let it all end soon!

Thursday, March 30
I got up in the morning not suspecting anything. You never know what the day has in store for you. Panic persists. Walek Eisenstein, commandant of the Jewish police, said that on Monday all the Jews from our Borysław camp are supposed to be evacuated to Jasło and Krosno. Daddy said to keep calm because the news has not been confirmed. Wuna came over in the afternoon. We talked. Hildebrand and Beitz[5] were holding an important meeting. Daddy said to get ready to leave. Through Władek, we sent all our clothes to Ewa Fedorow. Fearing the worst, people were jumping over the fence, escaping. Let them save themselves any way they can!

We were ordered to gather on the grounds of the camp. Hildeb-

---

5   On August 8, 1942, Berthold Beitz, as a manager of the German Karpathen oil company, saved 400 workers and 250 children from being sent to Bełżec death camp. In November 1942 Beitz aided Jews in their escape across the Hungarian border and was almost arrested himself. Beitz later testified that Fritz (Friedrich) Hildebrand, the SS commandant of the camp, "shut both his eyes" to Beitz's employment of forbidden Jewish workers. Sources: "Beitz Family," Yad Vashem's The Righteous Among the Nations Database. http://www.yadvashem.org/ and "Borysław," The United States Holocaust Memorial Museum Encyclopedia of Camps and Ghettos, 1933–1945. (Bloomington and Indianapolis: Indiana University Press, 2012). Vol. 2. Part A. 755–757.

rand reassured us that there was no immediate danger and no reason to leave. We were skeptical. Wuna is going into hiding. We said a tearful goodbye. Will our paths ever meet again? Maybe, after the war. I said goodbye to Dozia. Almighty God, help us meet again after the war. That is my one and only wish.

Friday, March 31

A beautiful day. Our room is completely empty. It looks sad. Nobody is around. I have no one to talk to. I went into the kitchen and started singing. I have to sing now because we are going into hiding today and I will no longer be able to sing or talk. I sang and remembered because every song reminded me of good times in the past.

Mummy and I are leaving the camp today. We will meet Daddy at his office outside the camp. He will take us to the hiding place. I met Janek and we said goodbye. Will I ever see my friends again? Elu approached me and asked me to intervene on his behalf and try to convince Dziunia to leave her mother and go into hiding with him. How can I assume such responsibility? Would I behave differently in her place? What a tragedy! I decided to do it, though. Her mother, with tears in her eyes, begged her to leave and save herself. But she told her mother that she would not. I felt that if I stayed any longer, I too would start crying, so I left. I went back to our room, said farewell to our apartment and left with Mummy.

Herman helped us to escape from camp under the cover of darkness. We crawled through a small opening in the fence and took off our armbands. No sooner had we covered a few steps than two of the guards took us back to camp. Herman intervened on our behalf with Walek, and we made another attempt. My friends were waving goodbye from a distance. "Bye, farewell, we'll meet again soon, after the war."

We met Daddy at the office and I broke down. I lost my composure and cried uncontrollably. Please don't be surprised. Don't ask me why. I am parting with freedom. Granted, you cannot call our existence freedom but, next to the prison I'll be living in, it was freedom. Now I will be confined to one room. I do not want you to think that I am complaining. No! I know that I am not allowed to complain, because there are many who would change places with me. I have only one wish. Let our whole family live together after the war. That is my dream.

Fearfully, we walked from the office to our hiding place. Daddy and Mummy went ahead and Dolek and I followed behind them. Dolek gave me a little brooch as a souvenir and asked me not to forget him. I will never forget you! How can I? It was almost dusk when we reached the house. We didn't even say goodbye. He just kissed me. Will I ever see him again? We said goodbye to Daddy. He went back to camp, where he and Olga will stay for now.

Facing me was the house, my prison. Silently, we walked up an outside staircase to the upper floor. A woman opened the door and showed us into her kitchen. Without a word, we followed her down a long dark hallway and into a room at the end of it. She closed the door behind us. A feeling of utter despair came over me.

Saturday, April 1
After the exhausting day yesterday, I slept soundly. I woke up at ten o'clock and looked around in bewilderment. The sparsely furnished room has one small window that faces another wall. Sadly, I looked through it. Freedom is on the other side. I am imprisoned. I realize that this is the only room in the house. It serves as a bedroom and living space for us and for the couple who is hiding us. We have been told not to walk around or raise our voices so as not to arouse the suspicions of the family living on the floor below.

Our landlord is a Polish truck driver; his Ukrainian wife looks after the house, garden, some chickens and a cow. There is also a grandmother, who sleeps in the attic in the hay. We have to pay for this hiding place. The money is being sent by Mr. Feliks Druszkiewicz, a colleague of my father's.[6] Ewa Fedorow will act as a courier, bringing the money every month from Warsaw, where he lives.

Our landlords went to Ewa's house to pick up our clothes. They were supposed to come back with Daddy and Olga, but didn't. Instead they brought a letter from Olga stating that the atmosphere at the camp is calmer and that they will stay there for now. Mr. Radecke, the director of the oil company, is trying to convince families that they should leave for Krosno and that their safety would be guaranteed. I don't know why but I sobbed uncontrollably upon reading the letter. Is it because, for the first time, we are not together? Or is it because, maybe, I could have stayed on the outside a little longer?

Mummy and I tiptoed into the kitchen, washed up with cold water, had breakfast and returned to our room. We played cards for almost the whole day. We had supper and went to sleep. How long are we going to live like this?

Today is April Fool's Day. It's a day I used to spend laughing, and today? Just the opposite — crying.

Sunday, April 2
Another day. There are guests in the kitchen, so we sat motionless, whispering quietly, locked up in our room. Why do I have to sit here, making sure that nobody notices me or hears me? Why? Oh, Irena! You are Jewish!

I look for something to do to pass the time. I read a little, write a little, sleep and eat. We waited for our landlady to bring us something hot to eat. Finally, she did. I think that our landlords are decent people.

---

6 Feliks Druszkiewicz was recognized as Righteous Among the Nations in 1985. See Yad Vashem's database at http://db.yadvashem.org/righteous/family.html?languag e=en&itemId=4014655.

Monday, April 3

While eating breakfast in the kitchen, I heard a knock at the door. We escaped to our room. It was Daddy. We were so happy to see him! He told us that the camp was almost empty, that the Soviet offensive had halted and that we shouldn't worry if he and Olga might one day be taken by truck to work in Jasło. It's strange that he was so calm about it. Does he think that Mummy and I will stay here while he and Olga suffer somewhere unknown? I don't even want to think about it. After he left, not knowing when we would see him again, I started thinking, maybe we should have gone into a bunker in the forest. I don't think that it would be as comfortable as here but maybe we would have a better chance of surviving. After all, if they search the forest, they might not find us. But in a house like this, our landlords may sooner or later give us away. Better not to think about it. I have to be positive!

Suddenly, at six o'clock, the landlord came in with a friend and started drinking. We became terribly frightened. If he gets drunk, he might blurt out the truth and tell on us! To our dismay, the friend insisted on sleeping over. There was no other solution but for Mummy and me to abandon our room and move into the attic. We cuddled close to each other, trying to give each other comfort, trembling from cold and fright. My dearest Mummy! She kept on saying, "Don't cry, Irusiu, I am here with you." At eleven o'clock, we went into the kitchen just to warm up a bit. We slept lightly, sitting up on chairs, listening. Finally, at three in the morning, we went back to the attic, covered ourselves with a blanket and fell asleep.

Tuesday, April 4

We slept until ten o'clock. We were both very upset because of the previous day's events. You never know. Our lives are in the hands of a drunk. One wrong word and we may be given away! It's another day. The routine is the same. I am slowly getting used to it. Hopefully, it won't be too long.

Wednesday, April 5

It's a beautiful day. I sat at the table and dreamed. Life could have been so different. But there are no answers. It is destiny that preordains our lives and that's all there is to it. The landlady brought us a letter from Daddy and again it started me thinking that maybe I could have stayed in camp a little longer. Human beings are so helpless. We live in emotional turmoil with no way out. Nothing makes any sense and there is no guidance to tell us which decision is the right one. I finished reading *Sylvia*, a beautiful book. In the afternoon, we got our dinner, a bowl of wheat with milk. Back home I wouldn't have eaten it, but here I finished it with gusto.

The planes were flying all night.

Thursday, April 6

It's cloudy outside. It is easier for me to be here when the weather is bad. It doesn't hurt as much. We asked the landlady to open the window but she said that she couldn't because her flowers would wilt and freeze. Isn't it funny? The fact that I've been here almost a week, wilting without air, doesn't seem to matter. Why am I surprised? For her, the flowers are more important. But I am not complaining about her. She is a decent, honest person with a good head on her shoulders.

Friday, April 7

It's been a week since we got here. I haven't seen Olga all this time. I cannot describe to you, my diary, my only friend, how I long for her. I would have never expected to miss her this much. Maybe because it is the first time during this war that we've been separated for a whole week. My dearest mother. I love her more than life. She comforts me all the time and keeps on asking me if it's that bad to be with her.

Saturday, April 8

As soon as we got up, the landlady brought my treasure box from Daddy. I am so happy! She also told me that my letter moved Olga to tears and that Daddy was coming to see us. Soon afterwards, he did. He told us about life on the outside. The Soviet offensive had stopped and the camp's evacuation was postponed. I asked Daddy to take me back to camp with him for a few days, but he absolutely refused, trying to convince me that I was much safer where I am. I know he is right, but I wonder if he understands how I feel.

Because of the holidays, the landlady served some vodka, bread, eggs and salami. It was nice of her. Daddy got a little tipsy and on his way out I asked him again to let me go with him. I started crying. Then I realized how much I was hurting my dearest Mummy. How insensitive of me to think only of myself. If I leave, would I leave her behind, alone?

It was five o'clock when Daddy left. It was getting dark. I lay down and started reminiscing. It was a year ago today that I met Janek. A whole year! I remember it as if it were yesterday. He was on the swing and I approached him. Janek, do you remember that?

Sunday, April 9
The second day of Easter holidays. We had to spend the day sitting in the attic because there were visitors in the house. Through a little window, I watched the world on the outside. It was a beautiful day. People in their Sunday clothes walked free and carefree. In the distance, I heard laughter and singing. Do they know that a war is on? We haven't eaten all day. I was hungry, but didn't want Mummy to worry so I kept reassuring her that I felt fine. At night, we went back to our room. The landlord came in and apologized, telling us how sorry he is that we have to be imprisoned like this. He seems to be a decent person. He refers to us as his guests.

Monday, April 10
Today is one of those days. I keep thinking that I should have stayed on the outside with Daddy and Olga. There is no logic to my thinking. To pass the time, I played cards with Mummy, read a little and prayed.

Tuesday, April 11

Days pass. One blends into the next. I sleep, I eat and I remember. A year ago? A swing, a song, Janek. When it got dark, I stood at the window, watching the people walk by. Free people!

Wednesday, April 12

Olga is supposed to come today. I waited for her with great anticipation. When she finally showed up, I was overcome with joy. She gave me letters from Tolek and Wuna. We talked and talked, and there was no end to my questions. Time was moving fast and I thought she was so fortunate to be able to walk out of here (risking her life by removing her armband), even if it meant going back to camp.

Suddenly, the landlady entered the room and gave us a letter from Daddy that had just been delivered by Ewa Fedorow. It read: "There are rumours that trains are at the station, ready to evacuate the camp. Therefore, do not let Olga leave your hiding place under any circumstances." Panic, uncertainty and helplessness overpowered us. There have been rumours before. Maybe this one will turn out to be false, too! What will happen to Daddy?

Thursday, April 13

No news. The day starts like any other. We assume that rumours will turn out to be just rumours. Olga gets ready to leave. But she cannot get out as the landlady has locked us in from the outside. Nobody realizes what a stroke of luck this is. Two notes are smuggled in to us. One of them is from Mr. Meszaros, a close friend of the family, the other from Ewa Fedorow. The news they contain is horrifying. The camp has been evacuated and Daddy was seen being taken away to the waiting trains, along with hundreds of others.

Just as we are sitting in shocked silence, the door opens and Daddy walks in, dirty, dishevelled and incoherent. "I escaped from the train," he says, his face white as a sheet. We realized then that had Olga been able to leave the house she would have been deported with him. He would never have left her behind.

My joy at seeing Daddy is mixed with sadness as he tells us his story. There was a roll call at the camp at 5:00 a.m. Everyone lined up in rows of three, then marched out of the camp toward the train station under heavy guard. Daddy boarded the train along with hundreds of other despairing people. Suddenly he noticed a man in uniform standing guard on the platform. He recognized him as someone he knew from his office. Trying to sound calm, Daddy approached him and explained that he had a set of office keys that he wanted to return. He spotted an opening in the fence and began walking toward it. The man looked the other way. Daddy passed through the opening and walked away, expecting to be shot any moment. In cold terror, he quickened his pace and made it to our hiding place. By another stroke of luck, the grandmother was home and let him in. How happy I am that we are all together!

Others also tried to escape, he says. They were shot. I ask Daddy about my friends — he says they were all taken away. Wuna with her father. Julek. Jozek with his family. Janek, Zygo, Tolek. Artek with his mother, and many, many others. Where are you, my friends?

It's beautiful outside. Spring is in the air. It is not meant for me, though. I can only look outside through a narrow opening in the window. I dream about being free one day, feeling young! I'd love to be dressed nicely and dance and be happy. In the meantime, our existence is very sad. I have been here for two weeks.

How much longer?


April 16 to 23

Don't be angry with me, my diary, for not writing for a whole week. I have so little patience. Everything seems to be a big undertaking; my life (if you can call it life) is so monotonous that I am forgetting who I am. I eat mechanically, sleep and move around like a robot. My thoughts and my dreams take up most of the day. I see myself being sixteen, dressed up and free. And I think about my friends. Where are they now? Are they working hard? Do they still remember me?

On Wednesday night, Ewa Fedorow came to visit. There is no news from the people who were deported. There are rumours that they are in a labour camp in Płaszów, near Krakow. Our camp is filling up again with people coming out of hiding. My thoughts are wandering again. Is anybody I know back at camp? While lying and reminiscing, I remembered that it was exactly a year ago today that I was kissed by a boy for the first time in my life. It seems irrelevant to remember such unimportant events in the context of our tragic lives, but I am only sixteen.

On Friday, April 21, our landlady brought us a letter from Mr. Meszaros. The Soviet offensive has been halted. It looks like we will be here forever! Do you think we stand a chance? Can we survive?

April 23 to 25

Books sent by Mr. Meszaros keep me alive. At least I can forget my own existence and live in an imaginary world, even if it is only for a short while.

Mummy and Daddy were in the kitchen one day when suddenly they tiptoed into our room and said the landlady's sister-in-law had seen them. We were all tremendously upset. Daddy blamed Mummy for not being cautious enough. She was supposed to be on the lookout. Mummy was feeling so guilty and I felt so sorry for her. The landlady was screaming and blaming her mother-in-law. The sister-in-law heard everything and now she may go to the police and denounce us. How will this end?

Wednesday, April 26

I looked through the letters from Janka and Niuta. My dear girls, how you've suffered! I've read your words over and over again: "We are still so young and would love to live. Our whole lives are ahead of us. It is not meant for us to see better times." Ewa Fedorow came to visit in the evening. No news from Dolek. I long to hear from him. I did not expect to miss him so much.

Saturday, April 29

Mr. Meszaros came to see us. He told us the news about the people that have been deported from our camp to Płaszów, where there are 13,000 Jews and 6,000 people of other nationalities. The barracks for men and women are separate. Nobody is allowed to leave the camp. Everyone has to work. The women work in factories while the men do physical, menial work. They work from 7:00 a.m. until 7:00 p.m.[7]

I get such childish, crazy thoughts: maybe I would like to be there with everybody. I do not think we will survive here either, so why be so confined? I know I'm being silly. In the evening, when the land-lady is not here, I look out the window and envy people who walk in the street. Young girls, happy, smiling, walking with boys. And me? Don't think so much about yourself! This is your fate and you have to accept it! But maybe you'll live it up after the war. Goodbye, my diary, my friend. Till next time!

Monday, May 1

The beautiful month of May. A month of happiness and sunshine, a month of blooming flowers and joy. But it is not meant for me. I cannot be part of it. I can peek through the crack in the window and watch others being happy. I've been telling myself over and over again that this is the way it has to be, but I cannot come to terms with it. The thought that if I survive I will make up for it does not console me. I also know that I am not allowed to complain. There are others much worse off than I am.

---

7  Created in 1942 as a forced labour camp, the Płaszów camp was reclassified a concentration camp in 1944 and divided into several sections, including a men's camp and a women's camp, and a labour education camp for Polish workers, to segregate the Jews from the Poles. The camp also contained barracks for the Germans, factories and warehouses. At its maximum capacity, the camp held over 20,000 people; thousands of prisoners were killed there. Source: "Plaszow," United States Holocaust Memorial Museum. https://www.ushmm.org/wlc/en/article.php?ModuleId=10005301.

Too bad, my diary, that you cannot talk! I have so much to tell you about the prison I am in, about understanding someone who has been sentenced. There's a difference, though. What have I done to be punished like this? I don't remember committing a crime, so why must I pay such a heavy price? I go to sleep asking God to end this nightmare. I get up in the morning and thank Him for the peaceful day. I hear you saying, my friend, that I shouldn't sin by complaining. I can wash up and I am not too hungry. But the humiliation is terrible.

Our lives are sad; we are dependent on the moods of our landlady. If I forget myself and talk a little louder or walk around the room, she comes running from the kitchen and scolds me. How can I expect her to know how I feel?

Tuesday, May 2
We went to sleep as usual but were awakened at eleven o'clock by the sound of planes. The sky lit up, followed by a thunder of bombs. At first, we got excited. A ray of hope! But then we realize that we cannot escape. We are trapped. We cannot run to hide. We are hiding, but not from bombs. The hissing sound is petrifying. The bombs are falling close by because the German artillery is somewhere nearby. It lasted until midnight. The rest of the night was uneventful.

After a long wait, Olga got a letter from Herman. I would like to hear from Dolek too. Everyone is frightened because of the bombing. Our landlords are running around like crazy. They've never experienced fear before. They don't know what a "roundup" is, that terrible word that represents the death of thousands of innocent people. We are not afraid of anything anymore.

And so the week goes by. The worst part is the feeling of helplessness. God only knows how much longer we'll have to be here. Sometimes, I think that it will always be like this and I'll be here forever.

The Soviet offensive has started but it doesn't look like the end is near. Something will happen, but when? In a week, a month, four months? I've been reading a lot. Mr. Meszaros supplies us with books. One of them was by Gabriele D'Annunzio, entitled *The Intruder*. The book is about an unhappy young couple. The other is by a Russian author and is about a correctional school for orphaned Russian boys. It is written with a sense of humour. Besides reading, we talk, discuss and reminisce. But most of the time, I think. I think about what life was like before, about all the boys in my path, always about Janka and Niuta, about Jo and Zygo who are in Płaszów, and everyone else. Sometimes, I wish I could join them, but then I discard the thought. If I leave this place, I want to be a free person. In the evening, when the landlady goes out and locks the door, I sneak out of the room to get a glimpse of another life. I watch the girls walking on the street, smiling, nicely dressed, and I feel pangs of jealousy. Then I stay up late into the night and dream. I live with the hope that we'll survive.

Sunday, May 7
Days blend into weeks and time passes aimlessly. I've been here six weeks, and who knows how much longer? I thought I was coming here for three or four weeks, just as the offensive was approaching. It looked as if we were going to be liberated any day. Now the offensive has stopped, the front has moved back and it looks like we may be here for months. I cannot allow myself to think in those terms. It becomes too unbearable.

Tuesday, May 9
Ewa Fedorow came to visit. She told us about the damage and aftereffects of the bombing attack. It doesn't impress me. I am prepared for the worst. I have days when nothing but black, dark thoughts engulf my unhappy existence. I try to chase them away, but in vain. It's hard for me to understand why Mummy is surprised to see me crying. She asks, "Why?" Don't I have reasons? No one understands me. That is when I like talking to you, my diary, my friend. What a pity you cannot answer.

Thursday, May 11

We had a terrible experience. Daddy briefly left our room and walked into the kitchen this morning, unaware that the milkman was sitting at the table. He backed off, but too late. He was noticed and the whole thing looked suspicious. Daddy was inconsolable in his guilt. We thought that now we would certainly have to leave this place. And leaving means deportation. If we are to go from here, we have to return to camp.

By some miracle, nothing happened. How I long to be free! I've never appreciated freedom, but now I understand its meaning. How I would love to experience that miracle.

May 14 to 20

After last week's incident, our vigilance has been doubled. Our landlady, as pleasant and accommodating as she was at the beginning, has changed. It is sad how dependent we are on her and her moods. How humiliating! We try to be as nice and polite as possible and do what we are told. We are allowed to be in the kitchen only in the morning, to wash up. The rest of the day we spend in our room. I feel alone with my thoughts. I enjoy reading. It keeps me distracted from my own sad life. I've read two books by Victor Hugo, *Hans of Iceland* and *The Last Day of a Condemned Man*.

I am terribly worried and concerned that I didn't attend high school. I am tormented by feelings of inadequacy.

Sunday, May 21

Ewa Fedorow came to visit. She is going to Warsaw again. Attractive, nicely dressed. It's amazing that there's life outside these walls.

Monday, May 22

Starting on Monday, May 22, we had one aggravation after another. The brother of the landlady lost his work permit, *Ausweis*, and accused us of stealing it. He didn't say it in as many words, but implied as much and threatened to go to the police if it wasn't found. Oh, what a sad life! To add to our unhappy existence, now this!

Tuesday, May 23
Daddy spoke to the brother of the landlady and explained to him that we did not take his *Ausweis*. He offered him money for his silence. The brother reassured us that he has no intention of giving us away, but can we trust him? Daddy told him that we have friends in the Underground who would hunt him if he were to denounce us to the police.

Since the Soviet offensive has stopped, people are coming back to camp. There are about five hundred people there now. As soon as there are enough people for deportation, there will be another transport going west.

Wednesday, May 24
Daddy's birthday. He is forty-eight years old. We asked the landlady to bring us some lilacs from the garden. At least I know that it's spring outside. Slowly, I am getting used to my sad existence. Maybe God is watching over us. Maybe He'll help us live through this and then I'll make up for all these years.

Thursday, May 25
A year ago today, Janka and Niuta were taken away to Dachówczarnia, a hard labour camp and brick factory in Drohobycz. I remember the day so well. My dearest girls, you are not with us any more. You suffered so much and it was all for nothing. How great my joy would have been if we could celebrate our liberation together. It is not to be!

Sunday, May 28
The weather is beautiful. The sun is shining and it's hot. How I'd love to go to the country with my friends and go swimming, dancing and running through the fields! Why am I dreaming? That is all I can do. Because of the crowded conditions and the lack of fresh air, the lice are eating us alive.

Monday, May 29

There isn't a day that goes by without some terrible excitement. Today, the landlady left as usual in the evening to visit Mr. Meszaros, who supplies us with books and news. She came back in less than an hour, dishevelled and in a state of hysteria. She was stopped and questioned by the patrolling police because she was out after curfew (nine o'clock). She was convinced that she was being followed. We got dressed and waited, prepared for the worst. But nobody came. Another miracle! It turned out the police are on the alert for partisans who are sabotaging oil refineries. The police regard everyone as a suspect.

June 4 to 8

On Monday, June 5, the landlady told us that an electrician would be coming to install a bell. She is paranoid about bombings and wants to be warned ahead of time by the neighbours downstairs. It's completely senseless, but she is beyond reason. We had to leave our room and go up to the attic. A partition at the end of a sloping tin roof gave us enough room to crouch down and hide. It was a scorching day. The sun beat down mercilessly. With no light or air, we were suffocating. It was a living inferno. We were there for six hours. Following the electric wires, the electrician stopped in front of the partition. Through the cracks, he suddenly saw four pairs of frightened eyes. Stunned, he turned away and left. He was supposed to have come back the following day, but he never did. He never installed the bell and he did not give us away. Who was this man? We will never know, but will be forever grateful to him.

Friday, June 9

Our landlady brought us a letter from Mr. Meszaros that the offensive on the western front — D-Day — had begun.[8] Maybe it won't be long now. My God! Help us survive! Romek's birthday. He would have been seventeen. How tragically he died. How often I think about him.

---

8  D-Day refers to the Allied invasion of the French coast on June 6, 1944.

June 11 to 18
It has been a quiet week. The landlady brought news from Mr. Meszaros that the Germans are losing on all fronts.

Thursday, June 22
Three years since the outbreak of the German-Soviet war. For the second time, everyone in our camp was deported. About 600 people were taken farther west.

June 25 to July 1
On Monday, June 26, at three in the afternoon, seventy American planes bombed Drohobycz, a neighbouring town. Five hundred people died. We expect a miracle any day. In the meantime, our suffering doesn't end.

July 1 to 9
We are worried. Ewa Fedorow was supposed to bring money from Mr. Druszkiewicz in Warsaw. We are expecting her every day. The landlord didn't get paid. They are rounding up Poles and Ukrainians and forcing them to join the German army. Our landlady informed us that if her husband is taken, she will no longer be able to keep us. There is no end to our problems.

July 9 to 16
Nothing is happening. The hopelessness is overwhelming. Fortunately, Ewa Fedorow showed up, but she brought only 5,000 złotys instead of 10,000, claiming that the remainder was taken from her. The landlady told us three times that we will have to leave. She called Daddy into the kitchen and told him categorically that she is too nervous and too afraid of being arrested and therefore we must go.

July 16 to 23
On Monday night, July 17, we panicked because someone came to pick up our landlords. The landlady is blackmailing us. She hardly

gives us anything to eat except potatoes and sour milk. We had asked
Mr. Meszaros to find us another hiding place. Finally, on Thursday,
the landlady told us that she had a fight with the neighbour and the
neighbour told her that she knows that our landlady is hiding Jews.
Daddy took a stand and told her not to terrorize us, that we would
leave as soon as we found another place, but in the meantime she had
to keep us. It worked. She has changed her attitude.

Saturday, July 22
Mr. Meszaros has let us know that the Russians are twenty-five kilo-
metres from Lwów. We learned that our camp was evacuated again.
Some people in camp were shot.

Tuesday, July 25
The *Schutzpolizei* and *Reiterpolizei*[9] have left. The Germans are retreating. My diary, my friend. Can I describe my happiness?

Sunday, July 30
We have been waiting in anticipation. From day to day, from hour to
hour. How difficult it is to be patient!

July 31 to August 6
Mr. Meszaros came on Wednesday. What a remarkable human being.
He brought two loaves of bread with him. The moment of truth is
near. Now every minute lasts forever. He tried to reassure us that the
retreating army would not blow up the refineries. Despite his assur-
ances, on Thursday, August 3, at 4:00 p.m. explosions not too far in
the distance shook our house. Maybe it will not be long now!

Friday and Saturday, we could hear the artillery — shots, explosions. We spent the night in our clothes, ready to leave any minute
if necessary. Tanks, soldiers — the commotion lasted all night. Our

---

9  Security police and cavalry.

sleep was interrupted. Tremendous explosions. Dust everywhere. The bridge nearby was blown up. Fighting takes place on the streets, the Soviet army is visible. Despite Mummy's pleas, Daddy goes out. You know, my diary, it is strange that instead of celebrating, I broke down and cried. My dear friends! Why can't you be here with me? Why didn't God help you live to the day of liberation?

Tuesday, August 8

This is a memorable day. Our city, Borysław, is liberated by the Soviet army as it advances victoriously toward Berlin. We are anxious to leave our hiding place, but the landlady asks us not to go before dark so that the neighbours will not see us. How sad that instead of being proud that she has saved our lives, she is embarrassed. We leave anyhow, and never look back. My legs, a little wobbly and weak, carry me outside as though I were in a dream. For the first time in four months, I feel wind and sun against my skin. I fill my lungs with fresh air and breathe freedom.

We meet other survivors also coming out of hiding. We all look pale, weak and tired from years of struggle. We hug and cry for the people who are not with us. How happy I was to see Dolek! How I have waited for this day to come! This is the beginning of a new life. I am alive and free. What joy! We have nothing and yet we have everything — our lives.

Miracles do happen.

POSTSCRIPT

World War II ended in Europe on May 8, 1945. Germany was defeated. More than thirty million civilians lost their lives. Six million of them were Jews, and of these, one and a half million were children.

Borysław, where we had been living after liberation, was annexed to the Soviet Union, and so we travelled west to Poland proper. We settled in Krakow, a beautiful medieval city that had been left undamaged by the war. It would become our home for the following four years.

I made up for three years of lost schooling and finished high school. After six years of war, my life was becoming normal again. It was free, fast and intense. I lived and I loved.

I visited Warsaw often with my sister, Olga. After a number of wartime uprisings, the city had been reduced to rubble. On April 19, 1948, five years to the day after the historic event, we took part in a ceremonial dedication of a monument to the fighters of the Warsaw Ghetto Uprising. Despite the solemn occasion, we marched through the streets with other survivors, singing and waving flags. The feeling of pride was indescribable. German prisoners of war who were clearing the rubble paused to watch us with curiosity. What bitter irony!

My father did not see any future in Poland for himself or his family. My mother's only surviving sister, Maria Zenwirth, helped us emigrate. She had left Poland with her family a week before the outbreak of war, living first in Palestine and then settling in Montreal. After hearing the joyous news that we were alive, she sent us sponsorship papers, thus enabling us to come to Canada.

In 1949, we left for the far-away land of Canada. I was twenty-one years old. Once again, I was uprooted. Once again, I left my friends behind.

With one life behind me, I began another. But that is another chapter, and another long story.

Montreal, 2004


*My gratitude to Sally Spilhaus for her patience, understanding and thoughtful insights while writing this memoir. Thank you, Sally, for your help in giving a voice to my experience and to war's silent victims.*

IN MEMORIAM

My aunt Stefa and her husband, Stefan Auber: Killed in a pogrom in Schodnica in July 1941.

My uncle Heniu Müller, his wife, Lola, and their daughter, Dorotka: The circumstances of their deaths are unknown. After escaping from the Warsaw ghetto in 1942, they lived as "Aryans" in the countryside.

My paternal grandmother, Babcia Koretz: Shot in the town square in Tarnów, August 1942.

My aunt Tynia, her husband, Jakób Lustgarten, their children, Rutka and Fredek, and Aunt Hela Müller: Perished in Bełżec death camp in August 1942.

Romek Engelberg (June 1927–August 1942): During a deportation from Borysław, Romek, his mother and others were hiding in the cellar of the German police station. They were denounced and sent to Bełżec death camp, where they perished.

Ewa Kessler (June 1929–1943?) Ewa was denounced and executed while a friend was taking her to a safe place by train.

Janka Teicher (November 1927–August 1943) and Niuta Teicher (December 1928–August 1943): On August 27, 1943, the Germans liquidated the Dachówczarnia camp in Drohobycz. While awaiting deportation, Janka, Niuta and their parents took their own lives by poisoning at the hand of their father, a physician.

Letter from Janka Teicher, smuggled from the camp shortly before her death at age fifteen. Translation by Irena Peritz.

*My dearest Irena,*

*I don't have the heart to write to you, yet I want to. I don't know if this is my first or last letter to you. However, we are still alive. I don't like to dwell on it for too long. What we have gone through and what we're going through is hard to put on paper. Yesterday's day and night of cry-*

*ing did not help. It is very hard to come to terms with our terrible fate. We live with our cousins, the Ornsteins, in one room — eight people. We were taken from our hiding place just in the clothes we were wearing. I did not even have time to take garters for my stockings. I had to hold up my stockings all the way. We have one summer dress between us.*

*Work will be hard, carrying bricks. Loading the kiln and firing them. Mummy and Daddy have to work too. Wakeup is at 5:30 a.m. We are counted and then taken to the factory. Work doesn't frighten me as much as watching my parents suffering. My father is a broken man. He cries like a little child. You wouldn't recognize him or Mummy. We, who are so used to comfort and hygiene, had to brush our teeth using one toothbrush someone had given us. Maybe it was meant to be. But I thank God we are all together and will die together.*

*If it weren't for us, Daddy would have been in Dachówczarnia and we in the next world. When we were in the movie hall with the other people gathered for deportation, Daddy's name was called, and we were told to stay behind. Ignoring the Germans and their dogs, we jumped over chairs to get to him. The Lieutenant agreed to let us go. It is so paradoxical that at that tragic moment we were happy to be together, even though being together meant that we would die together. Now I have lived to hear my father say, "My poor children, you are suffering because of me." Unfortunately, we do not have any poison with which to end it all.*

*My dear one, give my regards to everyone and remember us in your free moments.*

*Bye, be well. Hugs and kisses from your very unhappy,*
*Janka*

Irena (right) at age four, with her older sister, Olga. Warsaw, circa 1932.

The Koretz family before the war. From left to right: Irena's sister, Olga; her father, Józef; Irena; and her mother, Rozalia. Warsaw, 1939.

1 Irena (centre) and her close friends, Niuta (left) and Janka (right) Teicher. Borysław, Poland, circa 1941.
2 Irena's friend Romek Engelberg. Date unknown.
3 Irena's friend Ewa Kessler. Date unknown.

1  Irena and her husband, Simon.
2  Irena and her children, Paul, Nina and Ingrid, on Mother's Day, 2014.

1 Irena and her grandsons. From left to right: Darron, Daniel, Irena, Eric and Jonathan. Montreal, 2009.

2 Irena and Olga. February 2016.

# A Beacon of Light
# Eva Kuper

*To my mother, Fela Kupferblum, who was murdered at Treblinka; to my father, Anthony (Abram) Kuper, who against all odds escaped with me from the Warsaw ghetto; and to my two rescuers, Hanka Rembowska and Sister Klara Jaroszyńska, two women of uncommon courage and goodness.*

My parents, Fela and Abram, were both born in a beautiful town in Poland about two hundred kilometres southeast of Warsaw called Sandomierz, where 40 per cent of the city's population was Jewish. My family was extensive and very much a part of the life of the city. My paternal grandfather, Solomon, owned a shoe store that was located on the ground floor of the building in which his family lived and was very involved in the Jewish community. My maternal grandfather, David, owned a mill in partnership with his brother. My parents were distant cousins and grew up together, but my mother's family was financially more comfortable than my father's. My father had three brothers — Stanisław (Stach, or Stasiek), Leon and Moniek, and two sisters, Mina and Zosia (Sophie); my mother had a sister, Gucia (Gertrude), and two brothers, Hilek (Henry) and Leon. My father's parents did their best to educate all their children, but my father, as the oldest son, was the only one who had a university education at that time. As a Jew, he was not admitted to university in Poland to study chemical engineering and was sent to Belgium to study. My mother was trained as a teacher, but was also not able to work in her profession because she was Jewish and, therefore, worked in a bank.

In 1936, when my father returned from Belgium, my parents were married and they moved to Warsaw, where my father eventually started a small business as a chemical engineer, preparing the dyes for furs. He liked to play the lottery and on one occasion won a considerable sum of money. The money from the lottery made it financially possible to start a family, and I was born in 1940. My parents moved to a lovely new apartment in a suburb of Warsaw known as Bielany, where there was a lot of green space and fresh air for their new baby. They bought new furniture and settled into life in their new community. There was a small grocery store in the neighbourhood where my father would often stop to pick up whatever was needed at home. He made friends with the owners, the Rondio family, who were ethnic Germans. Mr. Rondio was employed as a policeman and his wife ran the store. One day, when my father stopped at the store, he found some men packing up the stock on the shelves. When he asked Mrs. Rondio what was happening, she tearfully explained that she had not been able to pay some debts and therefore her stock was being taken in payment. My father quickly offered to help by giving her the needed funds. This generosity sealed what would become an important friendship.

Unfortunately, the times were becoming increasingly turbulent as the world neared the beginning of World War II. The war broke out in September 1939 when Germany invaded and occupied Poland. The following year, the Nazis began to gather the Jews into a designated area of Warsaw: the ghetto.[1] Initially there were two ghettos — the

---

1   On October 12, 1940, the Germans issued an edict that established the ghetto, which was sealed in November 1940. It contained approximately 400,000 Jews, 30 per cent of the city's total population, in about 2.4 per cent of the city's total area. From July 22, 1942, to September 1942, 300,000 Jews were deported, mainly

small one where people lived and a larger one in which were found the commercial establishments, stores and factories as well as living quarters. The Poles and others who had occupied the area before it became a ghetto were forced out, and soon the ghetto was separated from the rest of the city by an encircling ten-foot-high wall topped by barbed wire.

When we moved to the ghetto, my parents left their new furniture with the Rondios, not wanting to take it to the squalor of the ghetto and still believing that the situation was only temporary and that they would soon return to their former life. The ghetto was unbelievably crowded, so we considered ourselves fortunate to secure a whole room for our small family, which now included five people — the three of us, as well as my mother's cousin and one of her daughters. My cousin's other daughter, Regina, was my mother's closest friend, and she worked as a guard in the ghetto prison. There was a phone in the cellar of our building that could be used to make calls, but not receive them. My father arranged with Regina that if an emergency arose, he would alert her by phone at the prison.

It is well documented that life in the ghetto became unbearable. The crowded conditions contributed to repeat outbreaks of many diseases, and the lack of food, clean water and decent sanitary conditions made life extremely difficult. It was not long before people began to die by the thousands. Yet at the same time there were others who, because of smuggling or paying off guards to look the other way, enjoyed a standard of living equal or even superior to conditions before the war. My father described peering into a restaurant

---

to Treblinka, where they were murdered on arrival. By the end of September, only 55,000 Jews remained in the ghetto and, on April 19, 1943, when new deportations were expected, they revolted. This was the largest and considered the most important Jewish uprising during World War II. By May 16, 1943, most Jews had been sent to forced labour camps. See "Key Dates: Warsaw Ghetto, Poland," United States Holocaust Memorial Museum. www.ushmm.org. Accessed on April 15, 2016.

one night only to hear music and see wine, champagne, fine delicacies and sumptuous decor. How could this be going on in the face of the horror experienced by the masses?

My father, as a chemist, worked in one of the German factories in the large ghetto. Because he was a key person, he enjoyed a somewhat privileged status, but we still had very little. He recalled that, at the beginning, there were corpses laid out in the street each morning for collection by carts belonging to the Jewish Burial Society. Even then the Jewish community was somewhat organized, with the Nazis forcing the Jewish community leaders to do their dirty work. Some did it to save themselves at least temporarily; others could not. The number of corpses increased dramatically, and each morning one could see masses of bodies awaiting collection. These corpses contributed to the diseases that ran rampant among a terribly compromised population. Eventually, huge holes were dug and bodies were buried in mass graves in an attempt to curb the spread of disease to some extent.

My father continued to work and, having some means, brought as much food as he could into the small ghetto from the large one. He would distribute the food to the neighbours and help as many people as he could. Years later, he remembered that I, as a small child, sat on the broad sill at the open window, handing out food to starving children waiting there who had distended abdomens and limbs that looked like sticks.

The Nazis would shoot people with little or no provocation. By the summer of 1942, at first every few weeks, then every few days, the Nazis would order the Jewish "authorities" to round up one hundred or two hundred or more people for transport or "resettlement," as it was called. The Jewish authorities could not refuse and the quota had to be met, or they themselves were forced to join the ranks of those who were "resettled." One morning, all the men in our section of the ghetto were ordered to report to the yard at the Többens factory.[2] My father had to go. The men were kept locked up with no explanation for several hours. It was only on his release and return to our room that my father found the entire area where we lived cleared of women and children. Everyone was gone! My father ran to phone Regina to alert her about what had happened and then ran to the *Umschlagplatz*, the loading platform where people were being herded by the hundreds onto cattle cars. He tried to find us but was prevented by the guards, who would not let him come near. He felt that if our family was being "resettled," he wanted to be with us. He persisted in trying and eventually was threatened by a Nazi with a gun. Meanwhile, Regina had raced to the loading yard and, incredibly, arrived in time to see my mother and me being loaded into one of the cattle cars. The timing was crucial. Had she arrived a moment earlier or later, she would not have seen us. She began to scream that I was her child, and maybe because she wore a uniform, or maybe because they still needed her at the prison, my mother was permitted to pass me hand-to-hand until I was thrown off the train into Regina's arms. A true miracle! My father found Regina sitting in her room, crying, with me on her lap. Regina, unfortunately, was not ultimately spared. As soon as she and others like her were no longer useful, they met the same fate as my mother.

The moment when my mother made the heroic decision to save me haunts me to this day. The natural inclination of mothers is to hold their children close when sensing danger or catastrophe. What did that decision cost her? How insightful of her to predict the horror that awaited those on the train, many of whom still believed the

---

2   The Többens textile factory, established in 1941 by Walter Többens and Fritz Emil Schultz, had two locations in the ghetto and, at its height, employed 15,000 Jewish slave labourers. The ghetto factories were part of a larger network of the company.

German "resettlement" story. How broken her heart must have been as she handed me off, believing that even that small chance was better than what awaited her.

My father began to plan our escape from the ghetto. At this time, however, I became sick with dysentery, which is very serious for a young child. Day after day, he watched as I got progressively sicker. He had three diapers that he washed repeatedly and put back on me, wet. I became dehydrated and lapsed into semi-consciousness. My father's friend Dr. Kalinowski came to see if he could help. Without a "physiological solution," he said, I would die within a few hours. In desperation, my father turned to the manager of the Többens factory where he worked, begging the manager, who was not Jewish and had access to the city outside the ghetto, to get the solution. He agreed and, within a few hours, I began to revive. Saved again! Once I recovered a little, it was definitely time to escape.

Each time there was a roundup, people scurried around searching for a place to hide. During one of the roundups, my father, with me in his arms, stood in the water-filled cellar of a factory building, along with a dozen others, while people were apprehended up above. The people hiding with us warned my father that, should we all survive the night, he would not find shelter among them again. It was too dangerous to hide with a small child whose cries could jeopardize the lives of everyone. My father knew the dangers and always carried two cyanide pills in his pocket, determined to kill both of us rather than be taken alive by the Nazis.

We had to leave the ghetto immediately, before another roundup. My father was convinced that the sewers were our only chance. He arranged with his sister Sophie, who, using false identity papers, was on the so-called Aryan side, to have someone pick us up once we emerged outside the ghetto. My father told me that the trip through the sewers was unimaginably horrible, with filth and rats as big as cats everywhere. It took two and a half hours.

When we emerged, a sorry sight I am sure, my aunt's friend took us to the home of the Rondios, who welcomed us warmly. Mr. Rondio, though he considered himself a Pole, had been badly treated by the Poles, who naturally distrusted and hated anyone German. Thus, the Rondios had moved into a German section of the city. They felt that they would not be suspected of hiding Jews, so they were not worried about having us there. Since we, in my father's words, "looked like death" and were pale as ghosts from being hidden so much, they had us lie on the floor of their dining room where the sun could warm our faces and help us look more normal. They fed us and helped us to catch our breath from the terrible ordeals we had lived through. They were very distressed to hear about my mother and to get a first-hand account of life in the ghetto. In spite of their willingness to offer us shelter, my father felt strongly that although we were not safe anywhere, he did not want to jeopardize their safety and very lives by our presence in their home.

My father turned to Dr. Lande, who had been the pediatrician who looked after the children of the fur trade union members. He had known my parents since my birth, and my father was sure that he would be sympathetic to our plight. He begged Dr. Lande to find a safe place for me; since my father could not work and hide his remaining family while caring for a young child, I could not be safe with him. Dr. Lande agreed and told my father that he would be in touch with him in a few days. True to his word, he placed me with Hanka Rembowska, an artist and illustrator of children's books who was a wonderful woman already caring for a little girl, Zosia, who, although not Jewish, had been orphaned by the events of the war. Hanka, who was suffering from tuberculosis, took care of us until she became too sick to do so. The antibiotics used to treat tuberculosis today were not yet known in 1942. Dr. Lande then took us to a farmhouse about 450 kilometres away in Zakopane in the Tatra Mountains, in the southern-most part of Poland.

My own somewhat vague memories begin in the farmhouse, which was located on a hill overlooking the town. There were many nuns, one priest and many blind children, all boys except for Zosia and me.[3] Times were very hard and there was not much food. I remember potatoes. All the children sat in a large circle outside, peeling potatoes. Since the boys could not see, they would peel as best as they could, then pass the potatoes to Zosia and me to remove the missed spots before putting them into the big pot filled with water, in the middle of the circle. Potatoes were the staple of our diet. There was also a cow that I loved. I remember going to get the cow from the pasture at the end of the day when it was time to bring her home for milking. I would hold the thick cord around her neck and pat her soft fur. That milk and the bit of butter that could be made from it were the only wholesome parts of our diet. I also remember sitting around a long rectangular table at meal times with all the other children, the nuns and the priest. The priest sat at the head of the table with me on his left side. He was the only one who would get a small square of butter for his bread. He would butter a piece of bread, cut it in half and pass me one half under the table. He did not have enough to go around. I was the lucky one. I was always very small for my age, marked for life by those early years of hunger and deprivation.

Whenever the Nazis invaded the village to renew their supplies and take whatever they wanted, someone would run up the hill to warn the nuns. Perhaps it was not because they knew that a Jewish child was being hidden there. It was good to know when the Nazis were around so that anything of value, such as food and supplies,

---

3   The farmhouse was connected to an Order that was established in 1918 by Elzbieta Czacka, a blind Polish nun of the Congregation of Franciscan Sisters Servants of the Cross. The Order had a facility in Zakopane during the war, and currently has residences in Laski, Poland, as well as Ukraine, Italy, Rwanda and South Africa. It is dedicated to the education and well-being of blind children. *Wartime Rescue of Jews by the Polish Catholic Clergy: The Testimony of Survivors*, compiled and edited by Mark Paul, Polish Educational Foundation in North America, 2009. http://www.savingjews.org/docs/clergy_rescue.pdf.

could be hidden before it was confiscated. Whenever this happened, I would also be hidden. I remember vaguely being outside in the pasture, in a hole that had been excavated for that purpose. I would climb in, a board would be placed over the opening and the sod would cover the board. I sat quietly in there until the danger passed. Strangely enough, I don't remember being frightened. I have no idea what might have been said to me to make it feel okay. I was used to being quiet. Somehow, I was made to feel safe, which is unbelievable to me now, since when I imagine placing my children or my grandchildren in such a situation, I am terrified at the psychological damage that would result. I lived in this farmhouse for three years and through to the end of the war.

After the war, my aunt Sophie found my name listed at one of the agencies that were compiling names of people who had been found. Not being sure that it was really me, Sophie did not tell my father, but came alone to get me. I don't remember this well, but my recollections do not match what she remembers. I remember her coming toward me as I led my beloved cow home for milking. She tells me that she found me in the convent building. I do not remember my feelings at being spirited away by my aunt, whom I did not remember at all. I do remember not being eager to leave my familiar and safe life, but I did not put up a fuss … hardly surprising, since I had long ago learned to be a quiet and accepting child. She recalls that the first thing I said to her was how lucky I was that I could see, since the other children were blind. Oddly enough, I don't even remember the meeting with my father, which must have been emotional.

～

After the war, we lived in a city called Bielsko, now known as Bielsko-Biała. My father was the director of a government fur-dyeing plant. He had an important position and, by the standards of the day, we were quite well off, having a housekeeper, a chauffeur and other servants. Of course, having a chauffeur in those days was not the same luxury it is today. All automobiles were old, somewhat reconditioned, and you could hardly travel a kilometre without some mechanical failure befalling you. My father was the least handy person alive … the chauffeur was a necessity if we were to have a car. My aunt Sophie, who had lost her husband during the war, lived with us in a lovely apartment. I remember that she was beautiful and lived life to the fullest, since everyone who had survived the horrors of the war tried to get the most out of life. There were parties, card games, outings, holidays and friends.

Even after the war, there was still a great deal of antisemitism in Poland. We lived as non-Jews, using my father's assumed wartime name of Kornacki, since it was not safe to live openly as Jews. I went to school where, among other subjects, I learned catechism. I had my first communion at the age of six, went to weekly confession and felt purified by the experience. My father never went to church, so I went with our housekeeper, whom I loved.

In 1948, my father met a woman named Barbara[4] and remarried, and he had to do some finagling to secure a passport and exit visa for my stepmother when our immigration to Canada was imminent. He had already arranged for our passports before his marriage. He felt that life as Jews in Poland would continue to be difficult, and I am sure that he was tired of the need for vigilant deception.

It was only on the ship crossing the Atlantic that my father told me that I was Jewish. It would have been dangerous to share this secret with a young child. I had learned in school that the Jews had crucified Jesus and that they were evil. I was horrified to learn that I was one of "them." It took many years before I became comfortable with the idea and many more before I felt pride in my heritage and in my people.

After the initial period of adjustment learning the new language

---

4  See Barbara Kuper's story in this anthology, pages 193–208.

and culture, I began to feel Canadian, just like all my friends. Since I was young and had an aptitude for languages, I learned to speak English without a Polish accent, and my life in Poland quickly began to fade in my memory.

My parents spoke little about the Holocaust and their experiences during the war. They did not want to burden me and wished for me to grow up without the horror of those memories. I asked few questions and was not terribly interested in the few stories that they did tell. I knew that my parents suffered from sleeplessness and flashbacks whenever they spoke of their experiences. I am sure that the spectre of the Holocaust remained with them even though I heard little about it. Nevertheless, the Holocaust, the loss of my mother and the deprivations of those years have had a profound effect on me and my family, even my children and grandchildren. My youngest daughter, Felisa, is named for my mother and since childhood she has had an abiding interest in that part of our past. When she reached young adulthood, Felisa was always keen to hear the stories, even though they were very difficult to hear and to tell. I had an uncle and aunt who spoke of the war years incessantly. Felisa was eager for me to go to Poland with her to retrace our family's history. I had no interest in going back. I had no fond memories and no love for the Poles or for researching the terror of those years.

Yet in 1998, I was approached by the Shoah Foundation to videotape my wartime experiences as part of the living testimony project initiated by Steven Spielberg, a request that started my own return to these past events. To prepare for the taping, I listened to audiotapes that I had begged my father to make for me about six months before he died. In them, he tells the story of how I was saved, recalling to the best of his ability, and with great pain, the events and horrors of those times. These tapes were the raw material from which this chronology emerged.

Beginning with the videotape, I began to prepare myself to approach my legacy of being a child survivor, a hidden child. My interest in this part of my life was reborn, and I became involved in Holocaust education at the school of which I was the principal — the Jewish People's and Peretz School in Montreal — and subsequently at the Hebrew Foundation School. In 2003, at a family gathering following the bar mitzvah of my cousin David's son Sam, the idea of a trip back to Poland with my husband, Harvey, and my cousin Joseph and his wife, Edith, was born. My daughter Felisa was very keen to make this trip with me, and eventually the plan evolved into spending two weeks tracing our roots with my husband and my cousins, after which Felisa would join me for twelve days to continue to search for my past and that of our family.

The evening before our departure on August 23, 2005, I attended a meeting of Auberge Shalom pour femmes, where I am active on the board and the executive. I took a seat near a former colleague and commented that I hoped that the meeting would not take long, since I was leaving the next day for a month-long trip to Prague, Budapest and Poland. Surprised, she told me that she too would be visiting Poland, in October. She gave me the name of an American, Yale Reisner, who was the director of the Jewish Historical Institute in Warsaw, and she gave me his telephone number. I took it but did not think that I would need his help since I had researched convents in Zakopane on the internet and had arranged an appointment with a nun in the one where I thought I had been hidden.

On arrival in Warsaw, however, I decided to phone Yale and told him a little about my history. He was eager to meet with me, so we trekked down to the institute to see him. He was busy but we decided to wait and visited the Jewish museum that was also housed in the former Jewish public library in Warsaw. After several hours, we were finally able to meet with Yale. I elaborated on my story, telling him that although my memory of the time in the convent was vague, I did know that there were blind children there. He bolted out of his seat and picked a book off his shelves. It was the Polish version of Ewa Kurek's published doctoral thesis, *Your Life Is Worth Mine: How Polish Nuns Saved Hundreds of Jewish Children in German-Occupied Poland, 1939–1945*. Flipping through the pages, he came upon this paragraph:

*Congregation of Franciscan Sisters Servants of the Cross: Polish order established in 1918 for the purpose of caring for the blind. In 1939, 106 sisters worked in 18 homes. In Zakopane, Sister Klara Jaroszyńska saved the life of a little Jewish girl.*

We were all speechless. This had to be the right convent, and the little Jewish girl had to be me!

The next day, armed with the telephone number, I tried to contact the convent in Warsaw, with no success. My husband returned to Canada, and while I waited for my daughter to arrive, I continued trying to get in touch with someone at the convent. Eventually I managed to contact a Sister Jana Pawła who was in Laski, twenty-five kilometres outside of Warsaw. Laski is the main establishment of this Order, where they continue to look after three hundred blind children to this day. I briefly told her the reason for my call and tentatively asked if it could be possible that someone who had been in Zakopane during the war was still alive. She was very warm and interested and told me the most astounding news: Sister Klara, then ninety-four years old, was alive and in Laski. Twice in two days, I was speechless, which does not happen often. I literally could not breathe. I recovered to ask about Sister Klara's state of health. Sister Jana Pawła assured me that, in spite of the fact that Sister Klara was herself now blind, her mind was clear, her memory intact and accurate and her sense of humour ever present. I was more than delighted, and we arranged a visit to Laski the very same day — September 8, 2005. Felisa was incredulous at this development, and we were both very excited.

We met Sister Jana Pawła in front of the convent's beautiful chapel situated in a forested area full of flowers and greenery. We entered the chapel for her to say a brief prayer, and then she led us to the house where Sister Klara lived, cared for by other nuns. Sister Klara, supported by Sister Rut, her close friend and archivist for the Order, came out of the house and opened her arms to embrace me. I went to her and we held each other close. Everyone was crying. I led her gently to a bench where we sat together, holding each other. She began to talk, recalling those terrible years.

She remembered me well and with great love. She told me that I was a tiny, dark-haired, bright-eyed little girl with whom she instantly fell in love. She recalled that I had come to the convent as a result of her meeting with Hanka Rembowska, whom she knew. Hanka had pleaded with her to take her little girls, as she had become too ill to look after us. Sister Klara told me that while they were speaking, I had been holding Hanka's hand, but I soon dropped it and ran to Sister Klara, putting my arms around her and asking her to pick me up. When she did, and I cuddled into her shoulder, she simply could not refuse. Sister Klara corroborated my own sketchy memories of that time and added detail and information previously unknown to me. Hearing her stories was a very emotional experience for me. Those three years in the convent had been an empty space in my life. I knew no one who could tell me what had happened and what I had been like as a three-year-old child under those difficult conditions.

Sister Klara described me as being the size of a two-year-old, bright, intelligent and very cooperative. She told me that I was very gentle with the other children, most of whom were blind except for Zosia and Sister Klara's three nieces. She told me that I was the smallest child they had in their care and everyone's favourite.

Sister Klara validated many of my memories and corrected others. She told me that when news reached her that the Nazis were nearby, if time allowed, I had indeed been hidden in a hole, but one that had been excavated beneath the earthen floor of the cellar. A board and a mat covered the hole, and a small table was placed on top. If time did not allow, she would put me into bed together with her little niece who, along with her mother and two other siblings, had taken refuge in the convent to escape the bombardment of Warsaw. Sister Klara's sister had three children, two of whom had blond hair, but one had darker hair more like mine. The two of us would hide under her covers and pretend to be sleeping until the danger passed.

I asked Sister Klara how she found the courage to risk the lives of the other children, the nuns, her own sister and her children for the sake of saving one child. She said, "I had to do it. It was right, and besides, God sent you to me, so there really was no choice." It was so simple, yet so very brave. She confessed to being very frightened many times. She told me that she used to carry me because I was so small, and when anyone approached, she would tell me to cuddle down into the fur collar on her coat and pretend to be asleep. I always wore a hat to cover my dark hair when outside the convent. She told me that I had a sense of the danger and always complied when told to. In a letter that followed from the correspondence we began after my visit, Sister Klara wrote that she loved me from the moment she met me. She recalled that the times she held me in her arms were moments of peace, as she felt that when I was so close to her, she could and would protect me from anything.

I feel that I was given life four times: the first when I was born; the second time when my mother passed me hand-to-hand and I was thrown from the cattle car going to Treblinka; the third time when I survived the near-death illness of dysentery; and the fourth time when Sister Klara agreed to hide me.

The miracle of finding Sister Klara came about because of so many coincidences and so many near misses. What if I had not gone to my meeting and learned about Yale Reisner? What if something had not compelled me to wait to see him for over four hours? I now believe that all these events were indeed *beshert*, destined.

I had no idea that I had been fortunate enough not only to find shelter and protection at the convent, but also to be so loved. During this very special visit, I felt as if a missing piece of my life had been put back in place. Sister Klara's sweetness and her beautiful smile as she remembered me at the convent was precious and meaningful to me. The fact that my daughter was there to witness, photograph and cry with us was an additional gift to both of us. I am convinced that the love and kindness of Sister Klara and the other nuns at that time is largely responsible for helping me to be the person I am today. After the loss of my mother and the separation from my father, it was the Sisters who taught me what it meant to love and be loved. It is a gift I treasure and benefit from every day of my life.

I was very eager to find some way to show Sister Klara my love and gratitude. She spent many hours alone each day, and I offered to cover the cost of having someone come to talk or read to her to alleviate her loneliness. However, Sister Rut told me that they could not accept because if Sister Klara had this luxury, all the other nuns would have to as well. A nun, as well, could not accept any monetary gift. We finally came upon the idea of them identifying a child in their care whose family was unable to help, someone desperately in need. I later transferred a sum of money to the Order for the purpose of helping a boy named Grzegorz, then aged thirteen, who was both blind and deaf; the Order was then able to provide him with various tools to assist in his learning, such as hearing aids and an adapted computer. I received a beautiful letter from Grzegorz in braille, which was translated by one of his teachers. He is now living independently, making his living as a massage therapist.

~

Ever since my trip to Poland, and particularly my most fortuitous reconnection with Sister Klara, I had regretted that my husband and my daughter Debbie and her family had not been with us for that momentous meeting. As life would have it, in July 2007 we were planning a family trip to Israel to celebrate my grandson Matthew's bar mitzvah, which had taken place in December 2006, and also my granddaughter Zoey's bat mitzvah, which would take place in Montreal that year. It occurred to us that we could take a detour to Poland on our way home from Israel. The idea took root and soon we had an entourage of eleven family members — my daughter Debbie and her husband, Ron, my grandson Matthew, my granddaughter Zoey, my cousin Joe and his wife, Edith, their daughter Tamara, my cousin David and his wife, Debra, and, of course, my husband, Harvey, and me — all of whom wanted to come along to meet Sister Klara.

We rented a large van with room for all and, with Ron at the wheel, we had a whirlwind tour of Poland in four days. Of course, the highlight of the trip was the three and a half hours we spent with Sister Klara. I was very emotional at seeing her again, and she was delighted to meet my whole family. I introduced her as each person hugged her and held her hands. As she spoke, either my cousin Joe or I translated for the non-Polish speakers. We had brought her a soft, warm blanket as a gift and three enormous, beautiful bouquets of fragrant flowers, wanting her to be able to smell them since she could not see their beauty. Sister Rut had organized a lunch for our whole gang, and we walked to another building that appeared to be a guest house, pushing Sister Klara in her chair through their lovely property.

We were served a lovely lunch in the pleasant dining room. Sister Klara sat beside me, holding my hand, and did not stop talking and smiling as we all ate. She was worried that there was not enough, that we had not eaten enough … just like a Jewish mother. I said that to her and she laughed and said that it was an honour to be like a Jewish mother. She told us many stories while Ron and my cousin Joe videotaped, Tamara took photos and Debbie wrote frantically, trying to note every detail as we translated. Sister Klara told us about the time we had spent together. I had heard many of the details before, but I loved hearing her voice telling the stories again. She said that she felt that we were one person, that only when she held me was I safe, and that I always seemed to sense how to behave in times of danger.

A new story she shared was how once a week she would take an empty sack and walk twenty kilometres to the surrounding farms to ask for food "for her children." The farmers would give her some carrots, onions, potatoes, whatever they could spare. Once, in a stroke of unbelievable luck, she heard about a woman who was both kind and rich. It is from this woman that Sister Klara got the cow I loved, which was supposedly pregnant, along with several sacks of carrots and other vegetables, and a wagon and a man to help her get all this back to us. The cow proved to be pregnant for all of the four years during which Sister Klara owned her, yet never produced a calf. The way she told this story brought gales of laughter from us, especially when she recounted how she was sued by the farmer who bought the cow from her, as a pregnant cow, at the end of the war. She also spoke of her many visits to Israel, the friends she had there and the love that she felt for the country.

We were very reticent to leave, and I felt so blessed to have been able to see Sister Klara again and to have had most of the people I love with me to meet her as well. My grandchildren were at just the right ages to understand and remember this experience for the rest of their lives, as we all will.

At ninety-six years old, Sister Klara had become more physically frail since our last meeting, but her spirit, her voice and her mind were very strong and vibrant. Her sense of humour and love of life, her optimism and her dignity, shone out of her face and one could not help but succumb to her charm and wit. I didn't know if I would ever see her again, but our relationship, even at a long distance, had become an integral part of my everyday life. What a blessing!

On October 10, 2007, Sister Klara, along with fifty-three other Poles who had been instrumental in saving Jewish lives, was honoured by the Polish government in a special ceremony at the Grand Theatre in Warsaw.[5] The president of Poland greeted each recipient

---

5   Sister Klara had been officially recognized as Righteous Among the Nations by Yad Vashem in 1981.

and personally pinned on medals of honour. The director of Yad Vashem attended, as did many dignitaries from the diplomatic core. Two children's choirs sang — one made up of youngsters from Polish schools, the other of Israeli children. At that time, 800 Righteous Poles were still alive, out of more than 6,000 who had been recognized. Obviously, all of them are in their very senior years.

When I spoke with Sister Klara the week before the ceremony she said to me, with her dry wit, "All my life, I was a simple, humble person. Now that I am old, they have made me a hero." It is a great pity that people like Sister Klara, who were great heroes in spite of terrible danger to themselves and those around them, had to wait over sixty years to be recognized. It is, however, better late than never.

In September 2008, I was contacted by email by Rachelle Goldstein, the editor of the Hidden Child Foundation, which had published my story in their newsletter in 2007. Rachelle, in turn, had been contacted by a German filmmaker, Kirsten Esch, who was interested in making a film to document the stories of three hidden children. After checking out the website of her film company, Kaspar Films, I agreed to speak with Kirsten on the telephone and communicate through email.

I liked Kirsten right from our first conversation, especially when I asked her about her motivation for making such a film. She explained that she was always curious about the events of the war; the failure of the German school system to teach children about it; and the reticence of her family to answer her questions and her growing interest. As an adult, Kirsten discovered the fact that her maternal grandfather, a well-loved physician and a concert pianist remembered with great fondness by his family, was involved in doing medical experiments on Jews in one of the camps during the war. Kirsten was shocked and very upset by her discovery, which disturbed her relationship with some of the members of her family and brought her great pain. She did understand, however, her family's unwillingness to discuss the war with her. Perhaps her mother was trying to protect Kirsten, or to protect herself. This history is very difficult and the issue of personal and collective guilt for the Holocaust rest very heavily on the shoulders of some Germans.

Kirsten and I had many conversations in the month prior to our actual meeting in Warsaw on October 21, 2008, for the week of filming. Our comfort and friendship grew with each conversation, and when we actually met at the airport in Warsaw, we were warm and comfortable with each other instantly. We spent the day of our arrival talking, discussing the film and our personal lives and histories. We walked the streets of the Old Town near our hotel, sat shivering outdoors at a café enjoying cappuccinos, and talked and talked.

The next day, we went to the Jewish Historical Institute building (the same one that housed Yale Reisner's office) to begin to research on the computer database in the archives office. Kirsten wanted to emphasize the fact that although her film would be chronicling the stories of three children, there were thousands of such children who were victims of the war. What we were looking for were three or four stories of children who had been liberated and whose testimonies were taken down in interviews when they were placed in children's homes or orphanages. These testimonies, which described their experiences and conditions at the time of the interview, were mostly written in Polish and in longhand, and that is how they were stored in the database. Few had photos attached to them, which was important because the film needed the visuals, and most were very difficult to read, not only because of the penmanship, but also because of the terrors they recounted. A list of about twenty names had been prepared for Kirsten by the staff of Mr. Jürgen Hensel, a German historian who has spent most of his life in Poland researching the Holocaust. We found only one case on this list that could be used in the film.

Kirsten's crew — Oliver, the cameraman, and Hek, the soundman — arrived later in the day. We met another of the institute's staff, Mr.

Jan Jablonski, a Jewish historian who had survived the war in Poland. Jan was about to publish a book, a photo essay that juxtaposed original photos taken in the Warsaw ghetto — mostly by Nazi officers for their own amusement — with current photos taken in the same locations in Warsaw today. Kirsten really liked this idea, and Jan allowed us to photocopy four of the original photos and gave us the current locations. Kirsten and Oliver decided that we would film there tomorrow.

The next day, we started off at the Jewish Historical Institute building again, where we filmed in the archival records room with me reading excerpts from the actual testimonies taken from hidden children found immediately after the war. I read from two or three, each accompanied by a photo of the child, some as young as eight years old. The stories were heartrending and extremely moving. I was repeatedly struck by the children's resilience and immense desire to live.

The day was once again grey and cold and so in order to capture the little light left, we set out to film the four scenes in the photos Jan had given us. I was to walk at the present site and glance at the spot where the original photo shows a person dying or barely alive. It was surreal to imagine, as I walked along the streets of today's bustling Warsaw, that the horrors depicted in the photos had actually taken place in those very spots.

It was very late when we reached the Jewish Historical Institute once more to recreate the amazing discovery of the book documenting the hundreds of children saved by nuns, which had led me to finding Sister Klara. Sitting in the reading room, I read the paragraph over and over until it was perfect. The building was dark and eerie when we finally went up to the second floor to film in the graphic photo exhibit that documented life in the Warsaw ghetto. Kirsten wanted to concentrate on photos of children, and I walked amid the haunting photos, stopping occasionally to answer her brief questions. At the photo of Jews being herded to the *Umschlagplatz*, where the

Jews were loaded into cattle cars for "resettlement" — death at Treblinka — and at another photo of the actual mass loading into the cattle cars, I answered Kirsten's questions through tears and sadness.

It was a difficult day, emotionally and physically. So many horrific stories in the testimonies, and the photos depicted terrible events. A testimony to man's inhumanity.

The following day we set out for Treblinka, arriving around 3:00 pm. A large group of Israeli teens was visiting at the same time. I cried immediately as we approached the main monument and saw these teens draped in Israeli flags, holding each other. They were visibly moved by their visit. Another grey, damp day of filming with scant sunlight as I walked among the stones commemorating all the places — towns, cities, villages — from which people had been brought to be murdered at this death camp. Treblinka has had the same effect on me in all three of my visits. There is an eerie kind of bizarre beauty there, a haunted silence where I feel that the stones are the ghosts among whom I am walking, the ghosts of those whose lives ended there, including my mother's. I cried through most of the day of walking, lighting candles and being interviewed. I had brought two boxes of matches and lit not only the memorial candles I had brought, but also all the other candles there, which had been extinguished by the elements.

Walking back toward the symbolic crematorium with its many original air vents, we saw another group of Israeli students standing in a large circle, with one boy playing a song on his guitar. The others stood close together, emotion written on their faces. I inquired of their teacher if we could film them and she agreed after learning that we were making a documentary about my experiences as a hidden child. While Oliver filmed, I asked if I could join the circle. The teacher put her arm around me and drew me close as we listened to the song the student had written for the occasion, swaying to the music while I cried. Several students stepped forward and read something they had prepared; others read the names of family members who had been murdered here and in other places during the war. They ended their commemorative service with the singing of *Hatikvah*, the national anthem of Israel, which further contributed to my sobbing.

How moving and meaningful. I felt the presence of the students around me — my people — as an affirmation of Jewish youth, of Jewish life in this place of Jewish death, a victory of great significance over Hitler and the Nazis. We turned to go back to the car and I could see the flickering flames of the candles: those lit by the students, the candle I had lit at the Sandomierz stone and the brave little flame of the candle I had lit for my mother lodged in the vertical crevice of the large monument. They were beacons of light and hope in the darkness.

On Saturday, October 25, we spent the day with Sister Klara and Sister Rut in Laski. Once more the day was damp, cloudy and cold. We were greeted by Sister Rut, who had to greet us several times while Oliver filmed the hugs and kisses. Sister Rut took us to Sister Klara's room, which I had not previously seen. It was tiny, with a small bed, a desk and bookshelf and a built-in cupboard, bulletin board and a sink behind the door. All around the room there were artifacts she had collected on her eight trips to Israel, including an Israeli flag, a "shalom" tile from the Arab market and two menorahs.

When I first saw Sister Klara, I was moved to tears. She held me and asked, "Why are you crying, my darling? Are you as happy to see me as I am to see you?" I introduced her to everyone and we chatted for a few minutes. I was glad to see where she lived, so that when I next called her I would be able to visualize her in her space. I gave Sister Rut the camera I had brought for her, a gift from Zoey; and for Sister Klara I brought some excellent Belgian chocolate with rum and liqueur.

We wrapped Sister Klara in the shawl we had brought for her in 2007, plus another blanket, and wheeled her out through the grounds to the cemetery where her sister and parents are buried. The grave was covered with flowers in preparation for the upcoming All Saints'

Day. Kirsten asked that Sister Klara tell us about her family. Her parents were also named as Righteous Among the Nations because they saved a Jewish family, while her sister Halina refused the award even though she also saved two of her Jewish friends. She did not want the honour, since she felt she had done what was right and deserved nothing in return. They are all truly righteous, courageous people with the highest moral standards of decency. Sister Klara told many stories, some with slightly different twists from the same stories told during the last visit. I learned even more of my story and of hers. We stayed at the gravesite for a long time and we were all frozen, except for Sister Klara. She was in high spirits when I finally turned her wheelchair toward home.

We returned to the reception room and talked some more. I wanted Sister Klara to rest, but she refused, saying, "I cannot rest today. You are here with me. I'll rest tomorrow." Throughout the visit, she held my hand, even when she finally drifted off for a little nap. She held my hand so tightly that my fingers were turning white. She is so wonderful and I love her to bits.

We filmed some old photos of Sister Klara's family taken when she was a beautiful young nun, with her parents, sister, brother-in-law and their five children. One of the children, Elzunia, had dark hair and was the one into whose bed I was put, pretending to be asleep if the Nazis made an unexpected visit.

On our second-last day in Warsaw, we filmed in the former ghetto area, beginning at the *Umschlagplatz*. The weather, although still cold, was not as grey and the sun shone weakly through the clouds. Oliver filmed me walking toward the monument bearing the names of people who had been deported from that terrible place. I touched my mother's name with tears streaming down my cheeks. The monument has a space separating two of the walls and a beautiful tree with lovely boughs hanging over the monument seems to be offering protection to the etched names. Oliver was determined to find a sewer with a manhole cover into which he planned to crawl and film from within, simulating my father's exit with me through the sewer after our escape from the ghetto. He finally did succeed, and we set about filming, with him crouching in the hole with the camera wedged under his arm as we slowly covered and uncovered the manhole, letting the light into the darkness.

Kirsten and I then attended a reception for Sister Klara's family, which was commemorating the father of her brother-in-law, who had been murdered by the Nazis and would have been one hundred years old. A special mass, a multimedia presentation of his extraordinary life and a lovely reception was being held at the home of one of Sister Klara's grand-nephews. I was delighted to be invited, to meet her family and especially to meet Elzunia, Sister Klara's niece, in whose bed I had been hidden. Elzunia is a judge and, of course, neither she nor I have any recollection of those events, but it was lovely to meet her. We did not have much time to get acquainted, as she was busy with the whole family. I stayed upstairs with Sister Klara, who was not able to descend the stairs to the basement, where the film was being shown, and we held hands and talked, each of us grateful for another chance to be together. It was very difficult to say goodbye to her when we left. I didn't know if we would see each other again, although I promised to return for her one-hundredth birthday, and she promised to wait for me.

~

I received the finished product of the film, *Hidden Children, Unknown Heroes*, in June 2009. I found it very impressive. Throughout the film, my story alternated with two others, with archival footage interspersed. The effect was powerfully moving and thought-provoking. I was so very fortunate to have had this opportunity and to have met all involved, especially Kirsten, who had become a friend. We had shared so much emotion and so much of our lives in our brief week together.

In November 2009, the film was shown as the final event in the

Montreal Memorial Holocaust Museum's Holocaust Education Series. The museum sponsored Kirsten's trip to Montreal during the week of the screening and she and I took the film on the road, showing it at several schools and venues. Each time, the audience was silent at the conclusion of the film, the emotional impact palpable. Kirsten stayed in my home during her time in Montreal and our friendship, deep connection and affection for one another was reinforced. Immediately following her visit to Montreal, Kirsten and I, accompanied by my two closest friends, flew to Germany for the screening of the film at the Jewish Museum in Berlin. We also saw Sister Klara for the last time. I was delighted to share her with my friends.

Since then I have been fortunate to show the film to different audiences, including students in elementary and high schools, CEGEPS, and in programs sponsored by community agencies, as well as to private groups. I have seen the film many times, yet its impact on me remains powerful. Usually, I introduce the film briefly and handle the questions from the audience following the screening. I am always impressed by the quality and perceptiveness of some of the questions. The film has given me a very precious tool for following my calling of Holocaust education, and I thank Kirsten for having the courage and the talent to create such a special film.

~

On October 20, 2010, my dear Sister Klara died, surrounded by her family and friends. She did not suffer long and died peacefully in her own bed. Her death left a large, empty space where her presence had been for me, but I am eternally grateful for the five years we had together, the depth of the long-distance relationship we forged, the four visits we shared and the frequent telephone conversations that kept our love for each other alive. I am also very grateful to Sister Rut Wosiek, Sister Klara's friend and mine, who made the telephone calls possible and arranged each visit since 2005.

1 The Kupferblum family and cousins in pre-war Sandomierz. Back row (left to right): Eva's father, Abram (Anthony); her aunt Mina; her uncle Henry; a cousin; and her uncle Stanisław (Stach). Middle row (left to right): cousin Jankiel; Eva's mother, Fela; Fela's cousin Regina Bankier; cousin Gershon; cousin Lotka; and cousin Zosia. In front: Eva's aunt Zosia (left) and her aunt Gertrude (right).

2 Eva's mother, Fela (right), with her cousin Regina Bankier, who saved Eva from the deportation in the Warsaw ghetto.

3 Eva's mother, age twenty-seven. Sandomierz, Poland.

1  Baby Eva with her parents, Fela and Abram (Anthony). Warsaw, 1940.
2  Eva at age eight to ten months. Warsaw ghetto, circa 1940.
3  Eva, age seven, after the war. Bielsko, 1947.

The first reunion between Eva and Sister Klara Jaroszyńska. Laski, September 8, 2005.

1 Eva and her family, 2002. Back row (left to right): Eva's husband, Harvey; her son-in-law Dwayne; her daughter Felisa; and her son-in-law Ron. In front (left to right): Eva's granddaughter, Zoey; Eva; her grandson, Matthew; her mother, Barbara; and her daughter Debbie.

2 Eva and Harvey outside the home of Eva's mother, Barbara. Montreal, circa 2001.

3 The family on vacation in Cape Town, South Africa, 2015. From left to right: Matthew, Zoey, Debbie, Ron, Eva, Dwayne and Felisa.

# Hidden by Hope
# Magda Sebestian

*To my children and grandchildren.*

I was the second child born into my family, the Neumans, in Sečovce, a town in eastern Slovakia. It was a small town of approximately 4,000 inhabitants with a large proportion of Jewish families.[1] My grandfather and my father owned a wholesale business of wine and alcoholic beverages. A subsidiary of the business was located in Trebišov, a town approximately twelve kilometres away, where my uncle Ernest owned the shop. We were a well-established, respected family in the town. We lived in a comfortable house that was divided into three areas. In the front of the house was the store, where my father, Bela, worked most of the day. Behind the store was my grandparents' apartment. I lived in the remaining portion of the house with my parents and my two brothers, Bandi and Robi. I loved our garden and backyard where our domestic animals — chickens, geese and two cows — were kept.

My mother, Aranka, was a very energetic, assertive woman who always spoke her mind. She had a good sense of humour, loved to read,

---

1  The population now is about 7,800. There is no source in English that identifies the breakdown of the population by religion in the twentieth century. The 2001 census indicates that there are no self-identified Jews in Sečovce.

liked to socialize and was always optimistic, even during the war when our fate was less than rosy. She kept us all in good spirits with her refreshing optimism and strength. My father was a hard-working man, and his entire life was devoted to his family. He was soft-spoken and very modest. My father repeatedly emphasized the importance of family staying close together. Unfortunately, my father suffered from severe heart disease. He was only forty years old when he had his first stroke, which left him with a damaged heart. He was diagnosed with angina, and these heart issues became more frequent and severe as time passed.

Otherwise, I had a very happy childhood and I felt loved and cherished by my parents and grandparents. My memories of playing with my brothers, Bandi and Robi, are fond ones. I remember how we used to entertain our parents and grandparents by dressing up in our parents' clothes and jumping around, singing and dancing. I was very close to my grandma, and she used to read to me before bedtime. She always comforted me when I was sick or was in any kind of trouble. My grandmother was a very kind and educated person. I remember she always had a book in her hands. My father adored her and would often put his needs aside in order to please her. This annoyed my mother at times, and she would often remind him that his first obligation was to his immediate family.

As a child, I was exposed to several languages — Slovak, German and Hungarian. I was quite fluent in German as a child; however, I lost it later when I was not practising it. My mother, who grew up under the Austro-Hungarian monarchy, attended Hungarian schools and spoke Hungarian at home.

I attended a Slovakian kindergarten and then a Jewish public school where all the Jewish children from the town were enrolled. The school had very good teachers and was known in the region for its high academic standards. In addition to the standard subjects, we enjoyed all kinds of extracurricular activities, such as drama and music. I always loved singing and dancing. We had a lot of school performances, especially during holidays, such as Purim and Pesach. Winters were filled with skating and tobogganing and summers were spent swimming and playing with girlfriends. My father owned a car, which was used mostly for business; however, once in a while he would drive us to Trebišov to visit my uncle Ernest. Sometimes we drove to the village of Bosnica for a picnic and a swim under the river dam.

Although my parents observed the Jewish holidays and kept a kosher household, it was my grandparents who were very religious, especially my grandpa, who used to pray daily in the synagogue. He was the last leader of the Jewish community until most of its members were taken to concentration camps.

I loved to sleep over at my grandparents'. My grandma prepared fantastic meals, and I could never resist grabbing a second helping of dinner. My mother was also a good cook, but it did not prevent me from walking over to my grandparents' after our family dinner and asking them, "Was habt ihr zum essen?" (What do you have to eat?), standing on my tiptoes and inspecting their dinner table.

Our life was simple but very happy until 1939. In March of that year, the German army occupied Bohemia and Moravia. The Slovak nationalists proclaimed an independent Slovakian state with the approval and support of Nazi Germany on March 14, 1939. That was the end of pre-war Czechoslovakia.

The fascist Slovakian government fully co-operated with Hitler's regime. The state officials and organizations launched vicious anti-Jewish propaganda and initiated a cruel persecution of the entire Jewish population in the new, so-called Independent Slovakia. The persecution of our family started in November 1940 when, in accordance with an anti-Jewish decree issued by the Slovakian government, our family business was "Aryanized"; that is, it was confiscated and given to an "Aryan" owner.[2]

---

2  The First Aryanization Act, which came into effect in Slovakia in June 1940, was the first attempt by the Slovak government in the process of confiscating the property of Jews. Following the Second Aryanization Act in November 1940, nearly all of the 12,500 Jewish shops and businesses in Slovakia were either

My father remained in the business as an employee. Most Jewish businesses in Slovakia were taken away from their rightful owners. This was the beginning of the cruel persecution of the Jews and our family. Vicious antisemitic propaganda and actions escalated during the following months and years. We were barred from cultural and public places such as restaurants, movie theatres, parks and promenades. By September 1941, we had to wear a yellow star as a sign of shame. Jewish children and youth were expelled from Slovakian schools. Education in Jewish public schools was tolerated until 1942; by that time, most of the Jewish teachers and pupils had been taken to concentration camps.[3]

In my case, I completed the first year of junior high school. I was not allowed to continue further, so I was forced to return to the Jewish primary school, which ran a special class for older students expelled from Slovakian schools. I was only twelve years old when my formal education was put on hold for the next five years. The situation for the Jews deteriorated as time passed. In March 1942, Slovakian "gardists"[4] started to round up Jewish teenagers to work in so-called labour camps. At that time, we

---

liquidated or Aryanized. See Jean-Marc Dreyfus and Eduard Nižňanský, "Jews and Non-Jews in the Aryanization Process: Comparison of France and the Slovak State, 1939–45" in Georgi Verbeeck and Beate Kosmala, *Facing the Catastrophe: Jews and Non-Jews in Europe During World War II* (Oxford: Berg, 2011), 24, and Anna Cichopek-Gajraj, *Beyond Violence: Jewish Survivors in Poland and Slovakia; 1944–48* (Cambridge: Cambridge University Press, 2014), 92.

3  One thousand and forty Jews were deported from Trebišov in 1940, most of whom were from Sečovce. See "Sečovce" in *Encyclopedia of Jewish Life Before and During the Holocaust*, eds. Shmuel Spector and Geoffrey Wigoder (New York University Press: New York, 2001), 1155.

4  Gardists, members of the Hlinka Guard, were the Slovakian equivalent of the SS. Founded in October 1938, the Hlinka Guard was a Slovakian paramilitary force that persecuted and terrorized Jews and other unwanted individuals. See Yeshavahu Jelinek, "Storm-troopers in Slovakia: the Rodobrana and the Hlinka Guard," *Journal of Contemporary History*, 1971, 6.3, 103–4 and Abraham L. Grussgot, "Bardejov Remembered," 187. www.jewishgen.org

did not know that the labour camps served as transitional points from which Jewish workers were transported en masse into concentration camps and death camps. My grandfather nearly agreed to send my older brother, Bandi, to a labour camp, but luckily my parents were opposed to this plan. My mother was terrified that the Slovakian police would find Bandi, so he stayed hidden in our warehouse until the transports of young people into labour camps were completed.

We found out much later that the Jewish teenagers in labour camps were among the first of the countless victims taken to the Nazi camps in Poland; very few survived.

After a few months, the roundups of Jewish families began. By the end of 1942, close to sixty thousand Jews — two-thirds of the Jewish population in Slovakia — had been deported. A few families were able to avoid the roundups at this time because the Slovakian authorities considered them indispensable to the local economy. Our family was among the lucky ones; the new "Aryan" owner of our business was not capable of operating it without my father's assistance. Unfortunately, these official exceptions were not always respected by the fascist Slovakian guards, and many of the exempted families ended up in concentration camps nonetheless.

In 1942, when I was forced to say goodbye to my best friend, Valeria Schwartz, we shared a very sad moment. I was only thirteen years old, but I remember vividly our last moments together. We exchanged rings, and our final words to each other were, "L'hitraot b'Yisrael" (See you in Israel). We were most naive. I never saw her again. She and her entire family were taken in a cattle car to a concentration camp, where they were killed.

The roundups of Jews continued to intensify during 1942. Whole families were taken in cattle cars — seventy-five to ninety people in one car — to concentration camps and death camps. The Slovakian gardists marched from house to house to round up Jewish families several times a week. In spite of our exemption, we could not trust the gardists. We began to live in intermittent hiding. My older brother,

Bandi, was very resourceful. He built all kinds of artificial walls in our apartment and in the warehouse. Behind these walls were secret hiding spaces for the entire family. Some days and nights, when the word spread about an upcoming roundup of Jews, we went into hiding. My mother was busy preparing food for these days when we were concealed.

We were lucky that we managed to escape the gardists for some time. However, our fortune turned one day when Slovak gardists came to our house unexpectedly. They ordered us to pack our necessities and gave us ten minutes to do so. It was a terrifying experience. When my father asked one of the gardists some questions, the man responded by slapping my father, hard, on the face. They took my parents, my two brothers, me, my uncle, his wife, their four-year-old daughter and my grandparents. We marched with many other Jewish families through the town to the railway station. They shipped us in cattle cars to the sugar mill in the neighbouring town, Trebišov. The gardists herded us to the storage area, which was so packed that we spent all night sitting on the floor, unable to move. The next day, just before the people were ordered to board the cattle cars, one of the gardists pulled out a list from his pocket and read the names of the few families who were exempted from the transport. I still remember our profound relief when we heard our names. I never found out who rescued us from that terrible ordeal. Thankfully, we were allowed to return home this time.

We managed to stay in our town until the end of 1943. My father continued to work in his business as an employee. During this difficult period, I spent a lot of time reading and helping my mother with cooking and other household chores. I was even learning to sew, but I never made it as a seamstress; I was never even allowed to approach a sewing machine!

The Soviet army finally approached Slovakia in the spring of 1944. We were hoping that this terrible war would be ending soon. We did not know at the time how much more suffering we would have to endure. As the front came closer to eastern Slovakia, the remaining Jews

— who were considered unreliable and a threat to the fascist regime
— were forcefully evacuated to the western part of Slovakia. Armed
with false personal documents indicating that we were Christians,
we left our home and all of our belongings and fled to the western
part of the country. Our family settled temporarily in the designated
town of Hlohovec, near Bratislava.

In August 1944, the anti-fascist resistance groups, with the help of
Czech and Soviet partisans, organized an uprising in central Slovakia against the fascist regime. This uprising was later referred to as
the Slovak National Uprising.[5] The partisans succeeded in control-
ling a large part of central Slovakia. Many Jews, including our family,
moved to the liberated territory hoping that this signalled the defeat of the enemy. Unfortunately, our hopes were cruelly dashed. The
German army defeated the Uprising in October 1944, forcing the
partisans to retreat into the central Slovakia Mountains. The Jews,
out of self-preservation, followed the partisans into the mountains,
where they hid in bunkers built in forests and in the nearby mountain villages.

Our first hiding place was in the woods near Kalište, a small village high in the mountains. The bunker was built with a few branches. In the first weeks of hiding, the hardship was almost unbearable.
It was raining for days and our clothes and shoes were soaking wet.
We were starving but were afraid to go down to the village because of

---

5 Approximately 80,000 partisans from more than thirty countries fought in the
Slovak National Uprising, which was one of the largest anti-German uprisings in
Europe. Thousands of casualties resulted from the uprising, and Nazi troops destroyed ninety-three Slovak villages in retaliation for their suspected cooperation
with partisan forces. See Vilém Prečan, "The Slovak National Uprising: the most
dramatic moment in the nation's history" in Mikuláš Teich, Dušan Kováč, Martin
D. Brown, *Slovakia in History* (Cambridge University Press, 2011), 206–228 and
"The Museum of the Slovak National Uprising" at http://www.memorialmuse-
ums.org/eng/staettens/view/148/Museum-of-the-Slovak-National-Uprising#.

the frequent German raids. Eventually, we found the courage to descend to Kalište. We were happy to find some food and to warm up.
Later, the women and children were permitted to stay in the village
for several days. We tried to replenish our food supply and returned
to the bunker to join the men. I remember one night being invited
by a Slovak girl to sleep over in her house. I can distinctly recall the
delicious warmth and coziness of lying under the comforter of that
bed. It had been so long since I had experienced such luxury. As the
weeks passed in the bunker, conditions deteriorated as the autumn
rain was replaced by the harsh snow and winds of winter.

I remember one particularly terrifying episode during this time,
which could have had a catastrophic end for our family. I had spent
the night in the common room in the village with my grandmother, mother and little brother, Robi. When we woke up in the morning, we sensed a heightened nervousness around us. I asked a Polish
partisan what was going on. He told me that the German army was
believed to be approaching the village in order to fight the partisans
and round up the Jews. We pleaded with him to take my mother,
Robi and me to our bunker in the woods. Just as we were leaving the
village, we heard the unmistakable sound of heavy shooting coming
from the woods. Panicking, we started running in the deep snow.
Our guide disappeared in the forest. Suddenly, my mother noticed a
huge fallen tree in our tracks. All three of us jumped into the pit under the exposed roots. We were caught in the middle of the shooting
— gunfire came from all directions and lasted for many hours. We
were hungry and frozen but afraid to leave our hiding place. My poor
brother wet his pants and was crying inconsolably. We were very
frightened, but my mother continued to reassure us, telling us not
to worry, that everything would be fine, that we would all survive.

Finally, when it became dark, my mother decided that it was time
to move on. We walked a short distance and then came across two
partisans who told us the terrible news that the German SS had raided not only the village but the woods as well. They found the bunkers

where the Jews were hiding and rounded them up in the village. We crept closer to the village until we saw the house where my grandmother was staying, only a few metres away. A German soldier was walking nearby. As soon as he turned away, we ran into the house; to our immense relief, we found our grandmother safe and sound. At that moment, my brother Bandi, who was with the rest of the family in bunkers, arrived and told us what happened — the German soldiers had found the Jews, including some of our family, in the bunkers. As they were rounded up in the village, one of the soldiers revealed a soft spot for my little cousin Eva. She was a very cute little girl with red curly hair. The soldier decided to rescue her and her mother, Ibi. He separated them from the rest of the rounded-up Jews and led them into a house on the outskirts of the village. Eva's father, Erno, and the rest of our family managed to follow them inconspicuously into that house and thus this soldier saved their lives. That was a very close call. Later, we found out the terrible destiny of the other Jews who had been captured in the bunkers. They were all shot by the German SS and thrown into mass graves in Kremnička; this later came to be known as the Kremnička Massacre.[6]

A few days after this incident, we moved from Kalište, which we considered unsafe, to a lower-situated mountainous village, Podkonice. We found accommodation in the house of an elderly couple. We had one room for our entire family of ten people. We slept on the floor on straw, which we swept each morning into the corner of the room. Luckily, we were allowed to use the kitchen. We were hiding under the false name of Novy in order to hide our Jewish origin.

---

6   Seven hundred and forty-six people were killed, including 211 women and 58 children; over half were Jewish. The killers included Slovak fascists from the Hlinka Guard and Nazi Einsatzgruppe. This massacre continued from November 1944 to March 1945. See http://www.memorialmuseums.org/eng/denkmaeler/view/614/Memorial-at-the-Cemetery-of-the-Murdered-After-the-Suppression-of-the-Slovak-National-Uprising.

We heard that the local priest was sympathetic to Jewish refugees, so we asked him to introduce us in the church to the villagers as Christians. The priest promised to do so; however, he insisted that we first convert to Christianity. After listening to a few hours of lecturing about the basics of Catholicism, we were formally converted in the church by the priest. We had to attend church every Sunday for mass. We were quite successful in allaying suspicions of our true identities.

We had a hard time with the owner of the house where we stayed. The man was senile and unreasonably aggressive toward us. The village was a haven for partisans who frequently came down from the mountains to replenish their food supply and other necessities. As a result, the German soldiers or SS troops raided the village quite often, moving from house to house, and searching for partisans and Jews. It was terrifying to hear them yelling under the window, accompanied by their menacing looking German shepherd dogs. The village was alternately occupied by partisans or the SS troops. Our confused landlord never failed to cheer for the partisans when the Germans showed up and vice-versa. We tried desperately to explain his mental state to either the partisans or the Germans who showed up in the house to avoid further trouble.

The old senile man was not the only hazard in our crazy life. My younger brother, Robi, who was about nine years old at the time, provided us with a few close calls. One day, when the German SS men came in the house looking for partisans, Robi proudly presented to them his new watch made from an old discarded paper dial. One of the SS jokingly aimed his pistol toward Robi saying in German, "Pif-paf, this is for a Jewish head!" We all froze. After this incident, there was no more watch-parading on Robi's wrist.

The men in my family — my father, grandfather, uncle Ernest and brother Bandi — were not staying with us in the village during most of this period. They were hiding in the woods because it was too dangerous for them to be seen in the village. One night, when we were all together, my grandma lost consciousness and fell to the ground, and a few minutes later she passed away. Her body remained with us all night in our room until the next morning when the burial could be arranged. I remember how frightened I was, spending the whole night in the same room with her. This terrifying experience haunted me for many years, and I remember having nightmares and heart palpitations long after the end of the war. My grandma had a Christian funeral, which was necessitated by the circumstances. My grandfather was so upset by this that he refused to attend the funeral. When the dreadful war finally ended, my grandmother was reburied in the Jewish cemetery in our town.

I recall another frightening event in April 1945, a few weeks before we were liberated by the Soviet army. My mother developed heavy bleeding that forced her to stay in bed for several days. She lost a lot of blood and became very weak. I was only fifteen years old, but I knew that she had to be seen by a doctor immediately. My father was still hiding with the rest of our men in the woods, which meant that it was up to me to act on my mother's behalf.

The village was occupied by German soldiers at the time, who were retreating from the advancing Soviet and Romanian armies. The closest available doctor was in Slovenská Ľupča, a town about five kilometres from where we were in Podkonice. The only transportation available in the village was a horse-drawn wagon. The problems I faced were how to get it and who would take my mom to the doctor. I had no other choice but to ask the commander of the local German garrison for help. My German was reasonably good at that time, so I gathered my courage and knocked on the door of the commander's office. A young officer who was repairing a curtain on the window invited me in. The curtain fell to the floor. When I saw what happened, I could not help myself and said jokingly, "Geschicklichkeit, verlass' mich nicht!" which translates loosely as "Skill, don't abandon me!" a joke used when confronted with clumsiness. He was very friendly and asked me what part of Slovakia we came from. I told him we were Slovak refugees from the East, running from the advancing Russians. He showed me a map of Central Europe, the latest position of the German-Soviet front, and tried to reassure me that Germany would win the war. He also told me about some secret German weapons that would be used very soon. I enthusiastically agreed with his strategic analysis and managed to tell him at last about my mother being very ill. I asked him to help me to find a horse-drawn wagon for her transportation to the doctor. He explained how difficult this would be, as the army had confiscated all available horses, but he nevertheless accompanied me from house to house to search for one. I was terrified that somebody would turn me in as a Jewish girl. Fortunately, he found the transportation and arranged for two German soldiers to protect us from the partisans (what a joke) on our journey to the doctor.

I was both relieved and delighted — I had a hard time not bursting out laughing. Just imagine: Two German soldiers protecting a Jewish girl and her mother from the partisans! I felt great satisfaction after all the persecution, humiliation and suffering we had had to endure, and I was also proud of myself. We arrived in Slovenská Ľupča one hour later and found the doctor, who sent my mother to a hospital for a minor operation. She was discharged the next day, and we started our journey home. Two Hungarian officers gave us a ride for a short distance, but we still had to hike a few kilometres to our village. My mother was stabilized and gradually recovered from the blood loss.

~

In April 1945, we were finally liberated by the Soviet and Romanian armies. Our family was very fortunate. With the exception of my grandmother, we all survived this horrible war. We were devastated to learn how many Jewish families from our community were killed in the Nazi camps. From my class of forty-five children, only six survived with some members of their families.

We reunited back in Sečovce with my other paternal uncle, Michael (Miksa), the dentist, who was devastated at the loss of his mother. We found the front of our house in ruins but had no other place to live. Thus we started our new life in our old house. It was not a simple continuation of the pre-war life. We became painfully aware of the changes in our post-war town. Only a handful of Jewish families had survived the Holocaust. Our old community as we knew it had disappeared. Many Jewish survivors lost their faith in God, at least temporarily. My mother expressed her anger by refusing to cook kosher food.

My father suffered from frequent angina pain as a result of repeated heart attacks since his early forties. As a result, he resumed his business activities only on a part-time basis. My two brothers and I felt an urgency to resume our studies, which had been interrupted during the war years.

I was only a teenager, and yet my life story already felt like a long saga — wartime had affected my life horribly. My innocent, happy childhood in a loving and secure family had been brutally interrupted by the Nazi occupation and introduction of the anti-Jewish laws. The harsh persecution of my family and the whole Jewish community affected every aspect of my life. Needless to say, I was robbed of the normal life of a teenage girl — I had become prematurely occupied with more serious thoughts and problems. There were occasions when I had to assume responsibilities and make decisions not only for myself but for other members of my family. I had always dreamt about the day when this dreadful war would be over and we would live in a free society.

During the war, I came into contact with young people who were members of the anti-fascist movement in Slovakia. My strongest influence was my older cousin Edith who exposed me to a new world of political and social thought. I have wonderful memories of Edith, who was living with her parents in a neighbouring town, Michalovce. I was a frequent visitor to their family home during the war. Through my fifteen-year-old eyes, she represented everything positive and inspiring, since she was beautiful, mature and well-educated. Spending time with Edith and her friends was a highlight for me during those difficult times. They were well-read and liberal-minded young people, full of enthusiasm about the new life after the war. I remember listening to long and heated discussions about political, economic and social issues and being inspired by their visions of the new post-war world. Most of them were members of underground anti-fascist organizations. Undoubtedly, Edith and her friends had a major influence on my own developing perspective regarding political and social issues. I came to the conclusion, as did many other young people who suffered during the war, that socialism was the only system that would result in social justice and freedom for all people. I became an enthusiastic young socialist and promised myself that when the war was over I would be committed to helping build a wonderful and just new world.

Not all Holocaust survivors shared this view. Many families lost their trust in their homeland and decided to emigrate from Czechoslovakia and from Europe in general. The United States, Canada and Australia were favourite destinations for immigration. My uncle Ernest moved to Australia with his family in 1948. A group of mainly young and enthusiastic Zionists left for Palestine to build a Jewish state. In 1948, Israel was declared a new Jewish homeland.

My cousin Edith survived the Holocaust; however, both her parents perished in the camps. Her fiancé, who was a resistance fighter, never returned home. Edith got married shortly after the end of the war to a businessman, Micu, who was the brother of my aunt Ibi. They immigrated to Israel and later to Australia.

As I mentioned, my immediate challenge after the war was to focus and catch up on my studies. The new government introduced a wide range of courses for young people who had been deprived of their regular education during the war. My brother Bandi and I enrolled in one of these courses in Košice.

We found accommodation with our distant relative in Košice. In addition to the formal education, we had a wonderful private professor,

Mr. Sandor, who helped us to prepare for the exams, mainly in mathematics and physics. After a few months of intensive study, I passed the necessary examinations and I was eligible for the seventh grade of the *Gymnasium* (Grade 12 of high school). Our class was the first post-war class taught in the Slovak language. Our professors were mainly former supporters of the fascist Slovak state and many of them were openly antisemitic and hostile towards the Hungarian students. My friend Erika and I confronted our teachers many times in the classroom, openly criticizing their behaviour. Some of the professors glorified the Slovak fascist regime, which was very painful for us to listen to.

In the meantime, my parents also moved to Košice. My brother Bandi and I moved to our new family home. An important turning point in my life occurred when my aunt Rozsi invited me to visit her in Brno in the summer of 1945. I had a great time with my aunt and her family. When I mentioned to Rozsi that I was looking for someone to tutor me in chemistry for my upcoming exams, she immediately responded, "I know a young man in the neighbourhood, Ady, the son of Dr. Sebastian, who could teach you. I will introduce you to him." We liked each other immediately and became good friends. I have to confess that he was not very successful in teaching me chemistry, in the formal sense. However, chemistry was certainly in the air, and we eventually married in May 1949. We lived and studied in separate cities but we exchanged letters frequently. I loved the way he played the violin. I had always liked classical music, but he introduced me to the world of violin concertos.

Ady and his father were Holocaust survivors as well. They were liberated by the American army from the Ebensee concentration camp.[7] His mother and paternal grandmother had been killed by the Nazis when

---

7  The US Third Army liberated Ebensee on May 5, 1945. By that time, there were around 18,500 prisoners in the camp. Jews made up approximately one-third of the inmates.

the whole family was taken to the Auschwitz death camp in 1944 from Užhorod, Hungary, where they had been living during the war. Ady and his father returned to Brno and settled in the same apartment where they had lived before the war. His father, who was a medical practitioner, continued with his medical practice, and Ady successfully passed his high school graduation exams and enrolled in the faculty of electrical engineering at the University in Brno in the fall of 1945.

After I passed my exams, I enrolled in a girl's *Gymnasium* in Košice. I graduated in June 1948 and enrolled in the faculty of medicine at the University in Brno the same year. Ady and I married a year later and lived in Brno until Ady finished his studies at the Technical University in 1950. I moved back to my parents' house in Košice and continued my medical studies there as Ady was drafted into the Czechoslovakian army for two years. When he returned from the military service, I still had over one year of medical studies left. Ady started his career as an electrical engineer in Košice. I successfully completed my studies and became a medical doctor in November 1953.

Another joyful event happened in our family just a few months later when our first son, Ivan, was born in March 1954. I later started my internship in a university-affiliated pediatric hospital in Košice, and was very grateful to my mother, who helped me with Ivan's care. While I was working and studying for my pediatric specialty exam, which I passed in 1957, I was very fortunate in having a husband who always supported me in my professional life, sacrificing his free time and energy in order to help me to achieve my goals. When I had to attend a three-month course of pediatric cardiology in Prague in 1957, Ady and my mother agreed without hesitation to take care of Ivan. Sadly, that year my father died of a massive heart attack.

After returning from the cardiology course, I was in charge of the cardiology patients in the hospital. A few months later, when my good friend Dr. Mico Predmersky returned from his military duty, we both focused on patients with congenital and acquired heart diseases. I passed my post-graduate exams in pediatric cardiology in Bratislava in 1960.

That year, Mico and I organized cardiology seminars for doctors from out of town and published several medical articles. We were very enthusiastic about our work and joked that we were doing what we loved to do and were even getting paid for it. Mico was not only a good partner at work, but we also became friends. In the 1950s, when the political environment changed in the country and there was a backlash against Jewish intellectuals, Mico always defended me and helped me to overcome the unfair treatment I was often exposed to.

Our daughter, Tania, was born in October 1962. At this time we enjoyed a harmonious family life and interesting and fulfilling professional work, even though our recreation and travel options were limited due to government restrictions on our freedoms. The restrictions on our freedom became more obvious when we were finally allowed to travel to Yugoslavia (our car packed with canned food and other necessities) and were confronted with the huge discrepancies between our economic situation and that of our western neighbours. This injustice naturally infuriated us. How were our expectations of the new more "fair" life in post-war Czechoslovakia to be fulfilled? Both Ady and I believed, during the many years of living and working under the socialist system, that in spite of the many negative aspects of our lives, things would get better. We believed in socialism and sincerely thought that we were on the right track. In addition to our busy professional lives, we were also active in politics. As students, we had participated in several voluntary summer brigades to help rebuild the war-torn infrastructure, such as the railway communication *Trat' mládeže*, The Track of Youth, which connects two towns in Slovakia. Later, we helped with the rebuilding efforts in Ostrava during summer vacations. We were active in promoting socialist ideas in the workplace. We attributed all the negative experiences in our life to errors or wrongdoing of the people in charge, rather than to the system itself. When the political and economic situation got worse each year and we learned about the terrible details of Stalin's dictatorship and his era in the Soviet Union, we became very disappointed and eventually lost faith in our socialist ideas.

~

There was new hope in Czechoslovakia when Alexander Dubček[8] and a group supporting him in the Central Committee of the Communist Party openly revolted against the establishment. This revolt grew into a nationwide movement known as the Prague Spring of 1968. The enthusiasm of the people was phenomenal. The new progressive leadership abolished censorship, openly criticized the regime in the Soviet Union and published the truth about the mock political trials in the 1950s in Czechoslovakia, which had led to executions and long-term imprisonment of a number of innocent people, many Jews among them. Antisemitism flourished during the communist era in Czechoslovakia, especially in Slovakia. Unfortunately, with the Soviet invasion in August 1968, all hopes of Dubček's "socialism with a human face" died. At that point, we made the difficult decision to leave our homeland. We packed our belongings in our small car, and early in the morning on September 15, 1968, my whole family, including my mother, headed to Vienna, into the unknown, to start a new life in the West. I had to leave my home for the second time in my life, this time voluntarily. My dreams of building a just society were in shambles.

We often recall the risky moments of our escape. As we did not

---

8   Alexander Dubček (1921–1992) replaced Antonín Novotný as First Secretary of the Communist Party on January 5, 1968, and implemented a program of liberal reforms known as the Prague Spring. These political and economic reforms resulted in greater freedom for Czech citizens and aimed to replace the repressive, totalitarian style of communism with a more humane socialism. Dubček's April 1968 Action Program of democratic reforms included freedom of the press, freedom of speech and assembly, and greater freedom to travel. During his regime, which lasted only from January to August 1968, Dubček also federalized Czechoslovakia, creating the separate Czech Socialist Republic and Slovak Socialist Republic. The latter change was the only Dubček reform to survive the end of the Prague Spring.

have exit visas allowing us to travel to a western country, we couldn't tell anyone about our planned departure. We decided to use the border crossing to Hungary, not far from our hometown, and to pretend to be travelling to Romania; this trip did not require exit visas. Once in Hungary, we planned to drive to Vienna instead of Romania, hoping for the best. At the Hungarian border, a suspicious border guard challenged Ivan, asking him why he was travelling on vacation during his school year. Ivan was clever enough to reply that his parents had obtained permission for his absence from the school principal. The border guard tried to verify Ivan's statement by phoning the school; fortunately, it was a Saturday and the school was closed, so nobody answered. The guard, frustrated, waved us through the border crossing.

Vienna was the first destination for many emigrants from Czechoslovakia. Initially, our plan was to stay in Europe, where we felt familiar with the culture and customs. We tried the Swiss embassy first, but the line there was so long and the chance of success so slim that we gave up on further attempts. Germany was another option; however, we did not feel comfortable with the thought of living there. We learned about Canada as a friendly, very cosmopolitan country, where emigrants from all over the world were able to find a new homeland. At that time, Canada's Prime Minister, Pierre Trudeau, and his government were very supportive of Czechoslovakian emigrants, and we made the decision to build our new life there.

The Soviet invasion had been not only the catalyst for our emigration but also for our families to finally separate. My brother Bandi and his family ended up in New York and my younger brother, Robi, was stuck in Czechoslovakia for another eighteen years, following an unsuccessful attempt to leave the occupied country in 1968. He was finally able to leave in 1987 and joined us in Toronto with his family.

After spending a few weeks in Vienna, we landed in Toronto in October. The beginning was not easy, in spite of the financial support from the government. We certainly did not suffer from cold or hunger, but the psychological effects of immigration to a totally new world were distress and misery. The term "culture shock" best expresses the feelings we experienced as immigrants in a new country, and this culture shock lasted until we became familiar with the new customs and language — we struggled even to become accustomed to the surrounding streets and houses.

For a long time, I felt like a stranger in this new environment. I realized that I had lost my homeland, my friends; simply, I had lost my identity. We had to start to rebuild our lives from scratch. Not everybody was able to cope with this enormous stress, and we heard of tragic cases of fellow immigrants committing suicide. I was homesick for a long time, a feeling that lasted years, until I was able to accept and appreciate Canada as our new home.

We were lucky that Ady's university diploma was recognized in Canada. His English was fairly good, so he was job hunting just a few weeks after we arrived in Toronto. He started working as a draftsman in a private firm but, after a short time, found a permanent engineering job with the Ontario government. I had a more difficult professional road ahead of me. After passing an oral exam that tested four main clinical subjects, I started my internship a few months later at St. Joseph's Hospital in Toronto for one year. In the second year of my internship, I worked as a pediatric resident at St. Joseph's Hospital in Hamilton. I commuted from Toronto, and I had night duties almost every other day. After finishing the second year of my internship, I was eligible to write my medical licence examination, which I passed successfully in the spring of 1971. The next year I completed a fellowship at the Women's College Hospital in neonatology. When Dr. Llewellyn, who was in charge of the Neonatology Department, left the position, I assumed the position of acting chief, where I stayed for another two years. I opened my private practice in 1975 and worked as a private practitioner for twenty years. After closing my practice, I assumed a part-time position in a walk-in clinic for another three years and finally retired in 1999. When I reflect back, especially on those first difficult immigration years, I realize that I could not have succeeded in rebuilding my professional life without the help of my mother and Ady. Both of them shared the childcare and household responsibilities when I was working and studying for my exams. I will always appreciate their understanding and support.

My mother was very happy in Canada. She was determined to learn the English language and attended English courses for many years. She was very appreciative of the help she was getting from the government as a senior citizen and as an immigrant. My mother was very independent for her age and adjusted easily to her new lifestyle. She travelled all over Toronto on her own and made a lot of friends. She liked to write poetry in Hungarian. Some of those poems were published in the Jewish multilingual magazine at the Baycrest Geriatric Centre in Toronto, where she spent the final years of her life. She died of a heart attack in 1986 when she was eighty-two years old.

The children also adjusted to their new environment easily, especially Tania, who was just starting her first year of primary school. She learned English very quickly and was an enthusiastic student right from the beginning. Ivan, who was fourteen years old when we emigrated, had a harder time adjusting to his new circumstances. Unfortunately, the school he attended was not very supportive toward new immigrants at the time. There were very few immigrants at his high school and he often felt quite isolated. On the other hand, Ivan's academic knowledge in junior high school was superior to the Canadian students', which allowed him to spend more time learning English.

Sometimes I regret that we could not spend more time with our children, mainly in the first years of immigration, since we were so busy building a new life in our new country. I hope they understand and forgive us. We were so eager to travel that we did not miss any opportunities to spend vacations together, exploring our new surroundings. We purchased a second-hand car within a few months of our arrival. I remember our first big trip to Florida in those early years, and we have not stopped travelling since. Our children were happy to join us until a certain age. When they reached about seventeen, they refused to come with us anymore. I am sure, however, that they still have vivid memories of the wonderful places we visited together. Back home in Czechoslovakia, in spite of the beautiful countries so close to our home, we had not been allowed to travel, with the exception of the few socialist countries like Hungary, Poland and Yugoslavia, and there were severe limitations for visiting even these neighbouring countries.

Once we left our homeland, we were not allowed to visit. In fact, the government punished returning emigrants with a two-year jail term. It was only after the revolution in 1989 that the communist regime was overthrown in Czechoslovakia. We were ecstatic that freedom would finally prevail in the eastern European countries. It was hard to believe that this was happening during our lifetime. This new freedom in Czechoslovakia meant that we could visit our old country, twenty-two years after we fled. It was a very emotional visit for us. At the same time, it made us realize that we had found a new home in Canada and we would never return to live in our old homeland. For me, particularly, this return journey was meaningful, as I was able to resolve some of my ambivalent feelings and homesickness for the past. It helped me make peace emotionally and accept the finality of our emigration.

At the time we left Czechoslovakia in 1968, which we perceived as an emergency move, we were unsure of our destiny. After so many years living in Canada, we can say proudly and happily that we made the right choice. Our children are living in a free and democratic country and we don't have to worry, as we did back in Czechoslovakia, about their future. Both of our children are professionals; Ivan is a successful computer programmer and analyst and Tania has a master's degree in psychology. They are free to live their lives according to their abilities and ambitions. Ivan is married to Od, who is from Thailand. Tania is happily married to David, who we love as our son. David works as a senior information technology specialist with the provincial government. Tania and David's son, Matthew, and daughter, Jessica, are our dear grandchildren and give us tremendous happiness. Both of our grandchildren are very talented. Matthew recently graduated with distinction from high school and will begin his engineering studies at Queen's University in Kingston in the fall of 2016. Jessica is an excellent student in junior high school. Both our grandchildren study classical music. Jessica plays the piano and the French horn; Matthew plays the violin. His *Dido*, grandfather, is a violinist himself, and enjoys helping his grandson during their practice sessions. Jessica and Matthew are avid readers and very interested in world affairs; they have travelled extensively with their parents, who are doing an excellent job with their upbringing.

My life story is slowly coming to the end. We are enjoying our freedom to do the things we could not do while we were working, and are happy that we brought our children to a free, wonderful country where they have all the opportunities to grow and enjoy an active, productive and happy life. My husband and I had suffered such a blow after the war, when we believed that we were building a new and better world. We recognized only much later that our youthful enthusiasm was betrayed; that socialism is only a nice theory with a dark reality. This disillusionment forced us to leave our country and start our lives from scratch again. The political and economic failure of the totalitarian regime came to full disclosure in the early 1990s when the communist regime collapsed in the Soviet Union and the other Eastern Bloc countries under the Soviet domain.

I feel that we, the Holocaust survivors, have a duty to share our stories with our children and grandchildren so they know that all these terrible things really happened to innocent people whose sole crime was to be born Jewish. We learned from our own sad experiences that racism and xenophobia are extremely dangerous in any form and against any ethnic group. We must be tolerant of people with different backgrounds and beliefs. Living by this principle will ensure that the history of persecution and killing of innocent people because of their different ethnicity will never happen again.

1

2

1 Theatre performance at the Jewish public school in Sečovce. Magda is in the second row, second from the left, and her best friend, Valeria Schwartz, is in the front row, third from the left. 1938.

2 School performance, 1940. Magda is second from the right and Valeria is beside her on the far right.

1  Magda's high school graduation photo, 1948.
2  Ady Sebestian, circa 1948.
3  The Neuman family, 1949. Back row, left to right: Magda's fiancé, Ady; her older
   brother, Bandi; and her younger brother, Robi. In front, left to right: Magda's
   mother, Aranka; Magda; and her father, Bela. Košice, Czechoslovakia, 1949.

1 Magda's daughter, Tania, and her husband, David, on their wedding day, 1990.
2 Magda's son, Ivan, and his wife, Od, at their wedding, 1993.
3 Magda with her family. From left to right: Magda's daughter, Tania; Magda's son-in-law, David; Magda; her grandson, Matthew; her granddaughter, Jessica; her husband, Ady; and her son, Ivan. Toronto, 2014.

# In Memoriam
# Bianka Kraszewski

*For my parents, Paweł and Regina Rozenman, and for my brother, Ryszard (Rysio) Henryk, as well as all the members of my parents' families. I write here the things I remember best about these three most beloved beings of my childhood. Let this be their grave, their stone, their memorial. And I write for the millions of Jews massacred by the Nazis who have no graves, no stones, no memorials.*

## MY FATHER

May 5, 1990

Today is my father's birthday. He would be 101 years old, if he had survived the war. My thoughts are with him today.

My father, Paweł, was one of eight children, the first boy born after three sisters. He was only six years old when his father died of a heart attack at the age of thirty-nine. He could not finish school because he had to assume responsibility for his family quite early in his life. At the age of fourteen, he became an assistant bookkeeper at the firm where his father used to be head bookkeeper. But he continued his studies at night classes, and he was the best-informed person — in history, geography, math and languages — that I ever knew. My father was always a loving and devoted son and brother, who supported his mother and helped to support two of his unmarried sisters and his widowed sister and her two children, Sara and Henio. He was also a loving husband and father who adored my beautiful mother, and the only time I remember him spanking me was when I was disrespectful to her.

When I think about my father, there are a few memories that stand out. My father would invent stories as he was telling them to me, which he did almost every day after lunch. When he lay down to rest for a few minutes, I would be beside him listening to his tales of good little girls and bad little girls. I remember that when he sang a waltz or a cancan polka, he would hold me by the hands as I danced, turning me around him. Every Sunday, he would walk with me to a nearby café patisserie where I could choose one of the tasty European pastries: a Neapolitan, a *stefanka* (honey cake), a cream puff or a chocolate éclair. I ate while he perused the newspapers or talked to some acquaintances. Before the war, the talk was always about the political situation. In winter, when we walked there and my hands were cold, he would take my hand in his always-warm hand (he never wore gloves) and put it with his hand into his coat pocket. In the summer, he used to take me to the best Italian ice cream parlour for my absolute favourite treat.

My father travelled abroad two or three times a year on business and used to bring me beautiful hair ribbons from France and England. I remember a gorgeous white blouse, silk with silver threads, that he bought for my mother — how beautiful she looked in it!

When I had a bad case of whooping cough and I was choking, he used to get up in the middle of the night to comfort me, and once, when I was choking and panicking, I scratched him out of desperation.

My father liked company and he used to play cards from time to time with friends in his den. He made cherry-vodka in the kitchen, cooking the fruit and juice — the only times I saw him at the stove. He had a great sense of humour and joked with my mother's friend Mrs. Frenklowa, whom we called Frenlowcia. I imagine her first name must have been Maria, since he always greeted her in Russian, saying, "Zdravstvuyte, Maria Michailovna."

As I mentioned, my father was highly educated, and he spoke several languages. When he was young, Warsaw belonged to the part of Poland occupied by Russia, so his schooling was in Russian. He also studied Hebrew because my grandmother, an Orthodox woman, hoped that since he was the oldest son he would become a rabbi. As a young man, he went to one of the best private teachers in Poland to study German. In his travels and self-study, he learned some English. He also spent some time in France and could speak French. He spoke Yiddish as well. He was a self-made man who not only knew all these languages but also read widely in them. He was a great mathematician and music lover. He especially loved the violin and was very erudite on the history of music and world literature. He himself could play the violin, and he also had a yearly subscription to the Philharmonic Orchestra.

Before the war, we had many family members with whom we would visit. My mother's uncle Fabian Zakrzewski used to come visit us almost every day for afternoon tea — he was more or less the same age as my father and they were friends.

I often used to travel with my father from Lodz to Warsaw when he visited his mother and sisters, nephews and nieces. We used to take a *droshke*, a four-wheeled carriage drawn by horses, to the station and then a fast new train called a "torpedo," which got us there in an hour and a half. When we arrived at the large apartment where my paternal grandmother lived with her three daughters and her grandchildren, Sara and Henio, I used to hide in a big wardrobe as part of a family game. When my aunt or cousins came home from work there was always the same ritual: they asked if I had come, too, and my father would say, "No, I did not bring her." They would say how sorry they were to hear that, and at that moment, I would jump out from my hiding place and shout, "Surprise!"

MY MOTHER

My mother, Renia, was an extraordinarily beautiful woman, tall and slim with an oval face. She had almond-shaped brown eyes that seemed to dance; her hair was black, sprinkled with grey since the age of nineteen. Her eyebrows were very pronounced — a feature that I, my daughters and my grandchildren all inherited from her. She was graceful, had a long, swan-like neck and always looked elegant, often dressed in navy blue suits or dresses with boleros and blue, white or polka-dot blouses.

Of course, to me she was just my mother, the most familiar and most necessary person, and not until I was about nine years old did I realize from remarks I overheard that she was beautiful. After the war, I learned that there was a little girl in Włocławek (who later became my teacher in secret classes in the ghetto) who would stand waiting on the corner of the street to see this young woman, my mother, simply to catch a glimpse of her as she returned from her studies in Warsaw for her commerce degree.

Even when I was little, I was always afraid of losing my mother — I feared literally losing her in a crowd or on the street when I would jump ahead and suddenly not see her beside me, or when she was late by even a few minutes when picking me up from school or when she left me on the first day of school, alone among strangers. At a summer camp, I cried myself sick because I was alone — she was gone. Little did I know that, within a few short years, I would not only be without her forever but alone in the world, all on my own, and would have to cope with it and manage to live with my loneliness and a despair that would never leave.

My mother was born in February 1898 in a town called Włocławek in Poland. Her mother, Bianka, née Hirsch, came from a genteel Jewish family in Germany. Bianka and her sisters attended a finishing school for girls, where they learned subjects like French, embroidery and good manners. She met my grandfather, Aleksander Zakrzewski, a handsome, tall, energetic but not-so-genteel young man, who married her and took her to his native Poland. However, she never mastered the Polish language, so their four children were completely bilingual.

My grandfather started many businesses but somehow most did not succeed for long, and even when he was successful his enthusiasm prompted him to take new risks and to lose what he had achieved. I know that early on he had a dealership for agricultural equipment in Włocławek and, before World War II, he was a landowner with a manor house near Włocławek, in a village called Kobyla Łąka (Mare's Meadow), and had a peat factory nearby. We went there one summer and my grandfather had one of his farmhands take me around the garden on an old mare. One winter we went there by train and at the station a two-horse sleigh waited for us. Covered with warm blankets, we rode through the snow-covered countryside with the sleigh bells ringing.

My mother had two brothers, Leon and Karol, and one sister, Roma. Leon was the oldest, and Roma and Karol were younger than my mother, all about four years apart in age. During World War I, my maternal grandmother became sick with cancer of the liver, and my mother took her by train to the best specialists in Warsaw. She told us that she ordered the German soldiers on the train to make room for my grandmother and give her a seat, and, of course, they keenly obeyed this young beautiful woman (whom they would later kill in World War II for being a Jew). My grandmother died soon after. I think my mother was about twenty or twenty-one years old then and her two younger siblings were about seventeen and thirteen years old.

Sometimes my parents would reminisce, or at least my father would tease my mother, about the matchmaking that went on between her mother and a friend, the mother of a young Dr. Linke. However, my mother was not interested in him and that was that. I think it must have been after World War I that my mother left for Warsaw to go to Commercial College (the Wyższa Szkoła Handlowa, or Higher School of Commerce), where she graduated with a degree in commerce. In Warsaw, she was very close to a family of distant cousins, the Glocers. One of the daughters, Halina, was her very good friend.

She also met Janina Friedman in Warsaw, a young woman who was a few years older than her and who became Renia's stepmother as well as a good friend. In 1922, my mother's half-sister, Halina Zakrzewska, was born out of Janina and Aleksander's marriage; she was the only one of her siblings who survived the war. Halina married, had a daughter, Jasia, and a granddaughter, Nadine. She lived in Israel until January 15, 1992, when she died of cancer. Janina died after three or four years of marriage and eventually my grandfather married a third time, to a widow named Ruta.

There are two versions of the story of how my parents met. The first one is that they met at Janina's house. A renowned teacher of German, Klara Neuman, also lived there, and my father, wanting to perfect his knowledge of the language, was one of her students. The second version is that at the end of 1922, my mother travelled with her cousin Władek Glocer to Gdańsk (Danzig) to spend the New Year's Eve celebration with some friends of his. One of the guests was my father, who had his business office in Gdańsk.

Whichever story is true, their meeting resulted in what must have been a whirlwind romance. My father adored her, and they were married on June 5, 1923, in Gdańsk. They had been married for only nine months when, on March 5, 1924, my brother, Ryszard (Rysio) Henryk, was born in Warsaw in a private nursing home on Piękna Street. Both my brother and mother stayed at my grandma Rozenman's place until they were fit enough for my father to take them back to Gdańsk. Five years later, I was born at *babcia's*, grandmother's, apartment. I later heard the story that soon after my birth, my brother wanted to give me a herring because he didn't think I could survive on just milk.

We lived a good and prosperous life before the war. When I was little, we had a nanny and a maid who cleaned, cooked, ironed, washed and did the market shopping. My father's handyman brought coal for the fireplaces, sanded the parquet floors each year, carried the carpets to be beaten outside and occasionally walked me to school. My mother supervised all these activities, took care of the house on the maid's days off, cooked some dishes, did the baking, preserving and went shopping with me daily after school for rolls, pastries and other fresh foods. She also often answered incoming phone calls for my father, especially when he was away on one of his many trips abroad. She took me to the park, to the dressmaker and to the shoemaker. Her sister Roma's best friend would often come to visit. Or we would go to the café Ziemiańska, where she would meet a friend and I would get a pastry.

Sometimes guests came for a game of cards, or someone from our family in Warsaw — such as my aunt Rozia, her husband, Leon Teitelbaum, or my cousin Henio — would come for a visit. My grandpa Aleksander used to come from time to time and he always gave me a silver złoty. He suffered from angina and carried a box of tablets with him.

When I got up in the morning after a small party, I loved the lingering smell of cakes, candies and cigarette smoke in the dining room. The most exciting were the birthday parties — my brother's when I could watch the "big" boys playing games — and especially my own. I would wake up to find presents on the chair at my bedside from my parents, brother and Aunt Roma. Then my mother would take me to a patisserie to choose pastries and my favourite fondant candies. Then there was baking (and licking the spoons), setting the tables and dressing in a beautiful dress (dark blue, black or green, with a lace collar). Then, when my friends came, we'd play games, open presents, have fun and make noise, and scatter confetti. When I was nine, my mother invited the whole class of twenty from my private girls' school (which was named after the famous writer Eliza Orzeszkowa) and asked the nanny of my little cousin Gabrys, Roma's son, to come and organize the games.

There are many things I remember about my mother from when I was little. There were the times when I was sick in the middle of the night and my mother would sit me on the potty and cover me with her own crocheted green shawl; I can still smell my mother on this shawl that comforted me so much. There were the times after a bath when she would wrap me up well (there was no central heating), carry me to bed and serve me supper in bed — a soft-boiled egg and a roll. We would heat the water in the bathroom twice a week so that everyone could have a bath on those days and on other nights my mother used to wash me in a big basin. When I was sick with a cold (often enough) a doctor would come to cup my back, putting tiny glass cups on my back, while my mother held my hand. When I had to stay in bed, my mother would always buy me little presents to keep me occupied: booklets with a magic pencil to reveal a hidden picture, cut-outs, colouring books, books to read. She would sit beside my bed and read to me.

Every winter, she took me to an outdoor skating rink and I skated to music. She took me to the theatre to see children's plays and puppet shows. We always ate mandarins while we watched, and the theatre smelled of oranges. We went to the movies, and just before the war she went with me to a Deanna Durbin film — not a Shirley Temple or Laurel and Hardy one — and I felt very grown up. One day we were being vaccinated at school and because of the smell I felt faint. I was going down the stairs toward my waiting mother and I fainted, luckily into her arms.

In the summers, my brother went to a boys' camp, and my mother and I would go to a resort, where my father would join us on weekends. We stayed there all summer long. I played with other children in the river and sand. One day, I crawled under barbed wire with the other children and gouged my back from neck to waist, and my mother had to pour iodine on the wound. My mother would sometimes go to a spa in Ciechocinek, which I found out later must have been for her sciatica and gallstones.

MY BROTHER

March 8, 1992

My only and beloved brother, Rysio, would have been sixty-eight years old three days ago. As I mentioned, he was born in Warsaw on March 5, 1924. My aunt Chana, my father's older sister, told me in a letter she wrote from Israel in 1968 that when the time came for my mother to give birth, my father's brother, Uncle Anzelm, took her to the maternity clinic at 4:00 a.m.; my brother was born at 9:00 a.m. the next day. She stayed at the clinic for eight days and from there went back to my grandmother's apartment on Pawia Street. When Rysio was one month old, my father came and took him to Włocławek to my maternal grandfather's house. In Warsaw, my mother was visited by her father and sister, Roma. When my father was established in Gdańsk, my mother and brother joined him there.

Until I was six years old, my family and I lived at 42 Gdańska Street, in Lodz, but I have few specific recollections of Rysio at that time. I do remember that at about that age, in our new apartment at 4 Zamenhofa Street, we often played "pilot and his crew." We shared a big room. I had a normal-sized bed, but with slats all around it, like a big crib. My brother used to tie the sheet, or the coverlet, to these slats, fairly high up. We would go under it with just our heads above it, as if we were in a cockpit of a plane. My brother was the pilot, and I was the obedient happy crew. He would spell our names backwards and we became Draszyr and Aknaib Namnezor — a pair of fearless sheiks!

Often when he was still in bed, he would say, "Usia, please get a book for me," pointing to the books on his shelf. I did not want to get up either, but he made a game of it. "Okay," he would say, "I'll count to ten, and if you don't get it, I won't play with you." I would wait until the last moment, the count of nine-and-three-quarters, and then I would jump out of bed and hand it to him in the nick of time. He called me Usia (sometimes Usia-Siusa) or *Szmatka*, the Polish word for cloth or dishcloth. My mother sometimes asked him to take me to some children's movie but he was not too happy about going to the movies with a little sister in tow. Also, when his friends came to play I would always want to join in, even though his friends didn't welcome me there.

But otherwise, my brother doted on me and often played with me. He taught me many things: to whistle, balance a broom on my fingers, and play chess, checkers and many other games. He was an avid stamp collector and taught me how to put stamps in the album. At the same time, he enhanced my knowledge of geography, history and politics.

When I was eight years old, I had a severe case of whooping cough. My brother went to stay with my uncle Karol and his wife, Estka. But every day he would come into the courtyard after school so we could say hello to each other — I stood at the window and he looked up at me. At the time, he looked like he does in the two photos I have in my album, where I am with him. He was an excellent student, especially in math and science.

In 1937, my brother had his bar mitzvah. For his other birthdays, he had had a few friends over; they played games and ate cake. For his bar mitzvah, we went to the synagogue and heard him give his speech and later many people came to celebrate, not only Rysio's friends, but also members of my mother's family — her two uncles, the Danzigers, and her mother's cousins, all of whom I had never met before. There was a festive meal, and then the young boys played their games. One of the games I remember being particularly funny was called *dupnik*: you leaned over and covered your eyes, and one of the kids would give you a slap on the bottom, and you had to guess who it was.

Sometimes, in the winter, he went on a skiing trip to Zakopane. We spent our last summer before the war at this same resort. I shared a room with my mother, and my brother was allowed to bring a friend; they stayed in a room of their own because he was then fifteen and in September he was going to go to France to a *lycée*, a secondary school, as a boarding student. In the evening, my mother would often play cards with the other guests (since my father only came on the weekends) and I was afraid to sleep in the room on my own. Well, my brother devised a remedy for my fear. He would come into my room and say that, if I repeated a magical spell after him, nothing would happen to me. We both said in staccato voices, "Rum Tum Tum, Massa Kassa Hopsa Polbie, Rata Tata, Traszne, Mlasne, Polbie Trasne Boom Tcyk." After repeating this spell, I would fall asleep peacefully.

That summer was very memorable for me. The teenaged boys and girls would put records on in the evenings and dance while I sat in the garden, with the stars and moon shining, and the romantic melodies drifting from the lodge — "Habanera," "Donkey Serenade" and especially a song called "First Love Letter" with the lyrics "full of sadness and tears is but a memory today." It all seemed so romantic to me, and the young people inside dancing seemed so lucky, since I was so little and excluded from all this mystery.

That summer at the resort was the only bit of normal youth for my brother. When we returned to Lodz, everybody was talking about war. All the young people, including my brother, went to dig ditches and trenches. No time to think about sending him to France. My family thought that it was better to stay together, and if the war came we thought that the Germans would be defeated in a matter of days. How wrong everybody was.

## THE WAR

On September 1, 1939, there were suddenly air-raid alarms in Lodz. The games and other normal activities of our previous life were over. We were at war — Germany had invaded Poland.

We all ran to our neighbourhood café, Piatkowski, to get something to eat when the bombing stopped. We thought that the war would be over in a few days. During the raids we slept downstairs, on the ground floor at the apartment of the owners. On September 4, I was sleeping there, in the bed I shared with my brother, when I was awakened by my father taking me in his arms and saying goodbye to me. My brother was sitting at the table, dressed, with a knapsack on — my father and brother were leaving for Warsaw on foot, escaping before the Germans came. Everybody was saying that the Germans would kill Jewish men. My mother and I were to stay in Lodz.[1] And for the first time, I saw my father cry. We did not know when, or if, we would see each other again.

My father and brother left Lodz with other Jewish men who were running away from the Germans and heading toward the Soviet border. However, when they reached Warsaw, the Germans were already there, and there was no possible escape. They stayed with my grandmother and her daughters on Pawia Street.

On September 5, my cousin Gabrys' fourth birthday, his father, Uncle Olek, put on his lieutenant's uniform, and, as a volunteer, went to fight with the Polish army. He didn't have to go, as he had angina pectoris. We never saw him again: he was taken prisoner, with all the other officers, by the Soviets as they retreated from the German army, and he was shot in Kozielsk.[2]

After a short while, my father came back to us in Lodz, but Rysio stayed in Warsaw. However, in November 1939, when Lodz was an-

---

1  In general, Jewish families did not expect women and children to be victimized. Hence, men often fled, leaving their families behind. These families learned differently soon enough. Men who fled were also demoralized, unable to fulfill their roles as breadwinners and heads of the family.

2  Between April and May 1940, the Soviets massacred approximately 4,500 Polish military officers and policemen who had been in the prisoner-of-war camps at Kozielsk, Ostashkov and Starobelsk. The massacre took place in a forest near Katyn and became known as the Katyn massacre. The mass graves were discovered by the Germans in 1943. See Anna M. Cienciala, Wojciech Materski and N. S. Lebedeva *Katyn: A Crime Without Punishment* (New Haven: Yale University Press, 2007).

nexed into the Third Reich, Warsaw seemed safer because it was designated as occupied territory, so they decided we should all go to Warsaw. That month, I was sent on a train with a stranger, who took me
to my grandmother's in Warsaw. When I climbed to my grandmother's fourth-floor apartment, my brother opened the door. He shouted
"Szmatka!" and hugged and kissed me. Next, my father returned to
Warsaw, but my mother was left alone to close up the home and to
pack some things, until she too escaped to Warsaw in February 1940,
with only what she could carry with her on the bus. She arrived at my
grandmother's apartment pale, frightened and frozen. The Germans
had stopped the bus on the way, told everyone to get out and stand at
a wall ready to be shot — one of their sick jokes to frighten people to
death. After her ordeal, she went to bed for two days.

We started a precarious existence in the big living room of my
grandmother's house. That one room was for the four of us, with
hardly any of our possessions from Lodz. But we felt lucky to have
a big room to ourselves, even if everyone had to pass through it to
get to the two bedrooms. We had a dining table, a wood stove and a
wardrobe. We also had four beds put in the room — my father slept
on the couch, and my mother, Rysio and I slept on cots. We discovered bed bugs in those mattresses and we used carbolic and boiled
water to try and get rid of them, but they returned every time.

All of the windows were broken from the bombing and covered
with newspapers, and there was no electricity. So we had carbide
lamps and relied on the stove. We could not know exactly how lucky
we were to still be together. The apartment was on a street assigned to
the Jewish ghetto, which had been established in October 1940. There
was no work for my father in the ghetto, even though he had been a
successful businessman who represented both German and English
firms in Poland before the war. He was extremely worried about our
future and became despondent by the fact that he could not provide
for or save us.

In the ghetto, my mother was the one who was stronger and more enterprising than my father, who was a broken man. She started to sell lisle stockings to make some money. We cooked a big pot of soup once a day on the little wood stove in the middle of the living room (which we also used for warmth, without gas or electricity in the ghetto) and kept the soup warm by wrapping it in newspaper and in bed under eiderdowns. My mother would not let me peel the few potatoes that we sometimes had because of my frozen hands. It was so cold in the house because of the lack of fuel and the shattered windows that we wore gloves all the time and the water would freeze in the basin.

My brother and I went to secret classes in private rooming flats — in a different location every day — since Jews were no longer allowed to go to school. We each carried one book, hidden under our coats. We would have been killed if stopped by the Germans. My brother finished high school that way and then started his first year of electrical engineering. The best professors of the Warsaw University of Technology were in the ghetto, teaching in secret places. One of them was writing a book on mathematics for universities, and my brother, not quite eighteen yet, was helping him. The professor told Rysio that his name would be on the book when it was published after the war. Neither one of them survived the war.

My father stayed home and read. A typhus epidemic was raging in the ghetto, and my brother, who at this time was already extremely thin and undernourished, fell ill. If the Germans found out, he would have been taken away and murdered, so my grandmother and two aunts moved out of their rooms, and my brother and mother were installed there. She wore a nurse's coat inside and took it off when she left the room. Luckily, he survived and no one else contracted the disease. Afterwards, he was even thinner and very weak, and there was no nourishing food to give him — no meat, fruit or fresh vegetables, just the soup and some bread made of potato peels and sawdust with jam made of beets and saccharine.

Every day there were raids on the streets and men, especially, were captured and taken away in covered vans and were never heard from again. We were terrified any time my brother was even a little late coming home. We had friends in the ghetto with us, mostly living in the same block of apartments. I had my best, dearest friend, Rysia Perlberg, who went to secret classes with me. After the war, I heard that Rysia died of typhus and malnutrition in a concentration camp, after seeing her father taken to the gas chamber and her mother losing her mind.

I was sorry that Rysio had so little to eat and that I could not help him. But my brother was still full of humour and life. He taught me how to dance the "Lambeth Walk," the rage at the time. We could still take books out of the library and we read voraciously. Rysio read *The Picture of Dorian Gray* by Oscar Wilde while I was perusing Larousse's encyclopedia.[3]

In an attempt to escape the ghetto, a passport photo was taken of the four of us, but, in the last moments, we found out the passport was a hoax. (I hid this photo somehow, and it survived with me.)

In the late summer of 1942, when so many Jews had already been killed or sent to concentration camps,[4] those who remained were moved to three streets that contained "shops," or factories, for Jews who could work. A relatively small number of people were left to maintain these few repair shops for German uniforms in the ghetto. Luckily, a German, Friedrich Schultz, who was my father's handyman at his office years earlier, owned one of these factories and gave my father a job as a manager.

---

3  The full name of Pierre Larousse's encyclopedia, which was published in fifteen volumes between 1866 and 1876, is the *Grand dictionnaire universel du XIXe siècle* (*Great Universal Dictionary of the 19th Century*).

4  From July 22, 1942, to September 1942, 300,000 Jews were deported, mainly to Treblinka, where they were murdered on arrival. By the end of September, between 55,000 and 70,000 Jews remained in the ghetto. See Edelheit and Edelheit, *History of the Holocaust: A Handbook and Dictionary* (Boulder: Westview Press, 1994), 101–04.

The shops, which had been in operation for at least a year, were located on two streets of the ghetto, Nowolipie and Leszno, and there were a few houses with apartments designated for the workers. In each apartment, several people lived in one room, often all complete strangers. We all moved in there. My father arranged to employ or hide members of his family, as well as friends and strangers. Almost every day we got turnip soup and not much else to eat, but it was still paradise for me, since we were all together, a family.

These factories were only for adults, not for children or the elderly. My little cousin Gabrys, my friend Rysia, some of my other young cousins, my seventy-two-year-old grandfather, my eighty-year-old grandmother and I had to be hidden. Whenever the Germans inspected the factory, my brother was in charge of hiding us quickly and taking Gabrys and the other little children up to the space between the ceiling and the roof, covering them up with bales of sweaters. These little children, three or four years old, knew that they could not make a sound! My brother put my friend and me on a narrow shelf behind stacks of tied sweaters that were part of the German uniform and brought in from the battlefield for repairs. The sweaters arrived from the German front full of blood and lice. While hidden, we did not move; we breathed very quietly, half choking. There was always someone watching out in the courtyard to send a signal. How my parents must have worried about me!

One day the Germans dragged my grandmother from the toilet where she had hidden and took her away. We had to forcibly restrain my father from attacking the Germans. He went crazy and shouted. We had to hide him and cover his mouth. Later, we found out that they buried my grandmother alive — his beloved tiny "Mamele."

My brother was still quite emaciated from the typhus he got while we were living on Pawia Street. Rysio, at eighteen, was very tall and very thin; he was undernourished. He eventually moved out of our single room to be with people of his own age in one of the abandoned buildings. When my uncle Karol and his wife heard how sick Rysio was, they came back from the Soviet Union to help a little, since they still had some gold to sell for food. This helped nourish my brother back to health. They even bought a bottle of port to strengthen him. Later, they lost their lives because they had come back to Poland for us.

One day the Germans came and told us that the next day we would all have to go to another street for a selection. Since no children were supposed to be in the shop, we stuffed my mother's sister, Roma, and her six-year-old son, Gabrys, into a hole in the wall of the building and put bricks over it. A couple who had a three-year-old boy and a baby girl who had polio somehow managed to throw the boy over the wall in a sack to the "Aryan" side of Warsaw. They gave cyanide to the little girl by putting it in her milk bottle. When we returned after a day, the little girl sat in her stroller with a bullet through her head. The Germans had shot her.

My grandfather marched with us, trying to look straight and healthy. My family was very concerned about me because of how young I was, only thirteen. To avoid being selected, I had rouge on my cheeks to make me look healthy, my hair was put up in a bun to make me look older and I wore high heels. Many of the people from the shops did not come back after that day. As the columns of people were passing all night, we heard, listening from the house the Germans stuffed us all into, the cries and screams of children as they were being torn away from their parents and taken away to be killed; we saw the mothers trying to hang on to their children being hit over the head with rifles. We spent terrible nights in these abandoned buildings. When our turn came to march, I did not know that the Germans had slapped my father in the face. While we were waiting, I begged my mother not to let me go, and to come with me. We were lucky this time. We came back and dug Gabrys and his mother out from the wall. That's when we saw the baby in the stroller with a bullet in her head.

After this event, my aunt Roma's former housekeeper, Genia, smuggled my little cousin Gabrys to the "Aryan" side of town. Genia was a young woman from the village where my grandfather had his manor house. Soon my aunt, uncle Karol and his wife, Estka, followed, with some factory workers who marched out of the ghetto every day to work.

In November 1942, when we knew that the factory "shops" could not last much longer, my mother left the ghetto using false papers under the name Helena Siekierska and went to the "Aryan" side to find a place for us to hide. There, Genia, who was there with Gabrys, my two aunts and uncle Karol — all hidden in specially built hiding nooks in Genia's apartment — helped her to rent a room from someone. On November 30, 1942, I too joined them on the "Aryan" side.

But before I left, my brother came again to stay with us so that we would not be alone in the factory shop that night. There was a small fire one night and they almost deported my father because of it. My brother hovered over me; he somehow managed to buy a second-hand watch and a ham sandwich and gave them to me. We said goodbye at the ghetto wall and I left the ghetto secretly, with a group who worked outside the ghetto, to go into hiding in the "Aryan" part of Warsaw. That was the last time I saw my brother.

When Rysio became sick again with another bout of typhus only my father and his sisters were there to care for him, and they only had a thin turnip soup to give him. He got over the typhus and then succumbed again; he was so run down and starved by then. We wanted him to come over and hide with us on the other side, but he would not leave my father alone in the ghetto. And my father could not leave because if he did everyone in the shop would lose their jobs and be taken to the concentration camps. Rysio also had a girlfriend in the ghetto, his first love, and he wanted to be with her.

My mother and Genia obtained forged papers for me, and I stayed with my mother in a room in the flat of Mrs. Sobolewska. Soon, it was not safe to stay there anymore. Genia found us another place to stay, in a bigger apartment, where parents, two teenagers and a young girl in hiding lived. As it happened, this girl was the Glocers' daughter, the distant relatives I mentioned earlier. I never went outside and rarely even left our room. In the dark, I tried to read and memorize my new birth certificate, which was under the name Krstyna Warecka. Earlier, I had been Bolestowa-something. I was always shaking with fear.

By March 1943, notices had been sent to the factory shops that they were soon to be dismantled and that many Jews would be sent to the labour camps of Poniatowa and Trawniki[5] The Germans took away my brother and my parents' families, but somehow the owner, Schultz, put my father, against his will, into the trunk of his car and drove him to the "Aryan" side. My grandfather committed suicide before the Nazis could take him. I remember my mother saying, "What kind of world has it come to that a daughter should be thankful that her father has killed himself?"

When I went to get my father from the German's house, he was a ruin of a man; he did not want to be saved. He had begged them, on his knees, to save my brother, my good, brilliant, beautiful eighteen-year-old brother. I walked on one side of the street and father on the other and I led him to the place where we were hiding — but really only I was hiding, since my mother, with her forged papers and her so-called "good looks" (meaning she did not look Jewish), could walk around freely with no one suspecting she was Jewish.

We stayed hiding together for a short time, and then on Passover, April 19, 1943, there was the Ghetto Uprising.[6] The Germans were

---

5 Poniatowa, initially established to hold Soviet prisoners of war, was the site of a concentration camp between 1941 and 1943, when it was incorporated into the Majdanek concentration camp. Trawniki, in 1941, also held Soviet POWs, and was adapted into a forced labour camp for Jews from June 1942 until September 1943, at which point it became a subcamp of Majdanek. In both camps, some of the factory shops had been moved there from the Warsaw ghetto, where they continued to function under worsening conditions.

6 The Nazis had deported another 8,000 Jews from the Warsaw ghetto in January

bombing the ghetto, and the bombs flew over us. Everybody from the apartment house went down to the cellar. I wanted to run out to join them in the basement, but we had to stay hidden upstairs on the fifth or sixth floor so that nobody would see us. We were standing in the inner hallway at night, my father with his arms around my mother and me, while I tried to run away, screaming in terror as the bombs were falling over us. My father tried to comfort me by saying, "If we are to die, we will die here together."

It was getting too dangerous for us to stay there, so Genia arranged to take me to another hiding place, and then another and another.[7] I was separated from my parents and over the course of about twenty months I was hiding in seven different places. I usually saw my mother once a week as she was walking outside freely, with her false papers and her gentile looks. It was not until August 1943 that Genia found a safer place for me with a young couple who went to work and left me in their one-room apartment all day, alone. I was not allowed to go near the window or to flush the toilet, or to make any noise at all.

My parents had moved to Boernerowo, a suburb of Warsaw. On her weekly visits, my mother would bring me a clean towel and books from the library. I waited for her like for an angel of mercy. Sometimes she brought me a note from my father and herself, asking me not to cry, to be patient and in a good mood. She was working as a

---

1943. On April 19, 1943, the Nazis again entered the ghetto, thinking it would take only three days to deport the rest of the Jews, but the Jews resisted for about a month, until May 16, in what became known as the Warsaw Ghetto Uprising, the largest Jewish resistance effort during the war. *See* Edelheit and Edelheit, *History of the Holocaust: A Handbook and Dictionary* (Boulder: Westview Press, 1994), 101–04. See also Marilyn Harran, *The Holocaust Chronicle* (Lincolnwood, Ill: Publications International, 2000), 446–52.

7   Genowefa (Genia) Olczak was recognized as Righteous Among the Nations by Yad Vashem on July 15, 1981. For more information see the Yad Vashem database at http://db.yadvashem.org/righteous/family.html?language=en&item Id=4016666.

"housekeeper" for the person who was hiding my father and another Jewish man. (She was not really his housekeeper; she worked there only so that she could see my father, but to outsiders, her presence needed to be explained.)

One day in November 1943, she came to see me in my hiding place, terribly distraught. There was news that Poniatowa, the concentration camp where my brother was, had been destroyed, and everybody in the camp had been murdered. But just before this news, my brother had somehow smuggled out a letter from the camp to my parents, asking them to send him some warm clothing. My mother clung to the idea that he might have managed to escape to the forest and join the partisans. On that day, I lashed out at her and cried, "Why are you not doing something? How can you let him be killed?" My poor mother was tortured by the events, and here I was shouting at her. I was so desperate to get out of my hiding place and be with my parents. I begged her, over and over again, to take me there, but they thought it would be too dangerous for me.

I can recall one sunny moment with my mother at this time: Christmas in 1943. Genia somehow brought me at night, for a few hours, to her apartment, where my little cousins and my aunt, my uncle and his wife were all hiding. My mother came that night and we had dinner together — potato dumplings. I sat on the floor beside my mother and put my head on her lap and held her hand.

I had not seen my father since we separated after the bombings and I did not see him again until January 1944. By then my parents were hiding in the house from which they would later be taken from to be shot. Because she was worried about my father's safety, my mother had begged the people in whose apartment I was hiding to take my father for a couple of days while she tried to find a safer place. Those few days were so happy for me. After being alone, day in, day out, for months, locked alone in the flat, I had my father there. And even in those terrible days, what a wonderful companion he was. He knew so many poems by heart, German poems by Schiller, Goethe and Heine, as well as English, French and Polish poems. At the age of fourteen, after reading books day after day with no human contact, I heard his voice again and the beautiful poetry, which I wrote down in my copy books to comfort me later.

But the situation was too dangerous, and my father had to leave. They could not find him another place, and so he had to return to the previous hideout. My parents were completely broken people, especially now that they thought their son had probably been killed. They still had some hope, but not much. They also did not know if I would survive.

On February 1, 1944, at 10:00 p.m., on my mother's forty-sixth birthday, the Gestapo came to where my parents were hiding. The Gestapo took both of them away, my father and mother, with their host, Bronisław Przybysz, and two others who he was hiding, to a nearby field. There was a witness to this scene, a Polish passerby. Apparently, my father was the one who comforted the others. He said, "I hoped we would survive to see the end of the war, but this is it." The Gestapo told the Pole to dig graves and then directed a barrage of shots at my mother, my father, Bronisław Przybysz and the two others. The witness lost his ability to speak for two weeks. The only reason they were killed was because they were Jews and their host, Bronisław Przybysz, who was a Christian, was killed for hiding them in his house.[8] I found out about my parents from Genia about a month or so after their murder.

Earlier in the afternoon of that same day, because of her birthday, my mother had brought a treat she made for me, chocolates she made out of cocoa, and she also brought me my brother's winter coat. But I was locked inside by my host and could not open the door, could not say a word in case someone heard me. My mother, after knock-

---

8 Due to Bianka's efforts, Bronisław Przybysz was recognized by Yad Vashem as Righteous Among the Nations on December 2, 1991. For more information see the Yad Vashem database at http://db.yadvashem.org/righteous/family.html?lang uage=en&itemId=4017049.

ing, gave me a signal, clearing her throat, so that I would know she was there. She left the chocolates and coat with a neighbour, her last gift for me.

All I have left of my father is a little secret note he sent me in which he begged me not to cry, to try not to be lonely and to try to read, and in which he said that they were thinking about me all the time.

Did they worry in their last moments about me? Did they think that someone might have followed my mother that day to my place of hiding and come for me too?

How I wish they could, at the very least, know that I survived, had a normal life, had children and grandchildren. My parents live on through me, my children and my grandchildren.

~

The next day, I was taken to a house on Hoża Street, where a Mr. Zubnycki lived with his wife, son, daughter and nephew. I stayed there until the beginning of October 1944, which marked the end of the Warsaw Uprising.[9] During the Uprising, I was working with the partisans, carrying sacks of barley for soup from Haberbusch, a brewery, under Aleje Jerozolimskie (Jerusalem Avenue), through a tunnel to the partisans in the city centre. Once, during an air raid, I was in a cellar on Hoża Street when a bomb hit — half of the cellar caved in and I was taken out unconscious.

When the Uprising failed and Warsaw was surrendered to the Germans, Polish citizens of Warsaw were evacuated to Pruszków, a nearby town. In a courtyard, I saw a young couple with two children and decided to leave with them, thinking that I could take care of the

---

9  An uprising organized by the Polish Home Army in August 1944 to liberate Warsaw from German occupation and initiate the establishment of an independent Poland in the post-war period. By October 2, 1944, the attempt at liberation had been crushed and the results were devastating — more than 150,000 civilians had been killed, and more than 25 per cent of Warsaw had been destroyed.

children. We were put in an open freight car for a trip that took twenty-four hours — normally it would take no more than two — with no water or toilet, and I held the baby girl on my knees. In Pruszków we stayed in a huge, crowded barn-like building, where I got nits in the seams of my dress, the only one I had.

We were there a few days. Then the Germans started the selection: on the right went young people, apparently to work in the mines in Germany. To the left went children, mothers and the elderly, to be sent to the Polish countryside to help the farmers. I looked much younger than my age, and starved, yet the German motioned me to go to the right. But I ran to the left side under his rifle shouting, "My mother is over there!" and I joined this family again. We were taken on a bus that stopped at an inn where they had white bread with sour cream! Then we went to a cottage that the family had been to before. Once there, the farmer who owned the cottage greeted the family, but took the woman outside to talk to her. When she came back she said to me, "Krstyna [I was still using my false name], you can't stay here because the man said you look Jewish."

They told me to walk along the train tracks and at the end there would be an R.G.O. building (Rada Główna Opiekuńcza, or Central Welfare Council). When I got there, there was a father with a girl around my age, Mirka. I told them that I had lost my parents on the way and Mirka asked her father to take me with them. We went to the village of Tworzyjanki, where they had one room assigned to them in a villa. Her parents slept on one narrow bed, and Mirka and her grandmother on another. I slept on the floor, covered with my brother's school coat.

During the day, they worked digging potatoes but I was too weak to do it, so I went from one peasant's house to another, teaching children and getting food there. After awhile, I started coughing badly. Mirka's family said that I should go back to the main R.G.O. office in Krakow and that I would find help there, because they thought I had tuberculosis. I did not know what to do — it was too dangerous for me to be seen out walking and I was too weak and sick. However, in the same villa was a nice family, Mrs. Helena Kazimierczak, who was a teacher, her husband, their eleven-year-old daughter, Hania, and their son, three-year-old Januszek. The family took a liking to me and said that they would take me with them to their home in Koluszki. There, Mrs. Helena Kazimierczak took care of me, fed me and did not let me do anything in the house; she let me rest. I slept in the same bed as Hania but never told them about the nits in my only dress. I was afraid they would throw me out! Every evening I boiled a kettle of water and poured it over the seams of my dress to kill the nits. I stayed there until February or March 1945, when I found and joined Genia and Gabrys.

~

After the war, I looked for my brother. I hoped that the reason I couldn't find him was that he suffered from memory loss. I hoped that one day he would find me. Sometimes, I still keep hoping. Oh, my dear Rysio, all I can give you is my life; all of my life I have lived for you, so that you may live, so that my children are yours, too, and my grandchildren are your grandchildren. My big brother, now I, your little sister, am old, and you are eternally young.

In 1994, I learned that the prisoners of the Trawniki and Poniatowa camps were ordered, in late October 1943, to dig trenches in a long zig-zag formation for what they thought was a Soviet anti-tank manoeuvre. On November 3, about 43,000 inmates of the Trawniki, Poniatowa and Majdanek camps were shot and buried in these ditches in the so-called Harvest Festival Massacre.[10]

I only hope that my brother and cousins died fighting, but the probability of that is extremely low.

--------

10 The massacre of about 43,000 prisoners in Poniatowa, Trawniki and Majdanek by SS units occurred on November 3 and 4, 1943, as music was played through loudspeakers. At Poniatowa, the trenches that the inmates had been previously ordered to dig became the mass graves of approximately 14,000 inmates. The massacres were committed simultaneously under the codename *Aktion Erntefest*, or Operation Harvest Festival, at all the labour camps in the Lublin area.

1  Bianka's mother, Regina (Renia) Rozenman (née Zakrzewska), circa 1920s.
2  Bianka with her father, Paweł Rozenman. Lodz, circa 1932.
3 & 4  Bianka and her brother, Ryszard (Rysio), in Lodz, circa 1932 and 1938.

The Rozenman family in the Warsaw ghetto, 1940. This photo was originally taken as a passport photo when the family thought they could use it to escape the ghetto. They later found out that this was a hoax.

1  Bianka and her future husband, Ludek. Scotland, 1945.
2  Bianka and Ludek on their sixtieth wedding anniversary. Toronto, 2011.

1  Bianka and her daughters, Renata (centre) and Tamara (right). Toronto, 1990s.
2  Bianka and family, 2011. In the back row, left to right: Bianka; Ludek; and their grandson Mark. In front, left to right: Bianka's granddaughter, Nikki, her grandson David, and Ludek's nephew's sons, Tom and Matthew.

# Passing

# Foreword

In this section, we read the memoirs of four Polish women who were able to pass as non-Jews through a variety of techniques at deception. These four women had an advantage that men of the same age couldn't have — simply, they were female and therefore circumcision was not an issue. Genital identification was irrelevant for Jewish women; other traits and physical characteristics influenced how they were viewed — and judged. Namely, if they had blond hair, blue or green or grey eyes, spoke Polish or German without a Yiddish accent, and if they were clever and very, very lucky, they had a chance of passing as non-Jews. What also helped was their education at secular rather than at religious schools. At secular schools, they learned the vernacular fluently; they became aware of their nation's history and literature; they became more comfortable with the culture that surrounded them than did boys who, for the most part in many regions, were sent to religious schools, or *yeshivot*.

A woman also needed to relocate to an area where she was not known and yet behave as if she was familiar with the surroundings. She needed to be free of the possibility of being recognized. For the most part, this involved being alone, for a lone individual is much less conspicuous than a group.

Granted that the absence of a physical identifying trait and the presence of a secular education were the "givens" of "passing," a woman also needed courage and an intense degree of self-confidence to be successful at passing. A furtive glance, a hesitant way of walking or being unable to bluff her way through an interrogation rendered her suspicious and thus vulnerable to accusations by the Gestapo and other officials. Women who passed lived in a state of continuous terror; they risked their lives merely by leaving their apartments. Yet, they had to leave to survive. They were not hidden Jews; they were Jews who tried to look as if they led normal lives, albeit under frightening circumstances.

False identification papers helped because spontaneous raids were the norm, and each woman had to produce something to convince her interrogators that she was, if not "Aryan," at least non-Jewish. Of course, the risk of buying false papers involved getting papers that didn't look authentic and were not the papers of a living person, as was the case of Rachel, cited in Lenore Weitzman's chapter on passing.[1] In a routine registration, Rachel showed her false papers to a policeman who actually knew the person in the identification papers because she had been a maid in his parents' home and he had had sex with her. Because the policeman was taken by Rachel's looks, he let her go, expecting some sort of quid pro quo, to which Rachel agreed. He gave her a new identification card. Obviously, Rachel fled immediately. Rachel's experience was rare, although women did have the advantage, if it can even be called that, of using their bodies as commodities. To do so, however, was also to risk blackmail and betrayal, not to mention perpetual trauma.

In this section, Helen, Dyna, Barbara and Irene each passed by using tactics unique to her situation. Each was extraordinarily lucky. Indeed, each could have been caught at any point in her "hiding in

---

1   Original source is Rachel's son's testimony, #48 Fortunoff Video Archive, Yale University. Her son heard this exchange between his mother and the policeman as he waited for her just outside the office. Cited in Lenore J. Weitzman, "Living on the Aryan Side in Poland," in *Women and the Holocaust*, edited by Dalia Ofer and Lenore J. Weitzman (New Haven: Yale University Press, 1998), p. 214.

plain sight." Each clearly overcame terror and found the courage to take risks, time and time again.

Helen Mahut, who moved between Lwów and Warsaw and several places in-between, married a non-Jewish doctor in order to escape detection and deportation. However, he was caught as a member of the Underground and ultimately murdered. A friend of her dead husband gave Helen all the necessary documents to pass (birth and christening papers and nursing certificate) on the condition that Helen move away from Lwów, while she would remain there and declare that she had lost her papers. Helen soon joined the Underground and passed information through the Underground to London. She had several close calls that leaves one breathless but compelled to continue reading. Her memoir reveals the utter brutality of the SS and the profound bravery of the members of the Underground.

Dyna Perelmuter and her family were moved from a small town not very far from Warsaw to the Częstochowa ghetto. Her memoir conveys the despair of the inhabitants of the ghetto and her determination to escape from a labour camp to go into hiding, until she manages to obtain a *Kennkarte* of a deceased girl who had been close to her age. With false documents, she was then able to apply for a job as a farm girl. Her detailed encounter with a cow is a welcome distraction from her grim situation. Under her new identity, she grew confident enough to attend the local church regularly. After liberation, she travelled back to Częstochowa to find help from the United Nations Relief and Rehabilitation Administration (the UNRRA) and eventually moved to Warsaw. By 1959, fearful of the renewed rise of antisemitism, she and her new husband immigrated to Canada.

Barbara Meryn Kuper recalls being "rounded up and herded" into the Częstochowa ghetto, with its severe overcrowding and widespread starvation. Escape from the ghetto led to various hiding places and finally to Warsaw, where she rented a room in a house occupied by a Russian family. Barbara's blond hair and green eyes encouraged her to try to pass. She became a tutor to a boy who was preparing for high school entrance exams. She witnessed both the Warsaw Ghetto Uprising in 1943 and the Warsaw Uprising in 1944. When the war ended, she enrolled in Jagiellonian University to study chemistry. After her immigration to Canada, her expertise at a large paint company led to her development of the first formulas for acrylic paints. She explored other interests and became a well-regarded sculptor who had six solo exhibits in Montreal. Her work is found all over the world.

Finally, Irene Zoberman's memoir describes horrific treatment by the Nazis. Her life in the Sandomierz ghetto is replete with instances of Nazi brutality. Betrayed in a hiding place with dozens of others, they were gathered to be shot one by one. But Irene escaped and, despite some harrowing close calls and wandering for a time, homeless, she bought religious articles and a cross to add to her Christian papers. And that, she wrote, was how she became a Christian. Her months as a vagrant took their toll and she wound up hospitalized because of a kidney deficiency. In the hospital, she attended Catholic celebrations and masses. Upon her release, she became what can be described as a visiting nurse. She bluffed her way out of exposure as a Jew and, before long, became part of the Underground. She cleverly acquired birth certificates that would prove her Christian lineage dating back four generations. She tells some amusing stories that were anything but amusing when they happened. Caught in a round-up after the 1944 Warsaw Uprising, she was imprisoned in Stutthof, where she was assigned to the hospital. She managed another escape, this time to the partisans in the forest, where she helped establish a field hospital until finally, still living as a Christian, the war ended. Throughout her narrative, Irene questions God and His absence.

These four women lived through terror. Not only were their lives disrupted by the war and all the misery that accompanies war, but they also lived through the fear of being exposed for having stolen or bought identities and the consequent tortures that would have followed. We cannot know what courage it must have taken. We can only appreciate their remarkable survival.

# The Depth of Decency
# Helen Mahut

I think the dead would want us
To weep for what *they* have lost.
I think that our luck in continuing
Is what would affect them most.
But time would find them generous
And less self-engrossed.

*James Fenton*, from "For Andrew Wood"

The strength of the short story lies in what it leaves out.

*William Trevor*

A very close and old friend who fought with the Free French Forces
in 1944–1945 in France told me one day that I knew most of what was
worth knowing about his war and, yet, he knew very little about my
war. And so, this past November, 1998, suffering from a bad viral flu,
housebound with incessant rain and clouds in Paris, I set down to
write my chronology of events between 1939 and 1945.

THE SUMMER OF 1939
In the previous year, 1938, I had spent the summer vacation in a
friend's country house in Cornwall where her father, a country squire
and a Cambridge man, asked me quite seriously at dinner whether

I belonged to a communist cell in Warsaw — his knowledge of political geography did not extend east of the Rhine. In the summer of 1939, my father commanded me to return to Poland for my vacation, threatening to disinherit me should I remain in England. At that time, 1938–39, shortly after the catastrophe of Czechoslovakia, we were all donning gas masks and practicing evasion of bombs.[1] In that atmosphere, my friends bade me goodbye, crying and trying to convince me to remain in England because any day now the Germans might invade Poland. I had to return.

Our international train from Hook van Holland to Warsaw, known for its punctuality, reached the Polish border with an almost five-hour delay. The German customs and passport officers were extremely rude, muttering "Polnische Schweine," Polish pigs, when they examined the luggage of the sister of the Polish ambassador Józef Lipski in Berlin, and cut the soles of her slippers with razor blades. My father, who met me in Poznań, the first large city in the west of Poland, was dismayed by my stories, particularly when I told him that the train was late because military transports were continually swarming to the Polish border. I knew that war was imminent. "What war?" asked my father. "England has truly demoralized you!"

We left Warsaw a fortnight before the war broke out and travelled to the northeast segment of Poland, at the border of Lithuania, separated from it by a magnificent river, the Niemen. When we returned to Warsaw on September 3, we experienced the first heavy bombardment. We left Warsaw two days later. Our car was confiscated by Pol-

---

1   On September 30, 1938, in what ended up being a failed attempt at appeasing Nazi Germany, the Sudeten region of Czechoslovakia was ceded to Germany in the Munich Agreement, signed by France, Italy, Britain and Germany. The Sudetenland was of incalculable strategic and economic importance to Czechoslovakia — it was the location of most of the country's border defenses, many of its banks, 70 per cent of its iron and steel industry and 70 per cent of its electrical power. On March 15, 1939, Germany invaded and occupied the rest of Czechoslovakia.

ish officers who, we later learned, were on their way to Hungary. We continued by train, a journey that took four days instead of the three and a half hours it usually took. We were headed to join my father's sister, married to a Polish veterinarian, who lived on a property in the east of Poland, not far from the Soviet border. Since the rails were constantly bombarded, the train had to make detours. We travelled at night and hid in adjoining forests during the day. The last two cars carried our dead. The Red Army invaded the east of Poland, and we breathed a sigh of relief for having escaped the Nazis.[2] Life became "normal."

I soon got bored with nothing to do. Equipped with a backpack containing bread, salted lard and some sugar, I made my way to Lwów (renamed Lemberg by the Germans), the only university town free of the Germans where students from all other Polish universities converged. I arrived late one night on November 11, a Polish Day of Independence (1919), and found the streets empty. I was stopped by a Soviet patrol, who after I addressed them in Russian, were convinced that I was not their Polish enemy insurgent. They kindly walked me to the nearest student dormitory, which happened to be for medical students. I was nearly turned away by the Revolutionary Committee, who all agreed that I had the wrong "social origin," having studied in England. Only children of workers and peasants were gladly accepted. The role of the committee was to weed out any fascist students or professors.

1940–1941

Twice rejected, I was finally admitted to the university in the Department of Philology and Oriental Studies (Sanskrit, Urdu and Hindi).

---

2  In August 1939, Germany and the USSR concluded the Molotov-Ribbentrop Pact or the Hitler-Stalin Pact, officially called the German-Soviet Non-Aggression Pact. The Pact divided eastern Poland between Germany and the USSR. In June 1941, Hitler broke the Pact and invaded the USSR in Operation Barbarossa.

Civilian Soviet authorities took over from the army and, being prud-ish, they put an end to mixed-gender dorms. My committee decided that in order to keep me in a male medical students dorm, one of them should marry me since on the top floor there were to be rooms for married couples. Arthur Harlig decided to oblige. This marriage was to remain a friendly arrangement of convenience, and, in order not to embarrass me, he took night shift duties in the psychiatric hos-pital, where he was in charge of sixteen beds of schizophrenic women patients.

With the civilian Soviet authorities came the NKVD[3], who imme-diately began to arrest and send east all the refugees from the west-ern part of Poland under the pretense that there were German spies among the refugees (Polish and mostly Jewish). Arthur and I were exempted because he was a doctor and wore a red cross on his arm. However, his brother Zygmund, a crystallographer, and his wife, were arrested. Bear in mind that the Polish Communist Party had been "excommunicated" for "Trotskyite deviations" in 1937. Both Arthur and Zygmund were communists — sons of a rich industrialist who re-fused to take a penny from him and supported themselves by coach-ing less gifted students at the university. Upon hearing of their arrest, Arthur and I ran to the railway station where we saw all the arrested locked up in cattle cars — we found Zygmund who, through a small opening, consoled us by saying that they would come to no harm, after all, "The Party knows what it's doing!" This blind faith did not save the transport. Within a few hours east of Lwów, the transport was stopped by armed bands of Ukranians who, upon hearing that it contained Jews, massacred all the people in the entire train, includ-ing the Soviet guards.

---

3   The acronym of the Narodnyi Komissariat Vnutrennikh Del, meaning People's Commissariat for Internal Affairs. The NKVD functioned as the Soviet Union's security agency, secret police and intelligence agency from 1934 to 1954.

SUMMER OF 1941

On June 22, 1941, we experienced the first bombardment by the Germans — Operation Barbarossa had begun. At night, all the Red Army and civilian authorities fled. The German army entered Lwów one week later, greeted by songs and flowers from the Ukrainians dressed in their national costumes while Poles and Jews hid in basements, expecting the worst. It came: bands of very drunk Ukranians on horseback killed, raped and maimed any civilian they found. The German army stood by. After about six days, the German army put an end to this drunken and bloodthirsty behaviour by shooting the marauders. Some sort of order was reinstated. Armies don't like unregimented killing. If any killing had to be done, it had to be done by the army, in an orderly manner.

With friends, we hid in the basement of their apartment house. After several hours, I needed to escape, so I went upstairs to fetch a sweater and fell asleep. When I returned to the basement they were all dead — men and women mutilated. I moved in with other Polish friends while Arthur stayed in his hospital. I later learned from him that the Germans ordered him to kill his patients with an injection of petrol directly into the heart.

Arthur returned to our apartment, and I joined him. Because of his dark hair and brown eyes, it was not safe for him to be in the streets. I tried to obtain some food here and there, among other places, in a German officers' club, where a good Polish friend was a maître d'. One night, I came to the back door to get the usual soup, and the door was opened by an officer who informed me that my friend was off duty that night. Two of the officers, with guns resting at a nearby table, forced themselves on me and early in the morning, realizing that I was a virgin, blamed me for not telling them ("if we had known..."), apologized profusely and drove me home. Upon seeing me, Arthur exploded with pain and helplessness but then also asked me why, after a night with the Germans, I could not bring home white bread. He then went out and was almost immediately caught and interned in Janowska, a transit and concentration camp outside Lwów. Together with other doctors, he served as a "camp doctor," which meant issuing death certificates stating that the cause of death was heart attack for every inmate tortured to death by an SS *Obersturmbannführer*, a high-ranking officer.

Much later, when a typhus epidemic began to decimate the camp, the SS were terrified of getting sick, and several doctors, together with Arthur, put corpses onto trucks to take them to the city incinerators. Among the corpses, they hid living inmates, who preferred to risk contamination (infection, lice) in order to escape. In one of those transports, I saw Arthur for the last time. At the beginning of September 1942, during a large-scale liquidation, the SS killed hundreds of inmates along with the entire Jewish and Polish personnel. Some were hanged by hooks in the throat from a balcony on a busy street, Łokietka. Arthur was the second from the left, among some lawyers, professors and other doctors.

By July 1941, all the remaining Red Army soldiers had been captured and were put into the Citadel, locked up and left to die of thirst and hunger. Their cries were heard for a very long time. Four months later, the Jewish quarter began to be transformed into a ghetto. My Polish friends, Helena and Zdzisław Dziedziński, forbade me to put on a yellow armband and join the other Jews in the quarter. They hid me in their apartment and locked me up in my room when they had to go out. A former nurse who worked with Arthur eventually gave me all her documents (birth and christening certificates, nursing certificate and other papers that were impossible to buy even for a fortune) because, "not having been able to help the Doctor, [she] wanted to help [me]." All I had to do was leave Lwów and move to Warsaw, which was part of a different jurisdiction (General Government), and she would declare the loss of her papers later on. Her name was Helena Czechowicz — I still bear her given name.

My Polish friends found me a *Volksdeutsche* — an ethnic German living in Poland, who had certain privileges — who would accompany me on the train to Warsaw. In the fall of 1942, we left. We stopped in a small town near Krakow to visit his sister. It was the day when all the Jews were chased into a nearby forest for execution. We stood on the balcony watching and saw a young Luftwaffe soldier — not an SS officer or Gestapo — take a baby from a woman by its tiny legs and crash its skull against a wall. Just a young airman! We left, or, at least, attempted to take the next train to Warsaw, but because of the liquidation of the Jews, hundreds of SS were in the railway station checking every civilian. Profiting from the melee, my *Volksdeutsche* escaped with my suitcase and abandoned me.

I boarded the train fully aware of how dangerous it was to travel without luggage, particularly from that little town. I arrived in Warsaw and immediately went to see my mother's best friend, Lydia, who, like my mother, was a Russian gentile married to a Jew in hiding. Being a white Russian, she was permitted to remain in her huge apartment. She was in touch with my mother who, in the meantime, had moved with my father and twelve-year-old brother to Bialystok, a town in the north where Jews from many other towns were put into a ghetto. Lydia exchanged letters with my mother with the help of a black marketeer who traded between East Prussia (into which Bialystok was incorporated) and Warsaw. I asked Lydia to help me buy false papers for my father and brother so that they could escape with my mother. Lydia, whose husband owned the entire cotton industry in Żyrardów, Poland, was very rich, with hidden gold and jewels. But, like a penitent, simple Russian peasant, she prostrated herself on the floor with her arms in the shape of a cross, crying and beating her forehead on the wood, yet she refused to give me even one ring or one watch (this is all it would have taken) because "we don't know how long the war will last and the people who are hiding my husband are very expensive."

1942–1943

I rented a room with Mme. Adwentowicz, the estranged wife of a famous Polish theatre actor who was in jail because he had helped his Jewish mistress (also a known actress) to escape to Switzerland. My landlady was bitter, very religious and observant, and had one other lodger, a young woman named Danuta, whom I tried to avoid because her uncle, who frequently visited, struck me as a rabid anti-semite. Because this milieu belonged to the intelligentsia, nobody believed that I was a registered nurse, and I was frequently teased by references in French and English to literary works and authors. At the same time, with the exception of my landlady, all were agnostic, and I didn't have to pretend to be a practising Catholic like Danuta, who went to church regularly and who surrounded herself with holy pictures.

I supported myself by teaching English in an underground school for boys. Unlike France where cultural activities continued to flourish under the Nazis (Sartre put on plays, writers published books, night-clubs were open as was the university, films were being made), all ed-ucational institutions, including high schools, were closed in Poland, and teaching children in small groups gathered in private homes was punishable by death. This teaching put me in touch with the school priest and headmaster who helped me join the Polish Underground Resistance, the Armia Krajowa, or Home Army. I found my first du-ties offensively innocuous: having a good visual memory, I was to be at bus terminals on main highways to memorize the insignias on German army trucks (red triangle over a yellow square, for example) until it might become suspect that I missed too many buses. At the end of the day, I made notes and gave them to my lieutenant, not re-alizing that, with many of us doing this, London knew very quickly what was to be known about army movements from west to east. Lat-er, I was given the responsibility of listening to radio London (pun-ishable by death, of course) to take notes and translate them into Pol-ish to verify the communiqués aired in Polish. This involved carrying mimeograph paper and ink from here to there (including my notes in English and Polish). Incidentally, my lieutenant was the only one I could tell who I was because the Underground was afraid to take in Jews, since they were twice the risk.

One day, carrying an attaché case with paper, ink and other paraphernalia, my streetcar was stopped on a bridge — a usual procedure for the Germans to catch young Poles who were not working for the German war effort and did not carry the necessary papers. I had only a brief moment to make my decision: I could not abandon my briefcase because one never knew who was in the streetcar. Fortunately, I also carried my laundry carefully wrapped in paper. Coming out of the streetcar into the arms of two armed SS men, I handed the briefcase to one of them for safekeeping and, cursing all the while, I put my laundry into the snow and mud, which they kicked around with their boots. I gathered the laundry, took the briefcase handed to me by one of them and slowly, very slowly, walked away. It was only when I turned the corner that my knees gave out from under me.

One evening, when I came home just before curfew (7:00 p.m. in the winter months), my landlady tearfully informed me that the Gestapo had come to arrest Danuta and her uncle, who were denounced for being Jews. She begged me to move out because the apartment might be under observation and, as a young woman not working for the Germans, I could be taken to a labour camp. The next day, I moved in with my headmaster's family. The professor was a nice and decent family man who, unfortunately, began to recite surreptitious odes to my blue eyes. Eventually, I had to move out again and moved in this time with another professor from my school, a very odd, old retired history teacher who lived with his very old mother (the sister of Wanda Landowska[4]). She was almost blind and deaf, sat like an ef-

---

4  Famous Polish-French harpsichordist who fled France when Germany invaded. As a Jewish woman, she was targeted for incarceration. She later moved to the United States and successfully restarted her career.

figy at the table, had to be fed and put to bed and was called by her son, rather proudly, Seneca. The professor, in protest, had not gone out since 1939 but every morning he opened one of the windows facing the street and yelled, "Adolf is still here, Mother!"

The Underground began to send me adult students: members of the Underground who were told to learn English. Stefan Mahut was one of these students, but he did not want to learn lists of irregular English verbs when he came back to Warsaw after exercising in the forests or executing Nazi collaborators. I think he guessed that I was in trouble because, very discreetly, without giving anything away, he asked me to marry him. "Just think what my extended working-class family could do to protect you!" But it was one of those things one did not do, certainly not without the knowledge and consent of the family, because if it were discovered that he had married a Jew, his family would have been shot along with me. I declined.

APRIL 19, 1943 — GHETTO UPRISING

We heard shots, and the ghetto soon began to burn. From the Polish side, women with children, and some men, could be seen jumping from rooftops to the streets to avoid the flames. Individual members of the Resistance were encouraged to carry whatever arms they had into the ghetto through the sewers. Stefan was one of them. He made three trips and on the last one almost got caught because the Germans finally understood what was going on and began to throw grenades through the sewer openings in the streets. What he saw made him ill for a long time. What remained of my extended family — aunts, uncles and their children on my father's side — must have perished. In my immediate environment, the reaction was sober: "What is happening to the Jews will soon happen to us." Prophetic words, it appeared.

On April 21, I paid a visit to mother's friend Lydia to see if she had a letter from my mother, as the *Volksdeutsche* was supposed to be back on that day. I rested in the salon on a couch and fell asleep.

Later, I heard voices through the sliding glass door from the dining room: the man had returned but, unfortunately, he could not deliver Lydia's letter because he said that the day before, April 20, my mother, along with other Jewish families, had been herded into a small wooden schoolhouse, whose windows were barricaded, and the building was set on fire. The Germans shot only when people tried to escape through the barred windows. April 20 also happens to be my birthday.[5]

1943
On December 4, Saint Barbara's Day, I put a coat on over my nightgown and crossed the inner yard to visit a woman whose husband trained young men and women in the forest surrounding Warsaw; sometimes, he brought back some meat and cheese and she would signal that she could sell some to us. With me were two elderly ladies. Within minutes of my arrival, armed SS soldiers erupted into the apartment, began to beat the man to a pulp and proceeded to arrest the rest of us. In my case, a man in a civilian leather coat and boots ordered one of the SS men to accompany me to my apartment so that I could get dressed. The man dressed like a civilian also came with us. On my desk, he saw *Winnie-the-Pooh*, my only available text to teach my students, and a Polish-English dictionary. The two men were careful to turn their backs to me while I changed. We were put into a Black Maria with sirens; our destination was the Gestapo headquarters on political affairs. On the way, they finished off the young man, and he died. The two ladies were set free after a brief interrogation.

That night, my interrogations began. I faced a table at which sat about six or seven SS and Gestapo men, and one uniformed woman. I sat on a chair at arm's length from them. Whenever I fell asleep, I would be awakened by a knock on the head. One meal each day

---

5   April 20 is also Hitler's birthday.

(watery soup) and one visit to the bathroom. They did not believe me that I went to the apartment merely to buy some food. Why did I have an English-Polish dictionary? What were my ties to the Underground? The man in whose house I was arrested? One day, one of them took me up to the roof of the building (six or seven storeys) and pushed my head over the railing; I recoiled, quite sure that this was the end. I was taken back inside. The next day the man assured the others that I could not have been parachuted down because I looked green when he forced me to look down from the roof.

The uniformed woman looked at me with hatred, and I was sure that she began to suspect that I was Jewish. But this was the political branch of the Gestapo, and they were mildly irritated by her interruptions. Finally, one of them sighed and asked me to kneel down and pray, to which I reminded him that I had gone to a French high school where, since the French Revolution, there was a separation of state and church and, besides, even if I knew how to pray, surely this was not the right place for it. To which, with a smirk in the woman's direction, he put his thumb under his brown collar and informed me that he, too, used to be Catholic.

The woman was not popular, but to satisfy her they invited two uniformed doctors in, and I was told to undress down to my underwear while they proceeded to take measurements: forehead, neck, wrists, ankles, legs, waist, chest. Verdict: not only was I "Aryan" but some of my body dimensions were Nordic. The tone changed and I was spoken to more politely (*Sie* instead of *du*). Apologies were made for any inconvenience, and I was released into the care of the civilian, who had attended all the hearings without ever saying a word. He accompanied me to the guardroom where I retrieved my coat and my purse (with all my documents that looked as if they had been checked — Helena Czechowicz saved my life again). Coming down the white marble staircase the man said to me, "And yet, you are Jewish, aren't you?" — to which I said, "Yes." He grabbed my arm and said that he was glad I had not lied to him because "nobody lies to Wisniewski." Had I lied, he would have shot me right there "like a dog." He knew that I would want to change my address, but he advised me with a smile to remain in the same apartment "because those idiots upstairs can always guarantee that you are Aryan." I left and, on my way home, I promised myself that should I survive the war, which was doubtful, I would immediately insure my legs.

A real danger was posed when I got home. My old professor assured me that he would never tell anybody that I was so high up in the Underground that the Gestapo had exchanged me for one of their own, which he, of course, proceeded to do all over the block. Next evening, well after curfew, the man from Gestapo headquarters, Wisniewski, came to visit me with a pot of alpine violets. He put his gun on the desk and asked me to allow him to move me to the German district where "a lady" (he used the English word) like me should live instead of this hovel. He would dress me and feed me. In return, since the war was about to end, he said, all I would have to do is to testify that he saved my life and got me out of the hands of the Gestapo. He told me not to fear him "because I don't like women, I prefer men, which I discovered when I served in the Navy." My answer was that I would like nothing better than to move out of there and be fed, but "as a Polish citizen," I could not live in the German district, as he should understand. He kissed my hand and assured me that, once again, I proved to be a "real lady." He left promising to return. His visit convinced my doddering landlord that I had ties with the Gestapo and he was glad because "now, you can protect me and my mother"!

When I met my Underground lieutenant again in the local church on a Thursday at the appointed hour, he wanted to know where I had been for six days. I felt it was safe to describe the events to him. I noticed suddenly that he became very interested in the civilian and asked me to describe him in detail, his voice, his accent and so on. The following Thursday he told me that the Underground had been looking for that man for some time and had lost sight of him. He was tried in absentia and convicted for all the Resistance deaths for which he was responsible. One morning, they saw him come out of the Gestapo headquarters, got him into a car, and "You won't be getting visits from Wisniewski anymore," he told me with a pat on my shoulder and a rather cruel smile.

Three situations come to mind that illustrate some of the aspects of trying to survive in occupied Poland. In addition to the chronic lack of food, we lived through no heating during the long and severe winter months, and bedbugs coming out of wall crevasses required nightly pouring of hot water on the metal beds and searching the seams of mattresses every night. Hair and body lice were also common, frequently contracted on busy streetcars, a good remedy for which was petrol, as were very fine combs, which we used every day. Lice were more dangerous than bedbugs because they could infect anyone with typhus, which was relatively prevalent.

Situation 1: One day a seventeen-year-old pupil arrived for her lesson in a huff and wondered what to do about her mother. The student, Magda, had seen one of her schoolmates from before 1939, a Jew, who wore no yellow star and who, besides, was out of the ghetto. Magda got off the streetcar and called the passing Gestapo, who got the girl and shot her right there. When Magda went home to tell her mother about it, the mother had a hysterical fit. "How could you have that girl shot?" Magda was shocked and wondered what to do about her mother who, she understood, was a Jew-lover. By that time, I had learned not to blush or to show any outward signs of horror, yet somehow I had to respond to this and still be able to live with myself later. All I said was that her mother was right. Did Magda not know that, in 1942, the Polish government-in-exile in London had broadcast a message from General Sikorski: "Any Pole doing harm or denouncing Polish citizens of Jewish faith will be considered a collaborator with the enemy"? Therefore, her mother's reaction was not surprising. Ah, this was an acceptable explanation, and we began reading *Winnie-the-Pooh*.

Situation 2: One day, I was accosted by a very furtive young man, the son of the concierge in the pre-war apartment with whom I played as a child. "Your father was a Jew, and that makes you a half-Jew [he was wrong, according to the Nuremberg Laws, a half-Jew was still a Jew], so quickly give me your watch and I'll go away." I did, so he left, and that emphasized the importance of childhood friendships. After all, he did not betray me to Polish police or to the Germans.

Situation 3: On the other hand, a chance meeting, also in the street, with the janitor of my *lycée* (secondary school), Français de Varsovie, gave me necessary strength. He recognized me, hugged me and took me home with him to meet his family. He cried from joy that I had survived the bombardments. They fed me, they worried about me, but, when I left, I decided not to continue our meetings for they could prove to be dangerous in the long run to both them and me.

It was at about that time that I began to understand that human decency had little to do with social class or education. It was something much deeper, much more individual, just as physical and moral heroism had nothing to do with class or education. One exception, of course, was Father Kolbe, who in Auschwitz volunteered to take the place of a peasant, father of many, to be shot. The Germans did not like displays of courage, and it took Father Kolbe two long weeks to die. Much later, a Jesuit priest of my acquaintance explained to me that this was not "heroism" or "saintly" behaviour. It's just that priests were taught in seminaries all their lives that they were their brothers' keepers.[6]

WARSAW UPRISING 1944

The Soviet army was on the move, and rumour had it that it was about one hundred kilometres east of Warsaw. One day, we saw the

---

6   Father Maximillian Kolbe was canonized in 1982.

German army in retreat and we watched in silence with new hope. I was assigned to a group of twenty-four as liaison should there be an uprising on the orders from London, but that was in the near future.

One day, through the loudspeakers that the Germans used to give us daily reports of their "successes" on the eastern front ("planned withdrawals for strategic reasons"), we heard from General Bór-Komorowski, the leader of the Underground forces: "The Red Army is advancing; any day they will try to liberate Warsaw. We cannot allow this, we must free our capital before they come and we must put our flag on the Town Hall. If we do not succeed, let there be no Town Hall!" Upon hearing this, people began to cry and hug one another. We knew we were doomed by this jingoism independent from any orders from the Polish government-in-exile in London.

And so it happened: in response to the Polish uprising, the German retreat stopped, two tank divisions of the SS were called in and the carnage began. Three bombing sessions from the air every day — the heavy artillery of Big Berthas and tanks. We fought and built anti-tank barricades and dug holes in the walls of the adjacent buildings to be able to circulate when the Germans began to drop phosphorous bombs and Warsaw began to burn. Warsaw became very noisy, and we were hungry and thirsty. After one month of this, there suddenly appeared two silver birds high in the sky, patrolling and chasing German planes. Those two planes were Russian. But it was too late.

One day, the boys captured a wounded SS man, undressed him so that he could not escape, and because he was crying in pain from a contusion to his head they decided to put him out of his, and our, misery. Someone handed me the gun, but I could not shoot. My hesitation caused the beginnings of an ugly mood until one of the boys ran past me and whispered that I should begin to wretch and vomit. I did. Whereupon everybody relaxed, decided I had a weak stomach, and much to my relief someone else put an end to the man's suffering. Another time, I found myself in the basement of the Bank of Poland with many wounded boys, some of them near death. When an opening was dug out in one of the walls, we began to move the wounded. I looked after one schoolboy who fainted from pain every time I moved him. When he regained consciousness, he begged me to leave him alone because he could no longer bear his pain (flies were already settling in his open hip) but I persevered — whereupon he took my hand and, to calm me, he began to recite a Polish translation of a poem about the hanging of a thief by François Villon (*Ballade des pendus*).[7] This sixteen-year-old boy tried to rid me of my guilt should I leave him to die. I finally left, and within minutes we heard the German drills and sporadic shots. As long as I remember this boy, and I often do, I know he did not disappear forgotten from the face of this earth.

There remains much controversy about who authorized General Bór-Komorowski, the Commander of the Polish Home Army, to give the order to start the uprising. However, after the war he found his way to London, where he postured and was accepted as the great hero of the Polish Resistance. Much later, we learned that just before the uprising, a member of the Polish government-in-exile was smuggled to Warsaw to tell Bór-Komorowski *not* to start any insurgent activity before the Soviets were ready to liberate Warsaw. I believe that Bór-Komorowski misled the chiefs of the Resistance by exaggerating London's support of an early beginning. I began to hear rumours of this disastrous information in the 1960s, well after the general was dead and buried with honours in England.[8]

On October 2, after sixty-three days, Warsaw surrendered. The night before, uniforms, such as they were, armbands and general appearances were mended and spruced up. We each got a gold ten-dol-

---

7 Villon wrote the "Ballad of the Hanged" in prison while awaiting execution; it was published in 1489, after his death.
8 This is the author's opinion and what she heard from her sources at the time. The tone of many other narratives of the Uprising reveals Polish anger at the Soviets for not giving support to the Uprising, an attitude that has persisted to the twenty-first century.

lar coin in payment (courtesy of London), and women got promoted to officer grades because everyone was convinced that we were slated for officers' camps (*oflag*). When we filed out in the morning, with our flags, each of us supporting a weaker companion, General von dem Bach, who had been so brutal during the uprising, saluted our flag with full military honours, and we were photographed by Red Cross delegations from Sweden and Switzerland!

Civilians were evacuated to a transit camp and were eventually free to leave. The death toll was close to 200,000 Warsaw citizens, plus countless people from the suburbs and visitors who were caught in the unexpected uprising. When we arrived at the railway station, without cameras and red crosses present, we got put into cattle cars and locked up, destination: west. No *oflag* for us, that's for sure. Although the Wehrmacht guarded the train, our orders were issued by the Resistance — to abandon the train at the first opportunity, as long as we were still in Poland. At night, when the train slowed down, the boys removed some wood in the floors and we rolled out into the snowbanks. Many remained because they wanted to convince themselves that they were, indeed, going to an *oflag*. In our car, once the train started moving, the two soldiers shot twice into the air; they, too, were cold and tired and quite indifferent. We were ten kilometres west of Warsaw.

All night, we did our best to keep warm, and the snow tasted really good. My group consisted of about four or five men and three women. Early in the morning, when we left the forest for the surrounding field, we were triangulated by three armoured cars with Luftwaffe soldiers. Caught as Warsaw "bandits," we were taken to what had been a Polish airplane factory, with the SS quartered there. The men were assigned to various repair works and we women were taken into the kitchen to help the cook, Charlie, a Munich taxi driver who later told us that he had joined the SS only to escape the Russian front. There were ninety SS soldiers and six officers whose job was to drive trucks every day to Warsaw and dig in the basements in search of gold, silver, carpets, furs and other riches. And every day they brought their ample booty found in the ghetto and outside of it back to the barracks.

Charlie, the cook, was upset about my state of health and emaciated looks. He visited local peasants, requested their geese and forced me to drink two full tablespoons of melted goose fat every morning. After he slapped my face, I was able not to vomit and obediently drank the fat.

The routine was monotonous: up at 5:00 a.m. to peel sacks of potatoes, cut the meat, cook puddings in huge vats that had to be lifted before the pudding burnt, and wash wooden tables and floors after each meal had by SS-men in boots who carried in all the slush and mud from outside. In the evening, I had to keep Charlie company during his dinner (of which I could hardly partake) and drink every Schnapps toast. After that, he would lock me up in the storehouse (with food and booty from the ghetto) where I slept on a pile of carpets and covered myself with fur coats.

He became suspicious because I did not want to wear any of the clothes they brought back from Warsaw. I said that it would be too cumbersome and that the wooden clogs and white coat I wore over my underwear were quite sufficient. Charlie kept on insisting that at least once I should agree to come with him and other SS men to Warsaw "to meet some of his friends and, perhaps, choose something decent to wear." To allay possible suspicion by constant unwillingness to do so, I finally agreed. We were received by an assortment of SS men who were quartered very comfortably in one of the villas that had not been destroyed in what had been the German district. A high-ranking officer clicked his heels, kissed my hand and declared how flattered and happy they were to finally be able to receive a lady in their midst. A rich dinner was served with lots to drink and I was given a luxurious room in which to sleep. Just in case, Charlie locked my door and took the key with him.

The next day, I declined to accompany them into the ghetto

and elsewhere, citing extreme fatigue and, instead, walked around the dead city totally empty of people, ruins reaching at least two or three storeys; the occasional apartment house or building still stood, though even these were very scarred by the effects of fighting. Because of the ruins I couldn't even get to the street where we lived before the war. And yet it was not far from the SS villa where I was staying. In the evening we had a repetition of the night before, with heel-clicking and compliments. Charlie had not even told them that I slaved in his kitchen. We left the next morning, and I accepted a sweater and some leather boots that almost fit me. Of all that happened to me and around me, this was perhaps the most nightmarish scene of all whose irony, at the time, completely escaped me. I felt as if I were anaesthetized.

One of Charlie's pastimes, after many toasts, was to throw very sharp knives toward his beloved Irish setter, Senta, in order to corner her inside. He never missed his targets, nor did he miss when he once played the same game with me leaning against a wall. After he left, I had to clean and polish the kitchen and all the utensils. Sporadically, I shared my storehouse with one of the women with whom I was caught. Her name was Krystyna and she was a prostitute who worked before the uprising on a very elegant street. She left soon after our arrival, and Charlie told me with disgust that she had been "adopted" by the officers who quite illegally slept with her — the SS, for purity of Nordic blood, were not allowed to sleep with Slavs. Quite a populist was Charlie, with an endemic hatred of officers. However, every day, Krystyna dropped in on me and smuggled pieces of chocolate and other goodies.

At about 3:00 a.m. on January 12, 1945, all the windows in the factory began to shatter, the earth shook and the Germans fled in their trucks in panic; the Soviet barrage fire had begun, as did the final offensive east of Warsaw. Charlie, in full battle dress, unlocked my cubicle, pushed Krystyna in, threw to us our confiscated documents and suggested that we flee with them since the Red Army would rape and kill us. We refused, and he left after warning us to avoid the hangars because they were all mined. We did, with me still in my white coat and clogs and Krystyna under a sable coat that she shared with me.

We followed the railway tracks going east, toward Warsaw. Whenever we heard tanks, we jumped and hid in the piles of snow. Eventually we followed one of the secondary highways that snaked their way to villages and townships. After awhile, we heard explosions behind us and realized that Charlie had not been joking. Suddenly and unexpectedly, we heard a grating metallic noise and saw an elongated gun appear around a turn in the road. We hid in the snow thinking it might be a fleeing German tank. But no. A big red star was painted on the tank and a frightened, bearded and grimy face looked out of the open turret. I ran to the tank and hugged it only to be pulled up by the scruff of my neck by the soldier who alternately cursed me with colourful, three-tiered Russian curses or called me "my little soul" (*dushenka moya*) asking where were the Germans. I told him that they had fled west at 3:00 a.m., and the tank went on. Then Krystyna showed me my hand, which had no skin — it had remained stuck to the frozen metal of the tank — but I felt no pain. We were liberated!

After the encounter with the Red Army tank, Krystyna began to cry and hug me and tell me how terribly she had been worried about me since I was a Jew with false papers and she only hoped that no Germans would suspect it. "Why did you not tell me you knew?" I asked. She was surprised by my question and said that she figured as long as I thought that a streetwise Warsaw prostitute was fooled, I would have courage, and so she worried but never let me know what she had guessed. She was, of course, right.

That day we knocked at the door of the first little house and were admitted by a woman and her daughter. The last thing I remember was having my feet and hands submerged in icy water to prevent ice burns, after which I passed out, exhausted. Later, I was told that the Red Army, encircling the Germans, encountered our fleeing SS, stretched them on the highway and ran them over with tanks.

Krystyna and I were somewhat sorry for Charlie, who had protected us at the end. I woke up early in March. Apparently, I had slept for up to two months, did not talk and had to be fed and washed from time to time. Krystyna stayed with me.

I came to on a bright early spring morning, looked at Krystyna and announced to all that we must go to Warsaw to look for jobs. After a tearful parting from our railwayman's widow and her daughter, we walked until we reached the sight of the ruins of Warsaw. We crossed the Vistula by boat toward the eastern part of Warsaw, an industrial and poor section that was not destroyed because the Germans stayed on the western side liquidating the uprising, and I found out where we could find the Ministry of Foreign Affairs. The ministry was housed in a dingy apartment, where Mr. Mine, the Minister of Industry who came with the Polish government-in-exile, signed letters on a wall for lack of a desk. I was hired immediately: "There are not many people left who speak French and English and have presumably decent table manners." I would be sent abroad as soon as consulates opened either in England or France. In the meantime, Krystyna and I were lodged in a dorm, slept in a communal room on straw and ate at the ministry one meal a day distributed in their canteen.

By chance, we met Stefan Mahut one day. He was perhaps the only person of all those I knew who had survived the uprising and was not lost among millions returning on foot from Germany — a real march of nations in all directions. He suggested we go with his army detachment north to Gdynia, where a more or less normal life could be had. And so, I left the ministry and, piled high on trucks, we began our trek. At the end of it, Mahut got a beautiful villa facing the Baltic Sea in Sopot, a famous pre-war spa. It had been occupied by a middle-aged couple who presumably had fled, anticipating large-scale disciplinary exodus of every German citizen: Gdańsk (Danzig) and its environs were incorporated into the new Poland and all Germans were being thrown out as soon as possible.

Mahut did his thing with the army, and I became a teacher of

English at the Maritime Academy in Gdynia. Shortly afterwards, consuls from the US, England and Australia moved into a nearby hotel, and since their hotel frequently lacked hot water the consuls began to come to our villa to wash and chat. The US consul put me in touch with the newly opened branch of the United Nations Relief and Rehabilitation Administration (UNRRA), whose mission was to see that all the relief food, clothing and medication was distributed to the local population rather than finding its way to the Soviet Union. Thorley C. Mills of Shaker Heights, a suburb in Cleveland, Ohio, was my boss and he agreed that I could both teach and work with him as an interpreter, mediating between him and the local administrators. We did field trips as far as Königsberg in East Prussia (then also part of the new Poland) and, once a week, I typed our reports that went by diplomatic bag to the Warsaw UNRRA headquarters.

In the meantime, our villa was flooded with friends and friends of friends who began to migrate north, away from non-existent Warsaw. My UNRRA food parcels were sufficient to feed everyone. The first cinema in five years opened with *Casablanca*, and for two weeks we went every night and even forgave the Americans for presenting the Germans as credulous idiots. We knew the dialogue by heart.

Stefan Mahut and I married in the summer of 1945. He felt it was important to him, and I agreed this time. My feelings of friendship for him were limitless not only because he was one of the few surviving ties with the war but also because of his courage in the Resistance, his attitude to the ghetto uprising and his kindness and generosity.

Krystyna got along famously with all our visitors and house guests, but she became bored and restless. There was nothing much for her to do, as both Stefan and I were very busy. One day, she announced that she would go to Warsaw to look for some food and materials to make dresses with. At the time, she made me a dress out of a curtain and one for herself. She went and came back several days later with a suitcase full of the most wonderful and unobtainable meats and sausages. Apparently, she met a butcher who fell in love with her and presented her with a big diamond ring. At this point, it became clear to me that we would not be able to keep her with us. Soon after that first trip, she came to my room crying and told me that she would have to leave us. Warsaw was beckoning. She packed her belongings, and I saw her off to the railway station — she left us, this time for good.

Days were spent working and evenings were filled with parties at which we had lengthy discussions about "building a socialist Poland," until one day I was approached by a young man at the academy who wished to arrange private lessons with me. We agreed that I would visit him the next day in Gdynia so that we could arrive at some schedule and manner of payment (money was worthless). I went and the moment I entered the apartment, I knew I had made a serious mistake. There was no furniture, the young man was not there and the door was opened by somebody in a naval uniform. From the beginning to end, I found myself in a B-type movie: The first man who interrogated me wore a Polish naval officer's uniform but spoke accented Polish; the second man, wearing a similar uniform, did not even try to speak Polish but spoke a typical peasant Russian. I had to stand the whole time, while they sat next to an empty desk. What unnerved me most was the constant presence of a civilian in the room who never opened his mouth but stayed with us till 5:30 a.m. the next day. What did they want? Not much: Just a copy of our weekly reports to UNRRA HQ in Warsaw. Surely, I could make an extra copy? When I declined, they said that as a good Polish citizen I should let them know what our guests were thinking and talking about and, above all, our foreign consular guests "all of them western spies" (in that, he was not altogether wrong I eventually realized — but that was later). One moment they would offer me a cigarette from a box in the desk drawer and in another they would crush my fingers by shutting the drawer. My only reply was that after the Nazi occupation, there was very little that frightened me and, besides, I was not good material for spying — I was too tired of everything. They finally gave up. Before I was permitted to leave they made me sign a document in Russian that stated I was not to tell anyone about this encounter and should they suspect that I had done so, I would be "judged outside court proceedings," a euphemism for being shot. I left and then got really scared because though I guessed they would never shoot me in an apartment house they could easily do so on empty streets. As a result, I walked all the way to the train station sideways, with my back to the walls.

The growing political unease is best illustrated by the fact that when I got home, Stefan made me coffee and ran my bath but did not ask me where the hell I had been all night. Nor did I tell him, of course. I did tell Thorley Mills, my boss. And he was delighted. "We will prepare a copy for them, of course, we will." I did not go along with his game, but from that time on it became clear to me that we had to leave. There would be no socialism in this unfortunate and unhappy country, and the sooner we left, the better.

I established contact with smugglers from Krakow who helped people get across to what was still free Czechoslovakia. In turn, they put me in touch with the Haganah, a paramilitary force from British Mandate Palestine who were busy recruiting and smuggling young men to Genoa, Italy, and from there to Palestine in preparation for the war of independence to come. The fact that Stefan was not Jewish presented a serious problem; they thought that once it became known that he was a Pole he ran the risk of being lynched by our companions from concentration camps.

The preparations for leaving were made in secret. Thorley Mills knew, and arranged for me to have a job in the UNRRA in Vienna, should we ever reach it. He also gave me a Tissot wristwatch to be exchanged for money or food as the need arose. I still have it. We were to meet our smugglers and Haganah representatives in a small town near Krakow. The purpose of our trip, we told our friends, was to do some walking in the Carpathian Mountains. Strangely, they all believed us.

AUTUMN 1946

At night, we crossed into a small village in Czechoslovakia and were fed and given free passes for the train to the Austrian border. An enormous Soviet zone of occupation extended from there, without a single forest, just flat plains, and we had to invent reasons for strolling on the highways in plain sight. My Russian helped a few times. To get to the international zone of occupation in Vienna, we also had to deal with a Russian sentry at the head of a bridge over a narrow river. We could see the US, British and French flags on the other side, but we had to cross the bridge while the Russian sentry had doubts as to whether we were Austrians returning home. I explained to him why we needed to join some Russian relatives on the other side, so he let us go but kept watching us with his sub-machine gun at the ready. And so I made Stefan walk slowly, stop in the middle of the bridge to look at the water, throw little stones into it, then stroll slowly on. The last few metres, we ran into the arms of assorted MPs, with an American MP grabbing me, lifting me up and saying, "Why in hell did you stop in the middle of the bridge? He could have shot you!" I had to explain to him that we may have aroused more suspicion had we moved quickly or run.

We were finally free (or so we thought). Needless to say, Stefan immediately asked what had happened the night I did not come home from Gdynia. He surmised as much and that is why he had not questioned me at the time.

1946–1949

To get from the International sector of Vienna to the American zone, we were smuggled under an oil-cloth cover by an American Red Cross nurse in a jeep through the Soviet zone. There, the UNRRA suggested that I would be needed more at the JDC, the American Jewish Joint Distribution Committee, which took care of the five Jewish Displaced Persons (DP) camps. I had the necessary languages. This Jewish organization was very active in clothing, feeding and gen-

erally taking care of the Jewish DPs who were the only DPs exempt
from working for the Austrian economy (road building and other
heavy physical work). The Austrians were compelled by the American military authorities to supply 1,000 calories a day per person and
fresh milk for the children, elderly, pregnant women and tuberculosis
patients (of whom there were thousands). This supply of food had to
be closely supervised because of the Austrians' reluctance to comply
with the orders. JDC supplied medication and additional food, the
remaining 500–1,000 calories per day. We were also an administrative liaison between the camp committees, the JDC HQ in Vienna
and, more importantly, with the military governor of Upper Austria
residing in Salzburg.

The American Jews poured enormous amounts of money into
Jewish DP camps both in Upper Austria and the American zone
of occupation in Germany, with Munich as its headquarters. Many
thought that this represented "guilt" money on the part of American Jews who during the war did not exert the necessary pressure
when the *St. Louis*, a boat full of over 900 Jewish refugees, came into
an American port in 1938. The ship was turned back into the Nazis' arms in Western Europe. Nor did they insist that the Americans
bomb Auschwitz, when tens of thousands of Jews were incinerated
daily. They also seemed not to have reacted when the first news of
concentration camps began to reach the State Department from Switzerland. The attitude seemed to be one of "let's not rock the boat,"
which was just fine with the antisemitic State Department. There is
some truth, of course, to these views of American Jews during the
war. But many American Jews did not have the necessary political
clout and so many of them were engulfed in sectarian wars with each
other caused by their ties with communist Russia. Be that as it may,
they were helpful in the aftermath of the war. One of their branches
actively helped emigration from Austria and Germany, and that was
very important, too.

My boss, a lazy British social worker, took his weekends from

Thursday night to Monday night; many workers were demoralized by their enormous salaries and their new-found prestige (they stayed only in Allied hotels, wore Allied uniforms) so much so that much of the burden of running the five camps fell on me. The camps were filled with concentration camp survivors and many who had survived Siberia. Stefan and I were housed in a transit camp in Wegscheid, outside of Linz; about one hundred to one hundred and fifty were housed in each barracks, and American MPs guarded the entrance. To give me some prestige with the camp population, I was issued a UNRRA khaki uniform (but without insignia) and, in winter, I wore a German railwayman's coat. Quite a sight.

The black market flourished. Once, three train wagons with food coming via Switzerland vanished from the rails before they reached one of the camps. Some people did nothing but play cards and engage in the black market and procreation. My list of pregnant women grew from one day to another. One of my responsibilities was to be present, early in the morning, in the barracks that housed food and from which it was distributed. I could not manage to keep order — the strong and the young were winning. I was assigned an Austrian ex-German merchant marine sailor to help with the dangerous crowds. The only way he could preserve order was to hit the more pushy and aggressive men with a wooden plank while shouting in his mother tongue *Raus, verfluchte Juden* (out, accursed Jews) and, sadly and ironically, I was grateful. He had not been a Nazi, and sometimes he entertained me with American sailors' songs that he had learned before the war. We worked well together. He even added plywood sides to our open jeep, which was a blessing in winter.

At least two political aspects of post-war Austria served to undermine the already precarious morale in DP camps. One of them was the selective national amnesia for perpetrated war crimes. Upper Austria had been conquered and occupied by the Rainbow Division, the 42$^{nd}$ Infantry Division of the US Army, men who came through the bloody Italian campaigns and liberated Austrian concentration camps in the southern part of the country. No friends of the Austrians were they. However, they were soon rotated home and we lost good, trustworthy and battle-seasoned friends. The new recruits knew nothing of Austria's homegrown Nazism long before Hitler's army marched in to be enthusiastically greeted as long lost relatives and soulmates. Nor did they know that Austrians had participated in all phases of the war, from the army to all branches of political persecutions, terror and genocide. Thus, they readily believed the Austrians posturing as "victims of the German occupation." Jewish DPs, and other DPs in Germany, were at least spared this sickening duplicity.

The other was based on persistent rumours that some of the Nazi judges and sundry bureaucrats either returned to or continued in their posts. When returning former Austrian political prisoners, or DPs, pointed them out to the American authorities, no action was taken. "They are needed because of their knowledge of the terrain and their competence. After all, somebody has to run this country," was the usual response. The Austrians' cringing servility to their new masters thinly veiled their feelings of superiority. Possibly, these Austrians may have been perceived as easier to deal with than the "incomprehensibly" aggressive DPs who could not "forgive and forget" and who, among other "undesirable" characteristics, spoke in many tongues, none of them English. At times, Jewish and non-Jewish DPs would take matters into their own hands whenever they were sufficiently provoked by encountering ex-concentration camp or prison guards. However, by 1947, these painful events were gradually replaced by the demands of daily survival, hopes of emigration, vigorous black marketeering and other murky deeds.

The barracks were overcrowded and filthy. Out of despair, I used to wash the floor with very inadequate detergents and one day I simply snapped. I requested an audience with the assistant director of civil affairs, Lieutenant Colonel Howard Dellert, who resided in the castle in Salzburg. The audience was granted and off we went one sloshy winter day from Linz to Salzburg — my guard, our wooden jeep, my mongrel uniform and a lot of hope. As I passed consecutive halls of the Archbishop's ancient castle, I was greeted by more and more high-ranking officers until I came to the adjutant, a major, who even saluted and got up when I approached. He announced me and opened the door. Way at the end of a huge medieval hall I saw a green lampshade on a desk and, as I approached, a man got up slowly, greeted me and asked me to sit down. I could see only his elegant hands and rows of military honours on his breast pocket.

He politely asked me what he could do for me in a deep and intriguing voice with a marked accent that I later learned was southern. He did drawl his vowels, and I thought this was quite exotic. And so, without planning it, after I described the insalubrious conditions in the camps and asked for some decent liquid soap, I also asked for his cooperation in forcing the Austrians to deliver fresh milk, for some wire and army blankets so that we could fashion some privacy around the beds and for army stoves to put into the barracks and, before I knew it, I had also asked for contraceptives. This last request was greeted by a long silence followed by some statements about the war in the Pacific (Burma, mostly) with a resulting shortage of rubber and, "Surely, [you] can understand why, under the circumstances, the American soldiers and officers had to have priority." I couldn't understand the relevance of all this disquisition — why talk about Burma? I did not at the time have any idea as to what "contraceptives" were, except that, I imagined, when used by women they prevented pregnancies. At least I got my soap, wires, blankets and stoves. And, in my presence, he instructed his adjutant by phone to intervene in no uncertain terms with the Austrians about milk deliveries.

The next day, my secretary poked her head into my office with awe saying, "We are being invaded." In marched a tall American MP in white gaiters, as if on a racehorse, and wearing a white helmet, with the narrowest possible waist and hips, holding something in his left arm, and while saluting with his right arm he deposited with haste a package on my desk. "Will there be an answer, Ma'am?" The package was a pot of the most beautiful azaleas and a visiting card from the assistant director in which I was asked to dinner at the Allied hotel in Linz and warned that he would come in civilian clothes, but he would be able to recognize me. I accepted the invitation and this was the beginning of a very intense romantic interlude that remained platonic to the end. It was one filled with sporadic encounters and trips to the Tyrol in the French zone of occupation and dinners at the officers' clubs in which I saw my very first jukebox and discovered Benny Goodman and some American poets. We danced a lot, and he talked about his war; he had taken part in the landing in Toulon and had the brains of his best friend sputtered all over him. He said that he had no one to talk to, that he could not be himself with other officers and the officers' wives were a sorry lot. Nor could he fraternize with Austrian women, and I guess that left me. During one of the dinners, he told me how surprised and amused he had been when he realized that I knew absolutely nothing about the contraceptives I had requested. He remained amused by it for a long time.

My contact with him did not go unnoticed. One day, in came two British officers from Admont, another DP camp in the British zone of occupation. They both looked like stereotypical English officers, down to a clipped moustache and a cane under the elbow. I thought that any minute something very unpleasant would happen because the British did not allow emigration from their camps to Palestine and resented Americans for being either indifferent or downright unhelpful. They said that, given my contact with Dellert, all they wanted me to do was ask him for ten trucks and safe passage for the young Jewish DPs to Genoa, from where they would be shipped to Cyprus and, clandestinely, to Palestine. I must have looked both frightened and confused because one of the two took pity and introduced himself as Aryeh and his companion as Shlomo. They were both part of the Jewish Brigade of the British army in Palestine. Aryeh, for one, was a South African who had read law at Oxford.

There was no problem getting the trucks and, much later, when I was leaving for Canada, Aryeh came to my farewell party and presented me with a gold chain with a small Star of David, saying that though he disapproved of my going to Canada, one day I "might see the light and come home." I still have this chain.

While working, I was trying to arrange for emigration for Stefan and myself. The DP camps were really slave markets: the Australians were looking for hatters and furriers, as was New Zealand. England needed workers for the textile industry. Only France (the University of Nancy) sent me a warm letter assuring me that they would do everything in their power to expedite my emigration to France as a free person, a privilege granted to graduates of my French high school in Warsaw and a matriculation from that university. Unfortunately, they could do nothing for my husband. Of course, had it been the obverse, I could have easily joined him as his wife.

This frustrating period in Austria was not without its rewards. I became friends with two women from the UNRRA in Salzburg, one Norwegian and one English. I was able to assist at the very first Mozart festivals in Salzburg before they became jet-set territory. At one of them, while lining up to buy tickets, I was asked by an American officer whether I could lend him some schillings because, he said with dismay, the Austrians did not want to accept American army paper money. He was, at the time, one of the prosecutors at the Nuremberg war crimes trials. He later married an English woman, Lily, and we remained close friends.

And it was through Lily, who worked for a Jewish emigration agency in Vienna, that I heard that a delegation of the Canadian Labour Department was coming to find six engineers. Stefan had graduated just before the war as a civil engineer, and even though the Canadians were looking for electrical engineers, Stefan was put on the priority list. So, after two years wasted in Austria, he was able to go to Canada. Once established, with a bank account, he would then be able to bring me over as a dependent. A year after he left, my documents arrived, the UNRRA HQ gave me recommendation letters and the civil affairs office gave me the most precious document imaginable — a return visa to Austria, should I wish to return. Unheard of in the case of emigrants.

In March 1949 I left, first for Paris, where I had a key to a friend's apartment (the Norwegian UNRRA friend) on Rue de Grenelle, no less, close to Boulevard Raspail. I stayed there for five or six days. On one of the days, I got in touch with a JDC representative in Paris whose name and telephone number I had been given in Austria. He had a car at his disposal, which enabled us to drink red wine on the terrace of the famous cabaret Lapin Agile in Montmartre and to visit Versailles. Knowing more or less what to expect inside the château, I preferred to look at and stroll in the gardens. Familiar until then only with cozy and protective English gardens, I was unexpectedly moved by the impersonal, self-sufficient and almost arrogant symmetry of the French gardens. It was there that I realized that I was about to exile myself from Europe and that I may never return from unknown and distant Canada. That night, for the first time in eight years, I could afford to cry myself to sleep.

Spring was full-blown even though it was the beginning of March, and bundled-up women sold mimosas at street corners. I drank coffee at every turn and visited with strong feelings the Lutetia Hotel, where I knew that all the prisoners of war and those who returned from concentration or labour camps were housed for free while relatives and wives and friends came every day looking for news of their loved ones. I so approved of the hotel for doing this and it was only much later that I learned that during the occupation this very same hotel housed an assortment of German officers and even the more sinister types of occupying forces.

From Paris, I went to London, where I re-established contact with my English family, the children of my father's brother and his widow.

They were more interested in telling me about their hardships in London during the war than in hearing anything about my family or myself. And so, on good and polite terms, we parted.

I left London for Liverpool where I boarded the RMS *Ascania* for Halifax, with first-class passage paid for by the JDC and train fares by UNRRA. I arrived on March 11, 1949. Stefan awaited me in Montreal, where he rented a room on University Street for one month, left me all he could afford (fifty dollars) and returned to Hydro Ontario. I did not unpack for quite a long time, still crushed by a twenty-four-hour train ride from Halifax over desolate, snow-covered plains without the relief of even a single city on the way. As long as the money lasted, I went from cinema to cinema and at night sat on my sea-trunk and plotted my return to Austria. Fortunately, I had no money for the return trip and thus began to support myself by giving private English lessons to two couples who were recent Hungarian immigrants, with *Winnie-the-Pooh* as my tattered reading text. The two couples remained lifelong friends, as did their four children and their families.

In the fall, I became the secretary of the newly opened Consulate General of Israel. My lack of knowledge of Hebrew was unimportant because the Consul General himself did not know the language. Avraham Harman was an Oxford-educated South African. It was a very busy time, what with night school and my hands full during the day. Frequently, in the middle of the night, my phone would ring, transmitting by dictation press releases from the Israeli news agency. My special qualifications were a complete lack of ties with the Jewish community and the Canadian Zionist Organization. This ensured a political and financial independence of the diplomatic representatives of the newly born country.

I was also admitted to the graduate program in psychology at McGill, on condition that I take five courses in the evening program at Sir George Williams College (now Concordia University) in order to get a formal Bachelor of Arts degree. Two of the courses I chose were on the American Indian (very exotic), one on Shakespeare (not to have much work to do) and two of them were introductory courses in physiological and comparative psychology, taught by Don Hebb's[9] graduate students. Also, on Hebb's instructions, I read his book *The Organization of Behavior*. All this done, on September 8, 1950, I began to build a Hebb-Williams maze in the basement for an envisaged rat experiment.

In the fall of 1955, I received my PhD degree and obtained a friendly divorce. I became a Canadian citizen, which I remain today, out of both sentiment and predilection. I felt as though I had come home at last and that the European cemetery could be laid aside. And it was, until now, as I look back to remember.

---

9  Canadian psychologist Don Hebb (1904–1984) is known as the father of neuropsychology and neural networks.

Helen Mahut (then Walentyna Dudekzak) with her parents. Kiev, Russia, circa 1924.

1  Passing under the name of Helena Czechowicz. Warsaw, 1942.
2  Helen with an officer of the UNRRA witnessing the ruins of Danzig, Poland, after the war.
3  Helen at the beach by the Baltic Sea, across the street from where she was living with her fiancé, Stefan Mahut. Sopot, Poland, April 1945.
4  Helen and Stefan's wedding day at the Baltic Sea. Sopot, Poland, summer 1945.

1

2

3

1 Helen in her lab, experimenting with the Lashley Jumping Stand and waiting patiently for a rat to make up its mind to jump to one of two stimulus cards. McGill University, Montreal, 1949.

2 In the laboratory with one of her rats who preferred to jump on her shoulder rather than on a stimulus card. 1949.

3 Helen on the day that her MA thesis was accepted. Montreal, 1950.

# Mewa (Seagull)
# Dyna Perelmuter Reichental

*For my daughters, Sophia and Wendy; may they never encounter adversity. Life can be painted in different colours, and I pray that my children will be surrounded in the colours of peace.*

I would prefer to forget some episodes of my life but, alas, they are so vivid that I have decided to write down this unforgettable story.

I lived with my parents, Joseph and Zisl, and my seven siblings, Rifka, Avrum, Chajcza (Chaya), Fishel (Felix), Ruza (Shoshana), Shimshon (Sam), and Benjamin. Ours was a two-storey house; two rooms upstairs, one occupied by my brothers, the other by our parents. In the downstairs, facing the street, was a dry-goods store and a large kitchen. My sisters and I shared the two beds in the kitchen, and an annex served as a toilet and bathroom. In the backyard stood a small shack for breeding fowl, mostly geese, which were being fattened for the Jewish holidays.

In our small town of Bodzanów, situated eighty kilometres from Warsaw, life generally followed a peaceful course. My older sisters, Rifka and Ruza, moved to British Mandate Palestine about one year before the war, and my older brother Benjamin was in the Polish army. Until the outbreak of the war, we did not feel persecuted or isolated from ethnic Poles; our mutual relations were friendly and amicable. The eight of us were rather bright and intelligent. We were on very friendly terms with our neighbours and even with the parish priest, who patronized Jewish shops mostly for his household and clothing requirements.

I recall vividly an unusual incident preceding World War II that involved groups of homeless people who roamed around the small towns and villages. There were many small towns in the area around Warsaw, such as Wyszogród, Ciechanów, Płońsk, Nowogród and Pomiechówek. When the homeless came to a town, they would make a round of all Jewish and Polish stores, where they were often each given ten grosze (Polish currency) and some food. The begging over, they continued to the next small town. If they happened to arrive late at night, they were given the key to a low building behind the synagogue to spend the night. The building was reserved for homeless people, regardless of their origin or religion. It held six mattresses made of thick canvas filled with straw, small pillows and grey blankets. In the centre stood an iron stove with a pipe fitted into the chimney and close to the window was a pail of water and a cup.

One night, they came very late, and the *shames*, the caretaker, gave them the key to the shelter. They lit the stove and went to bed. By some ill luck a heavy snowstorm began that night, and snow blocked the chimney on the roof. In the morning, the *shames* who was in charge of the synagogue and shelter opened the door to see how the people were faring, and he nearly fainted. Six corpses lay on those six beds. They had suffocated overnight. All the people of our small town were in shock. The men were buried in the Jewish cemetery, some special prayers were said, and for a few weeks we lived in sorrow.

In September 1939, World War II broke out. In our town, the first victim was Polewski, the water carrier. He was standing in the middle of the street with a broom when some armed German motorcyclists rode by. They shot him as they would shoot a dog and rushed on to spread terror in another small town. Such was the onset of German tyranny. As an initial move, the Germans shut all Jewish stores and transported all the goods looted from the Jews to Germany. Fear and panic prevailed. No more hope for a peaceful life. People were moving like shadows, neighbourly chatter turned into whispers. No one had any idea what lay in store. Some sensible young folk fled to Bialystok and from there to the Soviet Union.

We sensed that something dreadful was about to happen, and it did. In the spring of 1940, the Germans occupied the parish priest's presbytery and they ordered the synagogue to be pulled down immediately. Indeed, it was done within a few days. My close friend and schoolmate Cesia Kornacka always repeated the priest's sermons to me and I learned that he had said, "The Germans ordered you to dismantle the synagogue, but why did you do it? The place where people pray is sacred!" Soon after, both the priest and the organist were deported, vanishing forever.

People no longer believed in a miracle, or that the war would soon end. We were being haunted day and night; we were segregated into the Jewish quarter and heard rumours about deportations to a different ghetto. Soon enough, in the spring of 1941, the Jewish population of the town of Bodzanów, about 1,300 people, was loaded into a truck and driven to the towns of Nowy Dwór and to Działdowo. From Działdowo, my parents, my sister Chaya and I were soon sent on a cattle train to the ghetto in Częstochowa. The Jewish delegation from Bodzanów, the so-called Judenrat, boarded our wagon together with young Jews in police uniforms. It seemed things would not be too bad in the ghetto, with an organized Judenrat leadership.

The journey lasted two days with no food and no stopovers. My older brother Fishel, who managed to get married before the war, was on another train with his wife and young child. We never found out what happened to them. My three other brothers, Avrum, Shimshon and Benjamin, fled to the Soviet Union; Shimshon and Benjamin survived and Avrum was lost without a trace.

⁓

Once released from the cattle wagons, we were allocated to various Jewish families. We had to make do in the densely overcrowded ghetto. We were assigned a room in an apartment with a woman named Mrs. Sabina Lerner and her young child; she had two rooms, the larger occupied by her and her child, and the four of us — mama, father, my sister and I — took the smaller room.

The Częstochowa ghetto was ruled by the strict orders of German fiends. Poles were allowed in and out, but Jews were not allowed to leave. Jewish policemen were posted at the gates, watching that nobody left the ghetto. In due course, the Srebrnik family, to whom we were somehow related on mother's side, heard about us. They were quite well-off and started helping us with food. They also found a job for me, since I did not look too Jewish: they ran a business supplying toys to Polish shops outside of the ghetto. I was adventurous and not easily intimidated — I took the Star of David off and carried the parcels with toys to their destination. The Jewish police did not stop me, since I was unfamiliar to them and did not belong to the Jews of Częstochowa. Sometime later, we received a few parcels from my father's sister Sara Landau in Warsaw, which must have been an extraordinary undertaking. Sara, together with her husband, owned a knitting factory. They also imported shells from abroad, which they used for manufacturing pearl buttons. In 1942, as the liquidation of the Warsaw ghetto proceeded rapidly, we no longer received packages and we had to manage as best we could.

On Nadrzeczna Street in Częstochowa's ghetto, there was a small marketplace where most Jews brought various wares for sale or trade, enabling them to buy food from Poles. Father met some kindly Jews there who were ashamed to put their goods out on the market, and consequently gave father a variety of things for sale. From that, we were paid a certain fee. The situation, however, involved some risk: considering that we were not allowed to leave the ghetto, the goods had to be entrusted to the Poles who came shopping and would resell them outside the ghetto; the person would either return and pay, or the goods would be lost. By some lucky coincidence, my father met a most honest female customer, Mrs. Bozkowa, who fetched the goods and brought back money or food in exchange.

In the fall of 1942, the situation in the ghetto changed; we heard rumours that the Częstochowa ghetto would be liquidated. It was quite obvious that the ghetto was dying; hence, the last exchange with Mrs. Bozkowa took place not at the market but in our apartment. The rumour about the liquidation of the ghetto had reached the Polish part of town. Mrs. Bozkowa was quite upset and sympathetic — something else she heard must have hurt her deeply. She simply said, "I cannot help you anymore. Danka, you do not look Jewish. If ever you manage to escape from the ghetto, memorize my address — Limbowa 14 — and I'll try to hide you." I shall not forget that address till I die.

A curfew was introduced in the ghetto; no one was allowed out in the street after 6:00 p.m. Consequently, people got together in backyards. Everybody was in utter despair — women and children wept, and a deep sorrow marked the faces of men. My father calmly stated he did not need food anymore, that he preferred to be weak so that the Germans would not torture him too long.

In our backyard, a shattering incident occurred during the liquidation of the ghetto. In the house next to ours was a bakery, and the baker must have decided to bake bread one last time because that day an aroma tickled everyone's noses. Among the tenants of our house was a family with five children and the eldest, a sixteen-year-old boy, decided to go next door and try to get some bread. A little frightened, we watched through a gap in the gate for the armed German to turn around. It seemed he turned, and the boy rushed next door. Suddenly we heard a shot and the boy collapsed. His father opened the gate and pulled him into the centre of the courtyard. We all gathered around the wounded boy. Nobody tried to stop the bleeding from his chest. His face grew ashen as his mother approached, shutting her eyes in horror at the sight of her dying son.

Someone summoned a hearse, and when it arrived they threw the boy on a heap of other victims. Nobody wept. Everyone dispersed, with deadpan expressions. So quickly the life of a youth had been snuffed! Only a puddle of blood remained in the backyard. I will never forget that sight.

The first liquidation of the Częstochowa ghetto went on for two weeks, from September 22 to October 8, 1942. The people on our street, Garibaldi, were one of the last to be rounded up. It wasn't until mid-1943 that we were ordered to leave the apartments and stand in rows four deep, in the street; whoever could hold a few things in a bundle on their back did so. Armed policemen, mostly Ukrainian, stood every few steps apart. I have no idea what prompted them to assist those German criminals. Toward the end of the war, after all, the Germans probably killed those "assistants" too. As to the line-up of Jews, row upon row, I doubt any writer could accurately depict our despair as we stared, hopelessly, at the calm sky. Father looked totally helpless; before leaving home, he had cried like a baby. It was the first time in my life I had seen my father cry so desperately. Mother's eyes looked almost insane — she stared vacantly ahead. I was standing in front of her. Supporting my small backpack, mother told me, "Danka, say T'hilim [psalms of David]. You might survive still." These were my mother's last words to me and they echo in my ears until this very day.

We were marched to the Horowicz metal factory. The Germans posted there were armed with machine guns and dogs equally as vicious as their owners. The soldiers examined and appraised us as if we were cattle, segregating us into two groups. A German would command: "Right! Left!" Nobody knew what was awaiting us on either side. In due time, I noticed that I was with a group of young people, and I never saw my parents again. We were later told that they were packed into a train headed for Treblinka.

From the Horowicz factory we were taken to a former textile factory called Pelcery, also known as Pelcowizna, which became a munitions factory and forced labour camp under the HASAG Company.[1] There, grenades and other weapons were manufactured, and we had to file them to a smooth surface. Of that time, I distinctly remember the cauldron of black soup made from vetch, a crop generally used to feed animals. It tasted like boiled pepper and burned my throat horribly. This, with the addition of a slice of black bread, was our daily diet.

At the camp, I met some friends from the ghetto as well as my cousin Rachel Majzlisz; she was a young, beautiful, tall and slim blond. Together, we started planning our escape from the camp with help from two Polish sisters, Natalia and Celina Markowska, whom we had met through our work at the camp. They lived with their mother, Maria, in the railwaymen's quarters, right next to the rail line. My cousin, perhaps not wanting to take the risk, did not escape with me, but I was able to sneak out of the camp by posing as a Polish worker. The Markowskas received me quite warmly. They lived in a one-room apartment on the second floor, and I hid behind a trap door leading to the attic. I felt amazed at the courage they displayed for my sake; they could have been killed on the spot if someone reported me.

In this way, 1943 came to an end. From their home, I planned to find my way to the address I had memorized for Mrs. Bozkowa, who had earlier agreed to hide me. Early in 1944, however, there was a great tragedy: Mrs. Bozkowa's brother, who belonged to the White Eagle underground organization, was captured. He owned a small house in the suburbs of Częstochowa and manufactured arms in his cellar. Someone must have reported him, because the Germans found the arms, beat up the whole family and deported the adults to a camp from which they never returned. Mrs. Bozkowa took care of their

---

1  An acronym for Hugo Schneider Aktiengesellschaft, a German firm founded in 1863 that used forced labourers and concentration camp prisoners to mass produce armaments during World War II.

children. This was a serious blow for me, as her family now became twice as vulnerable.

I decided to stay at the home of Mrs. Maria Markowska. I often walked with her daughters, Celina and Natalia, to the Jasna Góra monastery and religious shrine, so that neighbours would not wonder who I was and what I was doing there. At this point, there were partisan groups — the White Eagle, Armia Krajowa (Home Army) and Armia Ludowa (People's Army) — fighting the Germans in the forests. Many Jews who were hiding in the forest joined the Armia Ludowa. From a resistance organization to which my adoptive sisters belonged, I eventually received an official German document called a *Kennkarte*[2] copied from the documents of a deceased girl more or less my age, with a photo of me on it, as well as my fingerprint. I still have the *Kennkarte*, stamped by the German *Arbeitsamt*, employment bureau, and issued in the name of Zofia Suska. Now, I felt more confident about my "Aryan" origin, but even though it was rumoured that the Soviet army was close to the Polish border, my joy did not last long.

During my stay with Mrs. Maria Markowska, I got a shock beyond any description. One day, Mrs. Maria opened a letter that contained only one sentence: "You shall perish if you do not get rid of that alien person." It was signed, "A friend." Pale with horror, she showed me the unfortunate letter. Dear God, may the good earth swallow me! Each day, I begged God not to wake up anymore. I truly dreaded the Gestapo and their tortures. Once again it was time for a decision — what was to be done? How should I vanish from the surface of the earth? Mrs. Maria kept her cool; she gave me a multicoloured Łowicz cape, worn by countrywomen, and said, "Perhaps you should buy a

---

2  During World War II the Germans used *Kennkarten* as identity documents; they were issued to various groups and distinguished by colour: grey for Poles, yellow for Jews and Romas, and blue for Russians and other non-Polish Slavic peoples.

newspaper and find a job. The situation is very serious; you see, we might all die."

With fear in my heart and faith in providence, I had to part from this truly decent and god-fearing family. I walked to town and found a newspaper stand. The paper was full of various advertisements, but one in particular drew my attention. "Wanted — a girl for housework on a small farm — Olsztyn past Częstochowa, Dutkiewicz farm." The question arose: in what direction was Olsztyn? After a long deliberation, I stopped an elderly gentleman, asking for the way. "Follow Warszawska Street till the end," he said. "It's another few kilometres. A royal castle once stood there. It's a beautiful village." I thanked him for the information and went off to Olsztyn. It was only about twelve kilometres away, and I reached it within a couple of hours. As I entered the village, my soul simply burst with joy; it was a beautiful place with tall trees, houses scattered in the woods and a church that loomed far off in a magnificent clearing. Would anyone believe that two days earlier I had seen that clearing in my dream?

I quickly went to look for the place where household help was needed and was hired. The farm was small, and an elderly couple had lived there. The Germans had taken the man away to work in a mill, and the woman could not cope by herself. The farm consisted of one cow, ducks, hens and geese. The problem for the woman was that there was no well close to the farm; consequently, one had to take two pails and go to the nearest neighbour to fetch water for the fowl and the cow. The task was arduous, but satisfying; with the German *Kennkarte* I felt more secure, and the fear I had felt in the city slowly vanished.

Milking was the worst job. I had to take a large jug and fetch milk from the vestry, and I had been told to assist the milkmaid. I looked on as the woman indicated a very low stool, saying, "You must pull very hard on the udder for milk to start flowing." When I was hired, I told the elderly woman that I had lived on a small farm, with no cows, and that my parents had been deported by the Germans. These were the details I had been told on receipt of the German *Kennkarte*. So, after the milking demonstration, I sat down, trying to jerk the cow's udder as hard as I could. I often got hit on the head by a cow's tail, but I gradually gained experience in milking. It helped that there was a sack in the far corner of the barn containing large circular pieces of linseed cake that looked like pressed grain of a cereal and poppy seed. When I fed the cow a piece of linseed cake, she stood still and did not wag her tail at me.

Olsztyn was a small town with a nice, well-preserved church with a cemetery behind it. Each Sunday, I went to church, as was expected of me. The priest said mass without any political allusions. He talked instead about the life and suffering of Jesus. After mass, I liked to walk around the old cemetery of ancient tombstones. It was there that I found solace for my grief. I memorized many of the tombstone inscriptions; some were almost illegible and others were quite odd, almost shocking. I quote merely three: "Everything dearest lies in this grave." "Death took everything away, except pain." "Onto this grave I concentrated all my sorrowful fate and all the souls of my brothers and sisters." Another inscription seemed like an accusation: "You are what I have been; you shall be what I am, so let us pray for each other." Quite often there were quotations from Kochanowski's *Laments*[3], in an altered version; that is, instead of Urszulka, the names of the deceased were inserted, as, for instance, "Sleep in angelic sleep, dear Marysia. May your parents' tears bring Divine mercy." There, in that cemetery, I could cry safely, with no one to witness or ask why I was weeping.

Time passed quickly. As rumours abounded that the Soviet army was close to the Polish border, I kept busy with various farm chores and even made the acquaintance of a very nice girl, Krysia Zalewska,

---

3   Jan Kochanowski wrote *Laments* after the death of his young daughter, Urszula, in 1579. The book was published in 1580.

who provided me with books to read. Her father, a schoolmaster, had been deported by the Germans and never returned home. It was being said that the Germans wished to eradicate Polish intelligentsia, so that the plain folk left could do slave labour for the Germans.

Thus, I lived to see the year 1945. Once again, we heard that the Germans were withdrawing and the Soviet army was approaching. These rumours were confirmed by the fact that in early January some Germans knocked at the windows of our house one night, shouting, "Brot, Brot!" (Bread, bread!) They were tattered and coatless, obviously afraid to display their military ranks. I thought, what goes up must come down; go on, taste some of the misery and pain you yourselves have imposed on our Poland. The old woman threw them a chunk of stale bread. Shortly afterwards, a truck full of Soviet troops arrived. They seemed very much in a hurry; they rushed into houses, ordered potatoes to be boiled in their skins, snatched a pail of sauerkraut and, together with their commander, sang some very sad tunes and left.

Perhaps they were on their way to storm Berlin. I heard that British and US troops were pushing on Berlin from the other side. By mid-January 1945, Poland had been liberated, and occupied, by the Soviets. From my temporary home, I was still wary of returning to Częstochowa because there was no permanent government. Various organizations were settling their mutual accounts, and innocent victims were involved. It was a lawless time — in other words, a time of bitter reckoning and disappointment.

Amid all this news I learned that a Jewish committee had been established in Częstochowa, which, with the support of the American United Nations Relief and Rehabilitation Administration (UNRRA), was helping surviving Jews. I decided to leave the farm at once. I said goodbye to all my good friends and found transportation directly to Częstochowa.

There, I reported to the Jewish Committee, who helped by distributing clothing obtained from the UNRRA and gave me some money. It was encouraging to be given the addresses of my friends who had survived at HASAG — Genia Bozuchowska Fajge and her husband, Jozek. The survivors I first heard about were Morys Steinman and his wife, from Bodzanów, and Abram Kohn of Częstochowa. The Fajges continued to live in Częstochowa, Morys Steiman left for Philadelphia and Kohn went to Israel.

Apartments were scarce in those days. I got in touch with friends and together we planned what was to be done. It was hard to accept the fact that none of my relatives came back. Yet, I was afraid to go to my hometown, since the situation was still not quite settled. Thus, I spent a few more months in Częstochowa.

I made the acquaintance of a fellow who wished that I would stay in Częstochowa at any cost. He was prepared to convert to Judaism, but I must confess that, in spite of my frequently close relationship with Catholics, I could not marry a non-Jew. I still had the image of my father and mother in front of my eyes. I imagined it would be a betrayal. And besides, I knew that I had relatives in America, and the urge to join them was far stronger than the temptation to stay in Poland after such a dreadful ordeal.

In those days, news was pouring in all the time from Jews seeking their relatives. One day, my name was on the list — relatives from Warsaw were inquiring about any Perelmuters living in Częstochowa. The Jewish Committee gave me the address of those seeking information, and early in 1946 I went to Warsaw. My relatives welcomed me with open arms and soon obtained an apartment for me in Praga, 8 Jagiellońska Street. It was an apartment owned before the war by a Jewish religious group and had been a *shtiebl*, a place where pious Jews gathered for daily prayer. I felt in high heaven. It was simply impossible to get an apartment in Warsaw at that time, since Warsaw had been bombed to smithereens. The Jewish Committee supplied me with a cot and a large suitcase, which served to hold my clothes in place of a wardrobe. The cellar of the apartment was full of books of Hebrew prayers. I managed to glue one together and I still have it.

It is a *mahzor*, a Hebrew-Polish High Holiday prayer book, published in Warsaw in 1933.

Gradually, I had to think of choosing a profession. In those days, all schools were made available to anyone willing to learn, and a few złotys were given as pocket money. Of my hometown acquaintances, I met the Sniedzinski family, who were extremely decent. Mr. Sniedzinski got a job in Warsaw as head of the general post office. After a few visits with them and with their patronage, I enrolled at a telecommunication college. I finished a two-year course and then found work at a post office in Praga. I felt, finally, as though my feet were well-planted on the ground. The other postal employees seemed like family to me. These friendly surroundings boosted my faith in a better future.

In 1951, at the post office, I met Moshe (Marian) Reichental, a properly tolerable fellow, and we married. In 1952, we had a baby girl. We called her Zofia, after my mother.

For a few years, we both worked in offices. After some time, however, the political situation rapidly changed in Poland, particularly after Khrushchev's visit from the Soviet Union. In 1956, his antisemitism provoked antagonism once again. As a result, many Jews who had survived in the Soviet Union and then settled in Poland after the war started to leave. The atmosphere of uncertainty and fear engulfed us, too. In 1959, we immigrated to Canada and settled in Montreal.

Life in Canada was difficult at first, as it would be in any foreign country without knowledge of the local language or a definite profession. Working hard, within a few years' time, we managed to reach a more or less stable existence. We had another daughter, Wendy, and with the help of a small government grant, my husband completed a three-year course at Laval University in the radiological institute. My husband worked for twenty-five years as an X-ray technician at the Jewish General Hospital, and I worked emergency registration at the Jewish General Hospital until 1985.

Once, in a private conversation, my colleague Dr. Karol Kuper-berg encouraged me to write down my story. He told me, "Write whenever you get an idea, at least one page a week. It would be a pity for such experiences to vanish without a trace." After my retirement, I felt more free, with my time no longer limited, and so I tried here to describe the most important events of my wartime story.

~

In Canada, many feel freer from various racial persecutions. I believe that a multicultural population can find a common language and a peaceful coexistence. This is something very important and precious. As far as I am concerned, my children and my own mind order me to be happy, but my heart cannot obey. In dreams and in daytime, it wanders to the small town where a friend and friendships were true, as solid as a rock.

Half a century has passed since those events. Immediately after the war, there was not a single person who had not experienced a personal or family tragedy. One had to freeze those experiences and, in the hope of a better future, resume a normal life. Now is the time for a thaw, and these experiences are coming back as Bolesław Prus's returning wave.[4]

During sleepless nights, I carry on a dialogue with God, asking, Why did it happen? Why so much perversion, so much fratricide? I cannot find an answer. No rabbi, no priest can find a convincing an-swer. And, yet, in the world where I was brought up, people were full of compassion and responsibility. I remember our small town and

---

4  Born Aleksander Głowacki, Prus (1847–1912) was a renowned Polish writer and leading distinctive voice in literature, philosophy and journalism. His 1880 short novel *Powracajaca Fala*, which has been translated as *The Returning Wave*, used the metaphor of a wave returning to shore to describe people having their pasts come back to them.

my father, who on the occasion of any holiday picked a guest from among the homeless folk to share our meal with us. And most men did, too. Well, why did they all perish in such a dreadful manner? I explain it in the belief that it is people who are killing one another, while God does not walk among us and does not control our behaviour. He gave us life, reason and freedom, while the rest — conscience and responsibility — are up to us alone.

Danka (Dyna) Perelmuter (back row, centre) at age twelve with her sisters Shoshana (far left) and Chaya (front, centre) and her aunt Sara Landau (far right). Bodzanów, Poland, 1932.

Dyna's *Kennkarte* document issued in the name of Zofia Suska. Radom district, 1943.

1  Wedding photo of Dyna and Moshe (Marian) Reichental. Warsaw, 1951.
2  Dyna and Marian on the occasion of their daughter Sophia's graduation from
   Concordia University. Montreal, 1999.

1 Celebrating Rosh Hashanah, 2010. In back, Dyna's daughter Sophia (left) and Dyna. In front, Dyna's granddaughters Lauri and Rosalie.

2 Dyna and her daughter Wendy a few months after the birth of Dyna's first great-grandson. Montreal, 2010.

3 Sophia and Dyna at Dyna's art exhibit at Temple Emanu-El-Beth Sholom. Dyna's paintings can be seen in the background. Montreal, 2009.

# Life Lines
# Barbara Kuper

*To my family who was killed in the Holocaust: my mother, Franciszka Levenhoff Meryn, my father, Solomon Meryn, my sisters, Hania and Felcia (Fela), and my brother Henio (Henryk).*

I was born in Częstochowa, Poland, in 1920 to a wonderful, warm, loving family of five children, of whom I was the youngest. My mother, Franciszka Levenhoff Meryn, was a fantastic person, mother and teacher. Her father was her mother's second husband, and though he had other children from his first marriage, my mother was the only child of the second marriage. My grandmother's name was Mariana Pankofska. My maternal grandfather died before I was born, at age fifty-two, of cancer of the jaw. He was said to be a wonderful grandfather to my older siblings. My father's grandfather may have come from San Merino, Italy, hence the name Meryn.

My father, Solomon Meryn, was born in Kamienica Polska, a village of textile workers. His family ran a "cottage industry," providing looms for the manufacture of textiles. Father, who attended a textile school in Czechoslovakia, was talented and capable in many ways. He was very good at drawing and was an expert in pattern design for textiles.

In the early 1900s, my parents lived in Poraj, where my father was instrumental in building a railroad line between Poraj and Częstochowa. He was a jack of all trades and had many jobs. During

World War I, he managed a quarry, using about forty horses for the heavy work. One day, the Germans commandeered all his horses, leaving him with a worthless receipt. He also supplied meat to the German military. He was very well-liked and had many German friends at the time.

My parents must have been married before 1903, perhaps in 1902, since my oldest brother, Tadzio (Tadeusz), was born in 1903. My other siblings were Hania (Hanna), born in 1905; Felcia (Fela), born in 1912; and Henio (Henryk), who was born in 1916. I, Basia (Barbara), was the youngest, born in 1920. This made a seventeen-year difference between my brother Tadzio and me.

My sister Hania told us fairy tales, played games with us and made paper cut-out dolls. I remember sitting on one of her knees while Henio sat on the other. Hania had wanted to study dentistry, but this was impossible because of the lack of funds and because, as a Jew, she would not have been accepted, so she went to work in a bank.

Hania married Kuba Goldberg, her boyfriend since she was fourteen, in April 1930. I loved Kuba. He was very handsome and was closely attached to my family; he especially loved my mother. I remember that he often took me for walks, playing with me and paying a lot of attention to me even though I was just a little girl. Kuba got a position in a shipping company, and he and Hania both moved to Gdansk. However, he made some decisions with which the management did not agree and eventually lost his job. They then moved to Katowice, and I visited them there. They had a canary that had broken his leg, and Kuba, who was very capable, had put a cast on the bird's leg. I can still envision Hania's beautiful china that was stored in a large woven basket in our house, and which she never had a chance to use.

They eventually moved to Warsaw, where Kuba again worked in a shipping company. When the war broke out, Kuba, who was an officer in the Polish artillery, was supposed to report for duty. Instead, they fled to the Ukraine, where Kuba worked as a foreman in a construction company. It was in the Ukraine that they were later murdered, along with many other Jews.

My early memories are of our house being repeatedly for sale on auction. My father had many debts. He had borrowed złotys, Polish currency, from his aunt who demanded repayment in American dollars. This debt proved to be a great hardship. Our family struggled economically, and Henio and I were not properly nourished. As a consequence, Henio had to wear a metal brace to support his spine, and my legs were somewhat crooked. I remember being bathed in salt water by my mother, which was said to be helpful. In fact, my legs are now straight.

I was a very good student and attended a public elementary school. My favourite teacher, whom I loved as much as I loved school, was Mrs. Zebkowa. Although Henio and I were very close, he used to tease me about my teacher, whom he called Mrs. Parsnip. My mother belonged to the parents' association, and the school suggested that I apply for a scholarship to the Hebrew high school. I won a scholarship for the first year and paid a minimal sum for subsequent years, earning some money by tutoring classmates in my grade and in other grades.

At the high school, my classmates' families were much better off than mine. The girls were well dressed and wore valuable jewellery. When my class went on excursions, I couldn't go because my family could not afford the cost. One day, my uncle Leon dropped in and found me at home on a school day. When he asked why I was home, I told him about the excursion. He promised that he would cover the cost of any future class trips. I graduated from high school with very high marks. I remember my brother Tadzio bringing me a bouquet of hydrangeas for my graduation.

My brother Henio was studying law in Krakow. Since we had so little money, he basically studied at home from textbooks while he lived with and worked for our uncle Leon in Kamienica to help support himself. Henio really wanted to study medicine, but only the sons of Jewish doctors were admitted to medical school, and there were very severe quotas on admissions for Jews, known as *numerus clausus*.

I, too, wanted to go to university, and I registered in the Jagiellonian University in Krakow, an old and venerable university founded in 1364. I had wanted to study chemistry since I was eight years old. Science had always held a strong appeal for me. During the first year, I studied at home using texts and borrowed notes, just as Henio had. Nevertheless, I did so well on my exams that my professor commented, "It really shows that you attended my lectures."

During the second year, I had to live in Krakow because I had to be actively involved in laboratory work. Henio's work in Kamienica supported both of us. I also won scholarships that enabled me to remain at university for the second year. In Poland at that time, one did not need to have an undergraduate degree in order to work toward a master's degree. I completed my second year of the four-year program before the outbreak of World War II.

~

I was at home in Częstochowa when the war broke out on September 1, 1939. Two days later, Częstochowa was heavily bombed, and people ran for cover as they were strafed by bombs falling from low-flying planes. My family stayed in the house because my mother felt strongly that we could not escape death by fleeing amidst bombs.

Over the next years, the war affected us all in different ways. Tadzio, who was married to Janka, was ordered to report to the army. In April 1941, the Jews of Częstochowa were rounded up and herded into a ghetto. In the ghetto, Tadzio's wife, Janka, lived with my family. Janka, my sister Felcia and I knitted many things so we could sell them and support Janka's mother, who was staying elsewhere. Our house was within the walls of the ghetto and there were three stores as well as lodgings within the building. My father was not adept in business and he seldom collected the rent on time, and often not at all.

While in the ghetto, I volunteered in the hospital pharmacy after the pharmacist fled, where my training in chemistry was of great help. I also worked at the Jewish hospital as a volunteer nurse, having taken a training course. It was a terrible time of unbearable hardship and anxiety. People were dying from typhus, which was very common because of the terrible malnutrition, lack of hygiene and poverty. Lice were also a daily torment. Yet, at the hospital, the young people like me who worked together found relief in some laughter. My friend Irka Przysuskier worked with me. Her father had been the director of the Jewish technical school in Częstochowa before the war.

When the ghetto was being liquidated,[1] I was offered the opportunity to remain in the hospital, which would have been temporarily safer, but I wanted to be with my family. The Nazis herded thousands of Jews into railroad cattle cars. Henio had been working in a store owned by our German friends, who supplied goods to the Nazis, but he also returned home at the time of the liquidation, wanting to be with the family. My father was not with the rest of us when we were taken away. We were moving as a family group, heading for the trains, when a Nazi officer pushed me to the side and away from the group; perhaps this was because I was young and pretty. I was in tears as I was steered away from my family. That is how I found myself in the line of the living rather than the line marked for death. I was devastated as I watched my whole family move toward their inevitable death. At the time, we believed that people were being "resettled" in work camps.

The large ghetto had been emptied, but we were taken to the small ghetto where we were housed on the floor of the metallurgical factory. It was there that I met Adam Marian Magas, who wanted to take me to his family. Adam, who was not Jewish, worked in the metallur-

---

1  September 23, 1942, was the first of six large-scale roundups for deportation.

gical factory and had visited me when I worked at the hospital, which was also located in the factory. He later visited me in Warsaw, after which we lost track of each other.

Before the liquidation, my mother had sewn a gold bracelet into the sleeve of my sweater. It was stolen while I worked in the hospital. The wives of the doctors in the hospital stole many things, even the food that was assigned to me and the other young people who worked there. The doctors' wives called us "little dolls."

One day in the winter of 1942, my friend Irka, supposedly on a work detail from the small ghetto, went to the technical school because she remembered that her father had buried some money. She retrieved these coins, which provided us with the means of running away. We were also equipped with vials of fresh *cyjanek*, a cyanide poison, given to us by the chief doctor of the hospital who was a friend of Irka's family.[2] Before we left, Hela Gutterman, a friend of Tadzio's, had found a fur collar and sewed it into the collar of my coat. Since Jews were not permitted to wear fur, we hoped that this fur collar would help us appear to be gentiles and give us some minimum protection.

In December 1942, with the help of our friends Janek and Cesia, Irka and I escaped among a group of workers, first to a place near Jasna Góra monastery and later by train to Warsaw. Before leaving Jasna Góra, I went at considerable risk to the German store where Henio had worked to see if I could find out any news of my father, who I hoped had gone there to hide. The German owner of the store told me that my father had been there but had left, wanting to be with the family. I ran to my house, hoping against hope that I might find him there. He had apparently been picked up in the street. It was a hard blow and I broke down in tears, crying for hours.

---

2  During the war, some Jews in hiding or living under false identities held onto suicide capsules for various reasons — some felt that, if caught, they could not be tortured into revealing who had helped them; others felt that they would rather die than be subjected to a fate under the Nazis.

Janek and Cesia, who had led our escape from the ghetto, were Jewish but did not have a Semitic appearance. They were instrumental in helping many people escape, and Cesia, in fact, accompanied us on the train ride to Warsaw. We were dropped off right in front of the Nazi headquarters and walked in the street holding our small bags, until Cesia came back to take us to a hiding place. She took us first to the house of a tailor where there was a small room in which we organized ourselves as best we could.

At Christmas time, we bought a small tree that we decorated with candles, as was the custom at the time. When a nun came to visit the tailor's family, the family borrowed our little Christmas tree for the duration of her visit! Later, the candles ignited and caused a fire in our little space. Subsequently, we were moved to the home of Mrs. Stawicka, where there were approximately twelve other Jewish people hiding. We all hid in the attic whenever there was a threat of a "visit" by the Nazis. Since we did not have enough money to keep both of us hidden there, I went briefly to the house of a woman who, as an orphan, had been taken in and brought up by my aunt Helenka in Kamienica Polska.

From an ad we found in a newspaper, Irka and I then rented a room in a beautiful house occupied by a Russian family by the name of Kloczkowska, from St. Petersburg. We did not reveal that we were Jewish. I was blond, with green eyes, and did not look Jewish, although Irka did. The house, which was clean and filled with lovely furniture, belonged to the postal organization. The Russian woman was always elegant, so much so that even when there were bombing raids and we had to descend to the cellar, she wore her fox stole. On Sundays, she made tea in a samovar, a special device just for boiling and serving water for tea.

After a short time, we arranged to meet Irka's boyfriend, Jurek Konar, a convert from Judaism and a medical student whom I knew from Częstochowa. We met in a restaurant called Wiedenka so that he could hand us the "Aryan" papers that he had arranged for us. When I found out that a waitress was needed at the restaurant, I applied for the job right away. I had just received my new false identity documents, so when they asked for my name, I mixed it up, but landed the job anyway. My assumed name was Marcela Janina Murawinska.

I had to work to support us both since it was much more risky for Irka to venture out of hiding. Working at the restaurant was a good job because some food was available. I worked hard: peeling a whole sack of potatoes daily and washing the tablecloths by hand on a washboard were both part of my job description. I was paid no salary — my only income came from my tips, which supported us in our rented room. I still have the little book in which I carefully marked down the amounts of my tips. We struggled to secure food and had no money for luxuries. I remember standing in front of a display case of a bakery, gazing with longing as I looked at the pastries in the window.

One day when I did not return from work at the usual time, Irka became worried. She went into the entrance of the courtyard of our house, where there was an altar at which people gathered for special prayers for the month of May. This was very common, but she must have been seen and denounced by someone, because the next day the Gestapo came and arrested us at gunpoint. I remember that the Nazi officer was amazed that we did not protest, cry or beg. After robbing us of our watches, he let us go.

Now we had no place to stay. I found an ad in the newspaper advertising a position for a teacher to prepare a boy for high school entrance exams in Nieborów, near Łowicz. While I went to Nieborów to apply for the position, Irka went into hiding in a convent in Warsaw, where she was taken in by Sister Bernarda.[3]

---

3   For information on Sister Bernarda see http://collections.ushmm.org/search/catalog/irn37736.

In Nieborów, I got the job after showing Mr. Gajewski, the father of the boy whom I was to tutor, my university records with the name carefully altered to my new identity. Fortunately one of my grades was only "satisfactory" otherwise Mr. Gajewski might have suspected a forgery.

Irka was having a very hard time in the convent. One day she heard someone playing the piano and, to her surprise, discovered that it was my cousin Nusia, who was also hiding there, working as a washerwoman. Nusia's friend, a Christian woman named Zofia Wiewiorowska[4], was the director of a shelter for poor women, and had ensured Nusia's place at the convent.

Irka had been meeting with a young man, a Jew from a prominent family whom I met when I worked at the Wiedenka. I received a letter from Irka — it would be her last — in which she expressed her fear that this young man, whom we knew as Ziutek, may have been followed. I suspect that was the case, and that as he went to meet Irka he may have inadvertently led the Nazis to her. This made her hiding place no longer safe.

As soon as I received her letter, I went to Warsaw, walking the six kilometres to the train station in Nieborów. I searched for Irka, first going to Mrs. Klotchoska, who she had stayed with. Mrs. Klotchoska gave me Irka's ring, which she had left for me. I then went to the women's shelter where my cousin Nusia Wolfowitch was now hiding. Tragically, Irka was lost.

While in Warsaw, I stayed with Kasik Laski, my cousin Irena's boyfriend. Kasik lived in a cellar next door to a beggar who sang prayers incessantly. Since he worked as a night watchman, I slept in Kasik's bed while he was at work. When I had been to Warsaw previously for a few days in April 1943, I had witnessed the Ghetto

---

4 For information on Zofia Wiewiorowska: http://collections.ushmm.org/search/catalog/pa1177149.

Uprising and the tragic fire and death of the Uprising heroes. I remember riding on a streetcar as the ghetto burned and overhearing a conversation between two Poles who were discussing the fire. "Let them all burn," they said. I was devastated and horrified. After Irka's death, when I returned to Warsaw in August 1944, I witnessed the Warsaw Uprising, during which the partisans battled the Nazis while the Soviet army observed from the other bank of the Vistula River and did nothing to help.

I returned to Nieborów and my work as a tutor, where I remained until the end of the war. In early 1945, as the Soviet bombs fell and the Nazis retreated, I felt overwhelming joy. To me, the retreat of the Nazis represented freedom.

~

I left my few things in Nieborów and returned to Częstochowa, only to find that our house had been destroyed and replaced by an empty space. I found no other family, and I felt completely alone.

While in Częstochowa, I met some people who wanted me to transport some money from there to Warsaw, where I was going. In exchange for this service, they gave me a nightgown and a raincoat. I was pleased, since at this point I had practically nothing.

Not long after, I learned that my brother Tadzio had survived the war in the Soviet Union. I was overjoyed, and I went to Katowice where he was living with the friends with whom he had been during the war. When I arrived in Katowice, Tadzio's friends Ella and Edek greeted me very warmly. Edek was a lawyer and was very involved with the remnants of the Jewish community. He wanted to go to Switzerland to a Zionist conference but had no money, so I lent him the coins that Irka and I had so carefully hoarded. When he came back from Switzerland, he brought gifts and returned the money I had lent him.

I went back to Nieborów to collect my few belongings, and then I remembered the names of some people in Lodz to whom my uncle

Leon had been sending cotton yarn for dying before the war. I went to Lodz hoping to get some money or the yarn, which I could sell. They informed me that all the yarn had been sold and that they had purchased some art with the money. I was too stupid to ask for some of the art, which rightfully belonged to me, but they gave me some money that enabled me to return to Krakow to continue my studies.

I re-registered at the university and resumed my studies. I found accommodation at the students' residence, which was very fortunate as it was very difficult and costly to secure lodging there. I was lucky to have the help of a fellow student, Zygmund Woiciak, who was involved with the student government. Zygmund and I remained friends throughout my time at the university. I shared a room with two other female students who were very jealous of my relationship with Zygmund, who would steal flowers from city gardens and throw them through the ground-floor window of our room for me.

At the same time, I befriended two wonderful young women who also lived in the students' residence, Marysia Dlubak and Staszka Kozuchowna. Staszka was beautiful. We were like sisters, supporting each other in case of trouble and sharing all that was good. I tried to catch up with my studies that had been interrupted by the war.

Although I did not have money, I was awarded a government scholarship. I did very well in my exams and began to prepare the topic for my Master's work. I went to Professor Kamiensky, who taught physical chemistry and with whom I decided on the topic of my Master's thesis — "Sparks in Ultraviolet Light." First, I had to calibrate the spectroscope. During the war, all the instruments belonging to the university were either stolen by the Nazis or buried by university staff. My spectroscope was old, and I was almost blind by the time I completed the work, which had to be carried out in the absence of light.

Around this time I met Anthony Kuper, a chemical engineer considerably older than me who had graduated from University of Liège in Belgium before the war. He was the director of a government-owned fur dressing and dying factory in Bielsko, Poland. He was obviously interested in me, as he started to call me, send flowers and visit me during the weekends. I always prepared something interesting for us to do together during his visits — theatre, concerts and so on.

Anthony was a widower and had a seven-year-old daughter, Eva. Since I was the youngest in my family and had never had much to do with young children, I felt insecure about suddenly becoming the parent of a seven-year-old. My brother Tadzio reassured me, telling me that I should imagine that Eva was a small daughter left by my sister Hania. Anthony and I were married in Dzierżoniów, where the remnants of my family, the Prentkis, lived. My wedding consisted of a very small group of family members: my brother Tadzio, my cousins Dr. Leon Prentki, Stulka and Pinek, and my aunt Barbara Rozalia Prentka. Of Anthony's family there was only his brother, Stach, and Stach's wife, Marysia. The rabbi who presided over the ceremony was Orthodox and wanted me to go to the mikvah, but I had no intention of doing this, so Tadzio and Anthony bribed the woman at the mikvah to issue a certificate.

Eva, meanwhile, had been in Ciechocinek for a month. When we met for the first time, I asked her to call me by my name, Barbara. She wanted desperately to have a mother like all her friends and insisted on calling me *mamusia*, mama. Eva's birth mother had died during the Holocaust when Eva was a baby, and Eva's survival story is documented in film and in print.[5] I could not replace her mother, but I tried my best. I remember an incident when I asked her to do something and she refused, saying that I had no right to ask her because I was not her mother. I was very hurt. Eva now has her own children and grandchildren who are a great joy to me, but none of them resemble me or my family.

---

5 See pages 43–72.

We settled in Bielsko for one year after our wedding. Life was comfortable, since Anthony had a very good position. I prepared myself for my final exams for which I travelled to Krakow. Even though the war was over, we continued to live under Anthony's assumed wartime name, Kornacki. Antisemitism was alive and well, and pogroms were still happening in various parts of Poland, unbelievable as it seems. It was still not safe to live as a Jew. Eva, who had survived the war as a child hidden in a convent, did not realize that she was Jewish, and we did not tell her. In fact, she had her first communion and attended church regularly with our housekeeper.

Anthony refused to join the Communist Party, and since Poland was virtually occupied by the Soviet Union after the war, this was also a problem. He was arrested and detained overnight for this refusal. It was only after the intervention of his friend, who was a judge, that he was released. We decided that it was time to leave Poland.

Anthony had a passport and a visa for himself and for Eva. I did not have a visa and, having just completed my studies, my application was refused. Anthony had to bribe someone to provide me with a chest X-ray showing me to have advanced tuberculosis — I got my visa. I left Poland using the false X-ray and arrived in Canada using my own X-ray showing my healthy lungs. It was not permitted to take money out of the country, so we bought some diamonds and sewed them into the lining of Eva's coat. We managed to smuggle out some American dollars in the handle of an umbrella. Anthony had also sent some money, using the help of a consular employee, to his brother-in-law and sister-in-law in Richmond, Virginia.

In 1949, we arrived in Toronto, where Anthony had some distant cousins. We remained there for one year, spending most of our money. Anthony had been promised work in his field in Toronto, but the factory that was supposed to be built never materialized. Anthony felt that since he spoke fluent French and he had a friend from his university days in Montreal, we should relocate to Montreal, which we did in 1950.

We settled into life in Montreal with Anthony working at a well-known fur dressing and dying plant, Hollander Furs. I began to seek employment by going to a Jewish Community Agency for advice; they told me that it would be very difficult to find work as a chemist, given that I was a woman and Jewish, and they advised me not to reveal that I was Jewish when applying for work.

My first job, where I remained for five years, was at Milton Hersey Laboratories,[6] analyzing all kinds of substances: textiles, foods, oils. The work conditions were terrible. The draft cabinet was inadequate, and once when I was working with ether, it ignited and burned my face and eyebrows. My salary was $140.00 to $160.00 per month. The money only just about covered our rent.

During the next five years, I worked at International Paints, where my first chief chemist was a wonderful man who helped me to learn a great deal, sending me to conferences, meetings, and as a delegate to visit other installations. It was at International Paints that I developed the first formulas for the production of acrylic paints. My co-workers were very friendly, but again I did not reveal my Jewish identity. Nobody asked me and I did not say, heeding the warnings I had been given. Unfortunately, the chief chemist died prematurely and was replaced by a German. The situation became so unpleasant that since Anthony was doing well, having started his own factory, I was able to leave. Very shortly after I left, the new chief chemist was fired, not being permitted even to empty his desk.

Since our economic situation had much improved, I did not seek other work. Instead I took courses in nuclear magnetic resonance spectroscopy at McGill University and, at the same time, enrolled at Sir George Williams University (later Concordia), taking courses

---

6  Hersey labs, a lamp-testing company originally established by Thomas Edison in 1896, was eventually bought by and became part of Intertek, the largest tester for goods in the world.

in art, which had always interested me. I took life drawing as well as courses in sculpture with Professor Orson Wheeler, where I fell in love with stone and particularly marble. I took painting courses taught by a well-known artist in Montreal, Richard Billmeier, as well as sculpture courses at the Saidye Bronfman Centre (now the Segal Centre) with Stanley Lewis. Since then, I have pursued my work with a passion, which led me to have six solo exhibits of my sculptures at the prestigious Dominion Gallery in Montreal. Dr. Max Stern, the owner of the gallery and prominent art connoisseur, felt that I had talent and very good treatment of the material.

My work found a home all over the world, in places like the Ben-Gurion University of the Negev in Israel, New York, Quebec City and many private collections in the United States, Canada, France, Germany and Israel. I have travelled a great deal, visiting lands and cultures far removed from home — the Far East, Europe, Japan, Russia and the Caribbean — and I have also toured much of the United States and, of course, my wonderful adopted country, Canada. Everywhere I went, I visited museums and art galleries, learning, appreciating and absorbing beauty.

Unfortunately, my husband died in 1987, and as of the writing of this memoir, in 2007, I live a lonely life accompanied by my many memories, often painful. I have a great deal of satisfaction in learning, reading, listening to music and appreciating the beauty of nature. I am still keenly interested in world events, scientific progress and the wonderful advances in chemistry and medicine. I have given a great deal of thought to doing something to leave a legacy of good work by supporting various charities and causes to the best of my ability.

One of the legacies in which I take great pride came about on the advice of my late husband's physician, Dr. Larry Knight, a pulmonary specialist. I was particularly interested in this field of research because my husband suffered from emphysema and my granddaughter from asthma. I contacted Dr. Martin, Director of the Meakins-Christie Laboratories at McGill University, who informed me that there was a need for a particle research laboratory. I asked him to prepare a proposal outlining the project and the details of the equipment and materials needed. The cost came to $25,000, which it was my great pleasure to donate. Dr. Martin and his staff organized a lovely, warm dedication ceremony with many doctors, students and, of course, my family in attendance. It was very special, and since 1999 I have been an "honourary" member of the Meakins-Christie Laboratories. More recently, I have lent my support to the Segal Cancer Centre at the Jewish General Hospital in Montreal and to the Montreal Symphony Orchestra.

I am a member of the Sculptors Society of Canada and have been a member of the Chemical Institute of Canada for over fifty years. My work is cited in Guy Robert's book *Art actuel au Québec*. I am also listed in several editions of the Marquis *Who's Who* books — including American Women, International Intellectuals and Women of Distinction — and my biography appears in an edition of *Leading Intellectuals of the World* as well as on the website of the Sculptors Society of Canada.[7]

Of course, my greatest joy is being here to witness the growth of my family — my daughter, Eva, and son-in-law, Harvey, my two granddaughters, Debbie and Felisa, and their husbands, Ron and Dwayne, and my two wonderful great grandchildren, Matthew and Zoey. I have come to realize that life is not a bouquet of roses but am trying to learn from my daughter to make the most of each moment.

---

7   See Barbara Kuper's profile at the Sculptors Society of Canada at http://www. cansculpt.org/memberDetails.php?id=79&fn=%20Barbara&ln=Kuper.

Barbara Kuper (née Meryn) and her family before the war. From left to right (in back): Barbara's sister Hania (Hanna); her father, Solomon; Basia (Barbara); and her brothers, Henio (Henryk) and Tadzio (Tadeusz). In front: Barbara's mother, Franciszka, and her sister Felcia (Fela). Częstochowa, Poland, date unknown.

1

2

1  Barbara and Anthony Kuper, 1947.
2  In back, left to right: Barbara, Anthony, Anthony's sister Sophie and her husband, Zygmund. In front: Eva (left) and Zygmund's daughter, Irene. Bielsko, circa 1948.

1

2

3

1 Barbara Kuper, 1948.
2 Anthony Kuper, 1947.
3 Barbara and Eva after immigrating to Canada. Lake Simcoe, 1949.

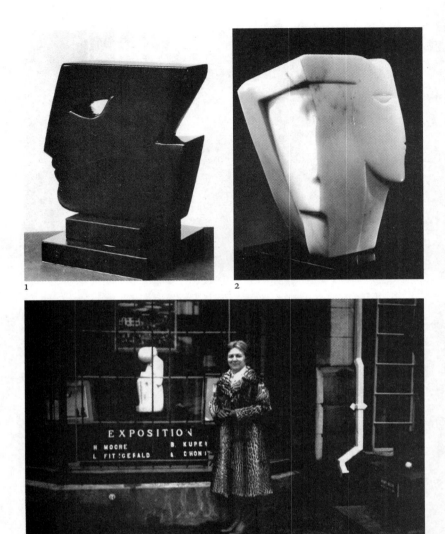

1

2

3

1 & 2  Two of Barbara's marble sculptures.

3  Barbara in front of the display window of Dominion Gallery just before the opening of one of her exhibitions. The sculpture in the window sold before the show even opened.

Barbara (front, left) at her great-granddaughter Zoey's (front, right) bat mitzvah.
In back: Eva (left) and Eva's daughter Debbie. Montreal, 2007.

# The Forces of Endurance
# Irene Zoberman

Translated from Polish by Marek W. Stobnicki (1992–1996)[1]

I was born in Sandomierz, Poland, in 1914. As far back as my memory can reach, I see my birthplace as a beautiful vista of this historical city: the Opatów Gate, the City Hall with its unique architecture, the prison that used to be the old King's castle, Saint Jadwiga's gorge, Salve

---

1 This memoir has a unique origin: In the early 1980s, the author's cousin, Dr. Bradley Strauss, was just four months out of medical school and discovering how to be an effective, empathetic doctor when he came across Irene Zoberman, a patient in the neurological intensive care unit. Though he had met Irene only a few times, she recognized him and was persistent that he visit her often. Irene was not always coherent at this point in her life, suffering from a brain tumour, but she often told Bradley that she "saved all of them" and that she had written her memoirs in Polish and that one day, when they were translated, he could read them. In a foreword to this memoir, Dr. Strauss wrote, "I would think of her tragic situation and wonder what had happened in Europe so many years ago that she continually returned to in her conversations." When Irene passed away, Dr. Strauss thought of her often, feeling that she had given him strength in dealing with his new role as a doctor. Sensing that she had entrusted him with the task of remembrance, the next time he was in Israel he visited Yad Vashem, where her Polish testimony was held (Irene had recorded it two months prior to her illness) and eventually had it translated into English.

Regina, and the Świętokrzyskie Mountains. But, above all, I still remember the streets full of people, the clean, shining houses. All these elements created almost perfect harmony. I had always been very proud that our city park was well maintained and that the meadows surrounding the city were full of colourful flowers, the grain fields full of red poppies waving in the wind, the green grassy hills and valleys, and the winding Vistula River. I was certain that my memory would forever keep that beautiful picture of the place where I grew up and which I considered as mine. I was young and I saw everything in rosy colours.

The population of our town was less than ten thousand people, of which about three thousand were Jews. The only small synagogue was located on Ulica Żydowska, Jewish Street. Sandomierz was a typical Catholic town, with its cathedral and seven other churches. There was also a seminary for Roman Catholic priests. The town's streets were full of them.

One wall in the cathedral was covered with a huge painting of Jews slaughtering Christian children before Easter to make matzo.[2] I remember when Rabbi Najem and my father, Yehoshua, who represented Jews on the city council, met with representatives of the Catholic church to ask that this picture be removed because it promoted an atmosphere of hatred and caused pogroms of innocent Jews. Even when the rabbi introduced documents showing that the painting depicted false ideas, the church's response was that this was the work of a very famous painter and it represented artistic values.

I tried to ignore this, as well as all the humiliating remarks referring to my Jewish origin, until the day the war began for us: Septem-

---

2    One of the paintings on the wall of the cathedral church in Sandomierz is titled "Ritual Murder by Jews," by the painter Carol de Prevot and commissioned by Sandomierz priest Stefan Żuchowski in the early eighteenth century. The painting reportedly still hangs in the cathedral, but its title has been amended to "Alleged Ritual Murder by Jews."

ber 9, 1939, eight days after the start of World War II. I remember the very first group of Jews who were treated like cattle on their way to Zochcin, a village with a population of 230. My father was in that group and later told me about being tortured in a half-dried pond. They were forced to jump over a fire, and the Germans were enjoying every time someone fell down. At the same time, the victims were forced to sing. For twelve days in Zochcin, Jews were mercilessly tortured and the smallest misstep was penalized with a beating on the head by a truncheon. Survivors returned home physically and mentally exhausted.

On September 21, the Germans gathered thirty Jews and selected seventeen for the Jewish Council, or Judenrat, appointing Henryk Goldberg as its head, or president. Mr. Applebaum, an owner of a printing shop, was nominated as his deputy. The Judenrat was charged with carrying out German orders. Among other duties, they were responsible for the cleanliness of the city in order to prevent the spread of contagious diseases. The president had to present himself at the police station, where he got a daily list of ever-growing demands, such as food, clothing and other items. The Germans wanted to have luxury in their offices as well as in their apartments. The president had to provide everything on these lists; otherwise, all members of the Jewish Council were threatened.[3]

Every day, our men and women were forced to do the most degrading jobs, such as cleaning communal sewage and public toilets, and cleaning floors using their own clothes instead of mops and rags. A lot of our people were hiding or leaving the city, but one day when not enough people reported for work, the SS drove the members of

---

3  Historians generally acknowledge that the occupation of Sandomierz was particularly harsh, abusive and murderous. See the *Encyclopedia of Camps and Ghettos*, v. 11, Part A, 301. 2012. Geoffrey P. Megargee, editor in chief; and *The Yad Vashem Encyclopedia of the Ghettos During the Holocaust*, Guy Miron, editor in chief, 2009: 688.

the Council out in front of their building. They beat them with clubs, and those who fell down got a double portion of the beating. Then, using their bare hands, they had to carry mud from one side of the road to another and back; they were beaten with clubs the entire time. Those who fell were kicked and their heads were clubbed.

My father was in this group. Later, he was prodded with a rifle butt and was ordered to clean the public toilets. When he finished, he was hit on the head and kicked into a dark cellar where he landed on a pile of coal. He could not move because his legs were swollen, but the German oppressor was not finished yet and hit his back. The German ordered him to bring coal to the third floor, giving him five minutes for this job.

The only thing my father thought about was his likely imminent death, but the remnants of his senses told him that he had to let his comrades know about his situation so they could notify his family. With much effort, he crawled to the door. He spotted his companions and realized they were in the same state that he was. In the meantime, the Germans bellowed at him and demanded the coal be brought upstairs. Then one of the Germans put his heavy military boot on my father's leg. And this time my father saw death coming to him. His last impulse was to stand up and hit the German, but a new group of SS men came and my father's oppressor left with them. My father, miraculously, managed to survive.

In early October, transports of Jews arrived from Opatów, Sieradz and Kalisz. They were half-dressed, stunned and unable to think logically since many of them had been dragged out of their beds in the middle of the night.

At the end of October, all Jews between the ages of sixteen and sixty were called to present themselves at the Town Hall at 6:00 a.m. Armed German soldiers pulled Jews from their homes and lined them up in rows in front of the Town Hall. They were forced to sing Jewish songs. All Jews who were bearded and were wearing the traditional long coats were separated and forced to clean up the street gutters with bare hands and then to march around the town market-place. All of this provided a lot of fun and joy to the Poles who were watching these unusual spectacles and, together with the Germans, were taking photographs.

Later, the bearded Jews had to stand opposite each other and cut their beards using little pocket knives. This was not only very humiliating but very painful as well. Hairs were being pulled out together with bleeding pieces of skin, but the Germans did not let anyone scream or cry. Any noise caused by the pain was penalized with forty lashes. Then, all those bleeding people had to run around the Town Hall seven times. Anyone who was slow was whipped or shot, and families of the victims were not allowed to approach them. Several people died that day. The religious Jews who brought with them their prayer shawls and holy books were carrying them back to their neighbourhoods covered with blood. Some of the Poles who witnessed these scenes showed their hatred toward Jews, watching with open joy. This experience disturbed my peace of mind for a very long time. I felt mutiny growing inside me and, for the first time in my life, I decided to never give in without a fight.

By December 1939, Jews were required to wear armbands with the Star of David and Jewish-owned shops had to display the Star of David in their windows. Infractions were punished harshly. In October and November 1940, the Nazis confiscated all Jewish real estate. A new law demanded that all the Jews in our region had three days to contribute half a million złotys. To raise the required sum of money, all valuables were gathered and sold to Poles for a pittance.

In the beginning, we all felt like stigmatized people who were waiting to be executed. We were not allowed to be seen on the streets between 6:00 p.m. and 6:00 a.m. We were not allowed to see non-Jewish doctors, and the only Jewish doctor in town had to publish an ad that he was forbidden to see any non-Jewish patients. We were also deprived of the right to ride trains. Gradually, Jewish shops and enterprises were confiscated and were given to *Volksdeutsche*, ethnic

Germans, and German sympathizers who had been longing for such a moment.

In June 1942, a ghetto was organized in the Jewish part of the city. Jews living outside the ghetto were evicted from their homes and forced to move to the ghetto. Jews were forbidden to use municipal telephone lines; instead, the Jewish Council was ordered to create a limited telephone exchange. Our only open link with other towns and parts of the country was our telephone exchange in the Council. That summer, three labour camps were created nearby, and we later heard reports about other labour camps being created in Skarżysko-Kamienna, Radom, Starachowice and Pionki.

As Jews from the surrounding villages had to abandon their homes, our ghetto became more crowded. The Council had to give shelter to all those people in the already overcrowded Jewish section, and several families had to be accommodated in one apartment. This overcrowding, and consequent lack of sanitary conditions, caused diseases to spread quickly, and we had very limited medical means.

In our tiny synagogue, we organized a soup kitchen, even though we had very little food, but, from time to time, we got help from people in Radom. We were able to provide about 1,000 lunches daily. Later, when the Germans liquidated the ghetto in Radom, food became even more scarce. Our spirits were down, and we prepared for a slow death. Diseases were spreading, which was made worse because the only Jewish doctor, Dr. Sztern, disappeared from the city, leaving us behind. The Council had only twelve members, since five had been tortured to death by Germans. Our situation became more and more tragic.

Soon, we got news from people who had managed to escape from Warsaw. They told us about famine and sickness in the ghetto, a situation beyond description. We learned that there were hundreds of dead bodies and thousands of dying, swollen from hunger. The

Warsaw ghetto, in which there were over 300,000[4] Jews in 1942, was slowly being liquidated through deaths and deportations. For us, this news was the final straw.

We knew that the end of the Jewish people's existence in Sandomierz was approaching. The men congregated in the synagogue and decided to bury the Torah scrolls to prevent them from getting into enemy hands. They wrapped them in white denim, placed them into wooden boxes and lowered them into the ground in the synagogue's backyard. Then we chanted the Kaddish, our prayers accompanied by convulsive cries. I asked myself, where will I be buried?

Parents organized meetings to discuss giving up their children before the liquidation of our ghetto. We were already witnessing sadistic Germans snatching children away from the hands of their mothers and shooting them in their little heads.

We started envying those who were deceased. Our existence was hopeless. Our stupefied brains searched for an answer to the question, does God exist? If yes, for whom? How can He silently watch German sadists grab scared Jewish children hiding in cellars and basements and then ask them to go to their mothers, only to then shoot those innocent children in front of their mothers? Religious Jews loudly prayed "El Rachamim," begging God for mercy.

In late October 1942, the Germans ordered all Jews to report in front of the town hall the next day, where the *Aktion* would begin. They drove hundreds of Jews to the town square and, together with Ukrainian and Latvian police, they shot into the crowd.[5] They also looted Jewish homes, murdering the elderly and sick people who

---

4   In November 1940, there were more than 460,000 Jews crowded into one square mile. The population fluctuated according to the number of deportations in 1942, primarily to Treblinka, at any one time. See Leni Yahil, *The Fate of European Jewry* (New York: Oxford University Press, 1990), 153, 215–218, 378–82, 479–83.

5   October 29, 1942, was the start of a two-week *Aktion*, during which approximately 3,000 Jews were deported from Sandomierz to the death camp of Bełżec.

were unable to walk. Jewish patients were dragged from hospitals and shot on the spot.

A section of the town was surrounded and basements and cellars searched. Those who were hiding and discovered were pulled out and led to the cemetery, where they had to dig their own graves. I heard that they were stripped, then had to face the grave, and then were shot in the back of the head. After they fell down, they were immediately covered with dirt without being checked to determine if some might still have been alive.

This *Aktion* meant the end of Jews in Sandomierz. We could hear the drunken noises of gendarmes, Ukrainians and Poles who were preparing for the liquidation of Jews. Why was God silent? Was the world paralyzed? When would it wake up?

Many people had managed to get false birth certificates that were given by or bought from local priests. Because these forged certificates identified the bearers as Christians, they were very often the most important means of survival. Those with such certificates ran away to take advantage of their last chance of survival.

My family — two of my sisters, Frania and Gucia, and my parents, Yehoshua and Matl — decided to stay in the ghetto, but I decided to go hide in a shelter. I got a birth certificate and I bid farewell to my family. We agreed that if any of us survived we would contact my father's friend, Mr. Berkowski, and from him we would know each other's fate.

There was room for only forty people in the shelter, but there were eighty of us — despairing victims. The superintendent of this house had been generously paid for letting us into this shelter. When all of us got down to the hiding place he closed us in, covering the opening with wooden boards and putting a box on top. The air was so dense that a match would not light. We began to suffocate in our own sweat. Next to me was my friend's mother, Mrs. Jedwabowa, who had a fever and complained that she was cold. I had worn a sweater, which I had knitted myself, so I took it off and gave it to her. She quieted down and got to sleep; she did not wake up again. A watch repairman's child began to cry, and his mother cuddled him and hugged him to prevent the noise from being heard outside the shelter. Silence followed, but we knew that many of us would not last under these conditions. We tried to keep our spirits high, and we consoled each other. Time seemed to go very slowly. We didn't know how long we had been sitting in this atmosphere of deadly tension. Suddenly, we heard the familiar voice of our superintendent talking to Germans, saying, "Here are the Jews I hid yesterday." In the next moment, we heard the wooden board break open and a voice bellowing, "Raus!"(Out!) The superintendent disappeared. He had done his job.

The Germans at first began to chase us away, but then they ordered us to stay in the corridor, close to an outside door. Many of us had not survived the shelter, due to asphyxiation. Two Germans started shooting people standing in the corridor. Each one who got shot was kicked out to the yard. I soon was not able to see over the growing pile of dead bodies. We all stood in the deadly silence awaiting execution, watching in dull fear. There were only four of us left — Renia Wilczek, her sister-in-law, a little boy, and me. At that moment, the Germans ran out of bullets, and the first one turned to the second one to bring more. He was strolling along the corridor waiting for the return of his comrade. Suddenly, I felt as if I had changed into a wolf. I had nothing to lose — I wouldn't be taken alive. We must fight! I yelled to the others, "Do not let them slaughter us like sheep. Run away!" I grabbed Renia's hand, and we ran into the open door of the Grozycznski family's apartment. Then we jumped through half-open windows to the outside lawn. I heard bullets whistling over our heads. We split up, each of us running in different directions. On the nearest street, I ran to the first house to hide. But when Mrs. Sznerch, whose daughter worked with my sister in a drugstore, opened the door, she immediately told me to leave her alone. I left and I felt that, after the whole night in the shelter, without enough air, I was weaker and weaker. A few more steps and I lost all my energy. I fell down and felt that I was rolling through some shrubs. Then I lost consciousness.

I remember that it was daylight when I ran from the shelter. I do not know how long I was lying unconscious. I opened my eyes because I felt a warm wind and some delicate touch on my face. It happened a few more times. I recognized, even though I still felt nauseated, that this was a dog. A German shepherd was licking my face. After a while, I heard some German voices calling the dog. He jumped over me and disappeared without barking. Then I heard the steps of heavy German boots going away. This dog had not betrayed my presence, thus saving my life.

I realized that I was lying next to a pig's shack, and there were shrubs around, which must have screened me from the Germans. I did not have any idea where I was. I couldn't make the slightest movement, and I was lying motionless for a long time. After some time, my hearing improved and I heard, and even recognized, the voice of Mrs. Fijalkowska. She was telling her neighbours that the shelter at Wilczek's place had been discovered and many Jews had been shot. Suddenly, to my surprise, I heard my name among those killed. I could not gather how Fijalkowska thought I was among the dead.

It was dark when I opened my eyes again. I tried to stand, but fell back on the ground. I had the feeling that hours passed before I was able to stand again and take a few steps. Clutching the shrub's branches, I started slowly to move, step after step, unsure where. There was not a soul around. Probably, it was after curfew. I stumbled on someone's legs and suddenly realized that it was a dead body. I kept walking ahead completely disoriented, speaking to myself: forward, forward, don't look back.

I wore a coat without the Jewish armband. In the pocket, I had the birth certificate. I had three hundred złotys. I had now been walking a long time. My legs were swollen, and I was very tired. Once I was out of town, I sat on the grass and after some time I heard a horse and buggy coming. I didn't know where this road led to, but I asked the coach for a ride. He asked if I wanted to go to Dwikozy[6] because he was going to the railway station. I nodded and I got on the straw in the cart. We had only driven a few kilometres when he whipped the horses and suddenly turned the buggy into the fields. There was something wrong with that, so I jumped off the buggy, clutching a bundle of straw, which eased my fall from the cart. The driver did not realize that I had disappeared.

I crawled to a ditch and lay there until I could no longer see the buggy. Checking to see if he would come back, I walked toward the railway station, which was quite close to where I was. Near the station, I noticed a crowd of people. I spotted someone who I used to know very well, so I stopped, but he signalled me to get away. I didn't know what this was all about, but, after a while, I heard voices of Poles who also warned me to stay away. Then I saw German gendarmes yelling at the crowds of helpless people they were forcing into the train cars.

When I asked the Poles what was going on, they answered sarcastically that, "At last, the time has come to clean up Poland from dirty Jews. Too long have they sucked our blood and slaughtered our children." In the railway station, there were people swarming to a teller, trying to buy train tickets. I asked a woman standing next to me if she could buy me a ticket, explaining that my legs were injured and I couldn't stand in the line. Then I entered the waiting room. I could still envision my people and their destiny. And the responses given to me by those Poles reverberated in my ears. I couldn't understand what had driven those people to such horrific hatred toward us.

The woman came to me with a ticket for the next train to Warsaw. She asked me if I also was a smuggler like the rest of them. I confirmed readily and squeezed myself into the train. I sat down and closed my eyes, pretending I was sleeping. Around me I heard drunk-

---

6  A village about seven kilometres from Sandomierz.

en voices openly expressing their joy at the liquidation of Jews. In this atmosphere, I got to Warsaw.

I had gotten the address for my cousin Zosia Kupferblum from her parents, who had asked me to inform her that they were underground and that a man whom they paid did not want to keep them longer, so they were asking her for help. Zosia got scared as soon as she opened the door and saw me. She suggested that we meet somewhere outside because I might endanger her and Dr. Stern's wife. They lived there as two Polish women and, of course, any undesirable visit could put them at risk. I told her about her parents and disappeared immediately.

I didn't have an address for a hotel, so I walked along, pulling my aching legs. I felt hungry and realized that I hadn't eaten anything for more than twenty-four hours. My recent experiences and nervous tension had completely taken away my appetite. As I was passing a cafeteria, the smell of food reminded me that I had to eat something. Inside, before I reached a table, I got the impression that everyone was looking at me, recognizing a Jew in me. I turned and left. Passing by a shop with religious articles, I went in and bought a few religious pictures and a cross. I learned about a hotel from the shop clerk, and went there. I checked in as one Irena Jagiełło, residing in Radom district, according to my phony birth certificate. This is how I became a Christian.

When I got into my room, I displayed all those saints' pictures on the night table. I tried to remember the names of my parents and birthplace and dates from my birth certificate. I was so exhausted, both physically and mentally, that I lay on the bed and slept on the spot. It was after midnight when I heard Germans beating on the door loudly and ordering me to open it.

At first, I did not know where I was, but before I was able to gather my thoughts the door was opened and three uniformed Germans burst into my room. One of them spoke Polish. They wanted to see my documents and they asked who I was and where I came from. My birth certificate was the only document I had. I explained that I had come to Warsaw to see a doctor because there was not a specialist in our village. To prove this, I showed them my swollen legs. They conversed among themselves and began looking for my things but I had with me only my coat and my robe. They became suspicious about that, so they ordered me to dress and go with them to the Gestapo office.

I got out of bed and put my robe on, but when I went to put my shoes on I could not because of my swollen legs. I sat back on the bed, gathered all those saint pictures from the bedside table and then made the sign of the cross and said that I would go with them barefoot and that Jesus would help me. They stood in the corner of my room and whispered something between themselves, and then the one who spoke Polish translated what they had told him: I was allowed to stay, on the condition that the next morning I go to the hospital for a checkup; they would be following up to find out if I really went. I thanked them and asked for the hospital address and then they left, leaving me alone in a sort of shock.

The next morning, I asked the room servant for scissors and strings. I cut the top of my shoes and, using string, I tied them to my feet. I had a small breakfast in the hotel cafeteria. I then took a horse and buggy in Zosia's direction but, after a short distance, I stopped the cart and got off and walked, just in case someone was following me. I left a note at Zosia's, informing her that I was going to the hospital under my new name. I took another horse and buggy to the hospital.

One hour later, I was checked by Dr. Stefan Schmidt and was admitted as an inpatient for further tests. The Germans kept their word and showed up, asking whether my health condition required treatment by a specialist. The physician was a good man and said that I really needed specific treatment. He told me that I would get the best care and that he would not let the Germans send me home until I was completely cured.

Zosia and Dr. Stern's wife paid me a visit in the hospital. They told me who from our family was in Warsaw. All of them were scattered across the city, hiding under phony names. It didn't occur to me to try to find their safe places, as I knew this would cause trouble for them.

Dr. Schmidt told me that the tests indicated some damage in my kidney and that treatment had to last for some time. I admitted that I couldn't afford prolonged treatment in hospital. He said not to worry and that he would contact a social organization that usually helped in such circumstances, and that after discharge I could work for them.

There were no suspicions that I was Jewish. I attended all masses in the hospital chapel, learning how to observe the ceremonies, and I even sang the religious songs; gradually, I began to get used to Catholic celebrations. The nuns were very helpful and sat me in a wheelchair when I could not walk. As soon as I got better, Dr. Schmidt told me that it would be appreciated if I helped the nuns care for other patients. He also gave me an address on Złota Street where there was a patient who would give me a room in exchange for my help. I agreed and moved to Złota Street.

Because one end of the hospital adjoined the Warsaw ghetto, as I went to work I could see groups of Jews being escorted from the ghetto to work. It is difficult to describe my feelings when I looked at these people and their misery. I sped up my steps to avoid a breakdown.

In the meantime, I wrote a letter to Mr. Berkowski, my father's friend, explaining whose daughter I was and that I was living on Złota Street, under a different name. I asked him, according to our agreement, for any information about my family and how I could contact them. After several weeks, I received a very confusing letter from my father, in which he wrote to tell me to stop making cruel jokes. He called me a blackmailer because, he said, his daughter had been killed by Germans, along with others in a shelter. He himself had been at the cemetery where his daughter was buried, he wrote. I couldn't interpret the meaning of this letter. In desperation, I made a very unreasonable step; I sent a photograph of myself to Berkowski, explaining that I was alive, had a job and wanted very much to contact them.

This time I did not wait long for an answer. I received a telegram, signed by my father, addressed to the Złota Street apartment: "Immediately run away from a burning house," it said. I told my patient that I had to go see my father who was sick. In the hospital, I told the same story to my doctor. For a few days, I was roaming about the Central Station, where I also spent nights with other tramps.

When I got back to Złota Street, I learned from the super that some Germans had been looking for Jewish women who were hiding there as well as a little Jew (in Polish, the term *zydek* is used — a derogatory description of a Jew) from Sandomierz. The super was promised five hundred złotys if he found this Jew. As I mentioned earlier, I had decided to fight and to not give up. I was playing this deadly game every day, and I believed that I would win. No super had a clear conscience, and I had nothing to lose so I turned to him and declared that I would go to the police and report this incident. I told him that I had never been to Sandomierz, that I must have been a victim of a *szmalcownik*[7] and that he might even be his accomplice. I forced him to go with me to the police station; otherwise, I told him, I would bring the Gestapo to him. This stunned him, and while we were walking to the station he kept saying that he too was a victim of misunderstanding.

At the station, they laughed us out, saying that the Germans had enough Jews here, and they would not bother to look for some Jewish girl from the middle of nowhere. I knew that my game was dangerous, but I had to show that I was not to be suspected as a Jew, since I had to return to my place. Through Berkowski, I notified my family not to write to me until I could change my address.

In the hospital, I felt tensions growing and surrounding me. I saw scenes from the ghetto that were breaking my heart. Yet, all the while,

---

7  A derogatory name given to a person who is blackmailing Jews in hiding.

230 BEFORE ALL MEMORY IS LOST

I was automatically following others in saying that it was time to finish once and for all the inhuman screams of tortured Jews and burn down this centre of contagious diseases. When some Jews from the ghetto came to the hospital for help, the nuns very often gave whatever they could. I supplied them with cotton, antiseptic, dressings and tablets.

One day, Dr. Schmidt invited me to his office, where he asked me if I wanted to cooperate with an anti-German organization. He said that we had to expect the same fate as the Jews. I agreed willingly. My task was to distribute leaflets with appeals to resist the Germans and to store medicines in the abandoned apartments. Because the mass arrests on the streets were more and more frequent, I was told to always wear a nurse's uniform and nurse's cap, and carry a bag with a red cross on it and drugs inside. Very often, I went across Trzech Krzyży (Three Crosses) Square, where I saw little boys selling cigarettes, and among them I was able to recognize Jewish children. One day, I asked one of them if they could get into the ghetto. When he fearfully confirmed that he could, I quieted him down and asked if he would carry some drugs needed in the ghetto. He promised to contact a doctor and provide me with a list.

In the meantime, I contacted the Edelmans, my relatives from Puławy. They had changed their names to Władek, Stanisław, Genek, Halina and Hela to sound more Polish. They told me that Aunt Estera lived somewhere in Saska Kępa, a southern suburb on the right bank of the Vistula River, together with her grandson Bolek. His parents had been murdered by Germans. I had unforgettable feelings after meeting my relatives. We all agreed to meet with our aunt once a week.

My cousin Hela and I decided to rent a flat on Krochmalna Street. It was located on the fourth floor and there was no elevator. No toilet, either. We had one room, which had a kitchen and one bed. We covered all the walls with religious pictures. Hela was employed in a German factory. Sometime later I met Hania Solomonowicz, who had changed her last name to Skotnicka. She told us that her son was together with her servant in a village not far from Warsaw. She visited us often and we soon accepted Hania as our roommate. We bought a mattress and took turns, with two of us sleeping in the bed, the third one on the mattress.

I had notified Berkowski that I changed my address, so now I was waiting for an answer. When I finally got one, I learned that my family had been sent to different labour camps. Berkowski wrote that they probably had my address and would try to contact me.

In the spring of 1943, there were a lot of rumours about preparation for an uprising in the ghetto. Then, one day in April, I heard the strong noise of explosions; the fight for life had begun. From my young cigarette traders, I knew that the resistance had some munitions. Olek Wasserman, whose brother was a physician in the ghetto, informed me that our people were waiting for further paid-for deliveries promised by Poles. I had hope in my heart that maybe, finally, Poles had realized that the Germans were more and more oppressive for the whole country and that they, the Poles, would help our people to liberate themselves from the murderers' hands. But my hopes were false. After a few days of horrible and desperate fights for freedom, the Poles showed the Germans where there were hidden weapons and munitions for our heroic fighters.

I saw the burning ghetto from my hospital window. People were jumping down from windows, not to be taken alive. My heart was bleeding as I watched mothers tighten their children to themselves and jump down from burning houses. It was a nightmarish spectacle — living fire falling down. The screams were unbearable. I felt that I would not be able to stand it physically or mentally anymore. Then, suddenly, the hospital started burning. The fire brigade arrived and there was total mess and disorder. People gathered and commented on this horrible scene. Their voices had tinges of joyous satisfaction that Jews were being killed.

I will never forget the Warsaw Ghetto Uprising and the people there who burned like living monuments. If God existed, He should have come at this moment, at least to close the mouths and eyes of the Poles who were watching. I will never forget. I will never forgive.

~

One of my patients from the hospital, Zofia Bereznicka, lived on Nowogrodzka Street. She asked me to come and give her daily injections after work. She was a very religious, aristocratic woman. Her daughter was married and was living somewhere in Warsaw and her son was a forest engineer and visited her quite often. From time to time, whenever she was not feeling well, I slept overnight at her apartment. One day, sirens announced a bombardment. This was a five-storey building, and my patient lived on the fourth floor. All the tenants started to run away to the opposite side of the street, where there was a bomb shelter. Normally, in such situations, a superintendent helped Zofia because her left hand and leg were paralyzed and she could not walk down the stairs, but this time it seemed that the superintendent had forgotten about her, so we stayed alone in the apartment. We were supposed to cover the windows and turn off the lights. As Zofia lay in bed she tried to convince me to leave her alone and run to the shelter. She believed the Holy Mother and Jesus Christ would not abandon her. I did not agree and sat next to her.

As we heard the approach of the planes, which were Soviet aircraft,[8] and then the deafening noise, I felt extremely anxious. My patient asked me to light a candle and to give her a card with a prayer on it, which had been given to her by her nephew, a cardinal in Rome. We prayed together. I got confused by some of the words a few times, but she corrected me, quietly saying that this prayer would let me

8   The author may be referring to a Soviet raid that took place on May 12, 1943, in which between 300 and 500 Polish citizens were killed. Soviet radio announced that the attack had targeted military bases. See Joshua D. Zimmerman, *The Polish Underground and the Jews* (New York: Cambridge University Press, 2015) 211–212.

survive. But there was a sudden explosion and our house was hit. We both lost consciousness. I woke up first, and I tried to give Zofia a few drops of her medicine into her tightly closed mouth. On the bed, there was a piece of plaster from the ceiling. I looked up and realized that there was a huge hole in the ceiling, through which I could see the daylight.

When Zofia finally opened her eyes, she kept repeating, "Pray, pray, Irena." After half an hour, the alarm was recalled and people began returning home. I got to a window and called the super for help. When people looked up and saw how the building looked, they started praying to the Holy Mother. The bomb had exploded in the post office, but some pieces of it had destroyed our house and the staircase looked like a skeleton. The firemen had to be called in order to get us down on the ladders. My patient believed that our survival was due to our prayers. She forced me to keep this prayer card with me all the time and never be without it. I took her to her sister and I had to promise that when she found a shelter I would stay with her.

I was now in contact with the anti-German organization, which began to act. We would hear daily that a German had been killed somewhere. Germans organized mass street arrests in response.

One day, Heniek Grynszpan, the husband of Cesia Sznajder, arrived. He had changed his name to Franek and was sporting a moustache and long boots in which he carried a gun. He admitted that he was a member of an underground organization and had a lot of contacts, so we decided to carry help to our people in the form of birth certificates and seals, which they wanted me to keep in a safe place. Heniek told me that Cesia was working as a maid in some country mansion and he left me his telephone number. I found a safe place to hide the papers and stamps, and we began to manufacture phony identity documents, both the Nazi German *Kennkarten* and birth certificates.

In the flat on Krochmalna Street, Hania, Hela and I had financial problems. We combined our money so we could buy some food, and

Władek provided us with coal that he stole from the railway station. Every Sunday, we met all our Jewish friends and acquaintances in a church. This was the safest place to meet. In this way, we were able to meet both escapees from the ghetto and the newly arrived.

Soon, there were new regulations in my hospital: every employee had to have an ID certified by German authorities in Krakow. Krakow was the capital of the *Generalgouvernement*, a part of Polish territory under German occupation. I had a document signed by Dr. Schmidt stating that I was working as a nurse, but the German authorities wanted to be sure that there were no Jews in my family for four generations back. I had to prove that with birth certificates of all of them, so I had to send a letter asking for the original certificates to the village where the owner of my certificate was born. I discussed the issue with Franek and he sent a letter to a priest, giving his address as the return one. He wrote that Irena Jagiełło was about to get married and she was asking the priest who baptized her for her original birth certificate. A few weeks later, Franek called and asked me to gather a group of our friends at his place, where he would read the letter from the priest. When we got together, Franek produced a bottle of moonshine vodka and read us the letter. It contained blessings in the name of Jesus and the Virgin Mary, together with a personal greeting from the prelate, who expressed his hope that the future husband would adopt an illegitimate child. It appeared that the owner of my certificate had an illegitimate baby. This evening was the first in a long, long time that we laughed loudly. I sent all the required papers to the health authorities in Krakow and I got back an official nurse ID. I still have it.

One day, my roommate Hela said that she had met a schoolmate from Puławy in the factory where she worked. She had recognized Hela and demanded a huge amount of money; otherwise, she would go to the authorities to tell them about her. We asked her to not go to the factory again, but she refused. A few days later when I came back from work, I saw a crowd on the street. I turned back, entered a corner store, and asked what was going on. I was told that the Gestapo had caught a Jewish woman in an apartment and that now they were waiting for her two other roommates. I waited for Hania on a nearby street corner. The two of us found ourselves without any shelter and with a terrible question in our minds: what would happen to Hela? Hania went to Zosia. I went to my aunt. We later found out that the Gestapo tortured Hela to get information about us, but she was very heroic and did not reveal anything. One day, they murdered her. She gave her life for us. I will never forget her sacrifice. Her father and our whole family could not return to normal for a long time.

~

The Germans decided to close the hospital and patients were moved to different ones. I next found a job at a store carrying glasses and china that belonged to one of the patients from the hospital. Hania and I found another apartment on Grzybowska Street, downtown, near the ghetto. On Sundays, I met my aunt at Saska Kępa, where the whole family gathered. Five-year-old Bolek stood in front of the shack as our lookout. Inside, our dear aunt prepared a huge pot of hot soup that we enjoyed very much. In the wintertime, we froze. No one had the appropriate clothes. Bolek had only shorts, and they were full of holes. I could not find the proper material for covering the holes, so I sewed a patch to his shorts from one of my gloves. Little Bolek studied medicine after the war and became Professor Boleslaw Goldman, an internist and highly regarded health professional in Israel.

There was a telephone in the store where I worked. The storeowners were very decent people and after some time they trusted me with the keys to the store; the majority of the time, I was working alone, which was very helpful when I wanted to contact my friends. Soon the store became a meeting point for anyone who needed help. One day Rachela (Ziutka) Lerner came for help. She lived with her husband, but her son was hiding in a Polish woman's apartment on the other side of the city. She asked me if I could contact that woman and give her some money. When I went there, I saw Aron, Ziutka's child, pressed against a wall, so scared, his black eyes open wide. My heart felt broken. His darting eyes were looking for someone he could trust. I hugged him and both of us burst into tears. Some time later, Aron was shot by the Germans while hiding in this apartment, and a bomb later destroyed the house, killing everyone inside. Ziutka survived and became a pediatrician in Warsaw.

Various situations occurred that required my help. One of our friends was working in the registry department and therefore had access to birth certificates of deceased persons. I forged signatures and Franek forged seals. I organized birth certificates for many people when their true identity was found out.

When someone snitched on both Chilek Cejlon and his wife, we organized separate birth certificates for them. We decided they should live apart, so they did and they visited each other regularly. After some time, Chilek's wife, Runia, came to us and said that her hostess, who was very attached to her, had advised her to marry this boy who was visiting her so often. We conferred and decided that they should get married. In this way, Chilek married his own wife, but this time in a church and with her hostess as her maid of honour. They started living together again, but this time legally, blessed by a priest. For a long time, we could not forget that farce.

A dentist, Genia Michalowska, was working as a cleaning woman in an orphanage run by nuns. Her husband was in hiding and she visited him often. Then, she got pregnant. In the orphanage, there was nothing unusual about Genia's pregnancy. She gave birth to an illegitimate boy, but the child had to be baptized. We decided I would be his godmother and Franek would be his godfather. Hania's maid, Zosia, instructed us on how to prepare for this ceremony and gave us books with prayers. Franek came by and for the whole night we taught him the necessary prayers. Close to dawn, Franek said he wouldn't do it unless he could get something strong to drink; he was afraid he would screw everything up. We managed somehow to get a bottle of vodka, and he drank it to the last drop. He got so drunk that he could not stand on his own. Franek held the baby, but when the priest asked, "What do you ask of God's church?" Franek answered, "A little vodka, a little vodka, Father." He stumbled and, at the last moment, I grabbed the baby from his arms and approached the priest. The priest probably had gotten used to his drunk sheep. He blessed us, then sprinkled the baby with holy water. We left the church full of fear; then we led Franek to his home. He slept for several hours and did not remember anything. Those tragic comedies kept us alive.

Finally, I got a letter from my youngest sister, Frania. She was in a camp in Radom. The Germans were closing this camp any day and redistributing all the people to concentration camps. I prepared birth certificates, stole a prayer book from a church, put the certificates inside the book's hard cover and sealed it without any trace. I sent it to the address I had gotten from Frania and wrote her that this book had been in our family for so many generations, and that she should pray often and be careful not to destroy the covers. She understood, took the certificates from the book and thanks to the help of Herszl Szlafsztan, who was in the same camp, she slipped away one morning when she was going to work. She found shelter and managed to arrive in Warsaw illegally by train. It is impossible to describe how joyful our meeting was. I learned that my father and my sister Gucia were in Pionki, and that Mama was in Starachowice, both of which were not too far from Warsaw. I made an effort to find a job for Frania and thanks to Abram, who was employed by Többen's fur shop, we found a job for her there. Hania, my roommate, also worked there.

Frania told me the story of what had happened with my letters to them. The first letter I sent to Berkowski got into my father's hands, but he was convinced that I was dead, hence the response where my father wrote that I was a blackmailer because he himself had buried his daughter. This was because he had been at the cemetery when people from my shelter were being buried in a mass grave and, although he could not see my body in the pile, he did see my sweater —

but this was the one I had lent to Mrs. Jedwabowa in the shelter. This sweater convinced my father that I was among the corpses. When Berkowski took my second letter, to which I attached my photograph, my family was at work, and the letter was taken by a kapo named Redelman. He promised that he would pass the letter on to my father, but since the Germans promised money to anyone for a Jewish head, when he saw my picture, that traitor decided to show my letter, with my address, to the camp's office. Luckily, in the same office was a young boy, Mendelbaum's son, who eavesdropped on the conversation. He ran to my father's work and said that he had just seen my photograph. At my father's request, he notified Berkowski, who had sent me the telegram that stated, "Immediately run away from a burning house." Let God bless dear Mendelbaum. I owe him my life. Redelman, responsible for sending a number of his own victims to the gas chambers, was eventually murdered there as well.

I learned that my cousins Abram, Stasiek (Stach) and Moniek Kupferblum were in hiding. One day, Abram showed up and asked me to bring money to Moniek. I knew where he was living so I went and encouraged him to come to the place where all our friends and fugitives were meeting. His mood improved when he saw other people sharing the same fate. He began to believe in a better tomorrow. Also, for all of us, these meetings boosted our spirits.

In the meantime, I was trying to find someone who could go to Pionki, where my father and Gucia were. I found a person, but it would be very costly, and I did not have enough money. I turned to my friends in Opatów who also had family in Pionki and wanted to rescue them. They agreed to share the cost, so I started to prepare birth certificates for my father using the name of Jan Zamojski, and for Gucia using the name Elzbieta Szymanska.

Late one evening when I was in my apartment with Hania and Frania, two men burst in through the door. They said they were from KRIPO (German criminal police) and that they knew we were Jews. They demanded money and then started to search the apartment, stealing all our savings. As they were leaving, they told us to disappear from this place; otherwise, someone else may come and we would end up in the hands of the Gestapo. We collected our belongings and went to Saska Kępa.

In the meantime, our relatives from Opatów arrived in Warsaw and, after acquiring IDs, they rented an apartment. Frania was living with them and also shopping for them because they were afraid to be on the streets. I met up with Sara and her younger brother, Chaimek, and I found an apartment for him. I also found an apartment for myself in Czerniaków, in the southern part of Warsaw, through an anti-German organization. Hania found something close to her son. Again, I turned to my friends from Opatów for help in paying this man who was supposed to go to Pionki. After much bargaining, we went there with him and brought back Father and Gucia. They moved into my place, which had one room and a kitchen. I had a single bed. The neighbours were not supposed to know that someone else was living in my apartment. Every morning when I left for work, I left them food on the table so that no one would hear them, as they were not allowed to go into the kitchen.

My father slept in the bed and Gucia on the straw mattress on the floor. Frania was working for the fur company, but both our salaries were not enough for food, especially now that we had to feed two more. Next to my workplace, there was a café that sold pastries. I asked the owner to sell me a few dozen and Frania took them to her job and sold them for a small profit. They were the pastries with cream, and I remember that we often opened boxes and, using a teaspoon, scooped the cream out of the box, so we had a replacement for the fat that we used to spread on our bread. I brought these home for my father and Gucia. They both looked terrible. We were living one day at a time, but we did not lose hope.

One day, my neighbours warned me that a German had been killed in our area, which meant that everybody was expecting that the Germans, come evening, would make home searches looking for men. The normal penalty for killing a German was that one hundred Poles were to be killed. I had to find a safe place for my father this one night. I went to the apartment that I had found for Sara's brother. The owner was a former patient and she agreed to hide my father. I brought my father at dusk and I promised him that I would come pick him up the next morning.

Indeed, Germans were doing the search, and they arrested several men in our area. As soon as it started to clear, I went for my father and found him on the street, standing against a lamppost. He was frozen and shaky from fear that someone could recognize the Jew in him. He explained that Sara had come to visit her brother, and when she saw my father she was very upset that the owner accepted another Jewish refugee, even for one night, thereby risking the safety of her brother. She forced my father to leave the apartment and wait for me outside. I cannot express how that made me feel, but I will not forgive Sara for as long as I live.

I brought my father home, trying to sneak him in so no one would see him. He was shaking for a long time before he got back to normal. I decided to take him and Gucia to my aunt in Saska Kępa so they could forget for a while and get some fresh air. There, they all joyfully hugged and kissed one another, while weeping as well. After a few minutes, a Pole suddenly appeared and when he saw Father and Gucia he said they looked suspicious and that it would be better if they went away. We did not need a second warning; we said goodbye to my aunt and left. We wandered until dusk so our neighbours wouldn't spot us. After this outing, neither of them wanted to leave the apartment.

Once, when I was at work, I heard the wailing sounds of fire engines. I soon learned that our house was on fire. Although Gucia had keys, she did not want anyone to know about their presence, so they almost suffocated completely. When I got back from work, both were lying on the floor and had not opened the windows or the door. The forces of human endurance are impossible to define.

I began to try to get my mother out of Starachowice. I found a few people who could help me financially and I sent over the same fellow who had brought my father and Gucia. He came back with the message that Mama did not want to leave the camp without her cousin Matylda Rosenburg from Opatów. Matylda's daughter Janka was in Warsaw, but Janka did not believe very much in her own survival, saying that her mother might have a better chance in the camp than here in hiding. It cost me a number of hours and sleepless nights to convince her daughter that she should risk it and live with a clear conscience. Finally, after long discussions, she agreed. I organized the required papers and we sent for them. Matylda moved into her daughter and son-in-law's apartment. I got my mother settled in Zofia Bereznicka's apartment; Zofia was such a good person and was still my patient. She now lived in the Mokotów district, on Tenisowa Street. My mother looked after her and they both got very friendly and attached to each other. Zofia wanted me to marry her son, the forest engineer. I promised her that as soon as the war was over, I would think about getting married. I tried to explain to her how difficult the times were and that no one was sure what tomorrow would bring. She considered me her future daughter-in-law. She and my mother lived together like two mothers-in-law, and she treated me and Frania, who also visited, as family members. Mother and Frania were using my last name, Jagiełło, so I created the Jagiełło Dynasty.[9] On Sundays or sometimes on a weekday, my mother managed to visit my apartment to see Father and Gucia.

My "mother-in-law" had a daughter, Ewa. She looked like a typical Jewish girl, and very often she said so to her mother. One day I got an urgent call from my "mother-in-law" asking me to show up immediately. She said that her daughter had been arrested on the street as

9  Jagiełło was the name of a Polish king who was an ancestor of royal dynasties in Czechoslovakia, Hungary and Germany.

a Jew and was taken by the Gestapo. She begged me to go to the Gestapo and tell them that her daughter was my sister-in-law, and that I had known her since we were children. As I approached the Gestapo I was laughing hysterically, so much so that tears were flowing down my cheeks, so when Ewa saw me, she thought that I was crying over her fate. Taking advantage of my "Aryan" face and using my cockiness, I made a scene that no actress could have topped.

In 1944, there were more and more mass arrests among Polish freedom fighters, who were everywhere in the city. Chilek Cejlon from Sandomierz told me that our acquaintance Romanski was in Warsaw with his pals looking for our brothers and sisters to extort money from us and finish us off. Romanski had seen Chilek on the street, pulled him into the nearest staircase and taken away all his money. Leaving him, he threatened they would meet once more.

One afternoon when I was at the shop, I heard behind me a familiar voice: "Finally I have got you, you Jew." I turned back and I spotted a young man from Sandomierz. Without any hesitation, he named the amount of money he wanted. He also warned me that they had a list of all our Jews who were hiding in Warsaw. At first, this took my speech away, but immediately I regained balance. I understood that I was at their mercy and I explained to him that I did not have the amount of money he wanted. I told him that since he knew my whereabouts, we could meet later, when I had the money. But he insisted that I collect the amount now and that I contact the other Jews, while he and a mob waited across the street. He hoped to catch more victims that way.

He left, and I saw from the shop window that the mob was observing the entrance to my shop. That day, my mother was supposed to visit me. The only hope was Franek. I called him from the office and, using a prearranged signal, I told him there was a fire and that he must come immediately, with firemen, to put the fire out. I closed the shop from the inside and was waiting for him. He soon showed up with a companion; both wore high boots in which they hid weapons.

Knowing that the mob on the other side of the street did not know Franek, I opened the door, explained the situation and I pointed to my "two friends." Franek told me to wait in the closed shop and to turn my mother back if she came. He approached Sobolewski and I saw them talking, and then all of them entered the ruins of a building, which had only a frontal wall. Franek's companion stopped for a while and looked around as if trying to find out whether they were being watched. Then he disappeared.

It seemed as if centuries passed. But, in the meantime, my mother came. I asked her to leave, but she said she would wait on the neighbouring street. She didn't want to go back to her apartment until the situation was clear. Finally, Franek showed up. He knocked on my door and said that everything was okay. He told me not to ask any questions and showed me a list of all my hidden friends and relatives and told me not to worry about the mob — I would not see them again. Mother came back and Franek told her not to be afraid.

Dear Franek was killed during the Warsaw Uprising as a heroic lieutenant. So many people owe him their lives. His wife, Cesia, who visited us from time to time, was always afraid that he was risking too much for other people and that one day he would go too far. But he never refused to help anyone. We survivors will never forget him; he always risked his life rescuing others. He was buried in the military cemetery, but after the war Cesia moved his body to the Jewish cemetery. His noble character will always be remembered by me and by those who knew and respected him.

Autumn was approaching and there was a lot of talk about an uprising.[10] Everyone was secretly preparing, and one could see other people's tense faces. We were listening to the news on illegal radios. There were a lot of rumours across the city — that the Soviets would come to help us, that there were armed partisans waiting for the proper moment to start an insurrection in Warsaw.

---

10 The Warsaw Uprising began on August 1, 1944.

Suddenly, one day it happened! It was August 1 when I was at work and heard the shooting. Everybody around closed shops and businesses and ran to the nearest streetcar to get home. I jumped into a running streetcar and I got home. Frania was already there, but Mother, who was with my "mother-in-law," had not come back yet. We were waiting, full of tension, for any news about her. A few hours passed, but still nothing. It was impossible to get to her; all transportation was interrupted. People who could not get back to their homes were trying to find shelter in the nearest houses to avoid being killed, or were trying to escape from burning houses set on fire by the Germans. And our mother was still absent.

We were in despair. There was nothing to eat, and shops had given away the last of their food. We were afraid of what would happen next. Frania and I had legal papers, but Father and Gucia had different last names, and their papers were, of course, phony. We had to be prepared for an explanation in case we were ordered to leave our homes. We decided to say that they were from a different part of the city and, caught in the uprising, could not get to their homes, so I had let them stay with us. We kept waiting for Mama, but she did not show up.

After a few days, the Germans came to our house and they forced everyone in Czerniaków from their homes. Then they burned down all the buildings. People were driven into a huge hall where thousands were already gathered. The Germans intended to send all of us to concentration camps, as Polish prisoners of war. As they began to check our IDs, I realized that on Father's and Gucia's documents I had missed certain numbers when making the documents with Franek. The numbers had been written with the red ink I had with me in my Red Cross kit, so I produced a needle and wrote down the numbers. No one noticed.

We tried to find my mother, but to no avail. We tried to spot anyone we knew — friends, relatives. In this crowd, we were all equal while waiting for the next step in our destination. We all felt hunger, thirst and nervous tension. The Germans ordered us into columns to march and we reached a train that took us to Pruszków, about twenty kilometres east of Warsaw, where we were selected — young to one side, the old on the other. Then they put us in barracks, where there were already hundreds of people. Some of them were crying; others were frantically looking for their closest friends and family.

The situation was horribly tragic. There were sick asking for help, but in this overcrowded place no one paid any attention. Everyone tried to hide from German eyes. We didn't wait long for our new orders. The Germans wanted to get rid of us; the sooner the better because in this place there were too many of us, and contagious diseases could spread very quickly.

They checked our IDs a second time, and I was ordered to report to a German doctor who immediately issued me a document (which I have kept for all these years) saying that I was a nurse. Next, he ordered me to go to the room with the sick people, who all had possible illnesses. The doctor forbade my contact with the other prisoners.

One day near the end of August, we heard the whistle of a train. People were herded into two groups. Gucia and Frania were pushed to one side, my father to the other, and I was told to get back to the sick. We didn't know where the trains were supposed to go, but we knew that segregation and separation of people did not forecast anything good. People started panicking and changing from group to group while the Germans were pushing the crowd into cattle wagons. I lost sight of my family, so I rushed to the train, running from one car to another and calling their names. Happily, they were not very far, and I managed to get onto the same train as they did. The Germans packed us in so tightly that they had problems locking the doors. It was impossible to sit down. Everyone tried to keep their balance and not get stepped on.

On the top of the wagon, there was a little window with iron bars. As the train passed some villages and towns, people on the outside were throwing small parcels of food, but the barred windows did not let a lot of it get inside. Whatever did was immediately grabbed by the lucky ones; the rest of us envied them. Inside the cattle wagon, we had difficulty breathing and, half-standing, leaning against each other, we tried not to faint. But many people fainted and fell, and we could not help them. There was no washroom and the train stopped for a while. I don't remember how long our journey lasted because the hunger and other awful, unhygienic conditions completely emptied my brain. Nobody was fully conscious when we arrived at our destination, which appeared to be a concentration camp called Stutthof.

We were thrown out into a large, open space. Germans and Ukrainians pushed us like animals until we were standing in columns. Then they counted us and checked to determine who was able to work. We had difficulty just standing straight. They counted about 1,600 people and then packed us into barracks. Here at least we could sit after the horrible journey in the dark. But we did not enjoy this for long. They drove us back outside, bellowing the whole time. We were told that everyone had to work, that we were allowed to move within a restricted area and that the smallest misdemeanour would be severely punished. One person started off toward the latrine and had taken only a few steps when he was spotted by a German and shot dead on the spot. I impulsively stepped forward, trying to help him, but a German pushed me back, yelling at me that I should never dare that again. Next, he ordered me to report daily on how many people were sick and said that everyone who had a contagious disease had to be removed from the barracks. I didn't realize then where those sick were removed to, but what I understood from his order was very scary.

We stood for hours and our legs grew weaker and weaker, bending under us. Whoever tried to sit was beaten with clubs, but if they tried to stand they fainted completely. Finally, they pushed us to where we got our food. Our food consisted of water with something floating in it and one hundred grams of bread. We were told that this would be everything until tomorrow.

Later on, I had the opportunity to look around. I noticed barbed wires around the camp. On the other side, I saw living human skeletons that were moving around like shadows. They wore striped prison uniforms. They were Jews. For the first time, we were confronted with the cruel reality.

People were assigned to miscellaneous jobs. I was sent to the hospital where I saw people in terrible septic conditions. There were few drugs at our disposal. There was one Polish doctor, one young boy as an orderly and myself as the only Polish nurse for 1,600 people. We tried to do our best to fulfill our duties. German nurses checked the situation, trying to detect anyone who had a contagious disease. Many among us suffered from diarrhea — we tried to hide this fact. When there was an outbreak of typhus we were supposed to report such cases immediately, but we learned that those people were sent to the gas chamber.

We had to stand straight, daily, until the Germans counted us, a procedure that lasted for hours. Then those who did not have any serious diseases were allowed to return to the barracks. From time to time, German nurses threatened that if those who were sick did not report to work on the next day, we — the doctor, orderly and I — would find ourselves on the other side of the fence, from where there was no return. And the smoking chimney was proof of that.

For me and my family, the fact that our Jewish people were on the other side did not let us sleep at night. The straw we were sleeping on was swarming with lice. Our clothes were stinking. We had to try and clean our bodies with RIF soap.[11]

---

11 The author is referring to soap that rumour had it was made from Jewish fat. The letters "RIF" on this soap were often mistaken for "RJF" and said to be short for *Reichs Juden Fett* (State Jewish Fat); in fact, RIF stands for "Reichsstelle fur industrielle Fettversorgung, or "National Center for Industrial Fat Provisioning," a German wartime industry responsible for soap distribution. This myth was persistent during the Holocaust and after; in the camps, Nazis perpetuated the myth to torture Jews. There is no evidence that the Nazis produced soap from human

Together with Frania, who had the same last name as I did, we pretended that Father and Gucia were our acquaintances. Our father had to be very careful not to have witnesses during his bath or while he was in the washroom, because he was circumcised. He was very nervous about this and did not talk during the day. Only during the night could we contact each other.

In Warsaw, I had worked with a surgeon who agreed to secretly perform plastic surgery on our men, with excellent results. There was no trace of circumcision after the operation. I personally knew five men who had this operation, and I had visited them in hiding, changing their dressings. Now, in my father's situation, the smallest carelessness could be fatal. We knew we had to be prepared for death and we only prayed not to be tortured when the time to leave this world came.

As more and more transports arrived at the camp, it was decided to send our Warsaw group to another camp. What next? For how long would we survive? Where was the whole world, which had been silent for so many years? Where was God and what was He waiting for?

Our IDs were checked and we were counted again to see how many of us were healthy and able to work. Again, segregation and the terrible wait for the sentence of who would be selected; we hoped that they would not separate us. The trains arrived and they packed us inside, as before. We were exhausted physically and mentally. Our eyes could not stop staring at the barbed wire with an electric current, and we knew that we would never see those human skeletons alive again.

The train started moving, and our mass, covered with lice, began to quarrel for a bit of free space for our tired bodies for the rest of the journey. Those who believed in God were loudly praying for a

---

remains. See "New Israeli Film Debunks Myth that Nazis Made Soap From Jews" at http://www.haaretz.com/jewish/features/.premium-1.527623 and "The Soap Myth" at http://www.jewishvirtuallibrary.org/jsource/Holocaust/soap.html.

prompt death. The rest were indifferent from exhaustion and inca-
pable of any reaction. The Polish doctor was not among us anymore.
There was only the male orderly and me. We both tried to hide any
pain we were experiencing because we knew that the Germans would
kill us and throw us from the train. So we kept together, cheating mu-
tually, and hiding the truth.

After a few days, we arrived at a place called Alt Folwark,[12] near
Grudziądz, a town in northern Poland halfway between Warsaw and
Gdańsk. A German camp there consisted of horse stables as barracks. The stables/ barracks were round, divided inside with wooden
boards, and the floor was covered with straw. They packed us into
numbered barracks, and again checked our documents.

In a short time, the Germans began to prepare us for the kind of
labour we could expect — digging ditches and trenches under strong
supervision. We were not allowed to even touch the weeds that were
growing in the field. We were starved and people often tried to steal
things from the field. The consequences were fatal. We were given, as
in Stutthof, one hundred grams of bread and a little soup, kind of a
lukewarm liquid, daily. Often our shaky hands spilled this soup before our lips even touched the edge of the metal can, which was our
only pot. There was no possibility of getting more rations. During
the bread distribution, one had to grab rations as quickly as possible. If this precious piece dropped on the ground, it had to be picked
up very quickly because people were stealing everything from one
another.

I was working in the ambulatory barracks together with two German nurses and a German doctor. They had separate, locked medicine cabinets. In ours, we had only the most necessary items for initial

---

12 Alt Folwark (also called Stary Folwark; Alt and Stary both mean old) is located
   about 145 kilometres south of Stutthof. It was a labour camp for 800 people and
   existed from July 1944 to January 10, 1945. Reference desk, USHMM, 2016.

treatment. Our bodies were covered with lice and we suffered from hunger, furuncles and bleeding rashes. A male nurse and I would try to steal some items from the medicine cabinet but we were seldom successful; besides, we were gambling with our lives.

Every morning and evening, Germans checked the number of people going to and returning from work. If somebody was missing, a German accompanied me and we walked through the barracks looking for the absentee. Very often, I was hit when I tried to hide the sick.

The straw we were sleeping on was so moist during the night that we woke up in the morning and went to work with wet hair and clothes. In the first days of winter, they gave us wooden clogs; until then we were walking in torn rags, and everyone tripped. We tried to cover our legs with paper or newspapers we found and tried to squeeze our feet into the clogs.

Sometimes, Germans living in the village approached the fence. Many of us asked them for something to eat. Some of us still had a watch or a wedding ring that could be exchanged for a piece of bread or a little milk. When winter came, we woke up with snow in our hair. We got blankets, but we tried to use one blanket for two people, and from the second blanket we sewed a kind of coat that we alternated wearing. From time to time, we could hear flying aircraft. Germans were running away to their shelters while we did quite the opposite — running out of our barracks, we were waving and crying to get their attention, but to no avail.

At Christmas, our representatives, with me as chairwoman, went to the commandant of the camp to ask for a permit to go to church. After a long discussion, they agreed to let us go to the church under heavy German security. During the Pastoral Mass, we had the occasion to meet, for the first time, the civilian population. A priest approached me and a few other people and whispered that he had contact with partisans and that he would try to get us medicines and documents in case someone decided to escape during work.

He arranged with me that one day at dusk he would come and also send us some medicine. We found out that the forests that surrounded our camps had a large number of partisans. From that moment, the spirit in the camp improved, a small spark of hope that we were not alone, that someone knew about us and that someday the awaited liberation would come. The first person who got documents from the church happily ran away, but the Germans immediately began to check our documents and seized all our *Kennkarten*, so we were left without any ID. In the meantime, we got some medicine from the priest. I remember that with those drugs we also got some petroleum jelly — sick and healthy begged me for a little so they could spread it on their bread, as a replacement for fat.

It was January 1945, and we heard from German guards that Hitler's forces had begun withdrawing from some occupied territories. More and more often, we heard aircraft and saw the Germans panic. More Germans arrived at our camp, making the guard even tighter. At night, we could hear shooting. The Germans ordered us to improve unfinished trenches. In February, they gathered all of us together, the sick on the sleighs, the rest of us at the front of the columns. They watched us from the rear so that no one could turn and run away to the forest. We were dragging our feet toward the unknown. We could hear shooting that was getting closer and closer. When we approached the forest, we started running in that direction and, even though we left many victims behind us, we managed to reach the partisan groups. They were Soviet and Polish soldiers. They were armed and gave us medication and food.

Immediately, we organized a field hospital, since there were a lot of wounded. We also had a Russian doctor. They settled us deep in the forest. The rest of the partisans fought for freedom and appealed for volunteer soldiers to join them. I had an occasion to see, for the first time, Russian sleigh ambulances. They were very well-supplied and were led by well-trained dogs that had first-aid kits hanging on their necks. The dogs pulled the wounded back to the partisans' camp.

I was full of admiration for our Russian liberators. They shared their food with us and cared for our wounded and sick. At the end of February, we came back to Warsaw[13] via Stutthof, where all the nightmares returned to us. We were led through all those halls where our dearest were gassed and we saw the crematorium where humans were burned.

Our journey by train took us a couple of days. The train was so packed with passengers that people were not only inside the train, but also on the roof. On our way, we gathered survivors from other camps. We thought only of how to get to a safe place. During the whole period when we were in the camps, we could not stop thinking about our Mama. As soon as we got to Warsaw, I immediately went to the Red Cross asking about a missing person. I gave the surname Jagiełło. We tried to find any Jewish community.

We didn't have anywhere to spend the night so we wandered the streets. All the places we used to live had been burned to the ground. We spotted people standing in line for food and joined them and got a warm lunch. It warmed not only our stomachs but also our spirits.

The next day when we were wandering the streets, we spotted a man who had a Jewish look, and he informed us that a Jewish Committee had been organized, and gave us the address. There, we found the names of our cousins from Puławy. Before we went to see them, we registered both our true and false names with the committee. We found our beloved aunt Estera from Saska Kępa with her son, Nolus. Also, there were Władek, Ludwik, Stanisław, Lodka, Halina and Genek. Still, the fact that Mama was missing spoiled our joy.

As a nurse, I was mobilized and had to go to Lodz, where a military hospital had been organized. My family and I left for Lodz, and here

---

13 Warsaw was liberated by the Soviets on January 17, 1945. Her route to Warsaw is confusing since Grudziądz is halfway between Stutthof and Warsaw.

we met other cousins from Opatów — Rosenburg with her daughter and son-in-law and her sister Fredzia. Their son-in-law was a doctor, and he invited us to his place, where four families lived together in a four-bedroom apartment. After a few months of work, I was given an apartment, but I was living in the hospital as Nurse Irena Jagiełło. And we still did not have our Mama with us.

The doctor I worked with was a Russian woman. No one knew that I was a Jew. One day, an officer came to our clinic and when he filled out an admitting chart he gave his name as Albert Zoberman. I glanced at him and I recognized a kind of familial likeness, although I did not know him at all. I told him to come after office hours because I would have to send him for an X-ray. When he reported later, I asked him whether he had any surviving relatives, because I had encountered the name Zoberman in a patient's home. He was very excited and I gave him the address of our family without telling him who I was. Our family lived on Południowa Street. When my father opened the door and learned why he had come, they started talking and soon found out that he was my father's nephew. When my father asked who sent him he said it was a nurse, a girl named Irena. They laughed when the truth came out. When he came back to the hospital, I asked him not to tell anyone that we were relatives. We had freedom, but after the war there were still pogroms and antisemitic incidents, and it was better to keep false papers for the sake of safety. Sad, but true. We could not trust some Poles. When many of our people came back to their homes to check if anyone survived, surprised Poles said things like, "You are alive and you want back your belongings? Go away and don't come back!"

I heard that Abram Kupferblum and his daughter survived as well as his sister Zosia (Sophie) and brother Stasiek and his wife, Mala (Marysia). Moniek was dead. Abram's daughter, Eva,[14] got out of the

---

14 See Eva and Barbara Kuper's memoirs in this anthology. Barbara married Abram (Anthony) Kuper after the war.

ghetto through a sewage canal; then she was hidden in a nun's convent. He found her after the Warsaw Uprising. A large number of survivors began to return. Late fall, our cousin Władek came to Lodz from Warsaw and said that a woman was waiting in the street, wanting to speak with us. He called to her and we spotted someone who looked like a living skeleton. She was bent, dressed in rags. Her face was full of wrinkles and tears were flowing down. I will never forget as long as I live this picture of our beloved, unforgettable Mama. She was in such a shape that probably no one would have recognized her.

During the Warsaw Uprising, Mama had been caught on the street and with many others she was sent to do hard labour in Germany. She was liberated from a German camp where she had been working, carrying bags of cement. After liberation, she either hiked or hitched rides on horse carts and came to Warsaw. There, she found our names at the Jewish Committee. I remember that for many months Mama hid a piece of bread under her pillow. Nobody took it away. She slowly adjusted to reality. Our father, however, was afraid to open the door for a long time and every time someone knocked he hid in the adjacent room. Gucia began to work in the Jewish Congress and Frania got a job in the Polish film industry, and we managed somehow. We didn't have any news about our oldest sister, Hania. She was a pharmacist, and had been living in the eastern part of Poland occupied by the Soviet army. We had heard that the Soviets had sent everybody to Siberia, and we tried to find out from the Red Cross if she was still alive.

Our cousin Zyta Kupferblum, who had survived the war in the forest as a partisan, had showed the Red Army how to get to Sandomierz in 1944. She got a very high reward for this and began to work in Lublin as a censor of letters. There, she found a letter directed to Sandomierz from our sister Hania. In this letter, Hania asked whether any member of the family was still alive. That was the way we found out she was in the Soviet Union. But, in 1945, there was still so much upheaval, and mail for civilians was highly unreliable. Times were still uncertain.

The doctor with whom I worked was going to the Soviet Union for vacation, so I gave her a letter to Hania to send from the Soviet side. After she came back, she brought me a letter from my sister. She wrote that she had been married and had a baby and that she was applying to return to Poland.

More and more survivors arrived. We tried to be in touch and help each other. Also with us was Renia Wilczek, who had run away with me from the shelter, and we talked a lot about our past experiences. Some time later, my roommate Hania Solomonowicz showed up in Lodz. She was with her son and maid, who had saved him. Many of our friends had contact with their relatives abroad; some of the braver ones tried to sneak through borders to be together with them.

I soon got a subpoena from Sandomierz, as did Renia. The supervisor of the house where we had been hiding back in 1942 and who had revealed our hiding spot to the Germans, leading to the murder of so many of us, was caught somewhere while he tried to cross a border. When I walked into the courthouse in my hometown, I had the feeling that I was stepping on the bleeding corpses of our relatives.

After our testimonies, the judge said that since we had not seen the super speak to the Germans but we had only heard his voice, we couldn't be sure that it had been him. When I asked why, then, had the super tried to run away from Poland, the patriotic judge said that this did not affect the case, and acquitted the executioner. So such was the justice: the traitor escaped from the gallows, and both Renia and I, the only two survivors of the massacre, left the courthouse imagining the piles of corpses from the shelter.

The day finally came when Hania returned from the Soviet Union. We had not seen each other for eight years. She came back with her sister-in-law and a few other people. We were so happy that we were able to have an open door for all who had survived. We were also in touch with our family in Canada and were waiting for the necessary papers. We knew that Abram had married and left for Canada. Zosia and her husband left for France. Our cousin Chilek Kupferblum arrived as the only survivor of his whole family. He decided to immigrate to the US to be with his sister, and he lived with us until his departure. Stasiek and Mala lived in Poznań and were in close contact.

In Poland, the situation became more and more tense under the communist regime. It is very sad that after the war we were forced to look for a safe roof over our heads — we had thought that the world after the war would be friendly, without hatred and racial differences. In 1948, my family immigrated to Canada.

~

I was raised in a traditional Jewish home. We kept kosher, but I have never been extremely religious. From my family home, I learned never to refuse help to anyone in need, and that one can always find a good neighbour. My conscience is clear because in spite of hunger and lack of money, I never refused help to another. I was swollen from hunger and my people knew about it and they did not help me even though they saw my condition. I do not hold onto any resentment toward them — one cannot change a stone to a heart. I risked my life and my health to rescue others and I am very proud of it. All events in this memoir are true — I am in possession of proof and there are still witnesses.

In the 1950s, when I was in Israel, it was the first time in my life that I felt I was where I belonged. I straightened my bent back and I walked with my head raised high, being certain that no one would point a finger at me with the words, "You Zydowa [Jew]." I was with my friend Cesia Sznajder and her child in Israel, and we shared our poverty and split each piece of bread between us; we never gave up. We always believed in a better tomorrow and we consoled each other that we were not alone and that as long as there was at least a single Jew in the world, our nation would not disappear. The time I spent in Israel was, and always will be, the best time in my life. Unfortunately, a family illness in Canada required that I return there, but the fact that Israel is my ultimate destiny will always stay in my mind and my heart.

During the first days after our arrival in Canada, I was sitting with my Mama and we were watching a TV program that was showing fragments based on a book in which there were scenes from the German occupation of Poland. I didn't understand English but I saw towns and villages with the names of Józefów and Puławy, where we used to have relatives. In the meantime, my mother fell asleep, and I could not find the name of the author of the book. When I told Mama what I saw, she laughed at me, saying that without knowing English I imagined all these scenes because they reminded me of our past experiences. It was very logical, but I could not shake it, so I called my aunt to ask her to contact the TV station to find out who the author of the book was.

My aunt was also very skeptical, but she called and then immediately let me know that the book, *The Child of the Holocaust*, was written by Jack Kuper from Toronto. She also gave me his telephone number. When I called and heard his voice, I asked him whether he was Jankiel Kuperblum; there was a silence on the line, and we both could hear our breaths. Finally, I told him that I was his cousin and that I wanted him to come to our place to meet family. He couldn't believe it and kept repeating that for so many years he had been searching for his family. He hadn't been able to find anyone because everybody had changed their last name to Cooper. When he arrived at our place, I gathered the whole family so he could see that he was not alone. And we chatted without end.

I was very moved when I found a Sandomierz society, a committee of Jews from Sandomierz, with Abraham Weisman as chairman. He tried to keep in touch with all the survivors. I know how much effort he spent sponsoring survivors of concentration camps. Still, there are a lot of folks from Sandomierz with whom I do not have contact.

I would like to thank my beloved family and relatives — Cooper, Milrad and Strauss — who brought us to Canada and looked after us. I had a very difficult time when my father died and also when my brother-in-law and my Mama died, my beloved mother with whom

I spent the last nineteen years. With her passed this priceless Jewish home — always open to everyone in need. For the first time in my life, I was depressed. Nobody will ever replace my mother, who always taught me, "Before you decide to do something, always check whether anyone would be hurt by your decision."

Dear brothers and sisters, open your eyes and hearts wide for all of those who need a warm word. Give a hand to those who are in need of your help and do not let them down. We can neither close nor erase the past from our lives if we do not stand firmly on our feet and teach our children and grandchildren to never deny their roots. Do not hide anything. We must stay together, supporting each other's spirits. I am grateful for all the help from family and friends. May they always be remembered.

1 The Zoberman family before the war. From left to right: Irene, her father, Yehoshua, her youngest sister, Frania, her mother, Matl, her oldest sister, Hania, and her sister Gucia (Gertrude). Sandomierz, Poland.

2 The family in 1948, the last time they were all together before everyone but Hania immigrated to Canada. Clockwise from left: Irene, Gertrude, Frania, Yehoshua, Matl, Hania holding her daughter, Ola, and Hania's husband, Fima. Lodz, Poland.

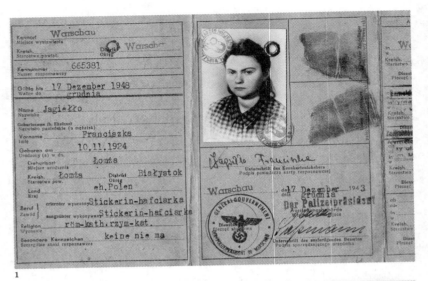

1

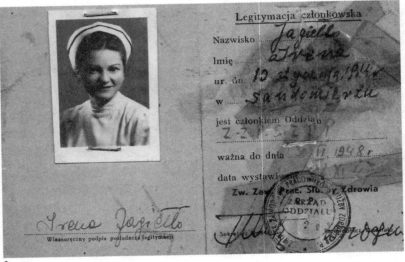

2

1 The front of Irene's sister Frania's *Kennkarte*, the false document that Irene procured for her in 1943 under the name Franciszke Jagiello.

2 Irene's post-war document with the photo that was on her false identity documents during the war. 1948.

Irene (seated in front, seventh from the left) after the war in the nursing sanatorium.

1   Irene, date unknown.
2   Irene, her mother, Matl, and her sister Frania at Yehoshua's (Joshua's) grave. 1960.
3   Irene with her nephew David (Gertrude's son) and her niece Jessica (Frania's
    daughter). Florida, 1979.

Camps

# Foreword

The women who wrote the memoirs in this section experienced concentration camps, labour camps and death camps, where they witnessed the process of selection. They watched their loved ones — the elderly, the sickly, the young and the women visibly pregnant — march to gas chambers. They watched young, healthy mothers carry their babies and toddlers to their deaths rather than abandon them to save themselves. And those not selected for death learned soon enough that their parents, grandparents, cousins, children, friends and neighbours would become a statistic that ballooned into the millions — six million, more or less.

Sarah Karpen Shapir reacted to the murder of her mother, Fradl Klinowski Karpen, by writing a heart-wrenching poem to her:

They ended your life, erased your name.
Choked the young years, hiding the trace.
You are one of the six million, from the past,
A part of a nation melted into ash.
And I was not gassed. I survived, alive.
Revived your being, whatever to come,
And gave you a future, in my born sons.
And you won, you exist, you are alive,
Mama, my Mama, you and your people will never die.[1]

---

1 Unpublished poem, "To my Mama" by Sarah Karpen Shapir. Montreal, Canada, summer 1999.

Shapir's sons and their descendants are the revitalization of her mother and the millions of others who were murdered. Ironically, says Shapir, the Nazis had limited, though devastating, success and did not succeed in erasing the Jews from memory or existence.

Beginning in March 1933, with the opening of Dachau to house real and imagined political opponents, the Germans established thousands of camps to facilitate the elimination of the Jews and other people they considered "life unworthy of living," a designation that included the handicapped, p o w s and Sinta and Roma (then referred to as Gypsies). Virtually all the camps fell under the jurisdiction of the SS, rendering them outside the laws of the state. The SS "leased" some of the camps to companies that manufactured essentials for the war effort, with the companies compensating the SS for the forced/slave labour they provided.[2] Often, these camps were temporary or short-lived. However, many stayed in business for years; for example, the Auschwitz labour camps provided prisoners for I.G. Farben, the company dedicated to manufacturing synthetic rubber and oil, or Degesch, which manufactured Zyklon B gas, or Siemens, Krupp, or any number of foundries and facilities making guns and ammunitions and other essentials for conducting war.[3]

---

2   I.G. Farben paid four marks a day for skilled labour and three marks for unskilled. The SS administration of Auschwitz received more than twelve million marks for a period of seven months of work by male prisoners and nine months of work by female prisoners. See *Auschwitz 1940–1945* (Albuquerque, NM: Route 66 Publishing, Ltd., 1995), p. 57; reprint of English language edition of the "Guide to the Museum" by Kazimierz Smolen. This book is the source of many of the details and statistics about Auschwitz-Birkenau in this essay, unless otherwise noted. It draws its information from primary sources found in the Auschwitz Archives as well as from the autobiography of Commandant Rudolf Höss, and trial records of Höss, Oswald Pohl, Dr. Josef Kremer, and Dr. Carl Clauberg.

3   It is important to note that forty subcamps of the Auschwitz complex provided between 500,000 and 600,000 prisoner-workers. Company representatives selected workers and paid the SS for such prisoner-workers. Oswald Pohl, Chief of the Economic Administration Head Office, ordered heads of camps to work

In contrast to the killing camps, whose only purpose was murder on arrival, the concentration camp system was designed to "eliminate" unwanted people through work[4]; it was an efficient system and expanded constantly throughout the war to reach the unimaginable number of over 40,000 camps of various types, which housed from several hundred to tens or hundreds of thousands of prisoners. For the SS, it was a profitable business; for the prisoners who were subjected to terrors from the moment they arrived in the camps, it was a dehumanizing existence that involved a struggle for survival against a system designed to annihilate them.

Some women who had advanced language and clerical skills were assigned work in the administration offices of the camps; others worked in the homes of SS officers as charwomen, cooks or seamstresses, while many were put to work in the factories that were, in essence, subcamps, always under the supervision of the SS.

Women were equal partners with men in subversive resistance activities, notably the four women who smuggled gunpowder from Auschwitz's Union Werke factory; these women were caught, tortured and hanged in full view of all the women prisoners on January 6, 1945, two weeks before the Nazis abandoned the camp. They were hanged because they supplied the gunpowder used in the October 7 uprising, which failed but destroyed Crematorium 4 and part of 5 in the process. Their names — Roza Robota, Ella Gartner, Estera Wajsblum and Regina Safir — and their heroism live on.[5]

the prisoners to exhaustion "in the full meaning of that word, so that maximum results be obtained. There should be no time limits to work hours...." p. 55.

4  Healthy pregnant women, and women thought to be pregnant, were gassed because they were considered unable to work. See Lucette M. Lagnado and Sheila C. Dekel, *Children of the Flames: The Untold Story of the Twins of Auschwitz* (New York: Penguin Books, 1991), p. 80.

5  Danuta Czech, *The Auschwitz Chronicle 1939–1945* (New York: Henry Holt and Company, 1997), pp. 728, 729, 775.

In Auschwitz,[6] women were subjected to medical experiments on sterilization, conducted primarily by Dr. Carl Clauberg, who strove to "attain the quickest method of biological extermination of the Slavs." He proudly wrote Heinrich Himmler, chief of the SS, that a "properly trained surgeon, working in a suitable equipped surgery, with perhaps 10 medical assistants, will most probably be in the position to sterilize several hundred or even 1,000 persons in the course of one day." Clauberg introduced a caustic substance directly into a woman's uterus to render her sterile.[7] Commandant Rudolf Höss labelled the experiments "unmedical activities". Other doctors, famously Dr. Josef Mengele in Auschwitz, conducted medical experiments on twins, including sewing them together to try to make them into Siamese twins.[8] Called the "Ravensbrück Rabbits," women in Ravensbrück, the concentration camp solely for women, were also subjected to "unmedical" experiments.

Women prisoners in Auschwitz and other camps were given the same assignments and punishments as were given to men. For example, in the penal colony in the village of Budy near Birkenau, women worked immersed in water to dredge lakes and remove rushes from fish ponds. In winter, they were forced to use ice picks to break patches of ice in order to get to the rushes. In concentration camps, women

6  I focus on Auschwitz-Birkenau primarily because it is the most well-known of all the camps and was simultaneously a killing, or death, camp, a labour camp and a concentration camp. Most of the women in this section were deported to Auschwitz at one time or another.

7  See also Danuta Czech, *The Auschwitz Chronicle 1939–1945* (New York: Henry Holt and Company, 1997), p. 414. This source provides a day-by-day chronology of events, including arrivals and departures, births and deaths, of the camp.

8  "The Angel of Death," www.auschwitz.dk. See also Anita Frankova, Anna Hyndrakov, Vera Hajkova and Frantiska Faktorova, *The World without Human Dimensions: Four Women's Memories*, The Menorah Series (Prague: State Jewish Museum, 1991); and Lagnado and Dekel.

were tortured — waterboarded, given injections into sensitive parts of their bodies, beaten, had their nails extracted.[9] Some women in Gross-Rosen were sent to the Bleischicht (lead-shift):

*The factory was a long ways off, we worked 12-hour shifts, and practically most of the day was spent getting there and back or standing at roll calls. We filled some sort of cartridges with hot explosive material — perhaps they were detonators. It was debilitating, dreary work.... Those who delayed even a second in screwing the cartridge onto a rotary conveyor system got a drop of hot, molten lead mixed with some filthy stuff on their hands and blisters that immediately started festering. We worked under the watchful eyes of SS-men and a German foreman. ...we dug pits for cisterns, dug sand in sand pits and loaded it on a narrow gauge track, which we always built ourselves.[10]*

In all camps, the appalling living conditions were the same, if not worse, for women as for men. In Birkenau, women prisoners were supervised by female guards hired and trained by SS personnel and by SS men who "being bored and wishing to enjoy themselves, ... baited the women prisoners with dogs."[11]

Several women in this section refer to an unfinished area in Birkenau called "Mexico," an area that housed thousands of Hungarian women prisoners. Their barracks were empty of bunks, so the women slept on the ground. The dresses they were given "were burnt by frequent delousing; they had been of silk or lace, evening dresses sometimes with low cut backs...almost gone to pieces. One sees women

---

9 Smolen, pp. 84–85. In October 1942, there was "an outbreak of mutiny" when women prisoners tried to escape Budy. During this attempt, the authorities murdered many women, and beat even more. Women who survived the "bloodbath" were murdered by shots of phenol to their heart.
10 Frankova et al, pp. 168–169.
11 Smolen, p. 104.

clad in a torn chemise only or covered with an apron, with nothing underneath."[12]

In fact, trial records indicate that 50,000 Hungarian Jewish women in "Mexico" deliberately received no clothing at all for two months even though the storehouses were bursting with clothes from murdered victims.[13] One guard's testimony reveals that women were desperate for water, begging him to bring some. When the guard asked his superior about the women's deplorable conditions he was told, "That's none of your business, it's high time for you to understand that these are Jews!"[14]

Overcrowding, starvation, disease, beatings, fear, thirst, degradation — all characterize life in the camps. Many women, however, coped by adapting skills they had acquired in their pre-deportation lives: they created "surrogate" families, adopting one another to offer consolation, assistance or even a slice of bread to a surrogate daughter, sister or mother. Before 1939, most European women had been part of women's groups in their synagogues, neighbourhoods, sewing/knitting circles and charity organizations. In the camps, they bonded as they had in pre-World War II days. In the isolation that followed deportation, they tended to recreate such family groups, many of which made the difference between life and death.[15]

Women in camps traded recipes, usually related to the Jewish holidays and Sabbath. In doing so, they taught one another how to prepare the most elaborate and intricate dishes, recalled, they said,

12 *Ibid.*, pp. 109–110.
13 Danuta Czech, p. 564. "Naked humans, especially women, feel defenseless and thus become unable to put up resistance."
14 Hermann Langbein, *People in Auschwitz* (Chapel Hill: The University of North Carolina Press in association with USHMM, 2005), p. 100.
15 Myrna Goldenberg, "Different Horrors, Same Hell: Women Remembering the Holocaust," in *Thinking the Unthinkable: Meanings of the Holocaust* (New York: Paulist Press, 1990), pp. 150–166.

from memory even though most of them later admitted that they had never cooked as well in the kitchen as they had with their mouths.[16] "Food talk" was a natural way of creating relationships. By sharing the recipes of their grandmothers, aunts and mothers, they kept the memory of these women alive. Since most Jewish cooking is related to a Jewish holiday, they were also transmitting Jewish learning along with cooking techniques.

In small but very significant ways, most women did what they could to resist and to survive: "small acts of rebellion...meant a lot: not obeying German orders, preserving one's own as well as national pride."[17]

~

The first memoir in this section is by Catherine Matyas, who kept a diary during her internment under the Nazis. She was sixteen years old when the Nazis invaded Hungary in March 1944 and she was detained in Debrecen,[18] her hometown. By June, along with 6,481 Jews from Debrecen, she was part of one of two transports that were shipped to a transit point in Strasshof, Vienna; from there, Catherine and her family were sent to the Lobau oil refinery, a labour camp near Vienna. Within a few months, she and her family were sent to a small concentration/labour camp in a school in Vienna, and then, in March 1945, to the concentration camp/ghetto of Terezín (Theresienstadt), from which they were liberated two months later.

The Strasshof transports were a result of negotiations between SS leader Adolf Eichmann and Hungarian Jewish lawyer Rudolf Kasztner. According to Yad Vashem, approximately 75 per cent of the Hun-

---

16 See Myrna Goldenberg, "Food Talk: Responses to Hunger in the Concentration Camps," in Elizabeth Baer and Myrna Goldenberg, eds. *Experience and Expression: Women, the Nazis, and the Holocaust* (Detroit: Wayne State University Press, 2003), pp. 161–179.

17 Frankova et al, p. 75.

18 The two ghettos in Debrecen held approximately 13,000 Jews.

garian Jews sent to Strasshof, including older people and children, survived.[19]

Auschwitz survivor Suzanne Katz Reich recounts her fear of Hungary's "armed hooligans" who terrorized her city and all its Jewish residents. She describes the Kisvárda ghetto as an "abysmal descent into hell on earth. A place where Satan — dressed in some German uniform — was the omnipotent ruler and rooster-feathered Hungarian gendarme demons served him only too willingly as lackeys with bayonets." When deportation was imminent, her mother and aunt baked money into dozens of cookies, hoping to use the money as bribes that would increase their chances of survival. On the way to Auschwitz, however, as the Nazis demanded money from the deportees and searched them and their baggage, her mother threw all the cookies out the narrow opening of the cattle wagon rather than give it to the Germans. Reich calls this her mother's act of defiance, an act of non-military resistance. Days later, they reached Auschwitz, where her grandmother was selected to die. Reich was numbed by the experience of the camp, "unsure whether I even existed. And then I was angry." Angry at her mother because she degraded herself by searching garbage heaps for "bits of raw potato skins...or a head of rotting cabbage she pilfered" to give to Suzanne for nourishment. She described her mother's "ingenuity" to find food to sneak to her and her sister, who was in a different part of Birkenau. When the Allies were near, she and others were evacuated to a bomb factory in Teplitz-Schönau where a surrogate family of sisters helped her survive until she was shipped to Oederan, an ammunition factory that was less strict than Teplitz-Schönau. Again, it was a surrogate family of sisters that made the difference in her experience.

---

19 This is the highest survival rate of Jews from Hungary. For more information on the Strasshof transports and their genesis, see Ester Farbstein's "Jews on Ice": A Look Inside the Labor Camps in Austria at http://www.misrachi.at/a%20look%20inside%20the%20labor%20camps%20in%20austria.pdf.

Telling her story so that she "could affect other people's choices to stand up and speak out against injustice" instead of choosing to be a bystander, Rebekah Schmerler-Katz explains that "suddenly" she and other Czechs became Hungarian citizens when Hitler took over the Sudetenland, the eastern part of Czechoslovakia. Katz details the loss of all civil rights as well as the struggle to remain optimistic, only to be rounded up for deportation to a town that had been mostly vacated to create a ghetto for Jews. Gathered together in a cemetery, the Jews were told, "By tonight all of you will smell the violets from the bottom." A few days later, however, they were all on trains bound for Auschwitz. These Hungarian women were assigned to "Mexico," where overcrowded and barbaric conditions were the norm, all of which Katz describes clearly in non-sentimental terms. She went through ten selections between May and August 1944, sometimes using the dye from red leather shoe tassels as rouge to make her forty-eight-year-old mother and herself appear healthy. She daydreamed about never being hungry again

Lodz was the birthplace of Fela Grachnik, whose memoir tracks a normal childhood in a low-income area through to life in the ghetto, with all its hardships and deprivations. Witness to "tragedies beyond anybody's imagination," she was deported with the remaining Lodz ghetto Jews in August 1944, to Auschwitz. She describes the selection, the shaving, the rags they were given and the numb reaction of the prisoners to their inhumane treatment. Two weeks later, she was selected to work in a slave labour ammunition factory, where she was fortunate enough to be assigned to the kitchen — a much better and safer prison environment than Auschwitz-Birkenau. In May 1945, the German guards marched the prisoners to Prague, hours away, and disappeared. Liberation had come after nearly six years of Nazi occupation and terror.

Babey Trepman lived in Šiauliai, Lithuania, under the Soviet and Nazi regimes. Under the Soviets, September 1939 to June 1941, her family suffered because they were not communists; under the Nazis, they suffered because they were Jews. Pogroms followed Operation Barbarossa, the invasion of the Nazis into Soviet Russia, as did the establishment of a ghetto. Trepman managed to get work outside the ghetto, where there were more opportunities to smuggle in food. For awhile, she worked as a maid for a decent Lithuanian policeman and his wife, but it was a subsequent job as a translator in a garage whose head was a German soldier from the Wehrmacht that provided her with food, warm clothing and other kindnesses. However, many of her jobs during this period were dreadful; for example, she dug trenches on the Šiauliai airfield during the cold winter months and suffered brutal physical beatings and extreme humiliations. She and her family were deported from the ghetto on the last transport in July 1944, as the Soviet army approached. She wound up in Stutthof, called by many a "little Auschwitz," where she endured more physical humiliations before transfer to a munitions factory and later to Bergen-Belsen, from which she was liberated.

Shuttled between Lodz and Krakow to avoid deportation, Ida Dimant and her first husband were ultimately unable to hide and were forced onto a train wagon built for horse transports. She describes her Auschwitz barracks and the latrine vividly: "like herrings in tins, we sat on broken cement floors" and the latrine was a "stable with toilet bowls and to sit down was like being in a movie....five minutes and out!" Dimant recalls the degradation and the daily visits from Mengele, who terrified her sister so much that she wanted to electrocute herself on the barbed wire. Mengele saved her the trouble by "selecting" her. Alone and bereft from the loss of her sister, Dimant was transferred to a camp where she was beaten and made to do hard labour for eating "a few of those little kohlrabis, like red radishes" she was picking. She considers her survival a miracle.

Lastly, Fela Yoskovitz-Ross' moving poem, "Auschwitz," opens this section on women in the Nazi camps.

# Auschwitz
## Fela Yoskovitz - Ross

It was a hazy September morning,
And the sun was peeking through the clouds.
When hundreds of trains came to a stop,
Trains for miles and miles.
Pouring out people, no greetings, no smiles.
A great number of trains had come to this station.
A voyage of no return was our destination.
No happy faces rushing here and there
No luggage needed only the things that you wear.
In a countless line of people
We stood deprived, in fear and fright
Waiting for a verdict without a trial.

Who will live to see a tomorrow?
The morning sun or smiling moon?
In their hands lie our fates to rule
To carry out orders, heartless and cruel.
Why do sheep bleat when to slaughter they go?
Why can't they be like people, silent?
Hearts wrapped in a veil of terror
While partings went on without violence.
What right do they have to take possession of our souls?
Why were we chosen to give life for free?

And pressing tightly my mother to my side
Among thousands we stood
In that judgment line.
How powerful was the wish for a miracle to come
Or heaven and earth to split in a deadly revenge.
But nothing of this, nothing was in sight all around
Only grief and sorrow and minutes of life to count.
And to the zone of death went also my mother.
Useless was pleading for her life.
With her went my painful heart.
Her memory to carry in that empty part.
Old people, young people, children with their mothers
There she went with all the others.
A world of love and affection swept away in a tide
Crushed and crumbled and gone from my sight.

Blindly we followed those pointing guns,
Driven on a road made of human blood.
Faces hungry and skinny everywhere,
Human destruction was in the air.

Then sitting closely to each other on a wet, dirty soil
A pit of half-naked bodies curled in a coil.
We are forgotten and erased from the globe,
Degraded morally and robbed of our rights.
Nothing but torment in one of its kind
Agony of body and agony of mind.
And up above over our heads,
Silhouettes of guards moved back and forth.
The sound of boots cut the still of the night.
And their guns reflected in the flickering light.
And when that sleepless night was about to decline
Surprising it was to see a tomorrow.

The moon was slowly replaced by the sun.
Stiff and chilled we got up without sound
And in the mist of daybreak we stood in despair.
Free of sins and innocent souls.
Horrified eyes looked up high
For rescue and salvation from the sky.

To a death march we were driven
Walking and limping in tired bare feet
Till dragging pain made them bleed.
A few lost birds were flying above
Singing freely with no hope in their tunes.
Are we souls waiting to be lifted to heaven?
Or are we bodies forgotten to fall?
Give me the power to step from this march
Or a bullet to bring an end to this torch
"Don't be a coward," somebody said.
"Our hope must be stronger than the will to die."

Fela Ross after the war. Hanover, Germany, circa 1945.

1   Fela in Hanover, circa 1946–1948.
2   Fela and her husband, Jacob, with their newborn, Michael. Hanover, 1947.

A page from Catherine Matyas's diary showing the poem "Where to?" March 8, 1945.

# To Live in Freedom: Excerpts from Catherine Matyas's Diary
## Catherine Matyas

Excerpts translated by Marietta Morry and Lynda Muir (2016)

While she was under Nazi occupation, Catherine kept a diary sporadically, writing prose entries about the people around her, foods she missed and foods she abhorred but ate to satisfy her hunger, the differences between celebrating the Jewish holidays at home and in her current reality and, of course, death, a presence that defined her surroundings. Her poems were often more narrowly focused; for example, she confronted God, whom she questioned but never doubted. In the poem "Sentiments," written February 25, 1945, she felt that "death [was] about to claim [her]" and, at the same time, she felt certain she'd be "set free" while "At other times that a captive I'll always be." In the next two quatrains of the poem, she identifies her desire to laugh and sing and "enjoy prosperity." Her last quatrain speaks volumes about her real needs:

Should I reduce my sentiments to one?
No opposite is needed for this one
I would just like to roam the world freely
In a word, what is my wish? Liberty.

Although the war was not over and liberation still out of reach, Catherine expresses an unexpected emotion in the following poem:

"PRAYER OF GRATITUDE" FEBRUARY 17, 1945

My God, I give thanks to you in a whisper.
My grateful heart demands I make it known.
My trembling heart murmurs a prayer
And You should hear it, You alone.

We live in a time of war, when millions fight.
We must endure a horrible ordeal.
Wounded hearts and shattered souls are such an awful plight.
The suffering that fate has dealt is real.

There are no miracles, they say?
Though they're visible to the eye,
So where can we see one today?
We're still alive is my reply.

A prayer of thanks I have to give.
May we look forward to good health again.
May we enjoy ourselves while we live.
Dear God, may we be happy again.

Transferred to a holding area on Hackengasse 11 in Vienna, Catherine wrote "A Yellow Building."

MARCH 6, 1945

A yellow building stands at the end of the street
It stands silent, in isolation complete.
Who its tenants are no one cares, no one knows;
Tell us, yellow building, whom do you enclose?

The doors are locked, the windows are sealed,
But through sighs much suffering is revealed.
Oh, what tales they could be recounting
The silent walls of this yellow building.

So much wailing and so much weeping
So much tormented silence seeping
Agonizing days creep slowly by
While all night you hear people softly cry.

And laughter, should you ever hear it
Rest assured it's counterfeit
And even if there's some good cheer
You mustn't think that it's sincere.

A lot of sufferers dwell inside
Here the stateless temporarily reside.
People, I ask you, if you pass by the place,
To this yellow building direct your gaze.

In March, she writes of Strasshof as a "place of shame."

"STRASSHOF" MARCH 7, 1945

I hate this place to the core
Its loathsome name I abhor
In my mind evermore
Strasshof, place of shame.

They've left their sense of shame at the door,
People losing their minds here is what's in store,
Strong emotions I can't find words for
Strasshof, place of shame.

Though we cry for food
We get beatings galore
And on us insults they pour
Strasshof, place of shame.

May I see you no more
Nor hear the name I deplore
I am trying to wipe you from the score
Strasshof, place of shame.

In March, on her way to Terezín, she recorded her fears in another sixteen-line poem:

"WHERE TO?" MARCH 8, 1945

In the pitch dark, in a speeding train, I sit and ponder
Where this fast machine is taking me. I have to wonder.
Slowly, slowly, I am losing strength, my limbs feel weak.
Where will I end up? In despair, an answer from God I seek.

They are taking me to the end of the world, forward we go
Whether to life or to the gallows, I don't know.
I dream of a laden table still
Will there be a day when I'll eat my fill?

Will there be a small place where I can rest,
Where perhaps with oblivion I will be blessed?
Oh, will there ever be any small place for me?
A small corner will do if need be.

The wheels of the train make a clacking sound
Along the endless tracks is where they're bound.
We have no time, no aim in view.
Only one question, where to?

In Terezín, her wish for "pretty clothes" and other items that teenagers everywhere yearn for takes second place to her wish for freedom. She implores God for help:

"WHY DO I DREAM?" MARCH 13, 1945

Why do I dream of pretty clothes?
Of Switzerland as refuge from Jewish woes?
Of posh Pullman cars and sweet repose?
Like a caged bird longing for green meadows?

How can I know this is reality?
Not something false or illusory
Because promises are cheap, you see,
Unless they're kept faithfully.

God, help me to keep dreaming, I ask you,
So that one day this dream of mine may come true,
Not for a dress that is pretty and new
But because to live and sing in freedom is my due.

On March 24, 1945, on the holiday of Passover and in the poem of the same name, Catherine describes the traditional celebration and then writes of her despair in the verses,

I am describing how it used to be
In every decent Jewish family.
Now we have no country, no home at all,
And we celebrate Passover crammed inside four walls.

This Passover we have many reasons to wail and moan;
Still, I would like to bring some good cheer of my own.
There's an experiment I think we all could do
Let's steal from God is my suggestion to you.

Let's take away his Afikomen, shall we,
Let's ask him for peace and victory,
Let's get on our knees to beseech him and implore
So that he'll come to help his chosen people once more.

Fellow Jews, I ask that my advice you heed
To pray to God for help in our hour of need
So that a new exodus there will be
And from Theresienstadt we can break free.

We are Jewish, and Jewish we will stay
We observe Passover, a Jewish holiday
Fellow Jews, honour this day and never cease
May you all be granted blessings and peace.

Catherine Matyas wrote three longer entries in her diary. A haunting
one, which she wrote from the labour camp of Lobau, prior to her
transport to Strasshof, closes this piece.

"ANNIHILATION" JANUARY 13, 1945

I have been thinking a lot about what annihilation is like. What, in
effect, is death? How is it at all possible that all of a sudden man ceases
to think, that his heart stops beating, and that he no longer exists as
far as the world is concerned? And what does death feel like, or is it
true that by then man doesn't feel a thing? I've been thinking about
this a lot, but I couldn't picture it at all. Even in childhood we were
familiar with the word death, because when we are disillusioned we
often wish for it, yet when it comes to dying we are overcome by fear
and dread, and we start praying. This summer I found out what it
felt like to be in death's maw. It is wartime, bombs are falling, and I
want to write about the third bombing of Lobau. It was a beautiful
sunny summer day. It was lunchtime, we came home from work, and

lunch was just being served when the factory's air raid siren sounded. We usually fled to the forest to take shelter from the bombing. My younger brother was sick and my grandfather didn't want to take him outside, so against my grandmother's wishes I decided to stay behind as well. That's how we remained, in dead silence, the three of us in our small wooden barracks in the premises vacated by all the others. I have to remark that I had some strange feelings, as if I had a premonition, because it had been more than two weeks since the last air raid, and before that we had regular bombings all the time. But I suppressed these thoughts that surfaced, convincing myself that God would help us and nothing would happen. God did come to our assistance, but there's a story to it. At the beginning, for a long while everything was quiet and we were glad that we hadn't gone out to the far away forest, since nothing was happening to us. However, soon I could hear the drone of planes. They have arrived, I warned my grandfather, and the three of us lay down close to each other. The first and the second waves were both horrible. The bombers must have been flying very low. There was a gigantic noise and we felt as if the whole barracks was travelling. I put the pillow over my head and plugged my ears so that I wouldn't hear a thing. It didn't make a difference, I could still hear it all. I was praying. And after a short pause came the third wave. There was a huge bang and I stopped feeling anything, but only for a second, because I didn't die, my heart kept on beating. I looked up at the sky. I saw an enormous cloud of dust and everything was flying through the air. I felt a pain at my waist and suddenly, not knowing how I summoned the strength, I lifted the side of the collapsed barracks that was pinning me down, and in an inexplicable, strange manner, through a divine miracle, managed to slide out from under it. I talked to my grandfather. He was as calm as always. I think I must have been wailing a bit, with tearful eyes. This lasted only a few moments. You could hear the heavy drone again. This was the most terrible part. Grandpa, I said in a feeble voice, they are coming again. I was overcome by dreadful bitterness. Oh God, now that I have managed to survive, and the wall of the barracks didn't crush me, I should die now? There was no time to do much thinking. I put the pillow back over my head, and boom, it started up again. The air pressure was tearing the pillow from my head, but I hung onto it with all my might. I was close to suffocating, but that also passed. And then there was quiet, so pleasing to the ear, but instead of daylight there was darkness, so troubling to the eye. I couldn't believe that it was over for good, and I was still alive. It was God's miracle, and all I could feel in my heart was gratitude. I got up. There was no strength left in my limbs. Every part of me was trembling, and I was cold. All I could see was destruction, fire and darkness. All the barracks had collapsed and the German barracks was in flames. And then, although exhausted and shattered, we started putting out the fires, together with the now homeless people who had returned from the forest. It was no small matter, what I went through. Unforgettable. And at the same time I learned that when you die you don't feel a thing. And the moment our barracks caved in on us, the moment of annihilation, was beautiful precisely because I didn't know about anything. It's only bad up until death arrives. Still, I was afraid of death, and after having escaped from it, I gave thanks to God for having helped me and letting me keep on living because, who knows, we might still have a beautiful life ahead of us.

Catherine at age five or six with her parents, Esther and Ignatz. Debrecen, circa 1934.

1 Catherine in Debrecen after the war. 1945.
2 Catherine, age twenty, in her passport photo. Paris, 1948.

The Matyas family at the wedding of Catherine's granddaughter Karine. Back row, from left to right: Catherine's granddaughters Talia and Aliza; her daughter Yvette; Yvette's husband, Alan; Catherine; Karine; Karine's partner, Jordan, holding their daughter, Nico; Catherine's granddaughter Shira; her daughter Hedy; and Hedy's husband, Paul. In front, Catherine's grandson, David (right) holding son, Jackson; and David's wife, Katie, holding their daughter, Sydney. September 2015.

# Sometimes I Can Dream Again
## Suzanne (Katz) Reich

My first recollection of antisemitism affecting me personally dates back to when, as a second-grader in elementary school, I overheard my parents whisper how they must have me transferred to another school the following fall. A school where the teacher would not make derogatory remarks about Jewish people, so that I would be kept in blissful ignorance about the very dark clouds gathering on our horizon.

And so it was. I was allowed to grow, to dream and to learn, encouraged in my awakening desire to look for beauty and harmony all around me. I started to read voraciously; then, awkwardly, at first, but with ever more enthusiasm I started to write poetry and essays. Not about great events, nor about lofty ideas, only about the beauty of my little world and of the love I had for it. My parents made a superhuman effort to shield me from seeing the ugly realities growing all around me in Hungary of the early 1940s.

Oh, there were signs, but I preferred not to acknowledge them or give them too much thought. To dream, to write, to read, to watch all that lived and grew on our land — to admire their beauty — certainly took preference over pondering about my aunts' frequent visits to our farm in Pátroha. Anyway, it was wonderful to see my aunts on these visits, and the fact that they actually came to help my father sell this family-owned land of ours, as we could no longer own it, refused to register in my mind.

Then one day, my uncle Henrik was drafted. But he still had his officer's uniform, so it must have only been because of the advancing state of war, and they needed all the doctors, so what was all this talk about a "forced labour army" of Jewish men?[1] And restrictions of every kind, even for us? I could not believe it. Isn't my sister still attending Mr. Petris Bruno's dancing classes with many other Jewish girls and boys, and isn't my mother getting a Dutch-girl costume ready for her for the recital? Surely, she would not do that if things were really so bad for Jewish people. Maybe elsewhere, far, far away, but not in Hungary. Why, I even heard some talk of a floor-length taffeta gown for my sister's high school graduation in a year or so in Nyiregyháza, in the spring of 1944.

But then, later, during the winter, my mother became forever glued to the radio, listening to how the fighting progressed near Stalingrad, near the Russian-Finnish front, or whatever fronts our news reported on. Such distant battles — why was she so concerned suddenly? Then one day as we passed my former teacher in the village, instead of raising his hat as he used to do, he raised his arm, shouting, "Heil Hitler!" and laughed heartily as he looked at us. What's the matter with him, I wondered?

Still later, we got a new Jewish girl in our class at middle school;

---

1　Hungary's military-related labour service system was first established in 1919 for those considered too "politically unreliable" for regular military service. After the labour service was made compulsory in 1939, Jewish men of military age were recruited to serve; however, having been deemed "unfit" to bear arms, they were equipped with tools and employed in mining, road and rail construction and maintenance work. Though the men were treated relatively well at first, the system became increasingly punitive in nature. By 1941, Jews in forced labour battalions were required to wear a yellow armband and civilian clothes; they had no formal rank and were unarmed; they were often mistreated by extremely anti-semitic supervisors; and their work included clearing minefields, causing their deaths. Between 20,000 and 40,000 Jewish men died during their forced labour service.

her name was Erika, and it was funny how badly she spoke Hungarian. There were rumours that she and her family had escaped from Poland. Strange. Then I noticed how my mother would wipe a tear from her eyes more and more often after whisperings with friends and visitors who came to our house.

Soon, my father's youngest brother, Uncle Imre, was drafted. No uniform for him, only a yellow band and shipment out to the front at the Ukraine. My father seemed sadder than I had ever seen him; could Uncle Imre have been sent to the forced labour army?

Then I overheard that the land my parents and my aunts had not sold a few years before would simply be taken away from us. No more Glück farmstead. We moved from our beloved farm in Pátroha to the town of Kisvárda and made a home for ourselves in one of the apartments in my grandmother's house.[2]

Still, I went to school, I continued to study, I wrote, I read and, yes, I still dreamed. It was only my father's life that seemed all changed now; all of a sudden, he had no work to do. But he looked cheerful most of the time, and established some sort of daily routine for himself. At least a dozen times a day he would say, "Don't worry my darlings, the war is almost over!"

On March 19, 1944, German troops, the SS and Adolf Eichmann in command, arrived in Hungary. I was thirteen years old. Within a week or two, the Germans announced that all Jewish students must stop attending classes. Confusion and immediate dismissal of classes followed. On my way home that day, I heard that Mr. Fried the pharmacist had committed suicide. Later, I heard that my grandmother's tenant, Mr. Moskovics the Hebrew teacher, had his beard yanked and

---

2 Pátroha's 141 Jews were actually considered part of Kisvárda's Jewish community of 3,558 in 1939. Kisvárda is about 300 kilometres northeast of Budapest. In 1940, Jewish men in the Kisvárda area were conscripted into forced labour battalions; in 1942, they were deported to the front, and, in April 1944, they were deported to Auschwitz. www.jewishgen.org.

pulled by Hungarian authorities. I also heard how these brigands in a nearby village took an elderly Jewish man off the train and squeezed him between two wagons. What was happening? Could these events really be true? Were some people really capable of such random cruelty? My father was stopped by a couple of German soldiers on Mail Street one day, and they asked him politely to interpret for them in a store, that's all. Wasn't that proof that those bad things may be exaggerated, after all?

The principal of our school sent my report home with a Christian classmate, and it was accompanied by a special award of excellence for "Creative Writing and Hungarian Literature." I was ecstatic and ran to show my mother this wonderful honour — she so knowledgeable of good literature and poetry — but she just smiled sadly and wiped her tears away.

At the beginning of April, we learned that we had to sew ourselves yellow stars and wear them on all our outer clothing at all times. The exact shade of yellow and exact dimensions were specified, and to deviate from the order would mean "strict punishment."

A few evenings later, several armed Hungarian hooligans came to our door and announced that the local magistrate wanted to move into our house immediately, so we had better pack some belongings right away. We had one hour to gather our things and move to another part of the town, to a house on Deák Ferenc Street, which would now be part of the ghetto. My grandmother would be in the small apartment, her tenants the Moskovics family in the side apartment; the elderly couple Mr. and Mrs. Schwarcz in the back apartment, and, of course, my mother, my father, my sister, Marica, and I would occupy the large central apartment of the house.

We were allowed to take one cartful of belongings with us, including food and provisions, and of the remainder of our possessions, they — the gendarmes — would make an inventory. They seated themselves at our dining-room table, pointing us to one end with their rifles and demanded a list of all we owned, starting with money and jewellery. Only my ailing grandmother was seated; my mother and my father stood on either side of her, my sister and I behind them; and with rifles pointing at all of us, "the inventory taking" began. These new masters of our belongings ground their burning cigarettes into our beautiful red Persian carpet; and, for their final act, they brutally ordered my mother to hand over her wedding band to their commander. Then it was time to leave.

The ghetto was only about five or six blocks away but for the six or seven thousand people who were herded there during the next few days, it was an abysmal descent into hell on earth. A place where Satan, dressed in some German uniform, was the omnipotent ruler and rooster-feathered Hungarian gendarme demons served him only too willingly as lackeys with bayonets. A place where if someone died of any kind of horrible illness, people said, "He is the lucky one." A place where my mother's sister Aunt Ilonka and her husband, Uncle Ernö, were brought from a nearby village a few days after us, and we made room for them in our corner among the nine people already there. A place where I heard Aunt Ilonka talk of suicide, and a place where a very familiar voice was speaking to her of hope and the end of the war soon. A place where I got very sick, and where my father got our family physician, Dr. Szöke, (himself now in the ghetto) to examine me as he had done many times in the past. A place where I heard my father say, "Dr. Szöke, heal my child and I'll pay tenfold for your services when we are out of here." And, finally, the Kisvárda ghetto was a place which, on the last day of May 1944, had to be evacuated of all the Jewish people there, so they could be sent to "work" at some unknown destination in Germany.

We were told to bring fifty Pengös and one bag of belongings with us; we carried our best things on our backs. My mother made my sister and me wear our three very best dresses, one on top of the other. She and Aunt Ilonka cooked black coffee and sugar together, until it had a soft and grainy fudge-like consistency; cut into squares, we all had to fill our bags with those. The two women also baked dozens of cookies, and there seemed to be some sort of secret about those cookies. It felt like all our family except my grandmother and I knew that secret.

Accompanied by dozens and dozens of heavily armed, rooster-feathered Hungarian gendarmes with fixed bayonets, our procession made its way through the streets of Kisvárda, towards the so-called "small-station." I fixed my eyes on the tip of my fairly new shoes and never raised them as we walked past the familiar streets, houses, people, schools, trees and gardens. "Deported" from our homes, "deported" from the places I knew and loved and wrote so lovingly about. My cheeks kept burning as if they were set on fire.

We were to board cattle cars, eighty or eighty-five of us in each wagon. Old people, women and children were in the majority as most men between the ages of eighteen and forty-five were already in the forced labour service. We had nothing to sit on and were given two pails per wagon, one filled with drinking-water and the other empty, to serve as a toilet. The wagon doors were slammed shut and chained, the tiny windows high up wired and boarded thickly. After a lot of shouting outside, the train started to roll. Our family of seven, including my grandmother, Aunt Ilonka and Uncle Ernö, together with the family of Professor Schück, our respected and much-liked religion teacher in middle school and in *Gymnasium*, plus the Moskovics family filled one corner of the wagon. With the help of some of our bags, a kind of a chair was made for my grandmother to sit on. Somehow the toilet pail got curtained off, assuring us a little privacy, a little dignity. Resting our heads on each other, trying to breathe the little air we had, we managed to pass the night. If some people perished during the night, or during the subsequent nights in the wagon, I could not know. My parents, my aunt and Professor Schück, with their own bodies, created a little wall next to me and my grandmother.

In the morning, as if it were the most natural thing to do, Professor Schück unwrapped his *tallis*, prayer shawl, and his *tefillin*, phylacteries, and led this anguished group of people in morning prayers. At

SOMETIMES I CAN DREAM AGAIN 299

that moment, an agonizing thought entered my mind, a thought that torments me and haunts me these forty-two years later and refuses to fade with the passing of time: Are those gentle, saintly old people — tall, white-bearded Emmanuel Katz, and his tiny, frail wife, Ida Angyal of Újfehértó, my very old and very sick grandmamma and grandpapa — are they sharing our fate in another ghetto, in another train?

I somehow climbed up to the window and looked out, saw the sky and the sun and fields and wildflowers and trees and mountains and rivers; and dear, dear, merciful God, please, I beseeched Him, take this thought out of my head!

From that moment on, I spent most of my time near that window, or near some tiny crack at the side of the wagon, shutting out the realities of life behind me, believing only what I saw on the outside: the beauty of the countryside on a day in late May.

When the trains reached the Hungarian-Slovakian town of Kassa, the rooster-feathered gendarme lackeys delivered the trainload of defenseless Jews to the SS and returned to Hungary for the next trainload of Jewish people, and the next, and the next.

The Germans immediately shouted their own orders and instructions; not wanting to be left out of some quick and easy gains, they too threatened us with torture and death if we didn't hand over the fifty Pengös we were told to bring, and whatever other valuables we may still have possessed. At this time, my sister tearfully begged my mother and aunt to give the SS all our money and not take any risks. My mother remained very quiet, handed them nothing, and only when the train was speeding through the open Czech countryside — my sister still very frightened and crying — did she throw the carefully baked cookies out one-by-one through the window.

I later learned that my mother was still hoping to provide for her family with the money she baked into those cookies. By choosing her own method of unavoidable surrender, this became the first of her many brave acts to defy the German command. I don't remember exactly how long this journey lasted, but after some days and nights in that wagon, the train came to a stop, and we arrived at our destination — Auschwitz-Birkenau.

It was night, a cool and rainy Friday night, when the wagon doors were opened. There were shouts and there were dogs, there were shootings and there were flames, there was smoke and there was a horrible smell, and there were SS, and men in striped pyjamas, and there were trucks.

The first order we heard shouted was that the old and the sick had to get out first, as they were to be taken by trucks to the place we had to go. My seventy-four-year-old grandmother, Fannie Groszmann, the mother of Aunt Ilonka and of my mother; mother of four other daughters and of one son; grandmother of nine children and widow of Antal Glück from Kisvárda, thus became the first member of our family to be "selected."

The trucks were quickly filled, and as one truck was hurriedly driven by, we heard my grandmother call out the name of her first-born daughter, "Ilonka, Ilonka, where are you?" My aunt Ilonka lived until 1980, but she was never again free of the feeling that on that evening she had abandoned her mother.

The next order shouted was for men to line up on one side, women and children on another side. "Leave your bags in the wagons, and do it fast, fast, you cursed Jews. Run or the bloodhounds will get you fast enough." As a matter of fact, the men were forced to the opposite side from us as soon as we were out of the wagons. My mother, Aunt Ilonka, my sister and I stood numb, bewildered, frightened and cold. On the other side, the men were being marched away to an unknown destination. Suddenly my mother whispered to us to look carefully, focus our eyes in the direction she had focused hers. There, in the midst of all that terror and confusion, my father remained calmly standing, tall and straight, his silver hair illuminated by a light, and he raised his hands in the priestly way of the *cohanim*. Turned toward us, his lips murmured the ancient blessing he intoned over our heads every Friday evening, "...as He has blessed Sarah, Rebecca, Rachel and Leah...."

Whether my father was punished or not for thus interrupting his march, I will never know. Although I later learned that he lived eight or nine months after this evening, for me this was the last time that I saw my father, forty-seven-year-old Sándor Katz from Újfehértó and from Pátroha, Hungary.

We next marched single file in front of an SS officer, and miraculously, all four of us were sent to the same side. At the time, I did not yet understand my mother's intense relief at having my sister and me by her side, nor did I ever fully comprehend the reality of this death factory all the while I was an inmate there.

We were told to undress, leave our clothing neatly folded in one area, including eyeglasses, and were shaved — our heads, underarms and pubic hair all shorn by the men in the striped pyjamas. Oh, how could my mother become so strange and frightening in just a matter of minutes? And all the others who were normal-looking human beings just a little while ago? "You'll get your clothes soon, after showers and disinfectants, you cursed Jews" were some of the words I understood.

In the showers, and during the many subsequent showers we were ordered to take together during the four months in Auschwitz, I was to see the same strange look of relief in my mother's eyes that I saw after that first selection. When we came out, our clothes were no longer where we left them, and we were ordered to line up in rows of five, naked, in the cool and rainy night. We stood like that for several hours until male prisoners brought us some warm, brownish liquid to drink and marched us to a barracks, where there was some clothing. Not our own, but it hardly seemed to matter anymore.

Now dressed in assorted, ill-fitting, filthy, lice-covered rags and shoes, we were marched to Lager C, Barracks 29, where Iris was the *Blockälteste*, the supervisor of the barracks and Frieda was her assistant. They were young Jewish women, one from Slovakia, the other from Poland; inmates of Auschwitz for approximately two years. Iris made some sort of a speech in German and in Hungarian, and though I understood the language fairly well, I had no idea what she was actually saying: "The C Lager is a death Lager, you'll stay here only until the next selection or the one after, or the one after that. You will become Muselmann here, and then you'll be marched away.[3] There is no need for you to be tattooed here. You came in through the door, but you'll be leaving through the chimney." What on earth could she be talking about?

That blessed fog, which enveloped my brain at the time I beseeched God to take the image of my suffering grandparents out of my mind, suddenly got even more opaque, and I looked up at the chimney of the barracks' fireplace and wondered how one could actually go out that way.

We were then directed to some kind of bunks, which became our "homes" for the next four months. They were made of rough wooden planks and there were three levels to them. Twelve women were to occupy each level, and the thirty-six women in those incredibly small areas had a *Stubendienst*, leader of that little room, appointed from their midst.

Besides the four members of our family, I can recall only three other women at our level of the bunk: A tall, stately woman in a roughly woven, tattered grey linen dress, who was reputed to be a Countess, long ago converted to Christianity; her quickly deteriorating sister-in-law, the first among us to contact typhus; and an unbelievably skinny woman, a lawyer by profession, from the western part of Hungary. There were one thousand women housed in each of these barracks, and Lager C contained thirty-two of such wooden structures.

In a few weeks' time, another sister of my mother, Aunt Erzsike, with her daughter, Hedy, arrived from a Budapest suburb to our bunk. My beautiful aunt Erzsike — she with the high forehead and

---

3  *Muselmann* (German; Muslim) is a slang term used by camp prisoners to describe prisoners who were near death and seemed to have lost the will to live. Some scholars attribute the use of the word to the fact that the prostrate and dying prisoners were reminiscent of devout Muslims at prayer.

the dimples and the flawless skin and the lovely smile, flashing the whitest teeth imaginable, always wearing such fashionable clothes, groomed so impeccably at all times. Now her luminous brown eyes were sunk deep; she was shaved bald; dressed in rags; her expression was that of despair. I saw and I didn't see. I suffered and I was angry. I loved little and hated much. And I was mostly just numb. Unaware. Unfeeling. Unsure whether I even existed. And then I was angry again.

In the next day or so, my mother's cousins Anna and Rózsi arrived, and Anna became *Stubendienst* for the bunk opposite ours, on the other side of the barracks. Anna had a little authority now, and with her authority, our family had acquired a little protection. Anna became friendly with Iris and Frieda, and from them she often gained a few minutes' advance notice of selections. My mother then quickly made me eat whatever meagre amount of her own miserable ration she put aside for just such an occasion, and then kept pinching my cheeks to get them rosy in time. If after all her frantic efforts I was moved to the bad side anyhow, miraculously she still found a tiny piece of stale, sawdust-bread in the folds of her dress, or perhaps a small cigarette-butt, which were treasures enough to be used as bribes to some of our own hungry guards. A bite of even that sawdust bread was worth taking the chance of letting a kid be pulled away quickly by her mother.

Anna usually was my mother's accomplice in these barters; together they did this on the seven occasions that I was sent to the side of the *Muselmann*. My mother's eyes became such perfect mirrors of utter despair, giving way to relief and hope during the few seconds that this took place, but I was simply unable to comprehend.

I was not grateful for their efforts — risking their own lives in order to save mine. Not because I despaired and wanted to die. No, I did not believe I would be killed; therefore, I was only angry. My anger was directed mostly toward my mother. Why was my mother so reduced to bribery and cheating? How was it that she searched the garbage cans for some bits of raw potato skins and begged me to eat that? Why? When she triumphantly ran with a whole head of rotting cabbage she pilfered, she was caught and was beaten for it.

This lady, who knew whole segments of Dante's *Divine Comedy* by heart, who could quote Goethe and Heine, who read Lin Yutang and Stefan Zweig, and Pearl Buck and A.J. Cronin; she now uses bribery? This lady, who made exotic tortes and baked French pastries, whose culinary achievements were known far and wide, and who used to be such a gracious hostess; she now digs in garbage cans? This lady who subscribed to glossy fashion magazines and then had her dresses made accordingly; she now wears lice-covered filthy rags? And this lady, who after lighting her Sabbath candles used to spend Friday evenings relaxing with the latest issue of the *Literary Journal*, now cheats?

I was unable to comprehend that she was desperately trying to cheat an unnatural Death itself, all the while reaffirming Life as best as she could. I was only angry. Anna, meanwhile, did her own cheating of unnatural Death with still another young member of our family. Anna somehow got information that my cousin Gaby — after being separated from her mother, Aunt Irénke, and tiny sister Marika — was now also in Lager C. But she was in the KinderBlock, children's barracks, at the other end of the Lager, and Anna heard that all one thousand of those children were destined to be "liquidated" during that very night. The barracks was locked and guarded that evening, but come morning, Gaby and Anna were miraculously with us in Block 29. Gaby was a robust child, and despite her extreme youth, she lived and was able to reunite with her father, Uncle Henrik, after the war. Anna we loved as our daring and cool "cousin-aunt" during our childhood in Hungary, and we loved her after the war, as our warm and loving cousin-aunt in New York.

We stood for endless hours of *Zählappell*, roll call, in Auschwitz. At dawn, we were herded outside the barracks to line up in rows of five, and at dusk we lined up again. About three hours each time. I watched the sun come up and I watched the sun go down. I kept my eyes on the sky as much as I could, and I learned of the beauty and infinite variety of sunrises and sunsets. But it rained also in Auschwitz, and then there was only mud and the horrible smell. We huddled together while we waited for SS *Oberscharfürerin* Irma Grese, accompanied by lesser-ranking women guards and SS men, and even by one or two Jewish women officials, who did the actual counting. Oh, how envious I was of the women guards' clean clothes and neat appearances. The crisply ironed sky-blue shirts evoked greater emotions in me than the menacing shouts of "Achtung!" (Attention!) or the never absent whips and dogs.

On one of those first days in Lager C, postcards were distributed among us and we were ordered to write simple messages of greetings and send them to friends or relatives in Hungary. Our domicile had to be written as "Waldsee." What a pretty-sounding name (Forest Lake) the Germans managed to dream up to fool our not-yet-deported relatives with!

Then, on another day, mail of a very different nature made its appearance. Women in neighbouring Lager B, separated from us by a high-voltage electric wire fence, were throwing dozens of small, flat pieces of wood across to us. They told us that the bits of wood were some sort of letter either for us or for women in the next Lager. My mother scrambled for them with the agility of an athlete (we had to be very fast, before the guard in the tower would notice and shoot) and she was rewarded with what was probably the last joy of her life: my father's carved message on one of those small pieces of wood! "Take care of yourselves my darlings, I am working, and I am well, and we'll meet again soon! I love you. Sándor Katz." Uncle Ernö too sent such a "letter," as did several other men. On that day in Auschwitz, the tears shed by many women were tears of suffering mixed with the tears of joy.

We had a few more "letters" and then they stopped coming. Whether my father and the other men were caught, thus defying the German efforts of dehumanization, or they were taken somewhere from where writing was no longer possible, I will never know.

In only a few weeks, most of our family could almost qualify as *Muselmann*, but somehow we endured. The brown liquid for breakfast, barley soup with all kinds of dirt in it for lunch, and a small piece of sawdust bread for supper as our total nourishment took their toll. Our gums were constantly bleeding; we had various sores on our skin; we were dehydrating; we were weak. Easy prey for the lice all over us; scabies spread between our fingers and toes; and dysentery and typhus were rampant in most barracks. The three women I remember from our bunk were all marched away after three different selections.

Our shaved heads started to grow hair that resembled stubble on the fields. To my utter horror, the ash-blond hair that was shaved off my thirty-nine-year-old mother's head only a few weeks ago was now replaced with hair growing in almost completely white, much whiter than her older sisters'. Trying to prevent two daughters from rapidly approaching the *Muselmann* state took incredible efforts on her part, and it was beginning to show. Her body — but never her spirit — was paying. She could no longer control the unbearable itch the lice and scabies caused her and there were scabs all over her body. She was getting much too thin, and she coughed frequently. Still, she kept fighting valiantly, endured bravely, and hoped fervently.

One day she even found a scheme for trying to involve me more in the business of living. I will never know how and where, but she managed to get hold of a small piece of paper and a pencil stub and bringing it to me, said, "Here, write." But since my inspirations in the past were the simple joys of everyday life and the beauty all around me, her efforts proved to no avail at all.

Then, on another day, my sister, Marica, got separated from us. The selection came with very little advance warning, and all of a sudden the orders were given about how we had to line up: Single file, naked and run one-by-one, with one hand held high, in front of the officer. He looked for girls with blond hair and long fingers. How many

evil and cynical ways the Germans found to amuse themselves! At
the end of that selection, my blond sister, my dark-haired cousins
Hedy and Gaby, plus a second-cousin, Magda, also dark-haired, were
all marched away from Lager C. The rest of us remained there, my
mother and Aunt Erzsike silently weeping.

A little later that day, just as we started to assemble outside for
the evening *Zählappell*, we noticed some commotion near the elec-
trified fence, which separated Lager C from Lager B. There, women
were shouting back and forth to one another (shout it had to be, as
getting too near the fence would have meant electrocution) and as we
looked over to the other side of the fence, incredible as this seems,
there we saw my sister, Marica, and cousins Hedy, Gaby and Magda.
They were there working, they shouted to us, they were together, they
had a good *Blockälteste*, and they would go daily to Birkenau to some
factory, and were already tattooed.

Now my mother had a new challenge. Beg, pilfer from the kitch-
ens, search the garbage cans, deprive herself of whatever food she
could, then find a way to get it to my sister. Otherwise, my mother
feared, my sister would not be able to do the heavy work she must
do now. My mother's ingenuity knew no bounds. She somehow got
a long stick and a little dish, and every evening after *Zählappell* she
waited by the fence for my sister to appear. When my sister finally did
show up, my mother would lie down on her stomach on the ground,
at a right angle to the fence, and instruct my sister to carefully do the
same on the other side. The fence was after all very highly charged;
one touch and you were dead. The guards in their towers could also
easily spot you and shoot. But, in this manner — and despite my sister's frightened protestations — with the aid of the stick, she managed
to push a little food under that highly charged electric fence to my
sister all the while we were in Auschwitz.

It must have been over three months since we had arrived, and
there were fewer and fewer familiar faces in our barracks. One group
went, another came, and then still more were taken away. We now

sometimes heard what sounded like artillery fire from the distance, and each time our spirits rose. "The Russians must be nearing from the East, and the war will soon be over," was repeated often by the older women.

The weather turned very cool, and we shivered in our rags during the *Zählappell*. Then a new rumour spread like wildfire through Lager C: yes, the front was getting closer, the Germans will empty Auschwitz, and all of us will be sent to work in ammunition factories farther west into Germany.

Iris and Frieda assembled us very nervously for the last time, and the selections were made. Although it all seemed an even hastier procedure than usual, a selection it was nevertheless. The weakest looking women were sent away in one group, and my two aunts, my mother and I were still together after the selection. It seemed that we were on our way to the trains out of Auschwitz. We had to go shower and get "disinfected" first. While we got undressed in the shower-place, an officer appeared for still another selection. This time he used a flashlight to subject us to one more of his evil ways, while scrutinizing our naked, emaciated bodies. My mother usually put me ahead of her in selections, just behind Ilonka and Erzsike.

Only after the first three members of our family were together in one group did we notice that my mother was being sent to another group. Oh, my God, what was happening? It cannot be! There must be a mistake. She could work the most, you monster, you brute, you evil destroyer; you idiot, don't you know how tenacious and how enduring she is, and how valiantly she fought all this time, and she is brave and resourceful? Let her live, let her work, let her come with us, we need her, we need her love, we need her hope, and above all, we need her indomitable spirit. But because she had scabs from the conditions you imposed on us, you scum of scums, on that night in September 1944, you found her unfit to work in one of Hitler's ammunition factories.

When I looked back, I saw her make one more attempt to join me, but the SS man proved stronger than she did, and I saw him hurl her back to the row. The Germans murdered my mother that night. They burned her body, but they did not destroy her spirit. It lives on, now in the five grandchildren of Heléna Glück and Sándorné Katz of Kisvárda and Pátroha.

In a matter of seconds, the gentle fog, that blessed, blessed fog, came to my help, and enveloped my mind ever thicker. Maybe my mother was sent to another group, to another camp, and maybe I could somehow find her. People led me by the hand from one group to the other — all groups destined to leave Auschwitz — to check whether I could see her. Her group must have been taken away, as I could not find her in any of those remaining.

Into the showers we went, and my two aunts had the strangest looks in their eyes. No relief afterwards either, as was so often the case with my mother. Only incredulity, despair, pain and misery.

We were given roughly woven grey overalls and a pair of wooden shoes and were ordered outside, to the same railway platform where we had arrived a few months earlier. There, some burly male prisoners, lined up assembly-line style, handed us each a piece of sausage, a piece of liverwurst and a piece of bread, and told us to hurry inside the wagons. Cattle cars again, but after such a long time of eating slop, this little food that we all recognized as food soon filled our stomachs and raised our spirits a little. Some of the young women, those approximately eighteen to twenty-five years old, wetted their short hair with spit, and tried to press waves into it. A raggedy but colourful old dress was found somewhere, and it was promptly torn into small bandana-sized pieces, adorning the heads of these young women.

I don't remember how long we travelled, nor the direction the train took us, but the name on the station where we stopped and were ordered out was Teplitz-Schönau. I guessed it to be in the Sudetenland of occupied Czechoslovakia. My recollections remain hazy from these days, as my mind seemed foggy, with only occasional periods of rational awareness.

We were only a few hundred half-starved, unarmed, defense-less women in that group, but once again we had a whole contingent of heavily armed, dog-accompanied SS soldiers awaiting us in Teplitz-Schönau. A gaunt, Prussian-type *Oberscharführer*, and one next in rank, briefed our group. We were brought there to work in a bomb factory, and we would be treated as slave labourers. We worked alongside other prisoners and shared the same foremen and supervisors in the factory, but our camp was separate, guarded day and night by the SS.

We were marched to our barracks, which were a big improvement over the barracks of Auschwitz. They were small, perhaps twelve or fourteen women were to occupy each, and we had bunks to sleep on, two women on each bunk. We were to get a meal of boiled potatoes soon, but first was the business of shaving. What shaving, our newly appointed *Blockälteste* protested, much to our amazement. Yet, the SS Commandant took a fancy to her, and her black curls remained untouched. The rest of us had a two-inch wide strip shaved in the middle of our heads, from the front to the back.

My two aunts were not housed in the same barracks as I was. The youngest girls were separated and were told that they would do farm work or work outside in the coal yards shovelling coal needed for the boilers of the factory. A few people got coats, but most didn't. I was among the latter.

By now, most everyone was left without family members, and we learned to rely on each other. I remember many people who became my friends in this camp. There were perhaps ten or twelve of us under the age of fifteen, and one way or another, most of the other women tried to help us. No one could possibly do more for me than Aunt Ilonka and Aunt Erzsike did. The two of them, because they worked in the dangerously toxic environment of the bomb-factory and probably because they worked alongside prisoners-of-war for whom rules of the Geneva Convention were perhaps followed, received a ration of milk daily. My aunts made sure that one-third of their milk ration was somehow smuggled to me each evening. Since I heartily disliked milk even while I was so very hungry, Aunt Ilonka showed me how to obtain a yogurt-like product by leaving my milk near the heating overnight. On one occasion, which would be difficult to forget, Aunt Ilonka and Aunt Erzsike brought me a few cubes of sugar they got from a prisoner, and I still cannot decide which one of us took the greatest delight in this unbelievable feat.

The outside work we did was hard, and we were always cold. November came, and December, and we still cleared the fields in our wooden shoes, without socks and without coats. True, we were sometimes rewarded in this arduous task by finding the odd carrot or potato left in the ground after harvesting, but more often we just kept yearning to be inside those cozy-looking farmhouses that bordered the fields so alluringly.

One day I got sick with fever. Our *Stubendienst*, a young woman from the Carpathian region of Slovakia, accompanied me to the infirmary. Mrs. Frankl from Kisvárda, a good acquaintance of our family, was in charge of the infirmary. There were no medicines, but it was clean and warm in there, and although my fever subsided very fast, Mrs. Frankl knew that I must remain in that place a few extra days. She had absolutely no hesitation about rubbing the thermometer quickly with her fingers until it registered some fever, and she showed it to the SS guard whenever he came to check on who was getting well enough to send out to work.

The Carpathian *Stubendienst* looked out for me, too. I remember many mornings when she went around screaming for all to hear how we must get out right away and line up for work while with her head and her eyes she motioned to me and to Ági, another thirteen- or fourteen-year-old, to hide wherever we could. Then, when the rest of the group had gone to work on the frozen fields, and there were still women needed to work in the warm boiler room, she would send Ági and me to that preferred workplace.

Ági, by this time, belonged to that rarest of rare phenomena of concentration camp inmates who was still together with her mother in Teplitz-Schönau. They had both survived all the selections in Auschwitz, and were regarded by most of us with a kind of loving awe.

My two aunts worked alongside Ági's mother in the bomb factory, so they were the first ones to know that the explosion one night in the factory took the life of Ági's mother, shattering the only live mother-and-child union in our midst.

Sometimes, if we lingered in the cold wash barracks a little longer than the few minutes it took us to wash ourselves with the icy water, we would encounter Edith. Edith, or "the Angel," as many of us referred to her, was a beautiful seventeen-year-old blond girl among us in this camp. No one knew much about her, as she never spoke a word, but she came often to the wash-barracks, perhaps to seek solitude there. She would have a faraway, empty look in her enormous grey eyes, until one such moment when that empty look would transform into something ethereal, and she would then suddenly leap high in the air. With her slender, lithe body she would do arabesques and grand jetés and pirouettes, and literally soar in that dismal, chilly place, just as we imagined an angel would soar, until she'd drop from exhaustion. Her eyes would then become empty once again while ours just welled with a heavy flood of tears.

Ági and I were becoming very close to each other, and soon we had a third friend, Heléne. Heléne came from the Carpathian city of Munkács, which once held the greatest number of Hasidic Jews in Slovakia. She was our age, but her dignity and social awareness elevated her to responsible adulthood and left an indelible mark on my memory.

One day while we were assembled in front of our barracks for *Zählappell*, a group of young German soldiers, barely twenty to twenty-five metres from us, were waiting for the rain to stop before marching us out to the fields. They were under cover, and all of them were eating apples. Red, shiny, crunchy apples. They chattered animatedly; then, just as if one of the soldiers had been telling a very funny joke, they all started to laugh heartily and looked in our direction. Within seconds, they pelted us with their apple cores and watched delightedly as the hungriest among us were unable to resist this almost forgotten delicacy. With all the authority that slight and fragile fourteen-year-old Heléne could command, she quietly but firmly said to Ági and me, "Don't pick up those apple cores; let us not provide them their entertainment." I have long ago forgotten what pangs of hunger feel like, but I will never forget how on this day Heléne helped to make me feel strong and full of dignity.

As winter started to give way to early spring, a truck pulled up in front of the camp and the *Oberscharführer* ordered eleven of the youngest inmates into the truck, Ági, Heléne and I among them. We were told that we'd be taken to a nearby camp for another kind of work, work that would be easier for us, and better use would be made of our efforts.

Trucks filled with the youngest people from camp brought dread to most of the women, and my two aunts hugged and kissed me, trying quickly to hide their tear-soaked faces. We travelled in that truck perhaps five hours, with only one elderly armed guard accompanying us. The truck was driven mostly on unpaved roads, and we came to a place that we were told was called Oederan. When we were ordered out, we saw a fair number of women standing outside, in the unmistakable rows of five of *Zählappell*.

What if? My heart started to pound, and as soon as we were told to join the women I began to ask, "Is there a Sándorné Katz here?" "Have you known anything about her? Has anybody met her in another camp perhaps?" "Would you know her?" "Did you see her?" My queries were answered with silent headshakes.

We were led inside a very large hall, all filled with wide bunks and small, night-table-like boxes next to each bunk. Four of us were to occupy each bunk, and Ági, Heléne and I were joined by tiny fourteen-year-old Sári from Máramaros-Sziget. During the next few months, the four of us managed to sustain one another with the kind of emotional and physical support that was as close to love as we were capable of giving.

We were to work in a cartridge factory on eight-hour shifts, changing shifts every three weeks. The 11:00 p.m. to 7:00 a.m. shift was particularly difficult since lights had to be out in that huge sleeping hall by eight o'clock in the evening. No matter how hard we tried to stay awake during night-shift weeks, we never managed it, and so every evening soon after we fell asleep, we were being awakened again.

The factory was immense and there were many prisoners-of-war working there. Even our camp doctor (there was one actually assigned to us here) was a Russian woman, captured some years before. She was morose and not talkative, in contrast to the men who were working in the factory. It was the first time that we had contact with male prisoners; although they were forbidden to talk to the Jewish slave labourers, there were many ways they found to communicate with us. There was one particularly handsome Czech man who always left the work area a few seconds after one of the young Jewish women from France left her lathe to go to the washroom.

The homelands of the Jewish women in this camp were more varied than in the camp near Teplitz-Schönau. Here in Oederan, there were Jewish women from Poland, France, Italy, Greece and, of course, from Hungary, Slovakia and Transylvania. It was the first time in my life that a Jewish woman from Poland befriended me, and I am still warmed by the glow of that friendship. Her name was Ruth, which for me alone bordered on the miraculous. A real biblical name by which she was actually called, and it was not only her "Jewish" name? I had not known of such things in rural Hungary, and I was truly enchanted by it. Ruth spent endless hours combing my uneven, short hair and trying to get rid of the lice in it.

Our work in the factory was indeed easier than the work we did in Teplitz-Schönau. We were to drill a small hole into the centre of the cartridges, and German political prisoners, who were our foremen, oversaw that we did it quickly and accurately. No matter that they themselves were prisoners, their sympathies were with the "Vater-land" (Fatherland), and they guarded us rigorously.

As children, we were in many ways less suspect of sabotage than were the adult workers. Our youth was quickly utilized by the French prisoners who taught us to drill the holes slightly off centre in the cartridges, rendering them completely useless. We followed their in-structions carefully and then delighted in making up stories about what would happen on the battlefield when these cartridges would be used by German soldiers.

It was in the storytelling that I eventually made my contribution to our small group of four friends. Sári was the most practical among us; she was quick and she was clever, and she lent a helping hand in much of the work we could not manage ourselves. Helping others came naturally to her. She even found a way to wash our overalls in the buckets of hot, soapy water under the huge lathes in the factory and did it with the speed of lightning so she was never discovered.

Ági, from Szekszárd, was sweet and gentle and breathtakingly beautiful. She was also a born peacemaker. If, in our misery about constantly being hungry or sleepy during the night-shift weeks, we had unjustly harsh words for each other, it was Ági's soft voice and gentle manner that helped us to understand a little and bear with one another better.

Heléne, from Munkács, not only brought her faith and her pride in Judaism to our little group, but she brought us her dignity and her social awareness at a time when those qualities were so difficult to come by.

I brought my stories of things beautiful. During long hours when we could neither sleep nor work and hunger tormented us and the only thing we could do was to kill bedbugs or lice, I would recall books of great literature I had read not so long ago. I would re-tell their contents in my own words, and my friends sat enthralled. Or I would talk about the farm and tell about watching the miracle of baby chicks and baby geese and ducklings hatching in the spring; or describe the graceful ritual of a wheat harvest festival in midsummer; or the feverish excitement of plum harvests and outdoor plum jam making in early autumn; or the joyful buzzing of the spinning room in the dead of winter. I dreamed, and I helped my friends to dream.

One day, I began to write poems again, at first only to help others in re-writing some popular songs into parodies of camp life and later, poems of my own. Poems of hope, of courage, of endurance and of liberation. I found my voice, and it was wonderful. The women who spoke Hungarian passed my little booklet of nine poems from one to another until it reached our *Blockälteste*. A few days later, the *Blockälteste* informed me that in order not to endanger us all, she had my little book of poems burned.

A young woman named Ilonka, perhaps twenty years old, led the group of Jewish women in Oederan in religious observances. We had no calendars, but somehow she always knew when each of the holidays were; she knew the days for Rosh Chodesh; she obtained bits of candles and she knew when to light them; and she knew the exact day we would observe Pesach in 1945. I had heard that she was a rabbi's daughter, and I heard that twice a week she did not eat her food rations at all but gave them to the weakest women in our group. When Pesach came, she gathered as many of us as she could around her, and by memory only, she recited most of the Haggadah. "...This year we are slaves; next year we may be free...."

Our freedom became a reality in a matter of a few weeks. When the sound of heavy artillery fire reached us loud and clear once again, the Germans did their thing and marched us to the trains. We were herded into open wagons, with four or five armed Germans to guard us in each wagon. We were shunted around for a few days, without food, without water, always alongside regular passenger-trains that carried German soldiers. On several occasions, the trains were attacked by machine-gun fire from low-flying airplanes. While our German guards ducked low, many of our women stood up and waved.

We got to Theresienstadt, together with other trainloads of prisoners from nearby camps. I later heard that plans were made to mine Theresienstadt with explosives, but time did not permit it. The Red Army of the Soviet Union liberated the city in May 1945. Some of the Russian soldiers who marched into Theresienstadt hugged us and kissed us and shared with us the only commodities they themselves had: cigarettes and vodka and champagne. I drank champagne for the first time in my life and was delirious with joy.

I will search and I will find, and I will rejoice and I will love, and I will forget and I will dream. It took me almost twenty years to fully comprehend the realities of Auschwitz. Twenty years to realize that I can never forget the horrors I saw there, and that my dreams in fact became shattered during those four months in Auschwitz.

It has taken a further twenty years of trying to put the shatters partially together — years of love and caring from my husband and from many other good people who helped me to love again, to rejoice again and sometimes even to dream again.

1

2

1  Suzanne's family before the war. In the back row, left to right: Suzanne's aunt
   Ilonka, who survived; her father, Sándor, and her mother, Heléna, both whom
   were murdered; her uncle Henrik, who survived, and her aunt, who perished. In
   the front row, left to right, are her sister, Marica (Mary), who survived, her cousin
   Gaby, who survived; her grandmother, who was murdered, and Suzanne.
2  Suzanne (right) with her sister, Mary, after the war. Circa 1946.

1  Suzanne after the war, date unknown.
2  Wedding photo of Suzanne and Peter Reich. Montreal, June 18, 1950.
3 & 4  Suzanne and Peter, circa 1950s.

1 At Mary's wedding. From left to right: Peter, Suzanne, Mary and her husband, Abe. Circa 1950.

2 Suzanne and Peter with their children, Edwina and Sandra. Circa 1963.

1  Suzanne (front, left) with family in New York, circa 1970s. Back row, left to right: Suzanne's cousin Gaby; her brother-in-law, Abe; and her sister, Mary. In front, beside Suzanne, is Gaby's daughter Irene.

2  Suzanne and Peter at their home in Montreal, circa 1990. In the background is one of the tapestries that Suzanne created.

3  Suzanne in the kitchen, expressing her joyful spirit and love of cooking. Montreal, circa 1992.

# If the World Had Only Acted Sooner
# Rebekah (Relli) Schmerler-Katz

*This testimony, a description of the darkest chapter of my life, is dedicated to my dearest children, grandchildren and generations to come.*
1996

I was born and raised in Rachov, a small town in Czechoslovakia, where I was a loyal citizen of a country that was one of the most democratic and progressive in those days in Europe. I loved Czechoslovakia and never lived anywhere else. We were a prosperous family of five: my most loving parents, Rose and Mordechai (Martin), my oldest sister, Sidonia (Sidi), who was only eighteen months older than me, and my brother, Mendi, who was four years younger than me. We were also surrounded by loving grandparents, aunts, uncles and cousins.

I was about twelve years old when the adults in our Jewish community started to express fear and concern about the rise of Adolf Hitler, the Chancellor of Germany. We saw very worried faces and heard terrible, frightful discussions about this dangerous dictator who promised his fellow Germans he would eliminate the Jewish race. We suddenly became little adults. I was no more the carefree little girl, the tomboy who loved to laugh and have fun. We were growing up very fast, scared and worried about what would happen to us next.

In March 1938, Hitler annexed and occupied Austria, the country of his birth, where his fellow Austrians welcomed him. It was September 1938 when he started to demand a part of Czechoslovakia called the Sudetenland, which was inhabited by a German majority. Little Czechoslovakia mobilized its army against the giant Hitler's Germany, but without any fight, Czechoslovakia was forced to give in to Hitler's demands and the German army marched in.[1] As Hitler's appetite grew and with the world standing by watching silently, in the spring of 1939, his armies also occupied the western part of Czechoslovakia. Germany and Hungary were allies and the eastern part of Czechoslovakia, where we lived, was ceded to Hungary in the spring of 1939.

Suddenly our town was called Rahó, we became Hungarian citizens, and every Jew had to have documents on hand as proof of Hungarian citizenship. It didn't matter how many generations back we had lived in this place. To obtain these papers, people faced great difficulties, knocking on closed doors, struggling with bureaucracies and, of course, great expenses. Poor people could not afford this. In July 1941, the people who had no papers were rounded up and sent across the border to Poland. Poland was war-torn, and poor, homeless people with only the clothes on their backs became easy prey for the antisemites.

The family of my sister Sidi's husband, Leibi, was deported at this time. Leibi's father had left for Budapest to try to obtain proof of Hungarian citizenship for the family, but to no avail. Leibi's six siblings and his mother perished in Poland. Leibi survived because he was in a labour camp and he only learned about the family's tragedy when he came home. He also found out that his father had been shot in Budapest and thrown into the Danube River.

---

1   The Sudetenland was the western border region of former Czechoslovakia that was inhabited primarily by ethnic Germans before World War II. In an attempt to prevent war from breaking out, Britain, France and Italy agreed to the annexation of the Sudetenland by the Third Reich as part of the Munich Agreement, which was signed on September 30, 1938.

In March 1944, Germany occupied Hungary, and we now faced many of the same laws other Jews had suffered under the Nazis. We had curfews and were allowed to leave our homes only at certain hours of the day. We had ration coupons for bread and certain groceries that were hard to obtain during the war and so when we were allowed to go shopping the shelves in the stores were already empty. After the curfew was lifted, our Hungarian mayor ran from store to store checking under the counters to see if, by any chance, a kind grocer had left any bread for sale to give to the persecuted Jews. He wanted to make sure there was none left for us.

We had to be recognizable as Jews by wearing a yellow Star of David of a certain size sewn on the left side of the chest. Our radios were confiscated and our permits for any business or trade had to be handed in. If a Jew had a store, any non-Jew had the right to put in a request for the business and the Jewish proprietor had to walk out without any compensation. The same thing applied to our residences. There were soldiers in the streets and, whenever they were in the mood, they beat up Jews. New laws against us came out every day.

We struggled to survive under terrible conditions — persecuted, living in fear, but considering ourselves fortunate that we were still at home. To survive, we tried to be optimistic. There were stories going around that the Soviet army was approaching our borders and we would soon be liberated. A little story here and there sparked hope in our very bleak situation. The Soviet army did come closer and closer. But too late for us Jews.

It was the spring of 1944, during Passover, when two German soldiers were stationed in our house. They didn't bother with us, and they even asked my brother to play chess with them, but we were terrified. We celebrated the two seders in our kitchen, praying so very, very quietly that we hardly heard each other. In the middle of Passover, the soldiers left for the battlefield. I wouldn't say that we were relieved because we didn't know what to expect the next hour.

It was six o'clock in the morning the day after Passover, April 16, 1944, when we were awakened by my uncle Sandor, my father's younger brother, who was under our window telling my father to go into hiding. Uncle Sandor had somehow managed to bribe some officials and become a "privileged" Jew, which meant that he had some connections. He had found out that the Germans wanted my father to help round up the Jews of Rachov; the Germans chose the more prominent Jews of the community for this job. Hearing this, my father rushed off into the mountains, where a reliable man who worked for us lived. Father promised that as soon as he arrived, he would send a message to us through this man.

Only an hour or two after Father left, two Jewish boys, friends of our family, knocked on our door with the following message, "Jews who are not in the synagogue by ten o'clock in the morning will be shot." We quickly packed a few necessities and some bedding. As we were leaving our house, there stood the Hungarian couple who had occupied our buildings and businesses, which were given to them by the government. The woman was laughing and yelling, "Look how they are taking the Jews away!" At this point, I couldn't resist and said, "Your turn will come, also." She started to scream, "Police, police!" Her husband seemed to quiet her down.

By ten o'clock, the Jews of our town, aside from my uncle and his family, were in the synagogue and in other buildings, wherever they were ordered to be. Meanwhile, the man who hid my father arrived with a message from him. We sent him back immediately with the news of our situation, and my father arrived just as we were approaching the synagogue. We spent a few days and nights in the synagogue sleeping on the floor, guarded by soldiers. At this point, our father told us that we must survive and eat anything, whether kosher or not, even pork. Again, we were moved to a school building for a few days. Then, we were lined up and taken to the train station. We were brought to a city in Hungary called Mátészalka. A part of this town had been designated for a ghetto.

We were moved to an attic of a big building with many more families, and our home became a few square yards on the attic floor. The majority of these families were from Hungary proper. Because we originally came from another country, we were foreigners to them. We were told that we would have to choose one person to be in charge of our affairs. In spite of being strangers to these Hungarian families, my father was elected for the job. The little bread we received daily had to be distributed equally among us. Poor us — our family got the worst deal, always getting the bread that was broken or that had pieces missing.

After two or three weeks in the ghetto, we were gathered and taken to a cemetery. We were a few hundred people lined up in fives, standing and waiting. It was the month of May, on a beautiful sunny and warm day. Everything was green and in full bloom. In spite of the hundreds of people lined up, there was no sound, except for the birds chirping and here and there a cry of a baby. In front of us, the Hungarian gendarmes started to line up machine guns. Every few minutes, they adjusted their guns aimed at us again and again. It seemed like those sadists enjoyed seeing the fear in our faces. Someone in the crowd dared to ask one of our tormentors what would happen to us. The gendarme answered clearly and loudly, "By tonight, all of you will smell the violets from the bottom." This inhuman explanation was not needed. We all understood what would follow.

I was young and loved spring, my favourite season of the year. I looked around and wanted to take in everything around me for the last time. But our journey didn't end at the cemetery. We were taken away one by one and our pockets and bodies were searched for valuables. I was standing next to my father. He had our five citizenship papers in his breast pocket. As I mentioned before, these papers meant life to us. When the police touched my father's breast pocket, he frantically uttered, "These are our citizenship papers." The police tore out the documents, threw them to the ground and yelled, "You will not need these anymore!"

The gendarmes marched us through some tents until we arrived at a field where there was a long freight train. We were counted and a number of people were sent into each railway car. The five of us were holding on to one another. As we were counted, they stopped right after my parents and my sister and loaded them into the boxcar. That meant my brother and I would have to go in the next one. At this point, my parents and I started to beg to be together. Although two people offered to change places with us, they were not allowed. Again, I pleaded with the gendarmes, and this time they beat me up with a club.

My brother was quiet and sad during the whole journey. He looked as if he knew that this was our last trip and that we would never see each other again. I told him to remember the words Duparquet, Quebec. This was a little mining town in Canada where my uncle, my mother's brother, lived. If we survived, I said, this should be our meeting place.

I can't recall how many days and nights we were on the train sleeping on the floor without any food, only stopping once a day when the pails, which were given to us to relieve ourselves, were emptied. We realized that we kept going north, toward Poland. We saw cities destroyed completely, only shells of buildings after heavy bombardments. I remember seeing the city of Krakow black from smoke and fire. We kept going north, and then west.

One early morning the train stopped. We looked out and saw young men in striped blue and grey pyjamas, cloth caps on their heads. I soon figured out that what I had considered to be pyjamas were prisoners' uniforms. It took a few hours until our turn came to be unloaded. My brother and I met with our parents on the platform. The men in the striped clothes helped us off the train. There was a lot of noise, screaming and yelling. We were completely confused. There were Germans in uniforms holding big dogs walking up and down the platform. The prisoners in the striped clothes were Polish Jews. They yelled and hurried to line us up by fives. Amid the terrible panic, I realized that our group was separated from the children, the older people and the men.

One of the prisoners looked at me and asked me to show him my mother. When he saw her he told me, "Kiss your mother; kiss her again." I suddenly realized that this was a goodbye forever. I asked him, "Will we stay alive?" He answered emphatically, "You young ones, yes." I don't know what happened to me in that moment. I understood what he meant and to this day I am embarrassed that I understood and yet, I felt that I wanted to live. It seems that life is precious even under the worst circumstances. At this moment, I was willing to part from my dearest mother, whom I loved so much. This young prisoner grabbed my mother and another mother, lined them up together and told them just to go ahead. Sidi, another girl and I were to follow behind them. The long line kept moving. From a distance we saw a tall young man in a uniform showing the moving line where to go. We had walked just a few yards when our mother slipped out of her line, grabbed Sidi and me, and said quietly to us, "I want to go with my children," and so she walked with us toward the uniformed man. We saw him looking at each person separately and gesturing them to the right or left. He was playing God. He decided who would live and who would die.

Sidi approached first, and he told her in German, "Right." Then came mother and I was behind her. I don't know how, but I lightly pushed her back to follow Sidi's direction. I did this in terrible fear and subconsciously. And the demon who played God told mother, "Right." That's all that mattered. I was in a daze. I was told the same and the rest was not important anymore. We were together. I don't even know when we parted from Father and our brother. It probably happened in the chaos on the platform.

Again, we were lined up by fives. SS men walked up and down and we were told to look in their direction. We were still wearing our own clothes and Sidi and I were wearing identical dresses that had a necktie attached on snaps. Sidi was two rows in front of me when she noticed that twins were being selected and taken away from us. Some people with blue eyes were also taken away. She turned around and whispered that I should unsnap my necktie. Only after the war did we find out that twins were selected for medical experiments. Next we were taken to a building where we were told to strip naked, leave our clothes there and keep only our shoes. Young Jewish prisoners who were forced to work for the Germans took us one by one, shaving our heads and pubic hair. Our shoes were wiped off with some disinfectant and we were chased into showers. After the shower we all got a grey cotton dress and were taken to barracks.

On our arrival, we were given a speech. We were told that our barracks was called Block 14A and that in Auschwitz-Birkenau we would be called only by numbers, not our names. Mother's number was 20838, Sidi's 20839 and mine was 20840. As a rule, we would have roll calls twice a day, but there could be exceptions when there would be more. When we heard the whistle, that meant *Zählappell*, roll call, and we would have to run as quickly as possible and line up by fives. We had to understand that the roll calls were the most important things in our miserable lives. God forbid if we were ever a moment late — this could cost us our lives. Most of these orders were given to us by Jewish girls who were supervised by the SS men and women. They were the prisoners from Poland and Slovakia who had been incarcerated from the beginning of the war and had built many of the barracks and other buildings in the camp. We considered these early arrivals to the camp as the "pioneers" of the camp.

We were shown our bunk beds (wooden planks) that had to accommodate about fourteen people on three tiers. Each tier was approximately two metres wide. Nobody could stretch out on an area so small, so we were sitting on top of one another. There were cries and even fights among the people accusing each other of sitting on one's arm or leg or even falling asleep on someone's head. People became animals.

It is hard to describe a day in Auschwitz. We were awakened early in the morning by a whistle and a cry of "Fast! Fast!" That meant we had to run quickly to the exit door where the girls in charge were standing with straps, and then line up for the roll call. An SS man or a woman guard counted us. After the roll call, we were taken to the latrines. We had to relieve ourselves very quickly because the supervisor was walking up and down between the latrines with a whip and hitting our naked bottoms. After that we were taken back to the yard around Block 14 and given our daily ration — a slice of bread, a pat of margarine or marmalade and a warm liquid with two or three pieces of turnip in it. We spent the rest of the days in our yard, except when we were taken for showers or for selections. Again, we had to march naked in single file in front of the SS men; the weaker ones were selected for the gas chambers.

One day as we were standing in the yard under the burning sun, we heard someone calling our names. Our auntie Rella, my mother's younger sister, appeared with her shaven head and with the same grey dress we had. Rella had been married before the war and had two little children, a girl of seven and a boy of three. She lived in a small town about 170 kilometres from ours, but we were a very close family and in constant contact. Since her husband was younger than my father, he had been recruited into the forced labour service, specifically for Jews, in December 1943. She didn't hear from him ever again and so she struggled all by herself with her two small children. She was one of the many people who were deported for not having citizenship papers. She had run from place to place with her little ones, hiding here and there. But fate had brought us together, and here she was with us in Auschwitz. We were looking at each other, hugging, kissing and crying. How could she have found us here in this hell, where no one deserved to be, where even a bird had no desire to visit? She explained that one day girls passed by her Block, carrying cans of soup. She heard her name being called and then someone told her that her sister, my mother, was in Block 14. Rella dared to sneak over, saw us and ran back to her yard in Block 1. This was a risky feat and could have cost her her life. When we asked about her children, she said that on their arrival she was separated from them. When she had begged the man in the uniform to go with her children, he said that she would be reunited with them on the weekend. Later, she saw him again. She ran after him, asking about her children. He answered, "It is too late."

We went through about ten selections while in Auschwitz between May and the end of July 1944. Our greatest fear was how Mother would survive because at the age of forty-eight, she was considered old. Most of her contemporaries had been selected for the gas chambers. We would rub her temples with the little margarine we had, so that the greyish hair that had started to grow would look dark.

One day we noticed a girl wearing a pair of red shoes with red leather tassels. We asked her for a tassel and she gladly gave it to us, but she wanted to know what use we had for it. We spat on the tassel, rubbed hard and some color rubbed off. This became rouge for mother's cheeks. The little tassel became our most treasured asset. But somewhere between the showers, latrines and selections, we lost the tassel. My sister and I couldn't stop blaming each other for the loss.

The days and nights in Auschwitz were more or less the same, and I don't know which were worse. Being outside the barracks during the day was a nightmare. It seemed that the Germans knew what site to choose for a death camp, because the climate there was hell. When the sun was out, it burned like in the desert. Many of our girls had second- and third-degree burns. When it rained, it rained non-stop and we were freezing. The *Lagerstrasse*, the paths between the barracks, were a sea of mud. We were barely able to lift our feet from the heavy mud that stuck to our shoes.

The nights on the bunk beds were also hell. We had been warned that if we were awakened in the middle of the night we were not to panic; we should just quietly follow orders. After being in Auschwitz only a short while, we understood that this meant the liquidation of all of us in our barracks. The girls I called the pioneers of Auschwitz knew very well that our days were numbered. Some of them were so cruel and callous that they pointed at the smoking chimneys of the crematoria, which were working overtime day and night, and yelled, "Where do you think you are? There are your parents in the chimney."

The only difference between the days and nights was when there were more selections, beatings or news of people who had run to the electric wires to kill themselves. Although we, too, became quite callous, there were certain episodes that touched me deeply that I will remember vividly for the rest of my life. There was a mother who was selected for the gas chamber in her daughter's presence. The daughter ran after her mother, fighting, screaming and crying, as the guards tried to hold her back. We never found out what happened to them. On another occasion, one of three sisters was selected for the gas chamber. The poor girl started to laugh hysterically. It seemed as though she had lost her mind on the spot.

Occasionally we saw a group of musicians, girls who were prisoners, marching through the camp blowing horns, trumpets, wind instruments and drums, acting as a happy, lively orchestra.

There were also times when we had to believe in miracles, because somehow they happened. Once, my sister suddenly developed a fever when we were going through a more thorough medical examination than usual. We were standing in a line as a doctor or nurse examined us. At my turn I was told to open my mouth. The woman touched my neck and ordered me to join the healthy group. It was Sidi's turn next and I knew that with a fever she had no chance to survive. I moved only a little farther and waited to see what would happen. As she touched Sidi's face, she said, "She has fever," and ordered her to join the sick group. Sidi was in shock. I don't know how it happened, but this is what I call a miracle: This so-called doctor or nurse was distracted for a split second and she didn't notice when I pinched Sidi's naked bottom and pushed her to the back where the healthy group was standing. I stepped in her place and opened my mouth, pretending that I still had to be examined. The woman slapped me on the face, hard, and yelled, "You stupid cow, I checked you already!" After we had all been examined, they counted the people who were considered sick. They realized that one was missing. We were at least seven hundred women, all naked, with shaven heads — we were barely recognizable from one another. The examiners started to yell that the sick person should give herself up. We were terrified. They walked up and down, looking at our faces, telling us that they would recognize the culprit and yelling that we would all go to the other side with the sick ones. There was not a sound. They were probably not ready to recheck so many people and it was also late in the evening and so, miraculously, my sister survived. Miracles were happening in Auschwitz every hour. Just staying alive was more than a miracle. I kept asking myself, how could we survive?

One day at the end of July, we were handed out some postcards and were told that we had write to relatives or friends and tell them that we were fine and were in a place called Waldsee.[2] Afterward, we were taken to a railway station and loaded into a long cattle car full of women prisoners, some who were Polish gentiles. We left Auschwitz knowing that a worse place on this planet probably couldn't exist and, so to speak, we were happy. At our first stop we saw a sign for Karlsruhe. From the size of the train station, I figured this must be a large city, probably a main artery leading to numerous cities. Our guards got off the train and walked up and down the platform. One left for

---

2   In the summer of 1944, Hungarian deportees were forced to write to their relatives and friends back home that all was well — they were working and healthy. The Nazis attempted to deceive the remaining Hungarian population in Budapest by stamping the word "Waldsee" (meaning "Forest Lake") on the postcards, which was the actual name of towns in Austria and Switzerland, to convey the feeling of calm and tranquility. Although the Nazis checked and censored the postcards, prisoners often managed to use coded language to warn their family members.

a while, then the other, taking turns. We were sitting on the floor with the doors wide open and were watching people rushing to the trains, normal activity in a busy station. I saw a young mother with a little girl of about six or seven years old. They were both well-dressed, wearing little hats and white gloves. As the mother was holding the child's hand and hurrying to a train, the little girl stopped and curiously looked at the interesting sight she saw — women on the floor of a cattle train, with shaven heads in grey rags. The mother blinked for a second, grabbed the child angrily and dragged her away. Didn't the German people know what was going on in their cities, towns and streets?

I can't recall how long this journey took us. One day the train stopped in a village called Rothau. We saw huge, white, rocky mountains and a quarry. Slave labourers were working, watched by uniformed guards. We felt optimistic and convinced each other that this would be a good place for us. We would work hard, not in a death camp but rather in a labour camp. After all, said Sidi, the eternal optimist, we were used to mountains, coming from a mountainous area. Then we saw that they were unloading the Polish women who appeared robust, in good physical condition. They left the train and we continued our journey. We were very saddened because we believed that since we were not chosen for the quarry work then something not as good was awaiting us, the Jewish girls.

Incidentally, after the war I had an experience that taught me again that destiny is really beyond anyone's control. On our way home from Germany, we met people of all kinds of nationalities who were trying to get home. One was a Hungarian man who had been one of the slave labourers in the quarry in Rothau. He told us that one day in the summer of 1944 there arrived a trainload of women from Auschwitz who had to work in the quarry. He believed that none of the women survived the terrible conditions there.

It is hard to remember how long our trip lasted until we arrived in a place called Geislingen an der Steige.[3] We were taken to a relatively small camp. Again, we were behind barbed wires, with watchtowers, but there was no comparison to Auschwitz — no crematoria with smoke and sparks coming out of chimneys day and night. In our barracks, each person had a bunk bed and received a blanket and towel. On each one was the stamp WMF, which stood for the company Wurttembergische Metallwarrenfabrik. Each of us received a grey and blue striped dress, a matching jacket and a pair of wooden shoes or sandals. We were told that we would work in a factory. In the past, this place had manufactured cutlery and kitchen utensils but it had been converted during the war into an ammunition factory. We were told that we would have roll calls, like in Auschwitz. We would work six days a week, twelve hours a day, one week on day shifts, the next on nights. The seventh day of the week we had all kinds of chores — cleaning the barracks, shovelling the snow in winter, taking the garbage to a city dump and so on. There was even some useless work to do, apparently just to keep us from getting spoiled and idle on Sundays.

In the factory, civilian men who had worked there before the war but were too old for the army supervised us. The women guards were cruising around watching us and whenever they felt like it, or out of boredom, they gave us a slap accompanied by a dirty name. In spite of everything, we were certainly better off than in Auschwitz. We felt that we had been delivered to a relative paradise. Our breakfast consisted of hot tea made of some weeds; lunch was hot soup with a few pieces of turnip and sometimes, if we were lucky, we could even fish

3  Geislingen an der Steige was one of fifty subcamps of the Natzweiler-Struthof concentration camp system. These were the only camps the Nazis built in the French territory of Alsace, which had been annexed to Germany in July 1940. On July 28, 1944, six hundred Hungarian Jewish women arrived in Geislingen from Auschwitz. *The USHMM Encyclopedia of Camps and Ghettos, 1933–1945.* (Bloomington and Indianapolis: Indiana University Press, 2012.) Vol.1 Part B, 1033–1034.

out a piece of potato; and supper was the same as lunch but in addition to the soup we received a slice of bread made of flour and sawdust, a tiny square of margarine and sometimes even a dot of jam made from beets.

And so the days passed by, going to work six days a week. We marched through the same residential streets, always at the same hour, in rows of five, SS men escorting us with rifles. Once, a civilian woman slipped in between our rows and spilled a few apples on the road. This must have been done intentionally, out of pity for us skeleton-like prisoners. Our people became wild and out of control, bending down and trying to catch a scattered apple. The SS soldiers yelled not to dare to pick up anything. They threatened the woman, asking if she wanted to join us.

A few times, in winter, as we were marching in the snow for the night shift, I noticed light in a building in an upstairs window. A woman was folding something that looked like a bedspread. She was obviously preparing the bed for the night. Feelings of a warm, cozy room, a normal life, a family, and probably even enough food in the house came over me. We were wearing open-toed wooden sandals, which we often lost in the snow while marching during the winter nights. It is hard to believe that after fifty years, often when I prepare for the night and fold our bedspread, the thought of the woman in the warm house still haunts me. Certain incidents remain with us forever. Like long after the war, my dear mother used to recall how a chicken once made its way under the wires and came in to our camp yard. As I was watching the chicken, envious of its freedom, I spoke out loud, telling it what a stupid chicken it was. "If I were a chicken I would never come close to such a place," I said.

But we still considered ourselves lucky after Auschwitz. The rest of the summer went by and as fall approached, somehow we decided, or knew, that the day of Yom Kippur was approaching. We were working in the factory, as usual, and we had to line up for lunch. We received our soup but since all of us were fasting, none of us touched our bowls. When the women guards noticed, they threatened us with punishments on our return to the camp. When our people explained to the commander of the camp that this was our holiday, to our surprise there was no mention of a punishment. He must have had some respect for people who were starved to death and still had some principles.

The days in Geislingen went by, if we were lucky, without any incidents. But some of our people became sick, skinnier and weaker day by day. One of those unfortunate ones was my sister. She developed large sores on her lower back that were full of pus and in no time her back was covered and infected with at least forty or fifty open, sticky sores. When we could not manage anymore, we realized that she had to be admitted to the infirmary. This was not an easy decision because we were afraid that one day the infirmary would be liquidated. My sister entered the so-called hospital where one of our girls, a nurse, worked. She told Sidi that if she were to have only one extra potato a day, her sores might heal better, since she was very undernourished.

In the previous few days, we had been assembled in the camp yard where the commander of the camp announced that if a prisoner were caught in the basement stealing potatoes, she would be shot. Yet, when I heard that my sister could be saved with a daily potato, I took a chance and stole some. Somebody up there must have been shielding me. After all, there was a soldier in the watchtower twenty-four hours a day who saw every move of ours. Again, a miracle.

As I mentioned, the infirmary was a dangerous place to be. One day a group of officers were inspecting the infirmary. Our nurse accompanied them as they checked every bunk bed. Sidi heard the nurse as she pointed out each bed that would become available. When the officers left, Sidi asked the nurse what she meant by an available bed. The answer was that if she wanted to survive she should check out immediately. Sidi went back to work.

One evening when we returned from our daily shift, we got some terrible news. The people who worked the night shift and spent the day in the camp told us that people from the infirmary and also one woman who was pregnant were picked up, loaded into a horse-drawn wagon and taken away. The girl who shared the news with us was so shaken up that she said that if she ever survived the war, she would never forget the people's lamenting, crying and begging for mercy. We happened to know the pregnant woman, who was married and had conceived at home. We knew of a few cases of pregnant women, but not in such an advanced stage that it showed when they were deported. They were secretly helped by some of our people, who artificially induced them to give birth prematurely. Then these women went back to work, diligently producing for Hitler's war machine.

We survived the winter. Some people with frozen toes, some with frozen fingers like myself. For two years after the war, I was still nursing my hands, where pus oozed out from under my cuticles. Some girls came back without fingers, which they had lost while working with heavy machinery.

Even through all this, we never worried about tomorrow. All we wished for was a thicker soup and a bigger slice of bread. I used to daydream, imagining how lucky I would be to be a beggar. I would knock on every door and would never be hungry again.

At the factory, there was an air strike one day, and we were rushed off to a bunker underneath the building. As we were running down the narrow stairs our *Oberscharführer*, a senior officer (we called him the Bird of Death), was standing on top of the stairs and in his anger was pummeling our backs and heads with the iron buckle of his belt. He was a vicious man and of course he knew that his enemies were our friends. After all, a bomb or many more didn't make a difference to us. Who needed this life?

~

Spring slowly approached. It must have been around March when, again, I don't know how, people decided, without any calendar, that it was the first day of Passover. Strangely enough, even in this terrible situation we still had some religious beliefs, and the majority of us didn't eat our bread the first day of Passover.

At the end of March 1945, on a day I had been working nights and was in camp during the day, I was surprised to see the gates of the camp open — a new transport of a few hundred women was arriving. In tattered clothes, tired, hungry and carrying tall sticks to support themselves, they had marched for God knows how long from another camp called Bergen-Belsen. Most of them were Polish Jewish women, but among them was a young Jewish girl from Hungary who was a medical doctor. My mother asked her if she thought we had a chance to survive. The answer was, "Yes, but only if an epidemic does not break out among us." By sad coincidence, she ended up being the first one who fell victim to typhus fever. How unpredictable destiny can be! This reminds me of our dear uncle Sandor, the one I mentioned who was the "privileged Jew." When the Jewish population from Rachov was deported to the ghetto, he was among the only Jews left in our town, along with his family and his mother — our grandmother. Being the only Jewish family left, they lived in terrible fear. But only a few days after our deportation, our uncle and his family were badly beaten, robbed and sent off to the ghetto where we were. I remember my aunt Rose, Uncle Sandor's wife, saying that her one wish was that at least one member of her family would survive. The irony of fate: Her wish never came true. On arrival in Auschwitz, their two wonderful sons, eighteen and twenty-two years old, approached the selection officer and told him that they wanted to go with their father, who had been sent to the left side; he gladly obliged. The whole family was sent to the gas chambers. The only cousin of ours who returned told us this sad story.

In early April, before we left for work one evening, we realized that many more SS soldiers than usual were accompanying us. We took a new, unfamiliar route to work. We grew suspicious, afraid of this change. This was not our daily routine. We marched in the dark in rows of five. On both sides of us, every step of the way, were SS soldiers with rifles. Then, we reached a train station. That meant we were leaving our labour camp. With broken hearts and terrible fear, we parted from Geislingen. We didn't expect anything better. A train arrived, a regular passenger train. As our crowd slowly boarded, we saw that this was a luxury train. We were going first class! This time we were not sitting on the floor of a boxcar, but instead, on beautiful upholstered seats — with springs sticking out and hurting our bare bones. The train must have been damaged in an air raid.

I don't know how long our journey took. When the train stopped and we were told to get off, it was a beautiful day and we were in a place that looked so nice and promising. Nature was awakening; there were green patches everywhere. It was quiet and the meadow scenery was beautiful. I was starting to build up my hopes. After all, there was still a world besides gas chambers and crematoria. There had to be something good in store for us, also.

We passed by an abandoned castle. In front of it was a lake with water lilies. Everything was so peaceful, not a trace of human existence. Completely uninhabited. Only later did we try to interpret the meaning of the abandoned castle. There must have been an important Nazi with his family living there and probably, as the Americans moved closer, the family evacuated. We continued marching with the SS accompanying us. After a mile or so, we noticed a sign pointing in the direction we were heading: Allach-Karlsfeld, seven kilometres to Dachau. All our hopes vanished. Our happiness hadn't lasted too long. The name Dachau was well known among European Jewry. It was one of the most notorious camps.

At the Dachau subcamp of Karlsfeld we received even less food than in the other camps, but each of us got a separate bunk bed. We became weaker by the day and since Mother could walk only with our support we realized that all our efforts had been in vain. If we couldn't survive, how could Mother? We could barely walk down to the washroom, which was close to the barracks.

Once, I saw girls leaning out the window of the washroom. I was curious to see what was going on there. Right under the window, along the walls, was a mountain of unclothed corpses. We were so calloused and indifferent by then; I just walked away without even exchanging words with the other girls.

But there was one pleasant surprise in store for us. Behind the barbed wire fence there was another camp and, for the first time, we saw male prisoners. So, there was hope that some of our men were still alive somewhere in some concentration camps. While we were spending our days in the yard between our barracks and the electric wire fences, we started to make contact with the male prisoners. We called loudly to each other, asking questions about who they were, where they came from and what they were doing there. Most of them were gentiles who had been deported from occupied parts of Europe and imprisoned in labour camps. They, too, went to work escorted by guards, as we had done, but they were not as starved as we were. Sometimes, they even threw a piece of bread over the fence to us. When one man found out that we were Czech, he ran and brought another Czech man over to the fence. He told us that he was a commercial artist and worked outside the camp in his profession. He also said that he would try to help us.

One day, when one of our girls was beaten up by our *Blockälteste*, the German woman in charge of us, the men on the other side of the fence happened to see it. One of them started to yell, waving a clenched fist and screaming, "Hands off! It is not 1940 anymore." The woman stopped right away and the news of the incident spread in no time over our whole camp. We felt encouraged by this, and also realized that we were not being guarded as strictly as in the past. We had no idea what the reason was. Who knew that the Germans were losing the war?

It was near the end of April 1945 when we suddenly heard that the camp was to be evacuated. When the men on the other side of the fence found out the news, our Czech friend showed up with a pair of wooden shoes and threw them over the fence — a present for our mother. The news of being evacuated became reality. We packed and were marched to a train station. Again, loaded into a freight train, sitting on each other on the floor. Near the door was a bench where two SS men sat, day and night. The train was moving at a slow pace. Days and nights passed by. We lost track of time. We kept going a few miles back and forth again and again. It seemed that the train had no destination. Our guards were up all night smoking, leaning on their rifles and quietly whispering to each other. Our mother, who was the oldest among us, told us quietly that there was something suspicious going on. At times the train stopped and we were taken by a guard into the field to relieve ourselves. While the train was not moving, our guards were walking nervously up and down the platform. At times, we heard distant thundering that sounded like bombardments. From a distance, we saw a fire that continued for a few days.

One morning our auntie, my father's sister, and her daughter Judy, both of whom were in the same boxcar with us, quietly shared some news with us. Our aunt said that during the night while we were half asleep, some men were negotiating something with our guards. She heard them saying that they were sent by the International Red Cross. Judy, who at fifteen felt very independent, a fresh little teenager, diagnosed her mother immediately. "Mother lost her mind," she said. We were just hoping that our auntie was right.

In the morning our guards timidly announced that they needed two people with two blankets to go with them to fetch something. The two girls came back carrying something heavy in the blankets. We were sitting on the floor and quietly waiting. We were all in shock when we saw the boxes — neatly sealed five-pound boxes, distributed to each of us. When we opened them we almost lost control; our emotions are impossible to describe. In each box, there was a can of dry milk, a small can of corned beef, a can of cheese, a package of chocolate, a pack of cigarettes and a package of biscuits. We were laughing and crying at the same time. Was it possible that there were still people who cared, who heard our cries, who believed in justice?

Was there any nation on earth who wanted to pamper us with such love? Were we still considered human beings? We tasted a little of everything, being careful not to be too extravagant, rationing the goods. When night approached, we made sure that no one would be tempted to steal our packages. We fastened our precious boxes to our bodies with the rope that served as a belt on our dresses.

The next morning, the SS men allowed us to come out of the train and move around a little. We couldn't understand the sudden change. Why were they being kind to us? Only when we were on the platform did we see that our train was endlessly long and that there were also male Jewish prisoners on it. They were very skinny, sick looking, unshaven and frail — walking skeletons in prisoner uniforms. I don't know where they obtained matches, but they made little fires near the train, added water to some powdered milk and boiled it. Suddenly, we heard familiar thundering and a whistle of the SS men calling us, "Children, everybody aboard."

The train tracks were running on elevated ground that descended into a field about twenty yards away. Along the field were very dense bushes that were hard to penetrate. Again, the so-called thundering became more and more frequent, and we saw a big fire from a distance. Then, our guards called us and asked us politely to come out of the train. We were in the doorway when we saw helmets and rifles aimed at us and then soldiers in uniforms pushed through the thick bushes. All this happened in seconds. We saw our guards taking off their belts with the pistols and bayonets and putting them down on the floor of our boxcar, almost touching our feet. They fell on their knees, with raised arms. My mother was standing near my sister and me, and she grabbed a little white kerchief I wore on my head, and started to wave it, calling, "We have to show them that we are surrendering." Fifty years after my mother's words, I still cry and laugh at that. Who had to surrender? Who was afraid of these tattered, defenseless walking corpses? It was long after the war when I still teased my dear mother, who was an exceptionally bright lady, about her excitement and the "surrender."

Now, out of nowhere, as if they were parachuting from the sky, our men from the other end of the train came running out welcoming the soldiers. In their excitement, they were foolishly yelling, "I have a brother in America!" or "I have an uncle in America!" Only after we heard the word America did we realize who our liberators were. The soldiers didn't bother with us, but lined up all the SS men and German soldiers who had been guarding this long train and marched them away.

All of a sudden, we realized that we were free; we could go and come as we pleased. Hundreds of us ran through a field, down a hill and we reached a road. We saw an army moving with trucks, tanks and heavy artillery. The soldiers were waving at us, throwing chewing gum and cigarettes. Now that we were free and on our own, what was next? The people who were strong enough decided that we must move on, find shelter and start to normalize our lives. To our greatest regret, we later found out that there were many sick people left unattended on our train, dying.

We reached a farming village called Staltach-iffeldorf. We saw the villagers hiding in their houses behind the curtains, afraid of the army and of us. We were starved and started to explore the village. Judging by the houses, barns and livestock we could tell that this was a small, but rich, farming community. There were chickens in every yard and our boys started to chase them. They wasted no time, and soon there was slaughtering and barbecuing. I too jumped over a fence and started to chase a chicken. An old woman came out of the house and yelled at me. I figured that if she was so brave, she must have someone in her house with a rifle. I chickened out, jumped back over the fence, and this was the end of my chicken chasing.

Then our crowd discovered a factory of baked goods. We just went in and picked up loaves of bread as the bakers were just standing there, without a word of resistance. This quiet little village had suddenly become busy like a beehive, with soldiers mingling with us ex-prisoners. In no time, we were sought out by Jewish American soldiers who were eager to ask questions. I don't think they needed too many answers. Just a glimpse at us answered everything. I remember one soldier saying, "Don't be afraid. I want to help you. Just tell me the truth." They also had something interesting to tell us. They said that not far away from the place we were liberated they found mass graves, which had most likely been prepared for us.

It was only a few hours after the occupation and the liberating army was still disorganized. April 30, 1945, the day of our liberation, was still not the end of the war. As the evening approached, one of the Jewish soldiers found a barn and placed a group of our people in the hay overnight. They also brought in big metal cans with milk for us. This proved to be a disaster. We drank all night and kept running all night, suffering from severe diarrhea. Whose stomach could tolerate this sudden change? During the night as I was lying in the hay, I kept planning how first thing in the morning we would take a train home, find our family, share our bitter experiences and rebuild our lives together. How naive I was!

We eagerly awaited daybreak. There were hundreds of soldiers roaming the streets and with them appeared men in long navy blue coats. On the backs of their coats were stamped two large white letters: KG, *Kriegsgefangener*, which meant prisoner of war. Also, seemingly out of nowhere, many partisans of mixed nationalities appeared. We had no difficulty communicating, since most of us spoke a few languages. Also, we had a lot in common to share — the language of misfortune. In no time, we all became good friends and together we were exploring the village. We found a huge storage room with dairy products, where there were porcelain containers, like bathtubs, filled with all kinds of cheeses and milk and cream. Another group of partisans joined us. They looked at our wooden shoes and told us to follow them. They brought us into an enormous warehouse with endless rows of crates of shoes and slippers. They broke open the crates by jumping up and down on them. We picked our shoes very carefully. For us we chose practical, sturdy, laced boots and slippers; for my father and our brother, two pairs of sturdy boots. We still wore our wooden shoes, saving the new leather boots we considered a luxury.

As the second day of our liberation progressed, the Americans also settled in. They tried to find temporary homes for us. A soldier brought us into a farmer's house and ordered the family to move out. The man tried to object but no explanation helped. We were told to feel at home there. We started to clean up, bathing, washing, burning our clothes and changing into whatever clean clothes we found in the house. But it was futile — no matter what we did, we were infested by lice. Only when soldiers came into the houses and sprayed us with DDT did we get rid of the parasites.

In the evening of the second day of the liberation an announcement was made that the army would serve us a hot meal. I was feeling very sick and was running a high fever, but how could I resist such a treat? I joined the rest and stood in line with hundreds of our men and women. We were given a bowl of delicious soup with generous pieces of beef floating in it. Every person also received a loaf of bread. The military kitchen was working extremely efficiently and we were taken care of as long as we stayed in this village. This lasted a couple of weeks. Meanwhile, I recuperated from pneumonia, according to a diagnosis of one of the doctors who my sister brought in.

Again, there was an announcement that we would be moved to another place. We were worried about every change. After all, we had such good food here every day. I still laugh when I recall how we ran every day for the loaf of bread, which we couldn't even consume. We hoarded those loaves, which, in the end, became mouldy, but we were always afraid of famine.

Anyway, on a beautiful May day the army brought in trucks and we left Iffeldorf. The trip didn't take long and we arrived in a most beautiful place called Feldafing. This was a resort in the mountains, with little lakes and many little villas, and had been the site of a summer camp for the Hitler Youth. On our arrival, we were greeted by American officers and German doctors. We had to undress and leave our clothes in a pile; our shoes were washed with a disinfectant and after showers we were examined by German doctors, with Americans supervising. We were asked if we had any complaints and if we felt well enough. We all received two pairs of light brown pyjamas and a pair of slippers. Then we were ushered into one of the villas with a huge bedroom that accommodated four of us. In every villa, there was a dining room, where we received three wholesome, excellent meals a day. A German doctor, accompanied by a nurse, visited us in our rooms every morning to check our temperature and ask questions about our health. It was hard to believe that, after we had reached the lowest level of human misery, our fate took a sudden turn and we were being treated like human beings, with justice and respect.

As we slowly recuperated, we started to become restless and wanted to go home. At the beginning of June, we heard that the first Czech official would visit our camp. He gave us a welcoming speech and told us how our country was ravaged by the German occupation and that we, the Czech citizens, were needed at home.

We were the first ones to leave Feldafing. The American trucks brought us to the Czech border and, after a warm farewell, we entered the first city in our homeland, called Plzeň, or Pilsen. From there, we started the painful journey home. To find a train in post-war Europe was practically impossible. The trains were running without any schedule and were full of Russian soldiers, civilians, political prisoners, prisoners of war, displaced persons or refugees. Thousands were heading home. There were also many robberies on the trains, most of them committed by Russian soldiers. If we were lucky to get a train, most of the time the train stopped in the middle of nowhere and we were told to get out. Often we were stranded in the middle of the night waiting for the next train, or for one the next day. It was chaos.

We finally reached Prague, the capital of Czechoslovakia. With identification cards issued by the Americans, we received preferential treatment. At the border, each of us had received a small amount of money, just to get by for a few days. In Prague, we were placed in the YMCA. This was a temporary solution; we didn't want to depend on charity. But, in spite of this, there was an occasion when we even received a meal from the nuns in a monastery.

With great difficulties, we reached Budapest, where the Jewish community was already active. Again, we were given a small amount of money and shelter, as well as help from one of the Zionist organizations. Meanwhile, more survivors kept coming, congregating around the Jewish community building, hoping to find some relatives. There were also posters put up with names of survivors. Occasionally, we saw people recognizing each other, kissing, hugging and crying.

We were not among the fortunate ones who were reuniting with lost family members. Later, we did find our cousin Icsu, who was with my father and brother in Melk, a concentration camp. After questioning him about their whereabouts, we realized that he was reluctant to talk about them. With terrible fear and suspicion, we pressured him and tried to extract information about them. He slowly revealed the devastating news to us. They both, my father and brother, had been working in a coal mine. One day, in the fall or winter of 1944, the mine caved in and both were badly injured. Since they were sick as a result of their injuries, they were separated. In front of my father, they threw my brother on a horse-drawn wagon, supposedly to take him to a hospital in Mauthausen. He passed away a few days before liberation, sometime in March 1945, at the age of seventeen. Our father died a while after he was separated from his son, sometime in December 1944, at the age of fifty-one. We never had the courage to find out more details. After this tragic blow, from which we never recovered, we realized that there was no reason for us to go home. There was nothing left for us. We had lost everything, including our home. With broken hearts and broken spirits, we decided to go back west to Czechoslovakia, from where there was a possibility to contact our uncle in Canada and leave Europe and the people who caused us so much pain.

1

2

3

1  Rebekah's mother, Rose, at age fifty-one, newly widowed after the Holocaust. 1946.
2  Rebekah and her mother, Rose, in Liberec, Czechoslovakia, while they were waiting to get their papers to come to Canada. Late 1946.
3  Wedding of Rebekah's sister, Sidi, in Czechoslovakia, 1947. In back, left to right: Rebekah's mother, Rose; Rebekah's aunt Rella; and Rebekah. In front, Sidi and her husband, Leibi.

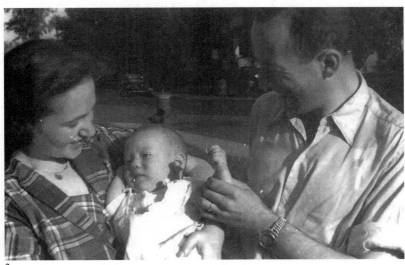

1  Rebekah and Sam Katz, circa 1950s.
2  With their baby daughter, Shirley, 1951.

The Katz family, 1998. In back: Shirley's husband, Norm, with their children Robert and Caroline. In front, left to right: Rebekah's daughter, Shirley; Rebekah; and her husband, Sam.

# With Great Pride
# Fela Zylberstajn Grachnik

I was born on May 24, 1924, in the city of Lodz, Poland. My parents' names were Mirla and Itzhak Boruch Zylberstajn. I was the second eldest of five children — my older brother's given name was Alter Ber; my given name was Faiga Miriam and I was called Faigale; my younger sister was Pesa; and my younger brothers were Aron Mayer and Shloimele. We lived in a working-class area of Lodz called Bałuty, where living conditions were hard. For example, we were seven people in the family, and we all shared one room in a large apartment building. There was no running water or indoor bathroom facilities, but everybody was comfortable and fairly happy because we didn't know any better. The majority of Jewish children in Bałuty attended public elementary school, as did I. Because of economic hardships of the time, very few children of Bałuty attended secondary school.

My parents ran a business selling coal and wood for heating, which was stored in a courtyard shed. Everybody in the family helped out, especially in the winter when it was very busy. I enjoyed getting together with friends to play different games, going to movies and ice skating during the winter months. I also belonged to a Zionist organization called Hashomer Hatzair, where I attended lectures about British Mandate Palestine. Since we didn't have a television, we spent much of the time reading. Friday nights, when our family sat around the table for Shabbat dinner, were especially enjoyable. After dinner, my father read some interesting, entertaining and even humorous stories to us from the newspaper.

Family was very important. In our home, there was a loving relationship between my parents and their children, and we had a close relationship with extended family members. I would say that life in pre-war Lodz was not easy, but it was full and rich.

This way of life came to an end on September 1, 1939, when the war broke out and a week later the Germans occupied Lodz. It didn't take long until the German Nazis started their horrific acts against Jews. They imposed a 5:00 p.m. curfew, and Jews were grabbed off the streets for forced labour. Whenever they saw a Jew with a beard, they were happy to cut it off. In November that year, it was the most terrible and heart-breaking sight to watch the Nazis burning the biggest and most popular synagogue in Lodz, the Altshtot Shul. I remember the black and red flames vividly. It was horrible to watch people crying and grasping their hands as they watched the synagogue burn.

My family started to live in terrible fear of what would happen to us. There were rumours that a ghetto would be established. Soon, the rumours came true. By February 1940, the entire area of Bałuty was sealed off with barbed wire and became the Lodz ghetto. Jews from all over Lodz were forced to move into the ghetto. My family did not have to move because we already lived there.

Chaim Rumkowski was the Jewish leader of the ghetto. Different sorts of factories — shoe, clothing, carpentry, watchmaking and many more — were set up that used Jewish slave labour for the German war industry. In all, ninety-six factories were set up. I worked in a straw factory where we made straw outer boots for the German soldiers. Men, women and even nine-year-old children were forced to work and be productive for the German murderers.

The ghetto soon became overcrowded and typhus broke out. There was no medicine to treat this disease. Food was severely rationed and hundreds of people died daily of starvation, sickness, exhaustion and freezing in the winter. I remember one terrible day known as the Bloody Thursday, March 7, 1940. During this pogrom, Jewish tenants living in a building on Piotrkowska Street, a prestigious street in Lodz, were given fifteen minutes to leave their houses. Well over one hundred people were shot.

We lived in constant fear of deportation from the ghetto. Then, in the beginning of 1942, my parents, my younger sister and two younger brothers were deported.[1] My older brother had been sent to a forced labour camp in 1940. I never saw my family again. I remained in the ghetto and continued to work under deteriorating conditions. Another family moved into our apartment. I missed my family very much and every night I cried myself to sleep and dreamt of being reunited with them.

I can never forget the *Sperre*, the massive roundup and deportation of September 1942. During one week of torture, the streets were stained with Jewish blood. The sick, elderly and children were the victims in every raid that the murderers carried out on the Jewish people. Thousands were deported out of the ghetto and sent to the Chełmno death camp. Many others were asphyxiated with carbon monoxide gas in the trucks that transported them. No matter how terrible it got during my time in the ghetto, 1942 was the darkest year, especially for me.

And so time passed, and we existed under worsening conditions. Every day I witnessed tragedies beyond anybody's imagination. From 1942 to 1944, we survived on rations that weren't enough to live on but not little enough to die on. The death toll was so high that it took three to four days for people to burn the dead bodies.

---

1   The first major deportations from the Lodz ghetto took place between January 1942 and May 1942 and then in September 1942, when over seventy thousand Jews and five thousand Roma were sent to the Chełmno death camp. The remaining seventy-five thousand Jews were deported to Auschwitz-Birkenau in August 1944 when the ghetto was shut down. See "Lodz" USHMM Holocaust Encyclopedia, https://www.ushmm.org.

In the beginning of August 1944, there was an announcement that there would be a total deportation, which meant the entire liquidation of the ghetto. To avoid panic, the chief of the German Nazi administration in charge of the Lodz ghetto, Hans Biebow, spread propaganda — he went around to the factories and gave speeches to calm people. In one of his speeches, Biebow said that the ghetto was only being transferred to another location. In doing so, he said, every effort would be made to save our lives. He assured everyone that families would not be separated. Biebow asked people to go to the transports of their own free will. Having high hopes and a strong will to survive this horrible and tragic time, most people believed the lying murderer and joined the transports.

During that month in 1944, transports with thousands of victims packed into cattle cars left the ghetto daily for an unknown destination. For many, this was their last journey. I was in one of these transports. Not only were we packed into these cattle cars, but we were treated worse than animals. There was no food, no water and no facilities to relieve ourselves. Cooking pots were used as toilets. With no fresh air, the smell was terrible. Every once in a while, someone fainted; a few people died.

After countless days, we arrived in Auschwitz-Birkenau. When the wagon doors opened, we heard a loud yelling: *Alles raus!* (Everybody out!) We crawled out exhausted, leaving the dead and our possessions behind. As we got to the gate of Birkenau, there was another traumatizing scene — the selection. Men were separated from women. Children were torn away from their mothers. The frail and elderly were immediately selected for the gas chambers. At the gate there was an SS man who was the master of life and death, pointing with his thumb as to which direction to go: left or right — life or death. We later learned he was Dr. Mengele.

After I was selected to live, I was taken with many other women to a shower. Our hair was shaved and we were given rags to wear that barely covered our bodies. We had no underwear. When we got out from the shower, we were numb and speechless. There were no tears. No one cried. We were absolutely frozen. We didn't recognize each other. We were then taken to barracks where conditions were horrific. We slept on the cold ground, were awakened during the night and forced to stand outdoors for long hours in thin clothing during the cold weather. We were slowly starved. One small bowl of soup fed five women. The air was filled with the smell of burning flesh. We were often beaten over our heads. After spending two weeks in Birkenau, there was another selection. I passed the selection and was again shipped to an unknown destination.

Upon arrival, I learned that this newly built camp was a slave labour ammunition camp in Bad Kudowa, on the Polish-Czech border. The German leaders of the camp picked Jewish Lager, or camp, personnel: a *Lagerälteste*, a leader, and girls whose duties included cleaning and other functions, such as serving the German staff. They also picked kitchen personnel. I was very lucky to be picked to work in the kitchen. The rest of the women were assigned to work in the ammunition factory.

We were put into barracks where we slept on bunk beds. Every morning, we were awakened at 6:00 a.m. to an *Appell*, a roll call during which we had to stand outside to be counted before we went to work. We were still slaves, but conditions were better than at Auschwitz. After a few weeks, I got sick with frequent gallstone attacks, but I was fortunate to have good friends around me, especially one close friend named Mala whom I knew from the ghetto. She took care of me, replacing me at work so as not to let the German authorities know that I was sick. The sick had to stay in the *Revier*, a special room that some called a hospital. Every once in a while, these rooms were emptied out and the sick were sent to the gas chambers at Auschwitz. And so life went on. My high hopes for a better tomorrow kept me going.

At the beginning of May 1945, the German guards took us out of the camp on a march. We marched for hours until we got to Prague,

Czechoslovakia, where we were put into a school. The German guards then disappeared. The next day we were liberated by the Soviet army. Finally, we had lived to see the unthinkable moment. To be liberated after almost five years of having been tortured physically and mentally. There was a great deal of excitement. This was a bittersweet time, filled with mixed emotions. But it was too soon to realize what we had lost.

I remained in Prague for almost two weeks. We were then informed that a transport with survivors was going to Poland. Hoping that maybe some of my family had survived and that I would meet them in Lodz, I, my best friend, Mala, and a group of friends registered with the transport and went back to Poland.

The second day after we arrived in Lodz, I went to see the house where I was born and where I lived all through the ghetto years. That was a devastating moment. The house was not occupied. We had lived on the ground floor, and when I opened the door there was a big hole in the ground that the Poles had dug out, probably while searching for valuables. Around the hole there was rubble and lots of dirt. When I started to move my foot around the dirt I found one of our family photos. I then found a whole bunch of pictures underneath the dirt. I broke down, crying my heart out, picking up these remnants. These photos were worth a fortune to me. I promised myself that I would treasure them for the rest of my life.

There was a Jewish institution in Lodz where every survivor who came back from concentration camps registered, which helped us find family and friends.[2] Mala and I found an apartment and moved

---

2   The Central Committee of Polish Jews (in Polish: Centralny Komitet Żydow Polsce, or CKŻP), also called the Jewish Committee, was an organization established in 1944 that sought to reconstruct post-war Jewish life in Poland. The CKŻP set up various departments to help survivors search for their families and document their testimonies. The organization also provided legal assistance, social services and health care, established orphanages, and disseminated reports and newsletters on the state of Jewish life in post-war Poland.

in together. Then I found a distant cousin who owned a stocking factory, and he hired me to work for him right away. While we stayed in Lodz, we went to the Jewish organization every day to check if any of our family members had survived and returned. I was always depressed because I found no one. Mala was fortunate to find out that her younger brother, Heniek, survived and had come back to Lodz. Then after a few weeks, her father and older brother, Moishe (Moniek), came back to Lodz. We all lived together as a kind of extended family.

After a few weeks, Mala married Abram, a childhood friend of Moniek who had come back from the Soviet Union. We all continued living in the same house like one big family. I started to spend time alone with Moniek, and we came to care for each other very much. I slowly started to come out of my depression. However, life in Lodz continued to be very hard on all of us emotionally. There was nothing left for us there — we experienced very strong antisemitism and knew that we had no future in Lodz, so our large family decided to leave.

At the end of August, my extended family and I packed up our belongings, one small bag each, and we left Lodz. We made our way through Czechoslovakia to Schwandorf in Bavaria, Germany, where there was a small Jewish community. There, a committee that took care of displaced persons welcomed us with open arms. The committee occupied a building that had a hostel and they organized different activities. We stayed there for a few weeks, until they found us an apartment. We were finally settled in Schwandorf.

Moniek and I got married on February 16, 1946. There was no elaborate wedding, just a simple ceremony with family and friends. My father-in-law and Heniek continued to live with us. Mala and Abram got their own apartment. Moniek became active in the Jewish community. He was a soccer player, which led him to help organize a soccer team; this was a big accomplishment for him. Abram was also a soccer player, and they played on the same team.

Somehow life became meaningful. On February 27, 1947, I gave birth to a beautiful baby girl. We named her Mirale Hena. Mirale was after my mother and Hena was after my husband's mother. She meant the world to us. I suddenly realized that there was a purpose to surviving the horrible tragedies that we went through. Our newborn daughter filled our lives with joy and the hope to build a good life for her. She was the first child of a new generation to carry on our legacy.

My father-in-law married Balcha, a very nice lady who was also a survivor. They got an apartment of their own, and Heniek moved in with them. For all of us, staying in Germany was temporary. We all dreamt of getting out of Germany and establishing a permanent home elsewhere, most likely in Israel.

In 1947, Heniek was the first of the family to go to Israel. He made Aliyah Bet, which was illegal immigration to Palestine. Then, a little later on, aliyah became legal.[3] Yet we still remained in Schwandorf. Little by little, people started to immigrate to Israel, the US and Canada. My brother-in-law Abram's sister Tobka, who survived the war in the Bergen-Belsen concentration camp, and her husband, Abram, came to live in Schwandorf, but then immigrated to Canada. My husband and I, along with Mala and Abram, decided that since our parents and brother were in Israel, we should go there too.

In April 1949, we made aliyah. We travelled almost a week by boat until we finally arrived in Israel. At that time, my father-in-law and Balcha occupied an Arabic house in Jaffa. We lived with them for a few weeks until we found a house of our own, again with Mala and Abram. There were two rooms with separate entrances and a kitchen to share. The house was in an Arab neighbourhood and Arabs had previously lived there. The conditions were very hard — there were mountains of sand in the area and the tough economic situation made life difficult. Everything was rationed.

The hot climate was also very hard on us. After a few weeks, my husband was fortunate to get help from the leaders of the soccer

---

3    The state of Israel was declared on May 14, 1948.

team, Hapoel Jaffo, and through them he found a job working in the engineering department of the city of Tel Aviv. There were no roads and no nearby transportation in the area where we lived. The nearest bus stop was over a kilometre away, a distance covered in deep sand. My husband was lucky to have a bicycle that we had brought from Germany. So he went to work by bike.

On September 24, 1950, I gave birth to a dear little baby boy. We named him Itzhak Boruch, after my father. Itzhakale — that's what we called him — brought more joy into our lives. However, the conditions were extremely hard for bringing up a baby. The baby carriage that we got as a gift, for example, was impossible to push through the deep sand. There was also no baby clinic in the area, so I had to carry Itzhakale in my arms to see a doctor for regular check-ups. We were lucky because we lived together with Mala and Abram, and we would help each other. They also had two children — Shlamek, a year and a half younger than our Mirale, and Sholek, nine months older than Itzhakale. Under the circumstances, we did our best to go on with our lives. After all, we were in Eretz Yisrael, our own country. We enrolled our Mirale in kindergarten. It was good to see her happy and making lots of friends.

At the end of 1952, Mala and Abram made their way to Montreal, Canada. Abram's sister sponsored them. We missed them very much, and things were not the same in Israel without them. From then on, we hoped to go to Canada some day. It was by accident or maybe fate that Abram's sister had met a school friend named Regina in Montreal. When Tobka found out where Regina had lived in Lodz before the war, she told her that her brother's sister-in-law (that was me) had lived there too and that we had been neighbours. She gave her my name. Regina was very excited to find out that I had survived the Holocaust. We got in touch and started to write letters to each other. In one, I asked her if it would be possible to sponsor us to come to Canada. Before we knew it, she sent us papers to fill out from the Canadian immigration department and that was it. Everything went faster than we had expected.

In the middle of September 1953, we left Israel. We took a boat to Holland because we had to stop there to see the Canadian consul to get our visas to enter Canada. At that time, there was no Canadian consul in Israel. We stayed in Holland for about two weeks until we got our Canadian visas. Then we took a boat to Canada, arriving in Halifax on October 11, 1953. From Halifax, we travelled by train for two days to Montreal. By that time, Mala and Abram had lived in Montreal for almost a year. They had a place to live and were pretty much settled. They took us in, and we stayed with them for two months until we found our own place.

We then faced a new country, a new start, a new language — another struggle. As soon as we moved into our own place on Saint Laurent Boulevard, I enrolled Mirale in Grade 1 at Fairmount School. It was heartbreaking for me watching Mirale when I brought her to school and picked her up from there. She was sad and didn't want to mingle with the children because she didn't know a word of English. But it didn't take long before Mirale started to speak English and have friends. We started to call Mirale by the name Myra. On the other hand, it was much easier with Itzhakale because, at only three years old, he was still too young to understand the changes we had made in our lives.

At that time, Moniek was searching for a job and feeling very discouraged. We were trying very hard to adjust to life in Canada. Moniek eventually found a job working in a factory as an operator sewing coats. Then we bought a sewing machine and I helped earn money by making linings for the coats. I worked at home because I had to take care of my two children.

As soon as we saved up some money, the first thing we did was buy a television set to make our children happy. And were they ever happy! I registered for night courses to learn English. And after a while, I was very satisfied to be able to communicate in English. In 1955, I enrolled Itzhakale in kindergarten. We then started to call him Issie. At that time, Issie hardly spoke any English, but it didn't take long for him to speak fluently.

We learned that there was an existing Lodzer Society, a *landsman-shaft* in Montreal. We joined and met many *landsleit*, townspeople, and with some we became very friendly. Meeting fellow *landsleit* with whom we had so much in common provided us with the opportunity to reminisce about the old times. I later became active in the Ladies Auxiliary of the Lodzer Society. At first I was secretary and then I took up the position of vice-president, which kept me busy and gave me satisfaction.

We grew very close to Tobka and her husband and to Regina and her husband, David. We continued to have a close relationship with Mala and Abram and their children, and our families did many things together, like Passover seders and Rosh Hashanah dinners.

In 1958, we were happy and proud to become Canadian citizens. We realized that Canada is a great country with many opportunities. On July 19, 1960, I gave birth to another beautiful little baby boy, who we named Alter, after my older brother. In English, Alter's name is Allan, and we called him Ally. Ally brought more joy and happiness into our family. Life went on and little by little became more meaningful. Six months after Ally's birth, Mala and Abram had a baby boy named Harry. In 1963, our dear Issie became a bar mitzvah. This was the first milestone in our lives. We created a beautiful nighttime event with our small immediate family, extended family and friends sharing our happiness. We felt a certain sadness because neither my parents nor any of my siblings could be with us to share our happiness.

In 1966, another delightful moment of happiness occurred when our dear daughter, Myra, announced that she and Simcoe were engaged. We held a beautiful engagement party with relatives from both sides, and soon started to get busy making wedding arrangements. On April 9, 1967, the wedding day arrived, another overwhelming time of rejoicing for our family. The wedding in the Shomrim Laboker synagogue was beautiful, but our daughter was an even more beautiful bride. We got richer by gaining a member to our immediate family, a dear son-in-law, Simcoe.

In 1969, my husband went into business with a partner and started a company called M & W Sportswear. Although they struggled in the beginning with this new business, after a short time there was improvement and Moniek started to make a better living.

On January 10, 1970, we were blessed with our first grandchild, a beautiful baby girl named Chana Esther; Chana was named after my aunt from Brazil and Esther after Simcoe's grandmother. Her English name is Andrea. It gave us a wonderful feeling to be grandparents. And the new addition to the family gave us a certain fulfillment. Two months after Andrea's birth, we had disturbing news. Simcoe's father, Jacob, had died suddenly of a heart attack. He had been a quiet and gentle man loved by all.

On April 8, 1972, we got another addition to our family, our second grandchild. Myra gave birth to a baby boy, named Jacob after Simcoe's father. His English name is Joel.

In August 1973, our dear son Ally became a bar mitzvah. We put on a beautiful luncheon with family and friends. It was wonderful and exciting to have my father-in-law and his wife come from Israel to visit and join us at our simcha. Their presence made the bar mitzvah much richer and more meaningful. In 1974, we had more wonderful news. Our son Issie announced that he and Terry were engaged. Terry's parents, Claire and Julius Weltman, held an engagement party in their house for family and some friends.

On May 18, 1975, the big day arrived — Terry and Issie's wedding, another wonderful time of rejoicing for the family. As for me, I couldn't help remembering my parents with an ache in my heart. How happy they would have been watching their grandson getting married. This was all I could do — to remember. And again we gained a member to our immediate family, a lovely daughter-in-law, Terry.

On January 10, 1976, I did something that I had been dreaming of for a very long time — I took a trip to Brazil. I went to see the family that had left for Brazil when I was a little girl. I remembered them well and I had corresponded with them ever since my liberation. Meeting with my family at the airport in Rio de Janeiro was profoundly emotional. There was a group of about fifteen people, first cousins and their families, who all came to greet me. When they immigrated to Brazil, these family members had left behind lots of relatives — grandparents, uncles, aunts and cousins in Lodz. I was the sole survivor of the entire family from this terrible period of time. I spent much of my time with my cousins reminiscing about our family in the old country. One of my cousins, Sarah Rivka, told me that my survival was the greatest miracle. How else would they be able to find out what had happened to our family? These connections gave me another sense of a purpose to my survival. This trip was a dream come true for me.

In 1976, Mala, Abram and their family moved from Montreal to Toronto. Parting with them was not easy for both our families. We had been together practically all of our lives. But Moniek and I considered ourselves lucky to have our own family together and to enjoy Friday nights with the children. In 1977 came another blow when our dear son Issie and his wife, Terry, moved to Toronto. We had a hard time and missed them very much, but as long as they were happy with the move, we were satisfied.

On July 17, 1978, we had another addition to our family. We were blessed with a new grandchild. Our dear daughter, Myra, gave birth to a beautiful girl, named Rachel Laya after my husband's younger sister. We call her Rhonda. On May 9, 1980, we had another addition of two grandchildren. We were blessed with twin boys, named Aron after my brother and David Benjamin after Terry's grandfather. They are called Adam and David. Two months after their birth, Terry's father, Julius, died after a lengthy illness. We were grieved by his death, for he had always made us feel so very comfortable in his presence.

The total number of people in our immediate family now stands at twelve. We are very proud of each and every one of them. We feel blessed and hope that our family tree will continue to grow.

I continued to be active in the Lodzer Society, advancing my position to chair the Ladies Auxiliary, which kept me very busy at times. I also joined the Holocaust Remembrance Committee and the Yom Hashoah (Holocaust Memorial Day) Committee, of which my daughter was the chairperson. With great pride, I attended the meetings under my daughter's chairpersonship.

The year 1983 was very hard for us because we were going back and forth to Toronto to visit Mala while she was sick with cancer. She died on September 19, 1983. For me, the situation was even more unfortunate and very painful because I couldn't attend her funeral. I was in the hospital after bladder surgery when she passed away.

In 1984, my husband gave up his business and retired. He couldn't get used to doing nothing and this big change for him brought on depression. This was difficult for the whole family, but, with the help of good doctors and good children, he improved and started to go on with life. On June 1, 1985, our grandson Joel became a bar mitzvah and we celebrated with lots of friends and relatives. We were overwhelmed with joy to have lived to experience our grandson's bar mitzvah.

But then three months later, there was another death in the family. Mala and Abram's youngest son, Harry, passed away. Again, there was sadness, but life went on. We kept ourselves busy. We enjoyed the *naches*, pride, from our children and grandchildren. With great joy, we attended their high school and university graduations.

On January 2, 1986, our brother-in-law Abram's sister, Tobka, passed away. Then two weeks later, on January 18, we received shocking news again: My father-in-law had passed away suddenly in Israel. My husband and I didn't waste time and we took the first flight we could to Israel. We made it to the funeral. We stayed five weeks, until the unveiling of the gravestone. In July 1994, his wife, Balcha, died. Our daughter, Myra, was in Israel at the time and represented our family at the funeral.

Despite the losses we had in the family, the ups and downs, life has been meaningful and worth living. We appreciate living in Canada, the country that gave us the opportunity to rebuild our lives. After my husband retired, we had more time to enjoy life in many ways. We started to go to Miami for two months in the winter and, as a matter of fact, I wrote this manuscript in the winter of 1996 in Miami, where I have lots of free time. The main reason for the good times we had in our lives was the *naches* our children gave us on many occasions like new births, bar mitzvahs and weddings in the family. I recall the tribute our dear daughter, Myra, was given by the Canadian Jewish Congress when she resigned as Chairperson of the Holocaust Remembrance Committee. We were extremely proud and our hearts were filled with joy.

As I said, life has had its joys and sorrows. In May 1993, our twin grandsons, Adam and David, became b'nai mitzvah in Toronto, and again we were overwhelmed with joy and pride. In November 1993, our family had a big shock and scare. My husband was diagnosed with a malignant tumour in his breast. He had an emergency operation that removed the tumour and most of the lymph nodes. He recovered quickly and is now cancer free. This was a real nightmare for the whole family.

I have continued to be involved in the activities of the Lodzer Society. On October 10, 1994, the Lodzer Society and Ladies Auxiliary organized a commemoration marking the fiftieth anniversary of the liquidation of the Lodz ghetto. The event was co-sponsored with the Montreal Holocaust Memorial Centre. It was the most dignified event in the Lodzer Society's history. Three generations participated in a candle-lighting ceremony and there were addresses by the second and third generations. This commemorative event was significant in transmitting the Holocaust legacy from the survivors to the younger generations. I was very proud to be the chairperson and one of the organizers of this important event. I was also very proud of Myra for her speech on behalf of the second generation.

There is one thing I need to emphasize before finishing my story: At every happy occasion in my family life, I never failed to think of my parents and siblings who were murdered by the Nazis during the Holocaust. They never lived to see their daughter Faigale get married, raise a family and become a mature woman. For a long time after the liberation, I wondered whether it was worth being the sole survivor from the big and loving family that I had once had. But now I can see that it was my fate to survive, to raise a family and to tell them that I was there. I witnessed the greatest tragedy in the history of humanity. This was my mission to fulfill, and I consider myself fortunate that my mission is complete.

1   Fela's parents, Mirla and Itzhak Zylberstajn, before the war.

2   Zylberstajn nuclear family in the countryside of Lodz, Poland, in 1934. In back, Fela's father, Itzhak (centre) and her mother, Mirla (right). In front, left to right: Fela's siblings, Alter Ber, Aron, Pesa and Shloimele. Fela is on the far right with her hand on her hip.

3   Fela's extended family in pre-war Lodz, 1934.

Fela and her husband, Moniek (Moishe), with their daughter Mirale (Myra). Schwandorf Displaced Persons camp, Bavaria, Germany, circa 1947.

1

2

3

1  Fela (right), Moishe, and Fela's best friend and sister-in-law, Mala (Grachnik)
   Herszkowicz (left). Florida, circa 1980s.
2  Fiftieth wedding anniversary party for Fela and Moishe. Montreal, 1996.
3  Fela and Moishe celebrating their anniversary with their family. Back row, left to
   right: their former son-in-law, Simcoe; their daughter-in-law Terry; their son Issie; Fela; Moishe; their daughter, Myra; and their son Allan. In front, left to right,
   are Fela and Moishe's five grandchildren, Joel, David, Rhonda, Andrea and Adam.
   Montreal, 1996.

# Living Every Minute
# Babey Widutschinsky Trepman

AUTHOR'S PREFACE
DECEMBER 1995

As we walked to the Bergen-Belsen K.Z. gate, we passed beautiful little houses in the village of Bergen with well-groomed lawns and flower gardens. People sat on their porches, relaxing. They saw very well the walking skeletons with bulging eyes and arms hanging down like sticks. After the liberation, when we confronted these same people, they said they knew nothing about what was happening — they saw nothing and heard nothing. People perished in the thousands right under their noses and they knew nothing. Amazing!

~

In the Yad Vashem museum there is an announcement displayed about Šiauliai, Lithuania, dated September 10, 1941, which states that most industries with important specialists are in Jewish hands, and that "we cannot do any work, especially in the shoe industry. We have to bring in young Lithuanians to learn the trade soon, so that the Jewish problem is solved without hurting the industry."

Did they know what the future for Jews would be?

~

I was born in Šiauliai, Lithuania, on August 20, 1924. We lived a fairly easy life as middle-class Jewish people in our town. My father was the secretary general of the Jewish community and, in the evenings, he spent a few hours as accountant for the Jewish Businessman's Association. I had two sisters — Dora was three years my senior and Sonia was six years younger than I. We all attended Jewish schools, had nice summer vacations in the country, belonged to youth organizations and took part in extracurricular activities. My mother was a housewife. We always had live-in help, which was very common in those days, especially for middle-class families. Housework wasn't as easy as it is nowadays. We owned only a wood-stove; there were no electric or gas stoves, and no vacuums. Our parents never had their own home, but we rented a beautiful house in a nice section of the city, we dressed well and our parents led a busy social life always surrounded by many friends.

In June 1940, the Soviet army entered Lithuania. It looked like a very friendly invasion, but later on I learned that the Lithuanians were waving and cheering and welcoming the German army in 1941 with no less enthusiasm, and no resistance. Our family did not belong to the very rich, but life for us was changed forever by the Soviet occupation. In order to keep his job, my father had made a written statement that he was not a communist, but that he sympathized with the masses in the Soviet Union. Later, when the Germans entered Lithuania, the Lithuanian police used my father's statement as a pretense to arrest him. Even though he would have been incarcerated anyway as a Jew, they used his written statement as an excuse to arrest him because they said he was a communist.

My father's arrest came so unexpectedly that he didn't even have time to think or do something about our situation. We happened to have good friends among some of the Lithuanians and maybe we could have gotten a place to hide during the German occupation. These thoughts come to mind when I think about these events, perhaps to try to lessen or reduce the pain inside of me. Unfortunately,

I will never be able to alleviate or diminish this pain. This is my life.

Children usually perceive parents or their friends as "older people," but when I think that our parents perished in their early forties, I get the shivers.

On June 24, 1941, we were awakened by sounds of heavy bombardment. It came very suddenly. The Germans attacked Lithuania on their way to the Soviet Union. The Russians didn't even seem to fight back. Maybe they were caught by surprise?[1] But two days later we saw the soldiers running and jumping over fences, leaving things behind them. The Lithuanians who were antisemitic did not even wait for the Germans to settle in. They carried out pogroms against the Jews immediately. They robbed Jews of their belongings and accused Jews of being communists to justify their deeds.

It did not take long before we were forced to wear the Jewish stars. We were sent out to do all kinds of jobs: cleaning streets, digging trenches, working on farms. The brutality toward Jews escalated every day.[2] We were prohibited from walking on sidewalks and instead had to walk in the middle of the road. Elderly and sick were gathered and taken to the big synagogue in Šiauliai. My grandfather and his unmarried daughter who took care of him were among that group. The rest of our family were still in the city, and my mother went to see my grandfather every day and bring them some food. My grand-

---

1  With the enactment of Operation Barbarossa in June 1941, which saw Germany invade the Soviet Union, Hitler surprised the Soviet army by breaking the Molotov-Ribbentrop Non-Aggression Pact forged in August 1939.

2  The Germans invaded the city of Šiauliai on June 26, 1941, and began mass killings at Kužiai forest twelve kilometres away on June 29. Lithuanian Jews were forced to wear the yellow star in the summer of 1941. A ghetto was formed in Šiauliai in July 1941, and all local Jews were ordered into ghettos on August 15, 1941. By the end of the war, about 500 of the 6,600 Jews of Šiauliai had survived. See "Šiauliai" in *The Encyclopedia of Jewish Life Before and During the Holocaust* and the online Holocaust Atlas of Lithuania, holocaustatlas.lt.

father and aunt stayed there for only a few days. One morning, my mother went to the synagogue and found the place empty. No one knew where the old and sick were taken, but rumours, which were later confirmed, were that they were taken a few kilometres out of the city and shot dead. Next came my father. One day he was arrested and taken out to work, and he never returned home. We found out that he was in jail with the rest of the group that had been recruited for work.

Shortly after, in July 1941, the Jews of Šiauliai were forced into a ghetto, surrounded by a barbed-wire fence and guards. The ghetto was established in the poorest neighbourhood. There were two parts to our ghetto, one called Kaukas, or Kavkaz, and the other Traku,[3] named for the long street bordering the jail. The four of us — me, my two sisters and my mother — were taken to Traku. I remember pulling a small cart with our belongings into the ghetto, all we had left of a beautiful household with nice dishes, linens, books, carpets and so on. By the time we went to the ghetto, the rest of our belongings had been stolen, plundered and robbed, so what was left could be carried by me, a sixteen-year-old, in a little cart.

The Traku ghetto was small, with about five streets. On one side was the city jail and on the other side was a big leather and shoe factory that belonged to the Frankels, a very wealthy and prominent Jewish family. Eventually, there was a passage made from the ghetto to the entrance of the factory, so that the Jewish workers did not have to go outside of the ghetto to enter their workplace. Lithuanians, Ukrainians, some SS officers and, later on, Hungarians were the guards. When the ghetto was first opened, we used to see our father being taken out with a group of people, loaded on a truck for work. They were usually brought back in the early evening, and our family would always be standing in the ghetto street waving to our father. One morning, my sister Dora saw Daddy being loaded on a truck, as usu-

---

3   Alternate spellings for the parts of the ghetto are Kawkas/Kaukazas and Trokaj.

al. We expected to see him again in the evening. That particular day, Dora had a funny feeling that she would never see Daddy again, and it so happened that her feelings were right. All of the Jewish prisoners in that truck were taken outside the city to the Kužiai forest, where they had to dig their own graves.

~

For a short time, my mother and I worked in the shoe factory, sewing the upper parts of ladies' shoes. This was considered a good job because it gave us an opportunity to exchange some leftover possessions for food with the Lithuanian workers. These exchanges helped to feed the four of us, as the rations we received were hardly enough to live on. Many people tried to get work outside the ghetto, where there were more opportunities to exchange food for some of our leftover items. My sister Dora worked in the ghetto administration office. Every morning, the girls in the office were on duty at the ghetto gate to count up the people in the working commandos.

Dora was trying to find a job for me on the outside. She had a Lithuanian "friend" who she met one summer on a student job. Now, a few years later, he had become a policeman and worked on the Šiauliai police force. As a matter of fact, he was one of the policemen who had come to arrest my father. After the arrest, Dora had gone to him and pleaded with him to do something to free our father. He promised to do his best, but the truth was he did nothing; he didn't even try. He found all kinds of excuses, and the bottom line was that he didn't want to show his friends that he even sympathized with Jews.

Now that I was trying to get work outside the ghetto, Dora tried again to get in touch with him and asked him whether he could help. This time he agreed. I think he felt guilty about our father. He gave me a job as a maid in his house to help his wife with the housework. In those miserable times, this position was a godsend. I cleaned the house and washed and ironed clothes. The policeman's wife was a good person who never let me go home empty-handed, and I always got some food to bring back into the ghetto.

There was a big problem though — how could I bring the food back into the ghetto without it being detected? We invented all kinds of ways to hide food on one's person. But sometimes one had a larger parcel and had to carry a bag. My mother was always waiting near the fence and sometimes it was possible to throw a parcel over when the guard at the gate turned his back. We also knew the guards as "the good one," "the one you can buy off," etcetera. Once, I had an incident with a chicken. I decided not to cut it up into pieces, but to take a chance and bring it in whole into the ghetto. My mother was waiting for me as usual and, lucky me, the "good guard" was on. I walked over to the fence and tried to hand the parcel to my mother, but she was afraid to take it. I had to push it right through the barbed wires into her hand and run off. Even with all that trouble and pain, in those life-and-death situations, there was also some humour. The way I handled the situation with the chicken was very humorous. As we used to say, "Father, you are laughing, woe to your laughter."

Life in the ghetto was very hard. Our ghetto was run by a group of well-known people in the community and our leaders were friendly and helpful, but not a day passed without something horrible happening. Everybody tried to help themselves in order to stay alive, and many people smuggled in food from their workplaces. One had to be really lucky to not get caught smuggling anything into the ghetto. One Jewish man named Mr. Mazavetsky was hanged for bringing in only a few packs of cigarettes. I will never forget the scene, how everyone in the ghetto was forced to come out to watch the spectacle of a man being hanged for a few packs of cigarettes.

Throughout August and September 1941, some selections took place in the ghetto. The elderly and sick were separated from their families; many were taken and just disappeared. A few days later their graves were discovered on the outskirts of Šiauliai. Everyday life hung in the air. No one knew what would happen next.

My job at the policeman's house did not last long. They had no children and the apartment was small, so they really did not need everyday help, but they recommended me to a friend, also a police officer, whose wife owned a farm; she spent her time there all week and came home only for the weekends. I had to prepare a meal for her husband and keep the house clean. The good thing about working there was that they owned a piano. I had studied piano with Mr. Vaniuunas, a teacher who had been on staff at the music school I had attended. He came from Riga, Latvia. Before we went to the ghetto, he told me that if I could manage to get to his house, he would give me free lessons any time. Unfortunately, it did not work out very well. I had a few lessons, but getting to them meant taking my life in my own hands. While I worked at that last job, I would remove the mandatory yellow star and run to Mr. Vaniuunas's house for a lesson. I would run on the sidewalk, but then forget myself and run down the middle of the road, where Jews were supposed to go. I was so nervous that I had to stop. What was the point? How long could I carry on like this? With all of the dangerous situations and death that we encountered, it made no sense. Why was I here playing the piano suddenly? But Mr. Vaniuunas was a wonderful human being. He surely meant well.

Another good job that I had during my ghetto years was working for a large garage that employed mechanics who fixed trucks for the German army. I was supposed to be the interpreter who translated the work sheet from German into Lithuanian. What did I know about car or truck parts, gears, tail pipes, steering wheels? But as we used to say, "A Jew manages somehow." A Jew always finds counsel, always gives himself advice. And so I did as well. I made friends among the workers, who helped each other understand my "translations." The head of the garage was a German from the Wehrmacht and not from the SS. He was very kind to the few Jewish workers and helped them many times with food and warm clothing. After the war, I tried to get in touch with him. He was from Aachen and during the war his house was bombed; even the City Hall was unable to help me find him. He should've been rewarded for his good deeds. There were not many like him.

Other times, I worked on terrible jobs. One of them was in Bubiai, a small village not far from our city, where we were sent to dig for peat that would be used as heating blocks. In the winter, this job was unbearable. Our bodies were frozen; we could not feel our skin when we touched it. My hands felt like two sticks and they hurt beyond description. I also worked, during the coldest weather, on the Šiauliai airfield digging trenches with a group of girls. Besides having to dig the hard, frozen ground, we also had to deal with vicious guards who hit and punched us whenever we stopped for a breather. Our bodies were bruised black-and-blue and our hands were dripping blood. But as bad as the beatings were, the humiliations were even harder to take. They had names for us that we did not know existed.

～

In the ghetto, many people were housed in one room but our family was separated in two different locations. There was no room for Dora and me where my mother and Sonia, my little sister, lived, because another woman and her young son shared that room as well. So Dora and I slept with another family, but of course we saw our mother every day.

Every morning, the adults lined up at the gate for their work outside the ghetto. Parents with young children had to leave their children on their own during the day. There were clandestine classes for different ages, an illegal school and other organized social groups. The children more or less looked after themselves and went to their appointed groups.

On November 5, 1943, there was a *Kinderaktion*, a roundup and deportation of Jewish children.[4] The commandant of our ghetto then was Foerster, a real murderer. That morning, Mother left for work at

---

4 The ghetto had been reclassified as a subcamp of the Kauen concentration camp in October 1943, and was run by the SS at this time.

the shoe factory before the *Kinderaktion* started, not knowing about it. Dora was on duty that morning at the gate. Before Dora left, we both decided to take our little sister and try to push her out with the group of people who were leaving the ghetto. I put on a large coat, squeezed Sonia partly under it, moved into the middle of the crowd and just went through the gate. We were lucky; it worked! Many things that occurred during those hard times were just unexplainable. *Mazal!* Something would work for some people, and then others would not be that lucky. Every day that passed was like a scale, up or down, life or death. We were lucky to have smuggled Sonia out. Ukrainian collaborators started to check every house in the ghetto to grab the children. The little boy who shared the room with our mother was taken away. His mother had a nervous breakdown.

Our mother soon came back from the factory; the rumour about the *Kinderaktion* had reached her workplace. By the time Dora ran to see her, she was in a daze, gripped by trauma. She did not know that Sonia had been saved; I did not come back home with Sonia until much later. Dora pleaded with my mother to believe her, trying to assure her that her baby was alive and well, but it did not help. My mother sat in the room like a glass sculpture, staring into oblivion. When I finally arrived home with Sonia, my mother looked at us and still did not believe that we were there. She acted like she was in a dream. It took a while for her to accept the truth. This story makes me think very often about how people survived. Where did they get the strength to live through such trying moments? I think that the only thing that helped them to go on was hope, hope for better days to come.

Our family (what was left of it) stayed in the ghetto until the last transport — the liquidation of the ghetto near the end of July 1944. We left by foot, walking to Pavenčiai, a small town about two hundred kilometres from Šiauliai. We were forced to leave the ghetto in a hurry because the Soviet army was closing in on Šiauliai and bombing it every day. Most of the bombs fell close to the ghetto, maybe because the jail and the shoe factory on either side were strategic points. What else was there in the small Lithuanian town? A bomb that fell in the Traku ghetto killed the head of our Jewish community, a wonderful man and important businessman in Lithuania, Mr. Mendel Leibovitch.

On the way to Pavenčiai, after all that bombing, people were disoriented and security was very lax. When I think back now, I ask myself, why didn't we try to run away? But where could we run to, surrounded by so many antisemitic Lithuanians? That would really have meant death, and that we had given up all hope.

After a long, hard journey, we arrived in Pavenčiai and were put in a large hall of a defunct sugar factory. We stayed there for a few days until the Germans acquired transportation to take us to Stutthof. Stutthof was a concentration camp where Jews from Latvia, Lithuania, Estonia and Poland went through hell. Many were selected as soon as they arrived and were sent to be gassed. The night we came to Stutthof, we were lined up and divided — one group of strong, young prisoners to the right, mothers with children up to thirteen years old to the left. Our family was cut in two: Dora and I to the right, Mother and Sonia to the left. I took courage, walked up to the SS guard and tried to tell him that my sister was fifteen years old and would he please let my mother come with us. He would not even listen to me. There were rumours that the group of mothers and children were taken to Auschwitz that same night and were gassed. Fifty years later, I got proof — I found out through a friend of mine that there is a museum in Stutthof with information in its archives about some of the inmates. I wrote to them and got my answers. The rumours were confirmed.

~

During my sleepless nights, another thought that comes to me: Life — how ironic! I could see my mother's happiness when we saved Sonia from the *Kinderaktion*, but then I think about what happened in Stutthof and I ponder that if Sonia had been taken away with the *Kinderaktion* our mother might have lived through the rest of the war with Dora and me. She was only forty-four years old, strong, tiny, smart, vivacious. Who knows? I have deliberated on those thoughts. They hurt; they do not let me rest.

～

The first night in Stutthof, we were all pushed into a large room, naked, and German gynecologists examined us internally in case we had hidden some jewels in our vaginas. What a degrading feeling and how humiliating to young people; they reduced us to dirt. Next, we were shoved into a shower room. We were told to wash up and as we exited the showers the officers threw clothes at us — dresses, shoes, coats. There were no questions asked of whether or not these items fit, and if one of us mentioned that the shoes were too tight, we were all barraged with hits and punches; we couldn't even anticipate where they would come from.

The next morning, we started to learn about the situation in Stutthof. One has to be an artist to be able to describe the atmosphere there, to make people understand or to even provide an idea of the place. It is impossible. It was the kind of experience that cannot be understood by those who did not live through it.

Dora and I assumed that we would not make it through one week if we stayed in Stutthof, so we tried to find out how to get into a work group. We heard that some girls were taken to do all kinds of jobs outside the camp, and this is what we aimed for. A few days later we heard that girls were wanted to work on farms during the harvest. Dora and I became two of the chosen lucky ones. Life on the farm was heaven. First of all, there was enough food, and second, the security was run by British prisoners of war. All we could wish for was for the war to end as soon as possible. But unfortunately, all good things come to an end. After the summer, the harvest was over, and we were sent back to Stutthof.

When we arrived back at Stutthof, Dora and I learned that we had missed one event: the shaving of the girls' heads. Dora and I stuck out like sore thumbs. My dress was very long, and so we decided to cut it off and use the material to make two headscarves. We wore them all the time, completely concealing our hair. Again a little luck — we saved our hair from being shaved.

Just a few days after we returned to Stutthof, the guards were choosing five hundred women to work in an ammunition factory in Ochsenzoll, near Hamburg. Dora and I looked really strong after the summer on the farm, so we had no trouble being chosen. Ochsenzoll was a fairly small camp. It contained two barracks with about 250 women in each. We worked in a factory, making ammunition, in two shifts. Overlooking the production were civilian Italian workers, and many of them helped us out with an extra piece of bread or other food items.

Our first commandant at Ochsenzoll was a real murderer. When we arrived back from work, he kept us for hours on the *Appellplatz*, the roll call place, counting us over and over again. We were lined up in rows of five, and while he was counting, the first person in each row was hit on the head with a thin stick that looked like a conductor's wand. Of course nobody wanted to stand in the front, and so *Appell* time was a disaster, with people shoving, pushing and falling, and that was what our commandant was waiting for. Then he really got outraged and started throwing punches and hitting people like a lunatic. One of our friends was made to stand all night on a pile of peat for "misbehaving." It was bitterly cold that evening, and it was a miracle that she came out of this ordeal alive.

We were really fortunate that he lasted only a few months at Ochsenzoll, and then we got a wonderful human being as commandant of our camp. Life became bearable. This was also only a few months before liberation, which helped. Every Sunday, our commandant chose a few women to dig potatoes for the kitchen. Most of us loved the job, because there was a chance to steal a few for the inmates. I wore a small sewn bag hanging from a belt, and while I was digging up pota-toes in the field, I also filled my bag. My coat was big and I put some potatoes in the bag around my waist as well as in my large pockets. One day when we returned from the potato field, we were stopped, asked to open our coats, and to leave all the stolen potatoes on the ground. My sister and the other girls watched through the bunk win-dows, shivering and wondering what was going to happen to us.

I walked into the bunk, opened my coat and yelled out trium-phantly, "May they all go to hell!" I still had my little bag full of po-tatoes hanging from my belt under my coat. When the commandant told us to empty our pockets and the rest of our clothes, I did so, but I took a chance and left the little bag in back full of potatoes. Dora wanted to kill me. She couldn't understand how I could take a chance like that. But we all cut up the potatoes, stuck them on the stove and enjoyed the special feast. After liberation, we said that we were the inventors of potato chips. We felt as though we were the first, making them in Ochsenzoll on our bunk oven.

We stayed in Ochsenzoll until about the beginning of April 1945. Hamburg was being bombed constantly, and one morning we were packed onto a train and shipped to Bergen-Belsen. The trains stopped in the village of Bergen and when we looked out, we saw a large field full of men sitting next to each other, legs crossed. We decided, for some reason, that there were no Jews in that group.

When we came to the Bergen-Belsen camp gate, the girls in our group started saying, "This is the end, we'll never survive this." Dora said, "It won't be so easy, they will make us suffer, torture us before they will be ready to let us die." And this was true. Bergen-Belsen, in the last days before liberation, was a camp that committed mass murder by plainly neglecting the inmates. By the time we came to Belsen, dead bodies were lying around one on top of the other like garbage piles. Corpses were found all over the place, rotting in the barracks and outside. This horrible situation was beyond anybody's imagination. The Nazis absolutely dehumanized us. People from different countries, different backgrounds, were brought together, confined in dirty, cramped bunks, deprived of all necessities, living in the most degrading conditions. All human weaknesses and passions are let loose in such situations and people's selfishness and mean behaviour are unimaginable.

The dirt, mud and lice made it impossible for us to keep clean. Our daily evening activity was to kill the lice. The elastic band of our underwear was full of them. The more you killed, the more came back the next day. It was a losing battle.

All day long people were shuffling about, carrying little cans (just in case they found some food), arguing constantly, swearing and making life intolerable. Meal time was a disaster. When the kapos turned up with cans of soup, which was more like dishwater, the inmates pushed one another as though they were ready to grab a treasure. The weak and sick ones got pushed and stepped on and could not even get near the soup. The Nazis turned us into animals; they drove us out of our minds. The sores of malnutrition — ulcers, boils — were an everyday occurrence. Epidemics were spreading. One day, the water was cut off. In the communal wash place, all of us stood close together, the wind blowing in from outside, the filth, refuse and excrement all over the place. Some cold water dribbled out of the taps and everyone fought for a drop.

Our food in the first few days was turnips and water — one bowl, if you were lucky. The systematic starvation in Belsen was atrocious. Auschwitz was a camp of mechanized genocide, but Belsen killed the inmates by starvation, violence, terror and the spread of infectious diseases.[5] Dysentery and typhus were widespread. The yards, washrooms and latrines, which were open holes, were permeated with

---

5  Bergen-Belsen began, in 1940, as a POW camp for Soviet, Belgian and French prisoners, but was converted into a concentration camp in 1943. It held no gas chambers, but Jews died of starvation, disease, exhaustion, brutality and medical experiments.

dirt. The guards watching from above, in their booths, laughed. They must have thought to themselves, "Look at those Jews, how dirty they are; they stink, they are worse than any scum of the earth." Even though the Nazis caused all of this, I tell myself now that I couldn't even blame those guards. To stand up there and look down on that horrible sight — what could anybody say or think about it?

I got typhus a few days after my arrival in Bergen-Belsen. This is a horrible disease. Your hunger disappears, the headaches are intolerable, you become delirious and you have diarrhea. You feel near death. My place in the bunk was on the top tier. When I got sick and tried to step down in order to go outside, the diarrhea took over. The people around me made my life miserable. They were so mean, called me a piece of shit and cursed me. I kept telling Dora to let me die, leave me alone, but she kept repeating, "You mustn't die, you have to hold on. What will Mama say after the war? She will look for us, and if she does not find us, she'll die. You have to keep fighting! Keep fighting! We must live to tell the story!" It took me fifty years to be ready to tell the story.

During the last few days in camp, we could feel the end of the war coming. It seemed close, but I couldn't even imagine what it would look or feel like. Rotting bodies were everywhere; fewer and fewer Nazis appeared. Where were they hiding? It was unbelievable when one morning Dora came into the bunk running and shouting, "We are free! We are free! Come, let's meet our liberators."[6] I was dragged down from my bunk and pulled outside closer to the gate. And there they were, near a beautiful tank. I raised my arms and then dropped down to the ground and fainted. Dora was always near me and always tried to help, but she was also weak since she had typhus as well. Luckily, we were liberated in time to survive.

---

6  The British and Canadian armies liberated the camp on April 15, 1945, and found 13,000 unburied corpses and 60,000 inmates. The camp was designed to hold 10,000. jewishvirtuallibrary.org

A hospital was immediately organized and all the sick were cleaned and taken there. It took weeks for us to get better and be strong enough to stand up. I got very hungry after I recovered, and I would drive Dora crazy asking her to go to the hospital kitchen to ask for more food. It is interesting that in camp people could kill each other for a bite of bread, but as soon as life became normalized, Dora was too shy to ask for food. She said, "Are you crazy? I'm not going to beg for food." The hospital kitchen was very careful not to let us over-eat. We had to get used to food very slowly. Approximately 14,000 people died in Belsen after the liberation because of overeating and other causes.

When we got well and started a more or less normal life, reality set in. Who was left of our family? There was only Dora and me and the part of our family that had immigrated to the US before the war. Hundreds of family members — aunts, uncles, cousins, great uncles, great aunts, Mama, Sonia, Daddy — had been killed. I felt so tiny and alone in this big, big world. And so as soon as we got our strength back, Dora and I tried to do something to get involved in the Bergen-Belsen cultural life. Soon a Central Committee was established, different organizations evolved and in July even a Yiddish theatre was set up — the Bergen-Belsen KZ, or Kazet — and Dora and I joined. Our director was Sami Feder, a Polish Jew who had been involved in Jewish theatre in Lodz before the war. Dora became an actress and dancer, and I worked as an accompanist and did all the musical backgrounds. I played the piano and accordion and wrote my own musical notations because there was no Jewish music available at the beginning. We, the group, even published an anthology of songs and poems from the ghettos and concentration camps. We collected those songs from people who remembered them. The anthology was edited by D. Rozental and Paul Trepman, and it was published in 1946 by the Central Committee in Bergen-Belsen.

Once the theatre group worked up a decent repertoire, we went on a tour to Belgium and France, which was arranged by the Joint, the American Jewish Joint Distribution Committee. In Paris, we performed in the Sarah Bernhardt Theatre. Where did we get the strength to start life all over again after such a disaster, after this genocide? Maybe loneliness helped. Because we were so alone, we tried to build a new world for ourselves. New families, children, grandchildren.

I was very lucky to meet such a wonderful young man like Paul Trepman. When I met him, he was already one of the editors of the newspaper *Unzer Sztyme* (Our Voice), the first Jewish newspaper in the British-occupied zone of Germany. As a correspondent for the newspaper, Paul had been sent to cover the Nuremberg trials. There he met a young journalist, J. Meskauskas, who had lived through the war in London, England, but who was originally from Šiauliai, Lithuania. When he heard that Trepman came from Belsen, he inquired whether there were any survivors from Lithuania there. Paul told him that he knew about two sisters by the name of Widutschinsky from Šiauliai who were performing in the KZ Theatre. Mr. Meskauskas happened to know our family and asked Trepman to please give us his regards and to ask if we knew anything about his own family. That is how I met my future husband. Paul and I were married March 28, 1946, almost a year after liberation.

Interestingly, when Paul and I first talked about our arrival in Bergen-Belsen, I found out that he was one of the men sitting in that large field I mentioned. It was true that most of the men in the group were not Jewish, but Paul was there because he had gone through the concentration camps as a non-Jew. Paul went through hell hiding with false papers as a Christian, working in the Polish underground and eventually ending up in seven concentration camps, about which he wrote in his book, *Among Men and Beasts* (published by the World Bergen-Belsen Association in 1978).

When our KZ Theatre was ready to go on tour, Paul came along as a correspondent of the paper. This gave him the chance to reunite with some members of his family who had lived through the war in Belgium and France. Through the newspaper, Paul was in touch with people from the *Canadian Jewish Eagle*, a Yiddish newspaper in Montreal, as well as many prominent Jewish writers. As a matter of fact, the *Eagle* sent us the necessary papers to immigrate to Canada.

We arrived in Montreal in July 1948 and a few weeks later were hired by the Jewish People's Schools to teach Yiddish and Hebrew studies. I taught only two years at the evening school because in 1950, our daughter, Charlotte, was born. After a year of absence I returned to teach at the Shaare Zion day school, which later changed its name to Solomon Schechter Academy. I taught there for forty years. In 1956, our son, Elly, was born. Paul taught for many years at the Jewish People's Schools and in the summers he was director of Unzer Camp in the Laurentian Mountains. Paul led a full, busy life, contributing to the Jewish community in Montreal. In his last thirteen years, he worked as director of the Jewish Public Library. He also wrote and published extensively and was involved in many aspects of Jewish life. Paul left an important imprint on our Montreal community.

Our two children, Charlotte and Elly, both got married and have children. Charlotte has four children and teaches English and music in New York. Elly has two daughters and is an orthopedic surgeon in Seattle.

When I think of how I lived my life, always running, always pushing, trying to live every minute of the day, I am sure it has something to do with my time in the concentration camps. I was always trying to make up for the lost time, always trying to catch up. For forty years, I was teaching as well as going to school myself, and I graduated cum laude from Concordia University. I also belonged to the YMHA, jogged, folk danced, played the piano and was involved in different organizations. I ask myself often, What made Babey run? I think you'll find the answer in here.

∼

Since the end of World War II, the conclusion of each year and the beginning of a new one makes me think of my Holocaust odyssey. I thank God for the good years in Canada, the country that accepted us and made us feel at home, and for my wonderful years with my late husband, Paul, and our two precious children. One could not ask for anything more. Since Paul's death on November 23, 1987, my life has not been the same. We had a marriage made in heaven. We came out of hell and started a new life together. We grew into this life and appreciated and cherished every moment of every day. Every new happening in our lives was regarded as a precious gift. Paul is in my thoughts every minute of every day. There are so many questions that I would like to discuss with him; he always had the right answer for me, and I miss him terribly.

It took fifty years for me to decide to finally put some thoughts of my war years into writing, even though the Holocaust was always present and discussed in our home. We never tried to overprotect our children and hide the pain that we felt from them. I firmly believe that our children grew up as well-adjusted adults because of our openness.

1 Babey Widutschinsky in Bergen-Belsen after the war.
2 Wedding photo of Babey in the Bergen-Belsen Kazet Theatre, where she married Paul Trepman in 1946. Backdrops from the theatre company's latest production are behind her.

Babey and Paul, circa 1947.

1   A trained classical pianist, Babey was the accompanist for the Kazet Theatre in Bergen-Belsen. After the war, she was a sought-after pianist for the Montreal Jewish community. As a teacher, she also incorporated music into her kindergarten program. Montreal, circa 1970s.

2   Babey (centre) with her husband, Paul, and sister, Dora. Florida, circa 1985.

1

2

1   At the 55th anniversary of the liberation of Bergen-Belsen. April 2000.
2   Babey (right) and Dora in Hawaii, 2005.

*Miracalously many like I survided who would believe in a Holocaust, with it we were at the one to tell about it*

*Dearest Lorraine and Sylvia:*                                                    *March 25, '86*

*Your thought of buying the tape recorder—and asking me to tape the story of my life for you, I appreciate much.* ▅▅▅▅▅▅▅▅▅▅▅▅▅▅▅▅▅▅▅▅▅▅▅▅▅▅▅▅▅▅▅▅▅▅▅▅▅▅

*My youth was nice. I liked school, I was in teachers and my classmates. Most of them came from fine homes. Some were richer, some middle class and some poor orphans whom I helped with things we had in our store. I remember all my teachers names. Our*

The first page of Ida Dimant's memoir, which the family discovered while they were sitting shiva for her in 1988.

# To My Daughters
# Ida Urbach Dimant

March 25, 1986

Dearest Lorraine and Sylvia,

I am writing to you, my daughters, because you asked me to tape record the story of my life. I appreciate that, but with my voice the way it is, I must wait until my health improves. Meanwhile, I will try to write my story for you, although I find it hard.

My childhood was not bad. We were comfortable, and I believe I had the basic things a child needed in those times. The most important thing I was lacking was my dear father, whom I don't remember and never had the honour to know. He died in his thirties and mom was left with six children — five daughters and a son. My older sister Rivka told me that my mother had to be watched after my dad's death because she thought of doing something foolish. She loved him so strongly and didn't think that she would be able to go on with her life without him. Later, she realized what that would have done to us and that she had to pull herself together.

My father, Shulem-Hersh, or Shalom-Zvi in Hebrew, had been a financier and also was in a leather business with a man who knew much about it, but it didn't work out and he gave it up. He wasn't meant for working in a grocery store like my mother, either. He had been a Talmudic scholar and a literary man and so was his father.

Zaide's name was Elias Urbach. I scarcely remember grandma, and cannot even remember her name. She died when I was little. If my father had lived, he would have taught Nathan Torah and Talmud and Nathan could have had a rabbinical doctorate. Regrettably, he was not fortunate in fulfilling this desire.

My mother's father was Benjamin Mayer Lessman. He was a beloved man, well-read and wise. He was more religious than my other Zaide and was very knowledgeable in the Talmud and in Polish. Uncle Nathan is the apple from that tree.... Grandpa Lessman's wife was the Boobie I knew and loved very much. She had personality and was respected by everyone who knew her. My mother loved her, too.

My mother, Shprinca, had been in business running a grocery store since before I was born and she was terrific at it. Our store was huge and carried many things a heart could desire. All of our customers liked my mother so much. They used to say they could trust her. My mother was honest and kind and such a good soul. She thought of the sick and the poor and always helped them. She worked hard until late at night — to provide for a family of seven was not easy. Mom had three brothers and three sisters, a family that had doubled precisely when her mother died (when Mom was ten years of age) and grandpa remarried. Then Mom was blessed with work to do from her teens on.

My father's aim was to give us all a good education and a good *Kinderstube*, upbringing. My oldest sister, Ruchel, attended one of the best Hebrew *Gymnasiums*, a high school, owned by Itzhak Katzenelson[1], a modern man. Bais Yaakov school was his, too. I liked school. Most of my classmates came from good homes. Some were rich, some

---

1  Itzhak Katzenelson was a well-known teacher as well as an author of essays, plays and poems, best known for the poem "Song of the Murdered Jewish People." He took part in the Warsaw Uprising and escaped afterwards, but was captured and murdered at Auschwitz in April 1944. See "Writers and Poets in the Ghettos," USHMM Holocaust Encyclopedia, https://www.ushmm.org.

middle class and some were poor orphans whom I helped by giving them things we had in the store. I remember all my teachers' names! Our principal was very strict and the school was one of the best, for girls only. Mostly, I did my homework with two of my best school friends: sometimes in their place, other times at our home. Their sisters and mine taught us how to "perform," which we did in many houses, selling about fifty tickets each time we performed a play. The money went to the poor.

I had four sisters — Regina, Ruchel, Rachel and Sally; Nathan was the only boy in the family. My oldest sister, Ruchel, was engaged at nineteen and married a year later. At her wedding, I wore a beautiful silk dress, white stockings and black patent shoes, and I had a white bow in my hair. My cousin Rivka made my dress. She was a very good dressmaker and had a large clientele. As if it were yesterday, I remember how I stood on a chair at the head table and made a speech about my sister's wedding day. I remember every word of it. Rivka's father, Henoch, was my mother's brother. He and his wife, Cipora, were very Orthodox. Uncle Henoch and two of his sons learned Torah day and night. One was tall, slim and handsome and wasn't religious. He escaped to the Soviet Union during the war but didn't come back. Rivka went to Canada in 1930 after she married Harry. The rest of the family perished. They were all married and had children. From eight in the family, she is the only one left. Harry also lost his parents and five brothers with their wives and children.

∼

In the building where we lived, there were eighty to one hundred families. We all grew up together and became like one large family. I still miss them all. Our place was clean and cozy and filled with love. My sisters took me to movies, theatres, the circus and to the huge and beautiful parks we had in our city, Lodz.

We had rich relatives, middle-class and poor, but all of them were fine people. Some of my aunts and uncles were in business; some hardly made a living, especially the aunts who were widowed. Cousin Miriam's father had a beautiful building and a huge store with tailors' supplies, but my poor uncle lost his vision as a young man. Cousin Salek's father had a store with ladies' accessories and ties for men. They were well-off.

My father's brother had disappeared in World War I. Aunt Hudes was my father's only sister. I saw a picture of my uncle at my cousin Ida's after the war, when I stayed with her. Ida and her husband, Mietek, had some photographs of her family because she and Mietek and their son Lucek (Luis) had survived on false "Aryan" papers during the war. Aunt Hudes's other children before the war were Helena, who died quite young, in her thirties, Jacob, Edmund, Abram and Mayerek. Jacob fell in love with a beautiful girl named Regina, who was from an Orthodox home. They were married and had two children. When Jacob was single, he used to play classical music for me, which I always liked to hear. All the children played the violin. Their son Edmund was a blond, very good-looking man who was madly in love with his brother-in-law's sister, Rena Krauser. She was a neighbour and very attractive and they knew each other from childhood. Their son Abram (Adek) was a ladies' man, a flirt, but still a fine, intelligent man. He married shortly before the war. He and his wife lived in the ghetto near us and came in every day on their way home from work. Their youngest son was Mayerek. He was silk and velvet. All of them perished in the gas chambers. I miss them so much. They were a beautiful example of a family and of a home.

My sister Sally and her husband, Elias Goldner, and little Tusia and their maid were deported in 1942–1943. I was so glad then that Tusia was with her parents and not deported with us. We were evacuated from our home for the first time three weeks after the Germans occupied Lodz in September 1939.[2] We were given ten minutes

---

2  After the occupation, Lodz was incorporated into the Third Reich and an ordinance was issued in December 1939 to deport Jews to the area known as the

to leave our place. My three-year-old niece was with us that day. How I dared to ask a high-ranking officer to let me take her to my sister (who lived a few streets from us), I still do not know. It was the beginning. I got permission and a guard took me there. I felt so relieved! In the meantime, my mother and sisters and my sister Regina's fiancé, Pinchas Engel, were already out of the house.

We were taken to Jasło, a shtetl in Galicia.[3] We were brought to a vacant courtyard, where there was a little bit of straw on the floor. We sat down, hungry and exhausted, stretched our legs, and wondered what they would do with us. Young people came with soup cans and meat, which was sent to us by the Jewish community and from private homes. After a few days there, the authorities told us we could go to Krakow at our own expense. Regina's fiancé, Pinchas, was from Krakow, so we all went to his parents' home. He had been at our place when they came to evacuate us because he worked in Lodz in his sister's business. We waited for a night train and we arrived at their place in Krakow, very exhausted. There, we met many of their other relatives who also were refugees from Lodz and who had been in our house at Regina's engagement party. We were all welcome to take a seat on the floor. They had three rooms: a large room, a smaller one and a kitchen. Thursday was my sister's wedding. It had been set for that day, and it had to go on. Pinchas' father was well-known among the Hasidim; prayers were said in his house in the morning and evenings. People brought food and helped with other things. One of his father's students took the young couple to his house and gave them a room. The celebration of the *Sheva Brachot*, seven blessings, took place the next day.

---

*Generalgouvernement.* Between December 13 and 17, 6,000 Jews were deported from Lodz. See Isaiah Trunk and Robert Moses Shapiro, *Lodz Ghetto: A History* (Bloomington: Indiana University Press, 2006), 11–12.

3   Jasło, a town in south-eastern Poland on the border with Slovakia, was almost entirely destroyed by the Germans in 1944, when it became the site of the frontline between Germany and the USSR.

I was sent to the home of a widow who had taken in a refugee from Germany. It was a comfortable place for the three of us. I finally slept in a bed with a warm cover and in the morning I got a kaiser roll with coffee and then went back to my family. We then met a neighbour from home who had two rooms and a kitchen. He said his wife would be glad to rent one, and so we did and were able to all live together.

We soon heard that people were being smuggled back to Lodz to their vacant homes. Nathan managed to find a smuggler for the two of us. We wanted to get back to our home to bring things to Krakow that we had left in Lodz. The journey was not an easy one. We walked in the darkness of night in fear, through woods, until we saw a Polish man with his wagon and horse. He took us to a village far away where another smuggler was supposed to pick us up in the morning and take us even farther. We stayed in a restaurant that night owned by Jewish people. We bought something to eat and sat down in the corridor on the floor. Next door was a Jewish family who had run away from Lodz. They invited us to sit on their floor; of course, it was warmer inside. Their daughter asked me where I came from and when she heard who I was, she screamed and said, "Mother, this girl is from that store you once sent me to buy flour when we couldn't get it anywhere but in their place." (My mother kept selling right up until the end, not thinking of herself.) This girl took me in her poor bed with a straw mattress; it seemed to me like I was in the best hotel. I thought of the others who spent the night on the floor.

In the morning, the next smuggler came, and we all got into his wagon. As we came close to a shtetl near Lodz, suddenly the wagon was in water, getting us, and all the things we had on our wagon, wet. The ice had cracked, and we had to get off. The man looked for a peasant and found one who, although he was afraid, took money for keeping our possessions in his small place until we could come back for them. The smuggler went home. We all walked — I was walking in my still-wet flannel shoes, until we reached the shtetl.

In front of a house stood a Jewish man with a white beard like Moses, with two of his daughters. All of them shed tears when they looked at us; they invited us in. The women dried our wet clothes and shoes and made us hot coffee and bread with cheese. I'll never forget that scene. It was Friday evening and most of the group had borrowed money from me on the way. I had hidden the money in the mouth of a fox fur I wore. But I didn't know where the group had gone and I was left with no money, and so an older woman took me to the Jewish Congress to ask if they would lend us some money to go home. They did.

I continued walking, and when I neared a streetcar that went to the city, to the street where my sister Sally lived, I saw the sign, "Jews are not allowed in streetcars." I took the yellow band from my arm, and in my wet flannel shoes, I got on. I sat next to a Polish woman and talked to her about the war. My heart was pounding, but I stayed calm. When I arrived at Sally's home, she was shocked to see me. Their maid and my grandmother were there. Tusia fell into my arms and we kissed and hugged.

Nathan ran to see what was going on at our place. I had eaten dinner, and I also went home. I saw two wagons at the front door and Germans who were taking everything from our store. Our hiding place was now open and the expensive things we had hidden were gone. I wasn't sure if the Germans had an order to take our things or were doing this on their own, so I went to the police station not far from us to ask if they had permission to ransack our store. A Gestapo officer looked it up in the books and told me that everything was "confiscated." With tears in my eyes and pain in my heart, I went back home. I went to the janitor, Anthony, and his wife, who knew me from childhood and who loved us all and could see what was being done to us. We had lots of soap hidden in our corridor. The Germans didn't know about it and I begged Anthony to take it down. He was terribly frightened but did it at night with the help of his niece and me. I gave him the confections we had hidden there and also some soap. I slept in their tiny room with them. The next morning I took the soap to Sally and she paid me for it; their store was still open. Ruchel's husband, Leon, came back later to do the same thing; she and her two children were away at his mother's place in another town.

Leon found a smuggler to take us back to Krakow. Before we left, we returned to our home once more. The Germans hadn't been in the rooms, so we took our quilts, pillows and a few other things. The smuggler took us to a small town where again we had to wait for another man to take us to Krakow. We waited and the Polish man came: I was afraid to look at him — a big Polish drunk, I thought! At sunset, we started our journey. On the way, the man stopped at a saloon, got drunk and started asking us for more money. It was bitterly cold and we didn't know what to do. Nathan and Leon put the man on his wagon with his two big horses and I sat in the front. The man fell asleep while they searched for a peasant to take us farther.

In the meantime, the horses started galloping; I was so scared and I screamed for help. I saw a very young boy, ten or twelve, pass by and begged him to hold the leather straps on the horses. He looked at me and said, "In the water with the Jews." However, a peasant came by and held the two horses back. Leon and Nathan were running toward me in tears; they hugged me and we cried. They asked this man to take the other drunken man to his house and let him sleep and then take us to the arranged destination. He was nice and also hungry for money so he took the wagon and went with us.

We came to a shtetl, Wolbrom, a few hours away, to a Jewish family who had a grocery store. I fell on my knees at the woman's feet and kissed her. I felt as though I had found my mother. She was so nice and so kind, taking us into her room and giving us a warm soup. The three of us slept on the floor with warm blankets underneath and on top of us. In the morning, we had breakfast and went to the train station. Leon went back to his mother's, where my sister Ruchel and their two children were staying.

The train was not on time; we froze the whole night outside and in the darkness I heard some Poles saying, "Good for them. Hitler will finish them!"

We returned to Krakow. My mother looked at us and started crying like a baby. We were worn and exhausted. But the room was warm and we had some food and soon came back to ourselves. It didn't take long before we again started thinking of going back home to Lodz. Many people were informed that they could go back and stay in their apartments, which were still empty. Nathan and I again were the first to go; then mother came with my sister Rachel. Regina and Pinchas stayed in Krakow and had a baby boy a year later.

My boyfriend, Abram, came back a few months later. First, food was rationed. Then the ghetto was created, which changed everything: in the ghetto, doctors and lawyers, and the rich and the poor were all the same.[4] After 7:00 p.m., we weren't allowed to be in the streets. Electricity was shut off. A few families lived in a single room. Conditions were very bad. We had to carry water from the well, and the weak became walking skeletons. The *klepsydra*[5] as we called it, the placards of death, were on their backs already.

Nathan and his friends couldn't stand the hunger and, on their own, registered for work. The Germans promised them good food and wages, which would be sent to their parents. Mother received forty-five RM (Reichsmark) monthly, which was later used as a reason to put her on the list to be sent away. Fortunately, Adek (Abram Motyl) saved her then, through a high-ranking friend.

"Aktions, aktions!"[6] One day, they took the children on the wag-

---

4 The Nazis established the Lodz ghetto on February 8, 1940. Barbed wire surrounded the ghetto, which was sealed on May 1.

5 *Klepsydra* is the Polish word for hourglass or obituaries.

6 The German word *Aktion* refers to a roundup for deportation. Jews were deported from the Lodz ghetto to the death camp of Chełmno beginning on January 6, 1942. From September 5 to 12, 1942, the *Gehsperre* action was a deportation of 15,000 Jews, mostly children and the elderly. For a time, the deportations

ons, the next day, the elderly. Lamentations from the rest of the families broke our hearts. We had to line up in the streets or in backyards. The sound of screaming still rings in my ears. People were running like wild animals to screams of "Alle Juden raus!" (All Jews out!) I hid mother in our shed in the yard and covered her with boards and *shmates*, rags, and while standing in the line, I heard the Germans yelling, "Alle Unterstände aufmachen!" (Open all the sheds!)

Evacuation lists with names of people to be sent away grew every day. My sister Ruchel, who had lived in the same building as we did, was deported with her husband, Leon, and two children, ages eight and twelve. We lost each other; they were in Rzeszów, near Krakow. Imagining that we must be in Krakow, they had tried to come and see us and that became a farewell forever. I think Sally and her family were taken to Treblinka. My sister Regina, her husband, Pinchas, and their baby were shot in Krakow on Passover night. They were taken away from the seder to go to their deaths. I learned that from a Hungarian rabbi in Bergen-Belsen, after the war.

The Nazi plan was to clear the ghetto and get rid of the Jews. Despite this, Abram asked my mother for her permission to marry me. He got it, of course, and mother asked a rabbi nearby to come over with his homemade chuppah, the wedding canopy. We were married; Abram was so happy and didn't want to think of what could or would happen the next day. We lived day to day and for the day. Thinking of tomorrow drove us mad. I married Abram Toter shortly before we were taken to Auschwitz. On August 28, 1944, it was our turn to walk to the train.

By then, we knew of the transports. Another one every day,

---

stopped; then, on June 19, 1944, Himmler ordered the liquidation of the ghetto and in June and July 3,000 Jews were sent to Chełmno. In August, the ghetto was liquidated and the remaining Jews were sent to Auschwitz. Life in the Lodz ghetto was characterized by starvation, overcrowding and forced hard labour. See "Lodz" at https://www.ushmm.org/wlc/en/article.php?ModuleId=10005071.

until it came to us. We weren't in our home the evening we were taken. Abram had a high temperature the night before. I gave him compresses often and he felt a bit better in the morning. He insisted on hiding and he found a place in the building where we lived, but we were discovered. I was afraid, but we all went down and lined up with hundreds of our fellow Jews in the street. To look at those murderers around us was awful.

We were taken to a barracks in a suburb near Lodz and were kept there for two days. Then we walked with the guards to the cattle trains. On the windows was written, *HIER SIND VERBRECHER* (Here Are Criminals). A pregnant woman in my line, who was in the late months, was asked by one German, "Who made that shit-poor thing?" She answered, "My husband." She disappeared. Bread was given to us and taken away before we got onto the train. How can one describe what it looked like? Mothers prepared candles to warm up something for their babies who couldn't stop crying. A big can, like a garbage can, was in the middle of the car. People were in such fear that they got diarrhea and had to use the can. For three days, we didn't have a sip of water.

They *shlepped* us for three days, until we arrived in Auschwitz-Birkenau.[7] At the gates, there were selections. My mother was taken away from my arms at the entrance. With her there was my husband, Abram, and my ten-year-old nephew, whom we had taken when his parents were deported in 1942 with three of their five children, thinking that we could save him. A five-year-old girl was with an aunt and the boy was with us. My sister Rachel and I were led to the *entlausung*, delousing, where they shaved our hair off and sent us to a shower room. When we got out, we couldn't recognize one another. Naked, we came out with a *shmate* and a number on our arms. Some, like me, weren't tattooed and the numbers, which were written on us, came off after we washed.

---

7  Lodz is about 210 kilometres from Auschwitz.

They showed us to barracks No. 31, with its broken floor and with little room to sit. Like herrings in tins, we sat on the broken cement floors. We couldn't stretch our arms or legs and, if one of us was loud, the *Blockälteste*, block elder, poured water on her or on all of us, so we had to stay quiet. We drank soup from a dirty pot, five or more people passing it around. We were paraded out on the roads. The Hitler Youth would line up like soldiers: some would laugh and others bowed their heads. Though we didn't have much food or drink, we still needed a washroom. When the doors of our barracks opened, we ran like cattle, and one person fell on the other. The washroom was a stable with toilet bowls and we had five minutes and out! No paper, no water for our needs. We were allowed to go only once a day, when the Nazis sent us. We ran to get on those toilet seats. After three minutes, the bell rang and, with their whips, the Nazis came in to see if all of us had left.

Dr. Mengele or the others who did selections visited us every day, in the morning and at night. And these were the cultured Germans of whom I had read? Josef Mengele was a doctor who turned out to be one of the biggest murderers in history. Whenever they arrived, Rachel trembled; she was so afraid and that frightened me. I could see how she had changed and how weak she was. Every day she begged me to go with her to the fence and touch the electrical wires and put an end to our miserable lives. I dissuaded her and told her to look at the other women we knew who were very intelligent and elegant, and how they hoped to survive and be with their husbands, sisters or brothers. She calmed down. One day after Yom Kippur, Mengele made a selection and took Rachel away from me. I prayed to die.

I was sent to another barracks with bunks in it. At night, I felt something on my head. Urine was pouring on me. Shortly afterwards, I was sent to work in a concentration camp far away.[8] I lost my

---

8  The author's family has not been able to establish the name of this camp.

TO MY DAUGHTERS 409

Polish women and was mostly with Hungarians and Czechoslovaks. My shoes were tight, no gloves, no warm coat. That's how I went to work. We dug ditches for the soldiers and dug up kohlrabi and ate the skin from it. Later, even that wasn't allowed. I was in Group 1. Our guard was an idiot, but he didn't hit us. He found me once with a couple of potatoes I picked up from the earth and asked me how I ate them. I said, "Raw, Herr Wachmeister!" He gave them back to me and said, "Lucky, God." Group 4 came with us one day. I'll never forget the name of their guard, Gerhard; he was a real bloodthirsty Hitler, with orders perhaps not to kill. When he hit someone, it was worse than killing. I prayed to be dead after he beat me with his rifle, over my legs, for seeing me with a few of those little kohlrabies. He slapped me and put me in a ditch with water in it. I had an ice-pick in my hands and was forced to do hard work until I couldn't breathe. I was bruised all over and found it hard to climb to my bunk. How I prayed to see that murderer being tortured like they tortured our people before they killed them.

It's a story with no end. I can use a hundred pages to tell you half of my ordeals. Miraculously, many, like me, survived. Who would believe the Holocaust happened if we weren't the ones to tell about it? We even asked the question, "Where was the Almighty?" I believe that the small number of survivors was meant to bring new Jewish generations to this world and to build a country where we would have friends.

~

In early 1945, the Soviets came and we were free. The war was still going on in Berlin. I began working in a hospital with four other girls from Lodz. Two of them I knew; the other two, Sonya and Lucia, came as young girls from the Soviet Union with their parents. We all shared one room and worked as nurses' aides. Sonya, a nurse, spoke Russian fluently. Her sister, Lucia, was quite intelligent, too. I was so good to the wounded men that some asked especially for me and waited for my shift. The head nurse gave me extra food. The Russian commandant forced us to come to the dances they held.

It took another four months until we were free to go back to Poland, with the help of the Red Cross. On arriving in Lodz, I met a neighbour at the station who told me that my brother, Nathan, was back. I found him five or six days later at Ida and Mietek's pastry shop. We all cried and hugged and kissed. Both Ida and Nathan said, "I knew that you would survive." It was the end of April, and since Ida's birthday was on May 1, Mietek gave me money to put on a nice party for her. High-ranking officials, with whom Mietek had dealt, were invited. Ida gave me a few of her dresses and shoes. My hair grew back and I looked like a *mensch* again.

Months later, I heard from a friend who was in a camp with my Abram that he was shot a day before the liberation while on a death march. At least I had found Nathan. Other people were left the sole survivors of their families. My mother's sisters and brother and their husbands and wives and so many of their children were murdered in the gas chambers. How can I forget my mother, who was taken from my arms in Auschwitz and who I never saw again? My sisters, who were so young, and their husbands and their children, whom I loved and miss? How can one forget one's flesh and blood?

Nathan went to Israel. In Poland, there were pogroms against the Jews again, just like in the nineteenth century. We ran wherever we could. I was the wandering Jew for the first time in my life. Then, I met your father and we were married after one week. We went to the Displaced Persons camp at Bergen-Belsen, where he had been liberated.

We came to Canada where I made a home with a good husband and three lovely children. Lorraine and Sylvia, you are my saviours, my healers; I hope to see you both happy, and your happiness will make me happy and give me joy.

∼

"'Tis Said Life Passes as in a Dream"

A dream has beauty,
The rest is just misery
Once I also had a dream so fair
Alas, it has passed so quickly
Like the "golden sheaves."

Oh, golden sheaves
Where have you abducted time?
Oh, golden sheaves,
For you I pine.

I lived and I laughed
And suffered much grief
Courage fled
Like the golden sheaves.

This big, beautiful world has no heart
From all its joys one is left apart
Why is one left so solitary?
Because people go where there is celebration
And not where there is lamentation.

*by Ida Dimant*

1   Ida Dimant at age nine or ten. Lodz, Poland, 1928.
2, 3 & 4  Three of Ida's sisters before the war. Lodz, circa 1935.

1   Ida and her fiancé, Abram Toter, whom she married in the Lodz ghetto. November 1939.

2 & 3   Ida after the war. Lodz, 1946.

1  One of the only photos of the Dimant family. Toronto, late 1950s. In back, Ida
and Abraham Dimant, who married in Bergen-Belsen at the beginning of 1947.
In front, from left to right, are Ida's daughters, Lorraine (born 1949); Sylvia (born
1952); and Sharon (born in Bergen-Belsen in 1947). Sharon died from complica-
tions of heart surgery on September 28, 1961.

2  A note that Ida wrote about her English classes and how immensely helpful they
were; the classes prompted her writing of her memoirs. Toronto, 1988.

3  Ida (standing fourth from the right) with her English class. Toronto, 1987.

1  Ida's daughters Lorraine (left) and Sylvia (right) with Nicole, Sylvia's daughter.
2  Ida and her granddaughter, Nicole.

Soviet Union

# Foreword

Father Patrick Desbois changed Holocaust history by focussing on the murder of Jews in Ukraine.[1] Until the 2008 publication of *The Holocaust by Bullets: A Priest's Journey to Uncover the Truth Behind the Murder of 1.5 Million Jews*, scant attention had been paid to the Holocaust in Ukraine and the rest of the Soviet Union.[2] Sources had been scarce, but not entirely absent, until the Shoah Foundation's collection of 52,000 interviews became relatively available.[3] (This website includes over 10,000 interviews of Ukrainian witnesses and survivors.) Indeed, at this point, there is abundant evidence of the "cacophony of violence" that followed — and sometimes preceded — Operation Barbarossa, the Nazi invasion of the USSR, in June 1941.[4] There were pogroms and extreme acts of violence in virtually every city, town and village.

---

1   Father Patrick Desbois, *The Holocaust by Bullets* (New York: Palgrave Macmillan, 2008).
2   An important exception is Jan T. Gross' *Neighbors: The Destruction of the Jewish Community in Jedwabne, Poland* (New York: Penguin, 2002). See also Timothy Snyder, *Bloodlines: Europe Between Hitler and Stalin* (New York: Basic Books, 2010).
3   See http://vhaonline.edu for access to the Shoah Foundation site and a limited number (1,600) of interviews as well as information about access to the rest of the interviews.
4   See Gross, 59.

The brutality of the killings by locals, coupled with the mass murders by the Einsatzgruppen, is expressed in both survivor memoirs and bystander testimonies. Einsatzgruppen squads, described by Father Desbois, murdered the Jews publicly, with the involvement of the locals, who whether by inclination to participate or ordered to participate, fell into one of more than twelve categories: teeth-pullers, cooks (the murderers needed to be fed during massacres that lasted a whole day or longer), clothes sorters, transporters of bodies or materials to facilitate the cremation of the victims, and so on.[5] Mass murder replaced mass deportation, which had been a systematic part of the genocidal process in the rest of Europe.[6]

One historian explains that the invading Germans "had no detailed plans" as to what a German-occupied Ukraine and Soviet Russia would look like. Responsibility for security was handed over to locals for a time, but ultimately "the occupation authorities considered the potential for recruiting appropriate candidates as very limited: 'Naturally, it is very difficult to find appropriate forces due to the complete lack of intelligence.'"[7]

Cooperation with the German officials inevitably led to collaboration, but one must not ignore the hundreds of Ukrainians who hid Jews or otherwise helped them survive, notably because of their religious convictions.[8] Ironically, after murdering Jews and thereby elim-

5  Father Patrick Desbois, "The Witnesses of Ukraine or Evidence from the Ground: The Research of Yahad-In Unum," in *The Holocaust in Ukraine: New Sources and Perspectives*. Conference Presentations. Washington, DC: United States Holocaust Memorial Museum (USHMM), 2013, 91–99.

6  Snyder, 214–215.

7  Markus Eikel, "Division of Labor and Cooperation: The Local Administration Under German Occupation in Central and Eastern Ukraine, 1941–1944" in *The Holocaust in Ukraine: New Sources and Perspectives* (USHMM: Center for Advanced Holocaust Studies, 2013), 112.

8  Crispin Brooks, "Visual History Archive Interviews on the Holocaust in Ukraine," in *The Holocaust in Ukraine*, 17–62.

inating their annual contributions to a town's or village's revenues, which declined dramatically, officials complained about the loss of such income.[9] However, the sale of confiscated Jewish property and goods added to the treasury. For many Ukrainians, mass killings were justified by Nazi propaganda that equated Jews with repressive Soviet actions, including the famine of the 1930s. Bolshevism and all that it inflicted was blamed on Jews.

*My Life in the Gulag*, a name given to a system of Soviet forced labour camps, is the title of Mina Wolkowicz's memoir, dedicated to "women martyrs, sisters murdered, tortured, degraded, deprived of their children and family in the Soviet gulag." Arrested soon after her husband was picked up on a false charge of spying, Wolkowicz describes the details of her arrest, imprisonment and classification as a political enemy of the people, i.e., Trotskyites are Bundists are Zionists.[10] Wolkowicz's ironic wit underscores the madness of the Soviet system and the oppression of Stalinism.

Svetlana Kogan-Rabinovich's harrowing narrative about her life, *In the Nazi Inferno*, describes the chaos that followed the bombings in June 1941, and the escape from town to town to evade being burnt or buried alive. Forced to uproot trees and load them onto train cars under constant beatings by both German and Romanian soldiers, she thought of suicide. Like other Tulchin ghetto prisoners, she was sent to Pechora, a camp distinguished by its method of death through starvation and hard labour.

Gitlia Popovsky escaped the mass killings in Babi Yar by leaving Kiev just as the Nazis took over the city. Her train headed for Kharkov, which was under bombardment. She and others were evacuated to Kazakhstan. From there, she went to Uzbekistan, living in a big tent with many other women until 1944, when she was able to return

---

9  See Eikel, 107–112.
10 Stalin equated his political rival, Leon Trotsky, with Jews who supported Zionism and Bundism, a secular social movement. Supporters of both Zionism and Bundism were persecuted under the communist regime.

to Kiev. Married to a Jewish tailor, Abraham, who was disillusioned with communism, Gitlia and her husband remained in post-war Soviet Russia, enduring the shortages of food and other staples as well as virulent antisemitism. Gitlia chose to immigrate to Canada when the opportunity arose.

Finally, Koine Schachter Rogel's ordeal reveals the randomness of survival under Soviet and then German occupation. Her journey in search of safety for her family and herself reflects the effects of occupation and war on ordinary people. Caught between Romanian and Soviet crossfire, hiding in plain sight while witnessing the rape of her friend, and finally finding the area in which other Jews were held, Rogel is overcome with loss. Hunger and thirst intensified her despair. She was ultimately reunited with her family and interned at Yedinitz until another ordeal, a death march, landed her in Bessarabia before she experienced liberation.

Given the testimonies of the women in this section, we can only conclude that the Holocaust in the Soviet Union, though more complicated and less "organized" than that in central or eastern Europe, was every bit as horrific and devastating. According to Wendy Lower, chaos notwithstanding, there was a discernible pattern and "pogroms became a common feature of the first days and months of the Nazi 'liberation' in the summer of 1941."[11] Jews were rounded up and thrown into burning synagogues; Jews were beaten at random with household and farm implements; and cartfuls of Ukrainian peasants arrived ready to plunder. Lower cites instances of Jews being slaughtered "to pay...for the sufferings of Ukrainians," and points to similar

---

11 Wendy Lower, "Anti-Jewish Violence in Ukraine, Summer 1941: Varied Histories and Explanations," in *The Holocaust in Ukraine*, 143–173.

patterns in Lithuania and Belorussia.[12] Other historians write about
the involvement of Ukrainian policemen in the mass murder and
rape of Jewish girls and women.[13]

Despite the suppression of documentation of Ukrainian involvement and other Soviet "cooperation" in the name of building a narrative of Ukrainian and Soviet victimhood and nationhood, "silence
or awkwardness" about this era is giving way to the publication of accurate histories.[14]

---

12 Lower, 147.

13 Anatoly Podolsky, "Collaboration in Ukraine During the Holocaust: Aspects of
Historiography and Research," in *The Holocaust in Ukraine*, 189.

14 Podolsky, 187–197.

# My Life in the Gulag
# Mina Wolkowicz

*Dedicated to all those prisoners who were with me in prison and camp*
*— women-martyrs, sisters murdered, tortured, degraded and deprived*
*of their children and family in the Soviet Gulag.*

EDITOR'S NOTE

Mina Wolkowicz's memoir only discusses her time while imprisoned in Kholodnaya Gora in Kharkov, for about a year and a half,
beginning in December 1939. Prior to this time period, Mina, born
in Piotrków Trybunalski, Poland, in 1920, had lived in France, studying at university there due to the rising antisemitism in Poland and
the *numerus clausus* restrictions. Mina and her husband, Herman
Geisler, lived in France from 1938 until August 1939, when they
moved to Białystok, Poland, due to the impossibilities of acquiring
French citizenship. Białystok came under Soviet rule in mid-Septem-
ber 1939, after the German invasion of Poland and the stipulations
of the Molotov-Ribbentrop Pact. Mina and Herman then moved to
Kharkov, where he worked as a bookkeeper and she at a newspaper
while also attending university classes. This was a difficult time, dur-

ing which immigrants and intelligentsia were arrested. In the late fall of 1939, Mina's husband was arrested, suspected of being a spy.[1]

## AUTHOR'S PREFACE

Men imprisoned in the Soviet Gulag[2] have written many books about the terror, the deprivation of basic human rights, the permanent hunger, slave work, and the acts of terror by the NKVD (the Narodnyi Komissariat Vnutrennikh Del, the People's Commissariat for Internal Affairs) and their mannekin-helpers,[3] but not many books are pub-

---

1   This information, as well as the information following the memoir, comes from an extensive interview between Mina and her son Nathan in 1995. Incidentally, Mina's hometown of Piotrków Trybunalski was the site of the first ghetto in Poland, in October 1939. *Numerus clausus* (Latin for closed number) was a quota system that limited admission to institutions or professions. In nineteenth and twentieth-century Eastern Europe, Jews were frequently restricted from entering universities, professional associations and public administration. For information on the Molotov-Ribbentrop Pact, see the glossary.

2   An acronym for *Glavnoe Upravlenie ispravitel'no-trudovykh Lagerei*, meaning Main Administration of Corrective Labour Camps, the term Gulag refers both to the bureaucracy that operated the Soviet system of forced labour camps in the Stalin era and to the camps themselves. Penal camps were established in 1917 but greatly grew in size during Stalin's campaign to modernize and industrialize the Soviet Union and to collectivize agriculture in the early 1930s; more than ten million citizens and foreigners were incarcerated. Gulag camps existed throughout the Soviet Union, but the largest camps lay in the most remote regions of the country (such as the Arctic north, the Siberian east and the Central Asian south). Prisoners endured hard labour, violence, extreme climate conditions, meagre food rations and unsanitary conditions, all of which resulted in high death rates.

3   The author is referring to staff who followed KGB directives. Other authors use the term *Chekists* for staff of KGB prisons, or *Chekas. Chekist* is a term of insult, connoting evil or unpleasantness. See Helene Celmina, *Women in Soviet Prisons* (New York: Paragon House Publishers, 1985), p. xiii.

lished about the tragic life of women in the Gulag. I have, here, tried to bring out my life experience in the Soviet prison and camp system. After World War ii, the world tried or prosecuted few Nazi leaders in Nuremberg for the murder of millions of people. In Soviet Russia, Stalin, with his helpers, annihilated between six and nine million people under his regime, through the gulag system, where between two to three million perished, the Great Terror (1937–1938) and the famine of 1930–1933, when about five million died. Hundreds of thousands were shot under Stalin's direction, but nobody was tried or prosecuted for their murder, even after the fall of Soviet Russia.[4]

$$\sim$$

In the late fall of 1939, when two NKVD officers arrested my husband as a spy, they assured me that he would be back home in no time, after only a short interrogation. They told us, "Don't take anything with you that you do not need," and my husband went away with only a towel and a toothbrush. In Soviet Russia, when somebody was arrested, the family, relatives and friends were immediately incriminated. After my husband's arrest, I became *persona non grata*. My friends and neighbours avoided me. Rumours were spreading about finding weapons and anti-Soviet literature in my house during the searches. Gossip like this was usually generated by the KGB to justify the arrest. "The NKVD doesn't make mistakes" was their motto.

A friend of mine, a student from my class at the university, advised me not to come to the university for a time, to avoid meeting anybody and to "avoid the humiliation." She told me that in the

---

4  The oft-quoted figure of deaths under Stalin's regime has been twenty million, which was the original figure stated in this manuscript. Recent access to Soviet archives have allowed for these figures to be updated. See Timothy Snyder's article "Hitler vs. Stalin: Who Killed More?" in the 2011 issue of *The New York Review of Books* at http://www.nybooks.com/articles/2011/03/10/hitler-vs-stalin-who-killed-more/

time of NEP (New Economic Policy) in the 1920s, her father was arrested as a capitalist. His children suffered discrimination and were deprived of the right to work and to education. She said, "We were told to go to Birobidzhan.[5] We lived in hunger and fear. Only in the 1930s did the situation change and we started to work again. I became a metal worker in a factory and now I am at the university." She never told me what eventually happened to her father.

My persecution started immediately. I was fired from my work at the university, where I was told it was only temporary, "until your husband is free." All my coupons and my card for bread and other food were taken away. I sold my personal belongings like clothes at the black market to buy bread.

For two weeks, I searched for my husband in the prisons, but without results. Every morning from five to six, I went to the Kholodnaya Gora prison[6] walls, where masses of people — women, children, the elderly — were looking, like myself, for their loved ones. All had red eyes and blue lips and were walking back and forth, speaking in whispers. Early in the morning, we signed our names on a list. All nationalities were represented near the prison wall. There, at the prison wall, was the true "internationalism"; there was the Comintern.[7] There we met friends; people we knew were whispering about the arrests, for example that last night was a "Polish night," a "German Night," "Hungarian," and so on. The line got longer and longer every morning. We named it the Arrestometre, or arrests measured by the

---

5  Territory in the far eastern reaches of the Soviet Union, close to Manchuria, designated in 1928 as the Jewish homeland and as a Yidishe Avtonomne Gegnt (Jewish autonomous region) in 1934. Yiddish was the territory's official language. It was a failed movement. See YIVO.com.
6  The Kholodnaya Gora ("cold mountain") prison was in the city of Kharkov.
7  The abbreviation for the Communist International, an organization founded by Lenin in 1919 that sought to promote communism worldwide and to control the international movement.

metre. More and more children came to the prison wall looking for their parents. We saw a seven-year-old-girl holding a five-year-old-boy by his hand, both crying, "Where are my mother and father?" All children at the wall were orphans, and all were crying in a whisper. It was forbidden to talk or cry loudly. The children! Stalin's new constitution about children stated that children from twelve years on were responsible to the law just as adults were.

The poet Anna Akhmatova, in "Requiem" (1935), writes that when she was standing in the prison line looking for her son, who had been arrested, an old woman with blue lips and red eyes whispered to her, "Could one ever describe this?" And she answered, 'I can.' It was then that something like a smile slid across what had previously been just a face."[8]

We all waited in the line, frozen, stiff and hungry, until noon, when a window opened, high in the wall, and a voice called out a name. Mostly, the answer was silence, but some were lucky. A woman heard her husband's name, an assurance that he was still alive. She smiled through tears. Now she was allowed to hand over a parcel for him, through another window. All the women and children held onto parcels they had prepared for their loved ones, knowing that its contents would be checked and rechecked. Only old clothes, short not long, were allowed, like shirts, underwear.

I found my husband more than two weeks after his arrest. Only one parcel was permitted every two weeks, but all of us came to the

---

8   Anna Akhmatova (1889–1966) is a renowned Russian poet. Although she was denounced during the Bolshevik era and her books were banned for fifteen years, she composed new works in secret. "Requiem" was written during this time (1935–1940), and clandestinely communicated to her friends, line by line. The poem, which describes waiting at Leningrad prison to find information on her son, was not published in full in Russia until 1989. See Akhmatova's full biography at https://www.poetryfoundation.org/poems-and-poets/poets/detail/anna-akhmatova.

prison wall every day. We met here as new and old friends, checking the Arrestometre. We met wives of doctors, engineers and other professionals. One woman doctor whispered to me, "Quo vadis? Where are they going? What are they doing? Only old people, women, children and all orphans, will be left." Another woman, the wife of a German journalist, said to me, "What's going on? Can you picture how Stalin will build his five-year plans when all specialists, all professionals, all men and women with education, are there in Potemkin's walls?[9] Stalin's Russia will from now on consist of old women, children, invalids."

At the prison gates one day, I met a student friend from my faculty, Shura. He ran over to me, stretching out his arms to me and cried. Shura told me that after my husband was arrested, a meeting of the Komsomol[10] was held at the university. He said that they were all told that "students must be very careful with immigrant students. All are spies coming to our country as saboteurs." After that, all immigrants were arrested. "I feel ashamed and guilty before you," he said.

Every night, I waited for the NKVD, knowing their ways toward the relatives of arrested people. I knew I would not survive the jackals. I was awake most of the time, or dozing. Any move or voice outside enraged me. I stopped undressing for bed, lying down in my clothes except for my coat, waiting for them. I packed my clothes and other things to take with to prison. It was sickening, waiting for them

---

9  The prison was built by Prince Potemkin during the reign of Catherine the Great (1762–1796).

10 The Komsomol (the Russian abbreviation of Kommunisticheskiy Soyuz Molodyozhi, Communist Union of Youth) was the youth movement of the Soviet Communist Party that was established in 1918 and geared toward youths between fourteen and twenty-eight. The Komsomol mainly functioned as a means of transmitting Party values to future members. Members were frequently favoured over non-members for scholarships and employment; becoming a young officer in Komsomol was often seen as a good way to rise in the Party ranks.

as if the prison was my aim in life. The waiting for the unavoidable was worse than the happening itself. My situation was tragic. I was all alone — no relatives, friends or work, with no way to get some food. Under Soviet concept, I was the real parasite and a parasite has no place in a Soviet Socialistic Society. I walked the street not even looking at people because I knew I was a *persona non grata* to everybody and, moreover, almost all my friends and neighbours were already locked up in the prison or dead. I was afraid of this world around me, so I was better off staying at the prison walls. I was in this desperate situation for over a month, awaiting the unavoidable.

Finally, one December night, I heard a whistle in the yard. Yes, "they" were here; the NKVD was here for me. I was ready for them, completely dressed, and only needed to put on my shoes and coat. I was ready to go to the Moloch.[11] The whistle was for the janitor; he was the witness to the arrest. It was two o'clock in the morning. At the knock on the door, I opened it and two NKVD *Vertukhai*[12] and the janitor came in. They didn't even show the arrest order but right away started the search, really the demolition, of the room. I didn't have the right to talk or to move; I could only sit on a chair. They, the jackals, threw all my books, notes, papers and photos into a big sack. When my husband was arrested, they had done the same thing. Now, they finished the robbery. They found photos of my family, and of my brothers in France together with me and my husband. "Look," said one *Vertukhai* to the other, "this is a picture of real bourgeois spies," and he threw it all into the bag. "They come to our country and eat our bread and spy for the fascists." The demolition ended and the janitor took my key to lock the door. He squeezed my hand very hard

---

11  This is a reference to the Biblical Moloch, a pagan god demanding sacrifice. In Russian culture, especially in the first half of the twentieth century, the name was often used figuratively to invoke the machinery of war, state terror or industrial production.
12  A Russian slang word for prison guards.

and looked me in the eyes, with tears in his. The two soldiers refused to take my parcel, which was quite big and heavy. "You don't need that much clothing; we are not taking it," they told me. I responded, "I will not go without my belongings. My husband you took empty-handed, telling him he would be right back, so I will not go without my parcel."

It was now 4:30 in the morning. They, the jackals, worked only at night. They had to deliver me to the prison and the NKVD before 5:00 a.m. One of the men went to make a call to the NKVD for advice. He came back with a truck and they helped me carry my very heavy sack because they were late. They cursed me in their very Russian dialect. The two men brought me in at 5:00 a.m., straight to the Kholodnaya Gora prison, and handed me over to another man in the office. He showed me a place in the next room and told me to wait. This room was foggy from tobacco smoke. Here were shadows of men in rags, dirty, holding up their pants because the NKVD had taken their belts away. They all looked as if they had been taken out of a dungeon or a coal mine. These were my husband's brothers returning from their interrogations. First, they looked at me with wonder, shaking their heads. Some were crying. Speaking to one another was not allowed, but they couldn't resist. One of them took a risk and sat on the floor near me. He recognized me as a newcomer, fresh from the living world with colour on her cheeks in contrast to their waxen faces.

I was more terrified that this would be the picture of my face tomorrow. One whispered to me, "So young, so young. Remember, dear, sign everything right away, everything that the interrogator asks; everything, don't hesitate, remember." I didn't understand him then; later, I did.[13] He was cold and he sent me a kiss with his hand.

---

13 In Mina's 1995 interview, she describes her interrogation period. The interrogation lasted five or six hours, during which she was asked why she was in France and was told that she had been arrested as a spy and a political criminal, for anti-Soviet activity. When she refused to sign the protocol she was given, which was an admission of her guilt as well as her husband's, she was forced into a

Another shadow whispered to me, "If you have some worthwhile items, try to hide them. Take only a few most necessary belongings with you in the cell. Give the rest to the prison storage." I told him that I had a gold Parker set — a pen and a pencil. He asked, "Do you have a cake of soap? Push the pen and the pencil into two flat pieces of soap." I asked, "How about my watch? It is also gold." He warned, "About your watch, forget it. They will hide it forever." He also told me about the interrogators. "Don't be smart with them, don't argue; everything is ready, even the verdict."

I was very skeptical. By 7:00 a.m., the prisoners were gone and I was alone in the room. The office *stukach*, informer, noticed me and yelled, "Why are you here? What are you doing here now?" "I am a new arrest from last night," I answered. "Your name?" I gave him my name. He found the arrest order and shouted, "Why didn't you come to my table right away? Why were you sitting here all night?" He was running in and out, calling somebody to take me to the cell. His night's work was finished. Another man came for me and took me to the basement to the repository where I gave away my parcel for safekeeping. I received a receipt for everything, even my gold watch, which I never saw again. From there, I was taken to a room. A woman told me to undress completely and she checked my body, my hair and my hairpins and ordered me to make two braids. Then she took photos of my face and profile. She ordered me to dip all my fingers in black ink to make fingerprints on the prepared list. The ink stayed on my fingers for months.

The *stukach* came to pick me up to take me to the cell. We were

---

corner for forty-eight hours, without access to food, water, or a washroom. She was then given the protocol again; she still refused to sign. Mina was then sent to a cell for another two days without food or water, and brought in again. This time, a "witness," an acquaintance from the university, told her to sign; next, her husband was brought in, beaten up, and told her in Polish, "Sign it, fast, it doesn't matter!" Mina still refused to sign. She was eventually taken to a cell. For more of the interview, visit http://www.math.uwaterloo.ca/~hwolkowi/henry/reports/previews.d/todo.d/mina.html#videos

wandering in a labyrinth of doors, gates, passages, buildings, stairs. An iron door opened, closed, then another gate. Every five metres was an observation post with a guard on the top. When we came near, the soldier at the post yelled, "Stop, who is there?" My guard gave some sign and we went through more gates, more yards and buildings and finally we came to a big red building where I was handed over to the building guard. He started to walk, with me in front of him, through a long no-end-in-sight hall. If he heard some noise or footsteps, he gave a few bangs on the metal buckle on his belt and he pushed me to the wall to let the oncoming party pass. The hall was illuminated with very strong lights but for me it was dark, like walking in a catacomb to nowhere. The hall smelled of carbolic acid and other cleaning chemicals. From both sides of the hall, prisoners were looking at me through big iron doors. "Which of those doors will swallow me?" I wondered. The hall ended and we came to wide stony steps. Again, a long hall and, at the end, we stopped near one of the iron doors. Here a young woman guard took over, and she opened the door with a bunch of keys hanging on her belt and pushed me in. This was my cell, Number 275. I saw nothing. A thick fog, a wave of choking air came into my face. I froze.

When I got used to the place, I saw a mass of human bodies shoulder to shoulder standing, whispering. Nobody even looked at me. I was completely lost. One of the waxen yellow figures pushed herself through the mass and came to me. I was shaking, and I stepped back. I heard her voice: "Don't be afraid, daughter. Here all are like you. Come with me, don't hesitate." Then she burst out in a cry. "Do I know you?" I asked. "Oh, yes. You know me well. I am Anna Green from Lodz. Our husbands are friends from Lodz. We met not long ago at Mietek's house."

"Oh! Is it really you? Oh yes, now I recognize you. How long have you been in this 'sanatorium?'" I asked. She replied, "Soon it will be three months in this prison, so well known for its strong, big, iron, brick and stone buildings with high windows covered from outside with tin 'glasses.' High on the top is a small opening for the light to come into the cell. We call the glasses dog muzzles."

The walls in the cell were painted dark red. She continued, "The prisoners, if they are not being punished, have the right to walk fifteen minutes in the yard every day. The sun is never there because of the high walls. The prisoners must walk in a circle, hands folded in back, head down, no talking. The inmates call the walls bloody because they are soaked in our blood. In normal times, there are five or six prisoners in a cell. Now, in Stalin's 'harvest,' the cells are made of 'rubber,' squeezing us in, not counting. The 'political' buildings are all overcrowded and they put the women prisoners in the criminals' buildings."

Anna Green was forty-eight years old, tall, blond and nice-looking. She had come to the Soviet Union from Lodz with her husband and two daughters in 1928. One daughter was a doctor, a medic. The other, an artist at the National Jewish Theatre in Kiev. And now, what would happen to her children, nobody knew. Her husband had been accused of Trotskyism, Bundism, Zionism. Anna told me that her interrogator had said, "Your husband is a Bundist. He came to Russia as a spy and because a Bundist is a Zionist, but he was afraid to cross the ocean, he came to Russia." Anna had answered him, "Oh, I know that this is Plekhanov's[14] joke." The interrogator had jumped up, banging the table, screaming at her, "Shut up, you Trotskyite, you Bundist. You are coming to us to spy, to sabotage our growing socialism." He sent me back to the cell. I have never seen him again but now I have another interrogator, just the same."

Stalin's sadists were, from time to time, changing the "decoration" in the cell. We, eighty to ninety or even more than one hundred in the

---

14 Georgi Valentinovich Plekhanov (1856–1918) was a Marxist theorist and revolutionary who opposed the 1917 Soviet regime and Lenin. Nonetheless, the Communist Party revered him as an exceptional thinker and prolific author.

cell, stood pressed to each other. We slept on a cement floor. Once, we came back from the *bania*, the bath, and in the cell were iron beds, cots, attached one to the other so close with no space to walk between them. From then on, we slept six and eight women on one cot, with our legs hanging down. No mattress, no bedspread, no pillow. I was very lucky because I still had my fur coat and used it as a cover for the whole bed for all six women. We were pressed together so that if one of us wanted to turn, the others would wake. Often an arm of a neighbour landed on the face of three others. During the day, we were forced to sit together on a piece of the cot; we were not allowed to sleep, talk too loud, sing or cry. In prison, we had to be quiet. We were reminded by the guards that in the door was a round small hole through which the *stukach* checked our moves in the cell. For any wrongdoing, we'd be put in the dungeon. In our cell were women from all over the world, all nationalities. He, the *stukach*, shifted them to other prisons and camps and the "International Comintern" was locked up in the Butyrka, Kholodnaya Gora, Kolyma and Karaganda prisons.

Stalin said that all classes would be liquidated in Soviet Russia. And he was right, because he put them all in the camps, prisons. Now, in Soviet Russia, the criminals were a privileged class, but he created a new class, *tyuremschiki*, a class of prisoners. The criminals were only incarcerated for "correction"; for them, the prison was a school, but the politicals were "enemies of the people and condemned by the people." They, the immigrants, were "homeless" cosmopoliticians — Father Stalin's definition for us. Stalin was called, "Father of the people" by his followers. He said that immigrants had run away from fascist oppression to "socialist" Russia and her Stalin then arrested them all, took away their passports, personal belongings and their children, and put the criminal bandits, murderers and thieves to be the watchdogs, the caretakers who would build socialism.

In prison, I didn't need a mirror because my neighbour was my mirror. The sense of beauty, of aesthetics, was dead in prison, but we were relatively clean because we realized that dirt was our worst enemy. We carefully watched each other, especially those with long hair. My hair was very long, in braids. Not enough water, not enough soap. When we went to the *bania* every second week, we received a small piece of soap; the first to wash were women with long hair. Very often, the water ran very hot and, then, very cold, and so on. Back in the cell, another prisoner helped the women with long hair comb and untangle their hair.

On the wall in the cell was a prominent scratch with some metal, a kind of an epithet: "Who went here will be, who was here will never forget" and another, "Better give in at once, I will get you anyway." Those scratches had been made by inmates. Also on the prison wall, under glass, hung a poster of regulations signed by Yagoda, then by Yezhov, now by Beria.[15]

The conditions in the cell were so miserable that every day there were people sick with heart problems, liver failure and other sicknesses. Most sicknesses happened in the summer because the air in the cell was so damp, so thick. We were unsuccessful in calling for help. It took so long for the nurse to come and the result was always one and only one medicine — aspirin. With a serious sickness like heart attack, they took out the sick woman and we never knew what happened to her. All day in the cell was the cry, "Where are my children? Who is taking care of my children?" Nearly all the women were

---

15 Genrikh Grigoryevich Yagoda was head of the NKVD between 1934 and 1936; he oversaw Stalin's show trials of Bolsheviks, eventually becoming Stalin's victim himself — during the beginning of Stalin's Great Purge, he was arrested and eventually executed. Yagoda was succeeded by Nikolai Yezhov, who from 1936–1938 directed the most violent years of the Great Purge and then also became its victim — he was arrested and was executed in 1940. Lavrentiy Beria (1899–1953) was Stalin's next chief of the NKVD; he presided over Soviet security during World War II and was Stalin's deputy premier after the war, from 1946–1953. After Stalin's death in 1953, Beria was arrested for treason and executed.

married with children. The NKVD took away children under twelve years old and placed them in government institutions and changed their names; they were never to be found again.

In the beginning, I couldn't sleep because every fifteen minutes the soldier high on the tower outside whistled and shouted, "Stop, who is there?" Then, a strong electrical light burned on the ceiling all night. With differences in character, behaviour and mentality, we comprehended that the first and most important need here was mutual tolerance and understanding. This aspect was the essence, the necessity to hold on to, so as not to fall into despair, resignation, capitulation. We told one another all kinds of stories about our children, our husbands, about everything — literature, movies, theatres, concerts. The most painful was the subject of children.

We talked about everything in the world but omitted the subject of politics. This was hanging over us like Damocles' sword. We knew Stalin's way: everywhere were his *stukaches* — spies and provocateurs. But the constant subject was children and food. The permanent hunger brought up the subject of food, and every women knew the secret of so many dishes unknown to others. They improvised menus and we felt the smell and the taste but swallowed our saliva. We begged one another not to talk about food, but we were like drunkards. We knew it was dangerous, and we promised not to, but we still did. This was a result of hunger hallucination but it was enough when one women started to cry, "Where are my children" and all of them followed.

The desperate situation was saved by two of our inmates — a professor of literature, Maria Slivniak from Warsaw, and Ekaterina Vladimirovna Morozova. They started our Prison University. Later, all inmates became "lecturers" at the "University." They were yesterday's professors, doctors, professionals. Katia was a *krasavitza*, an extraordinary beauty. Tall, slim, blond hair, blue eyes. She had been educated at the Mariinsky Women's Gymnasium, which was in Saint Petersburg. Katia finished the lyceum with the poet Anna Akhmatova. She recited Pushkin, Lermontov, Akhmatova and others by heart. We were deprived of books, paper and pencils, but from her memory she "read" to us Nekrasov's "The Railroad." Our university made us forget our tragic, helpless situation for awhile.

Katia's first husband had been a doctor in the Czar's army. In the time of the revolution, he fought against the Bolsheviks. He was later shot. Katia, to survive with her two children, later married a Soviet general. Now, in Stalin's "cleansing" years, the second husband was shot and Katia arrested. She expected the maximum verdict — death or a twenty-five-year sentence in a camp. Katia was an exceptional, extraordinary person. Always sober, a logical thinker, good-natured and always ready to help. She never cried.

One dark day, two women returned in the morning after a night of interrogation; they had been sadistically beaten, and our good, smart Katia came to their rescue. "Listen to me, please my dear sisters, we all are here in this 'sanatorium' with broken hearts and lives. I want to tell you about Leonid Andreyev's 'Day of Anger' [*Den Gneva*]. This is a story written by a genius about us, about the psychology of men, about the sinister ugly world we live in. I will retell the story, I will 'read' the story, improvise how much I still remember. We don't have any books here, but I will try."

In a moment of despair, when the whole cell was in tears, Katia was our saviour. "Day of Anger" by Andreyev is an elegy to freedom, liberty. For freedom, humanity fights eternity. Everyone is born free, but we are never sure how and when we can lose our freedom. The most beautiful creations — songs, music — are dedicated to freedom. In prison, thoughts about freedom were like balsam, essence. We cried, mourned and sang freedom songs. The prisoner, writes Andreyev, seeing the might, the colours of the prison, which men build to lock up freedom, doesn't even dream about freedom. He is afraid even to mention this word because the prisoner and freedom are closed up in these mighty prison walls. It is dangerous to call for freedom in prison because if you grabbed freedom for yourself, you would be dead.

"Once," writes Andreyev, "the prisoner heard extraordinary sounds, whispers, noises, buzzes, roars and then shakings, and at once the cell's door, this monster mighty iron door, flung open by itself; no, not by man's hand with a key, no, by itself burst open with a crack. We couldn't understand how a few of us were still alive, we were standing bewitched, frozen, couldn't move from this cursed, damned prison. We were seeing the mighty walls in ruins and we stood like dames wondering about the might that could tear this mighty prison into pieces like paper, together with the iron bars torn, bent, curved. Cement, iron, stone, crushed lying like rags. The iron bars that were forever strong and powerful and now torn! Only now we started to understand that we were free, free, free!"

Oh, Andreyev was a genius! His words, improvised by Katia, cheered us up and, at the same time, we were afraid of them. Would freedom never come to us by itself? Or would only a natural catastrophe, a higher might, give us liberty? Katia continued, "Our hearts now have windows, eyes, tears." We whispered and cried, calling for Andreyev's freedom. Freedom! Freedom! "If we could collect all the songs in the world and throw them into the air, take together all the children's laughter, mothers' love, a friend's hug; if we gathered all the flowers, collected all the lights from the cosmos, even then I am unable to describe you, crown you Oh Freedom! Liberty! Only those who lost you can describe you."

Katia didn't stop even when all of us were crying. "My dear sisters! I know it is very painful but Andreyev is giving us hope. Think about it: He is telling us that yes, freedom is far, but he is giving us hope that maybe it will not come by men of our time, but it will come unexpectedly." We were sitting squeezed together on Stalin's prison bed holding on to one another, whispering, forgetting for a minute our present situation.

One day, the iron door of our cell opened and the *stukach* pushed in a newcomer. When we saw her, we all, in one voice, shouted, "Who is this?" A woman dressed as if she was on a beach, in shorts and brassiere, which is unusual in Russia, came in. She jumped over all the beds and went right to the window. We had two windows in the cell, one facing the inside of a yard and the other facing the street of the prison gates. Both windows were covered inside with thick bars, and from the outside with tin nozzles. On the top was a small opening of the tin to let a little light into the cell. We reserved the bed near the window facing the street for sick people. In a dirty, underworld lexicon the newcomer yelled to the two sick women, "Out! This is my bed from now on. You Trotskyites, enemies of the people. From now on, I am the boss. My name is Motka Bandit and you will do everything I tell you. We are a class of *blatnye urki* — bandits, thieves.[16] We have the rights now, not you. We will teach you how to behave in our country."

She talked non-stop, and nobody reacted. Motka told us about the life of the criminals. "We, the thieves, robbers and so on are also in prison, but we are not enemies of our country like you all educated doctors and professors. You are spies for the fascists; you want to murder our Stalin. Because of this, so many of you are in prison and camps and we will re-educate you people to become Soviet patriots."

Motka was telling the truth. In the camps, the criminals were informants and instructors to the Article 58 political prisoners.[17] The criminals did not work in the camps; they were the brigadiers and

---

16 *Blatnye* were considered the highest caste in the prison hierarchy. The word *urki* means bandits or criminals.

17 Article 58 was the notorious 1928 statute in the Soviet Union's Penal Code that introduced the formal notion of the "enemy of workers" and was used by the Soviet secret police to arrest those suspected of "counter-revolutionary activities." The Article became the justification for the imprisonment and death of a huge number of innocent people. Sentences under the Article could last as long as twenty-five years and were often extended indefinitely without trial or consultation.

stole from the workers; they were the "watchers" over the "enemies of the people." They robbed the Article 58 politicals of everything: clothes, shoes and, most important, they stole goods from the political prisoners' accounts and put them on their own account. The camp administration approved the brutal robberies: they did not take any complaints from a "spy."

Motka became fresher because of our silence. We knew very well about the N K V D ways of putting spies and provocateurs into the cells of political prisoners, but to send a criminal monster into a political 58 cell was only to break us morally, to humiliate and abuse us. We knew we definitely could not capitulate to this provocation. We had to break her wings, but it wasn't so easy. Her first step was to be the "boss" of the cell. Until now, another inmate was the *starosta*, or monitor, and her function was to distribute the food, take care of the sick and so on.

Every day at noon, two criminal workers from the kitchen brought in the dinner in a tin kettle — always soup. Only the criminals were privileged to work in the kitchen or in the workshops; the political prisoners worked as slaves in the camps. The soup consisted of water and sometimes a few pieces of cabbage or potato. We use to joke that we needed a bathing suit to swim in the soup to find a piece of something. Now Motka declared that she was the monitor and would distribute the dinner. The first day we didn't object; we wanted to see how she would behave. Motka, first of all, took soup for herself, fishing out the few pieces of cabbage, then she started to choose whom she liked; at the end, many were left without dinner. The next day we chose our monitor, ignoring Motka's swearing completely. She started to knock on the door and, when the guard opened it, she gave him a report: "The Trotskyites are agitating here, whispering all the time. They are against me." The guard told her to listen better and, first of all, listen to the monitor. Motka was furious; she lay down on the cot singing her *blatnye* underworld songs about Odessa and its gangs. She asked questions and answered herself.

That day, our teacher Maria Slivniak was "reading" *Anna Karenina* by Leo Tolstoy. She told us about Anna's love for Vronsky, how she left her husband and child, how she suffered and wanted to see her child. Motka Bandit jumped over beds to the lecturer's cot, kneeling on the bed and listening very intently, open-mouthed, looking straight into Maria's face. Maria finished the "reading": Anna Karenina couldn't get her child, Vronsky changed his feelings toward her and she threw herself under a train. Motka was bitter, crying, stretching out her arms to Maria. "Dear dove, continue. I will be good from now on. I thought that you political prisoners were our enemies, as I was told." This was surprising to us. She said, crying, "I want to sleep with you together, I want to be your friend. I don't want the hospital bed for myself. Please, let the two sick women take back the bed." But we refused to let her sleep with us; also, the sick women refused to return to the window,

The next day Katia started the second part of Leonid Andreyev's "Day of Anger." "I described to you in my previous talk about the collapse of a prison building by an earthquake, about how a few saved prisoners were astonished. Now I will continue, trying to talk in Andreyev's language because his classic language is such a beauty that we used to learn it by heart. I will now 'sing' in Andreyev's words how much I remember: 'So the man is brutal, his hands are still shaking from yesterday's fear brought by the earthquake, but he is already grabbing the keys to lock the doors with a lock. When one hears the sound of gold, he must hear the sound of chains. How fast is man building prisons! Man has even locked heaven with his keys! But when you, man, will sleep peacefully with the keys in your hand, the underground mighty power will hurl, fling the keys from your hand. Your heart will grow ears and you shall hear the dead with your last breath and the watch will stop." We were talking through tears. "When will the underground power throw the prison keys from the jailer's hand? Will this happen in our time?"

Another lecturer recited a parody of "To be or not to be" from Shakespeare's *Hamlet*:

> *To be or not to be.*
> *To beat or not to beat.*
> *To howl or to scream or not to howl.*
> *To shit or not to shit.*
> *To live or not to live.*

And so, in Dante's Hell, we one hundred or so women with grieving hearts were again and again begging our Katia to "sing" Andreyev. Motka Bandit cried together with us. She knocked at the door, asking the guard to send her back to the kitchen to work. He told her to wait. "We will tell you when to go," he said. "I am a criminal monster. I am, you remember, the criminal Motka Bandit. I was working in the kitchen," she demanded. The next day Motka was taken out of our cell. She was crying bitterly, "I will not forget you, dear women."

Motka was now working in the kitchen and bringing us dinner every day. Every day, another "present" was hidden in her packet for the teacher and she would say through tears: "This is for today's teacher; why should she scuffle her throat for us for nothing?" Or she would bring a piece of bread, fish or potato and say, "This is for the hospital." This is why Motka had demanded to be sent back to work in the kitchen. Usually, the soup was now thicker and better. Motka worked in the kitchen from seven in the morning until two in the afternoon and then she came back to our cell. Our "prison civilization" became very popular in prison. All criminals from then on respected us. No more calling us "enemies" and "Trotskyites," no more throwing dirt on us through the window when we went for our walk in the prison yard.

Before Motka became our "patron," the criminals often abused us. Now the same prostitutes, thieves and murderers, instigated by the NKVD against the "political enemies of the people," threw presents to us through the same windows, an unbelievable change. More-over, Motka assured us: no more insults, no more names. "I told my friends," she said, "here is heaven — no stealing, no beating, no card playing; here is a school. You know, I never went to a school."

The other criminals brought breakfast or supper, always with a present. We begged them to be careful because we were Article 58 prisoners. Motka not only profited from us, as she used to say, but she "enriched" our lexicon-vocabulary with unknown words, epithets. We were often embarrassed, but it was fun, something extraordinary, new in our so-dark present. I doubt if Motka's juicy rich vocabulary would correspond appropriately to English. I shall bring a few "flow-ers" of Motka's wise, folksy quibbles: "Disaster doesn't walk alone." "My eyes saw it with my own hands." "A pauper is smart enough to invent anything." "Our life is poor, pitifully, we are bitten, smitten, but for us, nobody to touch." "For what you fought, that's what you got." "Kolyma[18] — wonderful planet with twelve months winter, the rest summer." "The nobles are fighting but, by the poor, the teeth are shak-ing." "Yesterday dirt — today prince — and this is the hall of liberty."

Motka' s vocabulary for us was a revelation; the resignation, pro-test, desperation of a prisoner, with almost no hope for freedom. Pris-oners can't revolt or protest against their oppressors, so they spit out their grief with specific, improvised vocabulary. We were often red in the face, confused with the accuracy of their synonyms. We never re-peated or used the criminals' lexicon. I would like very much to write the most interesting strong "dirty" words, but I can't. "You stinking vrediteli[19] sabotage enemies' intelligence with your golden tongue" was Motka's compliment for us.

---

18 Part of the Gulag system. An uninhabited, bitterly cold region in the northeastern section of Siberia that was known for its extreme repression and low survival rate.
19 The word vrediteli (plural; singular is vreditel) literally means "inflicting damage" or "harming" and is often translated as "sabotage." More precisely, its meaning was "wrecking" or "undermining" and was a sub-section of the Soviet Union's penal code of Article 58.

That necessity is the mother of invention was true in prison. We invented what we needed most in the cell. We were in desperate need of a needle. Our clothing was torn, burned in the delousing machine, and our stockings and other parts of our wardrobe were getting ruined. From time to time, we had a fish soup, *ucha,* in which there were only fish bones, never any fish, for dinner. We made use of the fish bones, particularly the long pointy ones. With a match from the cigarette smokers, we lit the wider part of the bone to make a small hole and we got a perfect needle. We also used the fish bones as a pen. Ink, we made from the scrubbed paint from the red wall mixed with a drop of soup. When we went to the bath every two weeks, we wrote our names on the bath wall with the red paint and also with a piece of soap. When I wrote my name on the prison bath wall, I reminded myself about another wall where I had written my name when we were in Paris. My husband, Herman, and I had gone to see the wall of the Paris Commune, the government during the French Revolution. On this wall, visitors had been putting their names for one hundred years from. "Anna," I called, "write your name here on the anti-Commune Wall." Every one of the prisoners did the same, but when we were finished, the criminals came to wash off all the writings. We were so sick of the life in prison, day and night sitting or lying with our legs down. We all wanted to end this hell faster. Nobody was even dreaming about freedom or home.

The definition for a concentration camp in a 1937 Soviet encyclopedia is "a closed up place in fascist states." For us Soviets, it was a continuation of prison. This was a place for revolutionaries. There was brutal terror against the prisoners. Arrested politicals were worse off than the criminals. "The fascists send the politicals to the camps without a court verdict." And we, the Soviet prisoners, asked and whispered, "How about Stalin's definition about a camp?" Stalin said that the Soviet prisons and camps are schools for workers to re-educate them." Mandelstam[20] wrote that Stalin re-made Russia into a Prison Re-education Camp. Marx[21] said that terror is the tactic of people who are themselves terrified.

EDITOR'S EPILOGUE

After spending about eighteen months in prison, Mina, along with ten others from her cell, was taken to an NKVD agent who quickly read out a sentencing verdict; in her panic, Mina thought she heard fifteen years. She would later find out that her sentence was in fact five years. Two days later, she was told to pack her belongings and was taken out to the yard, where black vans were waiting. Packed to capacity, she and others were driven to a station and loaded into *stolypin* wagons, in a compartment previously used to transport cattle. They travelled for six weeks with hardly any food or water. The transport arrived in the city of Almaty, Kazakhstan, where the prison was full, and then

20 Osip Mandelstam (1891–1938) was a Russian-Jewish writer who was educated in Paris and Germany, as well as at the University of Saint Petersburg. Mandelstam was eventually persecuted for not complying with communist directives, and was banned from publishing. In 1933 he was arrested and exiled, and he later died in a Soviet prison camp. For more information on Mandelstam, see https://www. poetryfoundation.org/poems-and-poets/poets/detail/osip-mandelstam.

21 Karl Marx (1818–1883) was a German philosopher, historian, sociologist and theorist who inspired the revolutionary communist ideology known as Marxism. According to Marx's vision, a communist society would be classless and state-less, based on a common ownership of the means of production, free access to the material goods that people need for wellbeing, and an end to wage labour and private property. In 1870, Marx wrote to Friedrich Engels — who co-founded Marxist theory — about the period of violence after the French Revolution, the Reign of Terror: "We think of this as the reign of people who inspire terror; on the contrary, it is the reign of people who are themselves terrified." See the full text of the letter at https://www.marxists.org/archive/marx/works/1870/letters/70_09_04.htm

went onto the city of Karaganda, where the transport was again refused, due to prison camp overcrowding. They were eventually taken to a prison camp nearby and put to work in the desert.

Mina was lucky and was sent to work in an office, where she had to oversee the production of the labourers who were digging for sulfur. Twice a year, the NKVD took her by train to the city of Almaty to give a work progress report to officials. During one of these trips, she heard a man speaking Polish. She managed to speak with him and discovered that he was Jewish and was the head of a Polish repatriation committee, organizing for when the war ended. He was in the process of registering all Polish citizens who had come to the Soviet Union, and he gave her a document stamped with her maiden name.

In early 1943, Mina managed to escape while on one of her visits to Almaty. She used the only identification she had — the document from the Polish man that stated she was a Polish refugee — and went deep into the Soviet Union, living on the run. Mina managed to acquire a false passport for her husband, who had been sent from the prison to a gulag camp with a twenty-five year sentence; she smuggled the passport to him and through bribery, he escaped the camp. Mina and Herman were briefly reunited. After Germany's defeat at Stalingrad in February 1943, Herman was drafted into the Soviet army; Mina registered with the Soviet army to work in the Ukraine, so that she could be nearer to the Polish border. In April, they parted: Mina was sent to Melitopol, Ukraine, far from the Polish border, where she worked at an agricultural institution. Herman was sent to the frontlines, where he was killed.

Mina and Herman's daughter, Lily, was born on December 22, 1943. In 1946, Mina and Lily escaped from the Soviet Union using false papers. They returned to Piotrków Trybunalski to search for her family; they did not find any survivors, but later reunited with Mina's sister Bronia, who had survived Auschwitz. Mina's parents, Laja and Hershel, and four of her sisters — Mala, Helena, Sara and Ester — were murdered during the Holocaust. Her sister Judith had im-

migrated to British Mandate Palestine in 1933, and her three brothers, Felix, Chaim and Jacob, survived the war. They all eventually reunited, some not until thirty years after seeing each other for the last
time.

Mina and Lily went to Lodz, where Mina met and married Pinchas Wolkowicz; their son Henry was born in February 1948. That
summer, the family left Poland, arriving in Czechoslovakia and then
Germany, where they were sent to the Feldafing Displaced Persons
camp. After several months, they managed to leave for France with
the help of Mina's brother Chaim in Paris. They eventually received
papers to be admitted to Canada, and arrived in Halifax on November 30, 1949.

1   Mina's parents, Laja and Hershel, before the war.
2   The immediate Herzlikowicz (also spelled as Hershlikowicz) family before the
    war. In the top row, left to right: Mina's siblings Helena, Felix, Sara and Bronia.
    In the middle row, left to right: Mina's sister Ester; her parents, Laja and Hershel;
    and her brother Jacob. In the bottom row, left to right: Mina's sister Judith; Mina;
    her brother Chaim; and her sister Mala.

1  Mina and her husband, Pinchas, with their son Henry. Lodz, 1948.
2  Mina, Pinchas and their daughter, Lily, in Canada, 1950.
3  Mina and her sons, Henry and Nathan. Montreal, circa 1951.
4  Mina and Pinchas in Florida, circa 1975.

One of the many soapstone sculptures by Mina Wolkowicz. Titled "Mother," this piece was made circa 1983.

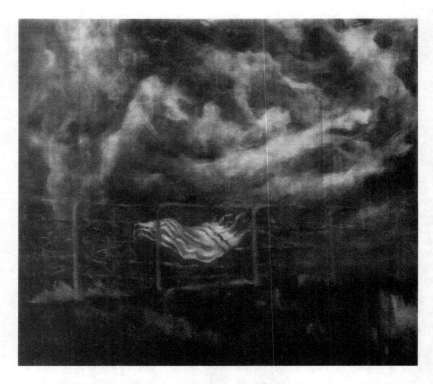

"Holocaust," a painting by Simkin Yefim Davidovich, cousin of Svetlana Kogan-Rabinovich. Canvas/oil, 1995.

# In the Inferno: the Dead Loop Concentration Camp
# Svetlana Kogan-Rabinovich

Translated from Russian by Irina Sadovina (2016)

Preface by G. Ressin

Svetlana Ilyinichna Kogan-Rabinovich was born in 1927 in the town of Tulchin, in Ukraine's Vinnitsa region.[1] Svetlana's mother, Menikha Izrailevna Vaisleib, the second eldest in a family of three brothers and four sisters, came from a well-known family of Breslov Hasidic rabbis. Menikha's grandfather, Tsvi-Gersh Vaisleib, also born in Tulchin, was the author of commentaries on the works of the great Rabbi Akiva.

Svetlana's great-grandfather, like other Breslov Hasidim,[2] preached education through labour. He had a great influence on the Jewish community, and all his life, he tried to convince people to move to Palestine. When he was asked why he didn't go himself, he responded that he was waiting for his two youngest sons, twins, to turn thirteen, the age of bar mitzvah. In 1881, after his sons Azril and Naftule reached the age of bar mitzvah, Svetlana's great-grandfather sent

---

1  In 1939, about 5,600 Jews lived in Tulchin, about 42 per cent of the population. In the 1990s, 150 Jews remained in the town.
2  A mystical and spiritual branch of Judaism, established in the seventeenth century.

them to a relative in Kishinev and he moved to Palestine, which, at the time, was controlled by the Turks. There, he shared in the difficult labour of the first settlers in one of the first kibbutzim.

In Kishinev, Azril and Naftule went to cheder and also mastered the shoemaking craft; they then returned to Tulchin. When Svetlana's future grandfather Azril turned eighteen, he was drafted to the Tsar's army. He married his niece, Chaya-Leah, and took her with him. In Belarus, they had a son, Nachman, named after the famous Hasidic *tzaddik* (holy, righteous) Rabbi Nachman of Breslov. Svetlana's grandmother came from the Barsky family, who descended from Rabbi Nachman. In the army, her grandfather observed Jewish religious law strictly — he ate only kosher food and did not trim his beard, among other things. He would get punished for disobedience, but once the higher authorities understood the situation, surprisingly they accommodated him. He would receive packed lunches and was moved to a shoemaking workshop.

After twenty-five years, he returned from the army and opened a shoemaking workshop and a school for children of religious Hasidic Jews in Gaisin.[3] He taught children the tanning craft, working with leather, along with the Torah and the Jewish tradition. From some Jews who immigrated to America, he bought a large two-storey house with columns and a balcony, where a sukkah hut would be constructed during Sukkot, the Feast of Tabernacles. This house stands there to this day.[4] Hasidic Jews eagerly brought their sons to

---

3  Gaisin, also known as Haisin or Gaysin, is 100 kilometres from the province's major city, Vinnitsa. This area was heavily populated with small villages, or shtetls, and small cities (such as Uman) in which many Jews lived in earlier centuries, until they were victims of severe pogroms. See the International Association of Jewish Genealogical Studies at IAJGSjewishcemeteryproject.org.

4  After the war, Svetlana tried to arrange to get back her grandfather's house in Gaisin, Ukraine, hoping to donate it to set up a Catastrophe Museum and a prayer house for the Breslov Hasidim; unfortunately, she was unable to reclaim the house.

him for education. He also took in and educated refugee boys. There were many such orphans in Ukraine after World War I.

In 1907, Svetlana's great-grandfather Tsvi-Gersh came from Palestine to visit his relatives. He invited them to come back with him. The relatives, for their part, tried to convince him to stay in Ukraine, but Tsvi-Gersh yearned to go back to Eretz Yisrael, the Land of Israel. One day, he went outside and did not come back. The family searched for him. A few days later, a horse-and-buggy coachman came by to ask for money. When Azril asked why, the coachman explained that he had given Tsvi-Gersh a lift to the nearest railway station, and that he had been told that his son would pay the fee. Tsvi-Gersh had gone back to Palestine. Three years later, in 1910, he passed away on the thirteenth of Nissan and was buried in the Jewish cemetery on the Mount of Olives. The family stayed behind and had to live through the pogroms at the hands of Petliura's army[5] and Grigoriev's gangs[6] during the Civil War, and they would later die as victims of the Nazi occupation. In this argument, great-grandfather Tsvi-Gersh turned out to be right.

During the years of the New Economic Policy (NEP),[7] business-minded people were arrested as capitalists and their property was

---

5  Symon Petliura (1879–1926), a nationalist leader and politician, advocated for an independent Ukraine between 1917 and 1921; he was head of state between 1919 and 1920. During the Civil War, Petliura's troops fought against both Bolshevik and White Russian forces. Petliura's legacy is controversial due to the Ukrainian army's pogroms against Jews during his time as leader, when an estimated 35,000 to 50,000 Jews were killed.

6  Nikifor Grigoriev (1885–1919) was a paramilitary leader of partisan forces during the Russian Civil War. Opposed to what he referred to as Jewish Bolshevik communists, he led a series of anti-Jewish pogroms in Kiev, Kherson and Poltava in 1919.

7  Between 1921 and 1928, Soviet policy changed from a socialist ideology to one of private ownership of small industry and nationalized, state-controlled large industry. See Helene M. Glaza, "Lenin's New Economic Policy: What it Was and How It Changed the Soviet Union," *Inquiries* 1.11 (2009) at http://www.inquiries-journal.com/articles/59/lenins-new-economic-policy-what-it-was-and-how-it-changed-the-soviet-union.

seized. Svetlana's grandfather was frequently arrested, and bail payments were demanded. He fled to the city of Rostov-on-Don, and his brother Naftule moved there as well. Her grandfather's spacious house was expropriated and the whole family was forced to move out. When the NEP campaign was over, her grandfather returned to Gaisin. He worked as a *shames*, a caretaker in a synagogue, and built a small house. He was widely respected, not just by the Jewish community, but by Russian and Ukrainian neighbours as well.

Svetlana continues the narrative about what happened to her and her family:

My father, Idel (Yutka) Peisakhovich Rabinovich, was born near Kiev. He was the nephew of the well-known writer Sholem Aleichem (the pen name of Solomon Nachumovich Rabinovich).[8] Father worked in the publishing house of the newspaper *Chervona Tulchyinschina*. He also knew the bookbinding craft. He had his own printing presses, which he received from Zeidel Spektor, a publisher who, in his time, used to print Hasidic religious works and the works of his friend Sholem Aleichem. During the Civil War, my father served in the army. At the Vapniarka station, Petliura's soldiers herded Jews into a shed surrounded by barbed wire. Father tried to save them. Because of this, the soldiers pierced his chest with a sword. When he was found, Mother nursed him to health. He suffered from lung issues for the rest of his life.

---

8  Sholem Aleichem (whose name is a Hebrew phrase meaning literally "Peace be upon you," and commonly translated as the greeting "How are you") was born in 1859 and is renowned as one of the founders of modern Yiddish literature. See "Sholem Aleichem" in the YIVO Encyclopedia of Jews in Eastern Europe at http://www.yivoencyclopedia.org/article.aspx/sholem_aleichem.

When World War II began, I was at home with Father.⁹ Mother and my elder brother and sister were away visiting relatives. I was thirteen. Bombings started on the very first night. As the Germans bombed the nearby Vapniarka station, Father was called into the printing office. When he was leaving, he told me not to go out of the house and, in case anything happened, to remember everything my parents had taught me. The windows were shaking from exploding shells. I was afraid. I lay face down under the big dining table and cried all night.

In the morning, Father came back. Following orders, we covered the windows with strips of paper, so that pieces of glass wouldn't fly in all directions if the windows shattered. The Red Army was retreating. Before the Germans' arrival, locals started looting shops and Jewish homes. They hauled things and food away in sacks. We were afraid to leave the house. Roads were crowded with refugees. Few people managed to evacuate in time; we had believed the propaganda that said the war would only last a month or two. Nobody among us thought that the Germans would reach us so fast, and we didn't know what they were capable of. Many could not abandon their sick elders. We tried to send a pregnant relative out of the city, but the trains were crammed. People were suffocating from the overcrowding. So she came back home. We later learned that airplanes bombed the refugee train.

Tulchin had no railroad. We, along with many other people, evacuated on horse-drawn carts, with the elderly and women with children walking behind us, through Gaisin, about fifty kilometres away, toward the city of Uman. Hasidic Jews were walking behind to pray on the grave of the Breslov Rebbe (Rabbi Nachman of Bratislava). During the bombings, people would scatter out into the forest. The

---

9  Germany invaded Ukraine on June 22, 1941.

horses were exhausted and hungry — there was no time to let them graze, and peasants didn't give them fodder.

The Germans, with their cars and motorcycles, moved very quickly. After we arrived in Gaisin, we soon heard German speech. Hasidic Jews prayed in Grandfather's house as a vegetable processing plant was being bombed nearby. The frontline was moving closer to Gaisin. Fighting broke out and lasted forty-eight hours. The Germans forced both the locals and refugees to clean the roads and to drag horse carcasses into the trenches that our retreating army had dug. Many who worked on clearing the roads never returned home. Those who dragged horse carcasses into the ditches were forced to climb inside, where they were shot and covered with soil. Across from the printing shop, the Germans hanged the shoemaker Yavorsky on an electric pole. Everyone regretted not having evacuated from the city.

We tried to stay together. One day, when I walked outside with a kettle to get some water from the river, a German caught me and sent me to work. I washed motorcycle wheels and was ordered to show up to work the next day. My parents had been worried, thinking I was no longer alive. In the evening, they decided to hide me in Grandfather's attic. The punishment for failing to show up at work was being shot. When the Germans arrived at our house, our hunchbacked neighbour, Shlima, got frightened and pointed out where I was hiding. A German dragged me from the attic by my braid. Mother ran after him and begged him to take her to work instead of me, but the German drove her away. He beat me with a ramrod. Everyone who hadn't come out to work was brought to the trenches by the bathhouse to be shot. Armed Germans and Ukrainian Polizei, the auxiliary police, were already standing there. I knew one of them; he used to work as a street sweeper. They made us stand in a row before the trenches. As we were waiting for the shot, we suddenly saw a tall, skinny red-haired German running toward us without his field tunic, waving his arm. He asked if anyone knew how to mend socks. Along with seven other people, I raised my hand. We were taken away. The others were shot.

We were taken to a bathhouse that my grandfather had built during the Civil War to combat the typhus epidemic. We washed the soldiers' wool socks. We were ordered to show up again the next day. For several days, we sorted, washed and mended socks. Most of those who mended the socks eventually died later.

Soon, an order was posted: "Everyone must remain in the location of their residences and registrations. Those who ran away from home are communists." My brother, Peysakh, who turned eighteen when the war began, was in Tulchin when he was drafted into the army. Mother was with him. Two weeks after the beginning of the war, she walked to Gaisin. My brother, like the majority of his peers born in 1922, died on the front lines.

In September, a ghetto for Jews was created in Tulchin, and we were ordered to move there. With the Hasidic Jews, we went from Gaisin to Tulchin through Ladyzhin.[10] We had to cross the Bug River in a ferry. The ferry was on our side of the river and there was no one on it, so we pulled up the rope ourselves. The air was filled with the smell of burned flesh and hair. Before we left, we walked up to the house of our relative Shlema Morgulis, which stood by the river. The blinds were drawn, but he heard us speaking in Yiddish and came

---

10 Ladyzhin, similar to other towns and cities in the Vinnitsa district — Gaisin, Tulchin, Uman, Bershad and Obodovka — was occupied by German troops in the summer of 1941. In Ladyzhin, Gaisin and Uman, more than twenty thousand Jews were murdered in September and October 1941. Soon after, this area was occupied by Romanian troops and was annexed into the zone of Transnistria, a 16,000-square-mile region between the Dniester and Bug rivers that originally had been part of Ukraine. The Romanians deported hundreds of thousands of Jews from Northern Bukovina and Bessarabia to Transnistria, an area comprised of ghettos, labour camps and concentration camps. From Ladyzhin and Tulchin, Jews were transferred to the Pechora camp. Transnistria, where between 150,000 and 250,000 Romanian and Ukrainian Jews were killed, was liberated by the Red Army in the spring of 1944. This extensive note illustrates the process of annihilation of the Jews in Ukraine and the Pale of Settlement by the Nazis and their collaborators.

down from the attic. He told us that the Germans had burned down houses in the township, that elderly Jews were dragged by their beards and thrown into the fire alive. His sister, Sara Goihman, came with us to Tulchin. A few days later, she went to the old market and found out that Shlema, not wanting to surrender to the Germans alive, had hanged himself in his attic. Like other young people, his daughters were rounded up to dig holes with spades, and, in those holes, they were buried alive. For several days, the ground was moving over the bodies of suffocating people. One of Morgulis's daughters was away in Odessa at the time and so she survived.

We found out that there was a mass shooting in Gaisin two weeks after our departure.[11] We were afraid to believe it. Ragged, dirty and hungry, we arrived at the Tulchin ghetto. Jews from the whole city had been herded into the ghetto. The Germans had moved beyond the Bug, leaving Romanians and Ukrainians in charge. All Jews were forced to live in horribly crammed conditions on Volodarsky Street. There was no water or food. Women were not allowed to leave the ghetto after 8:00 p.m.; men were not allowed to leave the ghetto at all. At the market, Jews were beaten by the Romanians and the local Polizei. We were not fed. We were doomed to die out.

We were rounded up to work on dismantling the ruins and debris left after the bombings. My sister Rakhil and I hauled rocks and uprooted trees in the forest, loading the logs into boxcars. At the labour exchange, we received 180 grams of bread per day. The Polizei and soldiers guarded us and often beat us with whips — iron rods covered with leather. These beatings, and our constant hunger, often led to suicidal thoughts. Resistance was out of the question. Not only were we constantly guarded by armed soldiers with dogs, but along with their weapons they also had gas wagons, and later crematoria

---

11 This massacre took place on September 16–17, 1941. *The Encyclopedia of Jewish Life*, 418.

and bone-crushing machines. In Gaisin, the Germans had ordered us to wear white armbands with a blue Star of David. Here, in Tulchin, the Romanians ordered us to wear a black circle with a yellow star on our chests.

A friend of Father's, Iona Reznik, a forty-five-year-old Hasidic Jew, lived with us because his house was not included in the ghetto. Before the war, he was a grain and fruit packer. As a packer, he had stored grain and fruit in the house of a disabled woman named Kilyna. I had helped her dig her garden before the war. As a believing Christian, Kilyna had earned Iona's respect. Her house was full of icons. Iona believed that she could be trusted, so he left his five-year-old daughter, Fira, with her, as well as all of his possessions. This girl was his only child, late and long awaited. It would turn out later that his trust had been misplaced.

In the fall of 1941, an order was posted in the ghetto: all of us were to be sent to the Pechora death camp known as the Dead Loop, and if we wanted to stay alive we needed to pay a ransom (a contribution), according to a list. Everyone tried to get on this list and pay the ransom; there was a long line. People pulled out their gold teeth with pliers. I brought a silver spoon, a gift from Grandmother. Obviously, the authorities were deceiving their victims. Regardless of the list and the payments, everyone was sent to the death camp. They just wanted to steal our valuables.

The Ukrainian Polizei, with the help of Romanians and Hungarians, herded us all into the school building. Their leader, Stoyanov, a former middle-school teacher and military instructor, was especially zealous. During house searches, he would shoot into the air to signal that there was nobody left in the house. The sick and elderly were carried out. Our seventeen-year-old neighbour, Motya Higer, hanged himself. Eighty people committed suicide; they were gathered and buried in the old Jewish cemetery in Tulchin in two graves, which, to this day, do not have any memorials.

We were kept in the school for three days. It was crowded, and we could only stand. We weren't fed or given water and we weren't let out to use the toilet. Finally, we were all led to the bathhouse, but not to wash. They ordered us to undress completely and gave us vaccinations against typhus and other infectious diseases. Then they ordered us to get dressed again and took us back to the school building. We stood there suffocating, thirty to forty people per room.

That November, exhausted, we were herded about forty kilometres to the Pechora camp, on foot, through the dirt.[12] Our feet got stuck in the cold clay. Many died along the way. When the mothers who were carrying their children got tired, the Polizei would force them to abandon their small children. They killed those who refused. They tore small children out of their mothers' hands and stomped them into the dirt. Heartbreaking cries filled the air. Elderly people had to walk, too. A man we knew, Hema Alter-Menashe, was shot before my eyes.

We walked all day surrounded by the Polizei and German shepherd dogs. Along the road, some locals gave us something to eat. Old Hasidic Jews who refused to eat non-kosher food collapsed in the dirt from weakness and emaciation, wrapped in their *talleisim*. They were trampled by the Polizei's horses. Along the way, the Polizei beat us, whipped us, forced us to walk faster. They gave us nothing to drink. We took wet dirt and licked it, licked our hands wet from the rain.

We marched through the village of Torkovo. Late in the evening, those of us who could still move were herded into a big cattle shed. Father and I stood in the cold cattle shed. I pressed myself against him to get warm. He stood wearing a *tallit* and *tefillin* and prayed the whole time. He was forty-two or forty-three-years old at the time. At daybreak, they forced us from the shed to the camp,[13] for which

---

12 On November 10, 1941, approximately 3,000 Jews were forced from Tulchin to Pechora (Pechera).

13 The village of Pechora is located along the southern Bug River in the Tulchin region (formerly Shpikov region) of the Vinnitsa Oblast (province); the camp

they had adapted the estate of Count Potocki, built in the style of a medieval fortress. In the centre there stood a castle and a Catholic church, surrounded by a cobblestone wall. The entrance to the camp was through large iron gates, beside which were watchtowers. Across from the gates was the gendarmerie. In order to look behind the wall, we would make mounds of dirt and stand on them.

The building we stayed in was unheated and cold. Everyone tried to get to the room on the second floor, which was warmer. There were forty people per room. The windows were frozen; condensation would drip from the windows and we lay in the puddles, pressed against each other. The weaker ones died. Men carried the corpses outside and took their clothes in an effort to warm themselves.

We weren't given any food or water in the camp. People were doomed to die.[14] The young ones would try to climb over the fence and secretly go over to the village of Torkovo to exchange people's remaining valuables. But the guards set up ambushes and took our valuables by force. They also caught messengers or smugglers and shot them. But they themselves sometimes asked us to exchange valuables for tobacco or groceries. A guard once beat me up with a ramrod and the butt of his rifle; I was covered in blood. But hunger would force us to climb over the wall again, overcoming the fear of death by bullets.

---

was located at the northeastern border of Transnistria, the territory in Ukraine under Romanian occupation during World War II. In December 1941, Jews from the surrounding regions – Tulchin, Bratslav, Shpikov, Trostyanets – and later from more distant regions – Mogilev-Podolsky (Mohyliv-Podilskyi), Bukovina and Bessarabia – were brought to Pechora. See Rebecca Golbert, "Holocaust Sites in Ukraine: The Politics of Memorialization," National Council for Eurasian and Eastern European Research, Washington, DC, November 10, 2002. Accessed from ucis.pitt.edu.

14 Between 6,500 and 11,000 Jews were deported to Pechora, which was known as the Dead Loop camp; more than 80 per cent died there. See http://kehilalinks. jewishgen.org/tulchyn/holocaust.asp.

We would gather rusty cans and try to bring back some water from the Bug River, even though the water was bloody; corpses were floating in it. Some couldn't bear the humiliations and drowned themselves. One day, our acquaintance Rabinovich threw himself in an ice-hole in the river. Shargorodsky from Vapniarka dragged him out, but two days later he died anyway. Rabinovich's wife froze to death in the ravine when she was looking for something to eat.

The village of Torkovo was located eight kilometres from Pechora. We would leave before dawn, in secret. People gave away their rings, watches, boots. Smugglers came and went secretly, so that the Germans wouldn't see. Peasants from the village didn't denounce us — they were interested in us bringing our remaining valuables to them. In return, they gave us potato skins and some chaff, husks of grain, that they were preparing to give to the cattle in the morning.

In the yard of the camp, men dug a hole and secretly stoked a fire. We would boil acacia leaves; sometimes, we would find some frozen cabbage, chestnuts, nettles, sorrel, saltbush. The most difficult thing was the constant, acute feeling of hunger. We sucked our own blood from our fingers to somewhat satisfy the hunger. Children's rectums stuck out. Everybody resembled skeletons covered in skin. Emaciated and atrophied people could barely move. Before my own eyes, a woman who had gone mad from hunger gnawed her dead neighbour's breast off. The Germans laughed and took photos of such occurrences.

At some point, a commission that included Doctor Beletsky, a man with a Polish background, and Smetansky, a Ukrainian Polizei, visited the camp. The doctor verified deaths of inmates. The fate of everyone in Pechora was to die from starvation.

In the spring of 1942, all those who were weakened from hunger were murdered. The rest were rounded up for work. We were moved to the Rakhny station of the Shpikov region, about eighty kilometres away, and herded there on foot. Along the way, we were made to kneel in the dirt, surrounded by German shepherd dogs. The commandant would fill out documents and then we would be driven farther. When mothers with little ones on their hands found it difficult to walk, their children were taken away and thrown in a pile. We badly wanted to drink. We walked past wells but were not allowed to drink. A guide accompanied our group, a Romanian man called Ion. He mocked us, saying, "It's not for you Jews that nature created water."

When we arrived in the camp in the village of Rakhny, an announcement was made: "There is no running away from here. Offenders will be hanged. Work conscientiously. Work starts at 5:00 a.m." The guides quickly finished their reports. Then, they finally gave us water. They drove up a water barrel, unbridled the bulls and uncorked the barrel. The water was spilling on the ground. We got on our knees, wet our hands and licked off the water.

Men were locked in the horse stables and women were locked in the cellar, where we slept on the straw floor. At dawn, we were rounded up for work. One day we worked in a forest nursery weeding the seedlings. Being inexperienced, I touched the roots of several seedlings. Polizei Tkachuk beat me up until I lost consciousness, swore at me. I lay there in a puddle of blood until lunchtime. My back was black from bruises. I was only fifteen years old and, like all the teenagers there, I was emaciated from hunger. When a cart drove up, they threw me in it and took me to the isolation barracks. There, I was thrown down by the doorstep with other "goners." I didn't want to live anymore. Nobody came back from isolation.

I was saved by Esfir Osipovna Svyatetskaya, who knew my father. Before the war, she had been a dentist. She was thirty-five at the time. She had been moved to the Pechora camp much later than I, from Kapustyany, where there was a sugar factory. Esfir had managed to take a bundle of valuables into the camp with her. Once, she lost it and cried. I found that bundle, and that is how we met. Esfir begged the police to carry me into the common barracks. She gave me some weak broth made with mangel beet and cabbage, which I found painful to swallow. She nursed me back to health.

We tried to stay together. When strength slowly returned to me, I resolved to escape the camp and I tried to convince Esfir to escape with me, but she was hoping for the help of a doctor she knew, Nizvetsky, who lived in Rakhny. Nizvetsky was a classmate of her husband's, who had been the head doctor of the Obod hospital. In 1941, Nizvetsky was wounded at the front but he had managed to get home. Esfir and her husband lived in the hospital and nursed him to health. They hid him in the cellar so he would not have to return to the army. He said that he would never forget that. When local women who worked in the camp handed us our broth through a window, Esfir asked them if they knew Doctor Nizvetsky. They replied that half the villagers were called Nizvetsky around there. Esfir established contact with the right family and sent them her bundle. They bought her boots, sent her bread. She always shared with me.

On November 8, 1942, both of us were severely beaten. We wouldn't live much longer if we stayed in the camp, so we both decided that we must escape, even though this would put us in mortal danger. We weren't usually allowed to go outside, but in the shed where we slept, there was no toilet, only wooden buckets. It was cold and windy, and nobody wanted to take out the buckets of feces. That evening, we carried out the buckets. A Romanian guard was sitting there, drunk. We came back and then walked out with the buckets again. It was raining and snowing as we threw the buckets in the hole and started walking toward the river. An icy plank had been thrown across the river, as a bridge. We were afraid we'd fall from it, so we walked across in the freezing water, and that saved us. It was difficult to walk because our legs were swollen. The night was so dark that we could barely see even one step ahead of us.

We lay low in the forest. Dogs had been following us, but they lost track of us at the river. We walked through the forest for two days until we reached a small farm. On entering the first house, we realized we were out of luck: a Polizei lived there; his uniform's armband was hanging on a nail. He beat us up and wanted to take us to the Gestapo — there was a reward offered for catching escaped prisoners. Esfir pleaded with him, said that I was her daughter. She was kissing the police guard's boots while he hit her in the face. The police guard's wife did not want to let him go to the Gestapo because she didn't want to stay alone with their sick child. The Polizei chased us out into the street.

We had no strength to continue our journey. We stopped by a house with a tall fence and knocked. The owner came out and invited us in, let us warm ourselves by the stone oven. His mother was elderly and his son had recently returned from German captivity, and this is why he treated us with compassion. But he said that he couldn't let us stay, since the villagers often visited him to ask his son whether he had run into their relatives. The owner gave us hot milk to drink and then hid us with the pigs in the pigpen, in the hay. We froze. We were afraid that someone would come and discover us.

At dawn, the owner gave us some bread and advised us not to walk on the road and to spend the night in the fields, in a haystack. We sat in a haystack for twenty-four hours. Then we walked to Tomashpol, a journey of approximately one hundred kilometres. We wanted to get to a market and find something to eat. We slipped in there secretly and hid under the counters, managing to gather cabbage leaves and bits of vegetables. From conversations we overheard, we found out that there was a ghetto in Tomashpol, but that many Jews had already been shot. We were looking for a place where we could hide from the cold wind when we saw a dilapidated hut. The house was being picked apart for firewood and we hid on top of a Russian stone oven.

Soon, a man approached us. He was a Ukrainian from Bershad. He said, "Don't be afraid of me — I won't turn you in. A Jewish girl from Bukovina, Romania, will come to see you here today. I agreed, in exchange for gold, to help her get to the Bershad ghetto, where she is hoping to find her brother." The Germans had forced Jews from Romania to Ukraine, transporting them like cattle in freight trains to Mogilev-Podolsky and then to Pechora. In the evening, the girl arrived. We talked in Yiddish. She had been left without relatives; they had all been killed in Mogilev-Podolsky. The guide said to Esfir, "You look Russian, you'll come with me through Obodovka to Bershad." And to me he said, "You look like a Jewess — you'll stay here."

Esfir gave me her last shirt and put a coat on her naked body. Our dresses had torn a long time ago. I had a skirt made from a bag, a little headscarf on my head to hide my long, dark braids. Esfir and I said our goodbyes. She went to Obodvka and I was left alone in a dilapidated house. I wailed all night.

In the morning, women from the ghetto came by. They had each contributed a little bit of food to bring me. They took me to the ghetto with them. My feet were swollen from hunger and cold. An elderly Jewish man, Zalman Soifer, took off his boots made out of rags and struggled to put them on my feet. He took me to his daughter. The little girl looked like an old nun, even though she was only sixteen years old. People would try to change the appearance of young girls, to hide them from the Polizei. (Forty years later, I found that woman's daughter, Musya, and then I found her mother, who lived in Siberia.)

There was fear of typhus. We heated up water in a *kazan*, a large cooking pot. We washed ourselves, but had nothing to dry ourselves with so would stand by the stove in the cellar. In the ghetto, they fed me some more, and I went to the village of Rozhniativka to look for work with the peasants. A couple of days later, I read a posting that the sugar factory director was looking for a housekeeper. He was a Russian called Vladimir Iks; his wife was Ukrainian, and they had two little boys and lived with a grandmother. I cleaned the stable, milked the cow, gathered saltbush for the cow and the pig. I had to learn how to do everything but the boys helped me. One day, Mashka the cow didn't come back from the herd. She had stumbled into a vegetable garden and caused damage. The owners of the garden tied her close to the ground by her horns. I begged the garden's owner to let the cow go. As I was leading her home, the cow struggled free and dragged me on the ground; her udder was swollen. I dislocated my shoulder and was afraid to go to the hospital, in case it was revealed that I was Jewish. The mistress took her jacket off my shoulders and put me out into the street. I didn't know where to go, and I cried.

It was now 1943, and the Germans began to retreat from the Volga River.[15] Romanian nuns gave me shelter in a hallway for two days. But then they also turned me out, since they were expecting monks from Odessa to visit. Next I found work with a Romanian whose surname was Purich. He was from the Dnepropetrovsk region. His wife, Tasya, was afraid of him, and they had two children. The master would send me out at night to steal coal; Romanian guards beat me up for that once. I would go see the master at the sugar factory where he worked, carry out some sugar, syrup and motor oil bit by bit, and sell it at the market, giving the money to the master. When he got drunk, he would shout that Jews in the Gulag knocked one of his teeth out and that he would kill me if he found out that I was a Jewess. One day when he was drunk, he got robbed and showed up at home naked. That night, he sent me out to look for his watch.

One day during a downpour I met a Jewish girl, a fellow countrywoman, in a partition between houses. She said that she and her little sister were alone. They had nowhere to live and nothing to eat. A legless beggar now gave them shelter in his den. He said that he would feed them if she slept with him. In order to survive and save her little sister, she agreed. From her, I learned that my parents had perished. She told me that my mother had escaped from the camp and had gone searching for me. In the woods, she had run into the people from the camp who disposed of corpses. A guard beat her up; her blood stained his coat. He ordered her to be thrown onto the pile of corpses and he kept beating her even more viciously. This is how my mother died. My father died a few days later after learning about her death. His sick heart couldn't stand the stress.

----

15  In February 1943, the German army surrendered to the Soviets at the end of the Battle of Stalingrad.

I decided to secretly find my way into the Potocki castle, where the Pechora camp was still located. I wouldn't give up the thought of finding some of my surviving relatives and I needed to confirm my loved ones' deaths for myself. My wanderings lasted eight months. I slept in empty houses. In late 1943, I met two emaciated Jewish children in the forest — a girl, Riva, and her younger brother, Zeidel, who had miraculously escaped a mass grave. The Germans would lead people to a ditch and shoot whole families. The bullets had flown above the children's heads. Although they were pushed into a common pit, the girl managed to crawl out from underneath the corpses and pull out her wounded little brother. They also had a little sister. She was also wounded and covered with corpses. She was still alive and asked them to save her, but the children didn't manage to drag her out.

Riva and Zeidel had lived in Kotovsk, near Odessa. They had been walking from the outskirts of Odessa, hiding from people, and had walked to Tomashpol through the forest. After the war, I met Riva again. She told me that her brother had made his way to the front as a volunteer and was killed. All that was left from him was a letter with a poem. But Riva herself did not live long either. She fell ill, lost her mind and died.

Eventually, I reached the Pechora camp. I hid there in an attic, dismantled the tiles on the roof and watched the troops moving. There were very few people left in the camp. Everybody had died from hunger or from the beatings. I made my way into the village, carried water for the peasants, helped take care of animals, earned my living. Peasants had been rounded up to dig a ravine for a grave. They said that this grave was for us, the ones who still remained alive.

In the spring of 1944, Soviet troops entered the city. The Germans retreated in a hurry and didn't have time to destroy the remaining prisoners of the Pechora camp. The first person to enter the camp was a colonel, a Jew. We couldn't believe that we were being liberated and were afraid to walk out. Many couldn't walk at all.

After the liberation, in the hopes of finding some of my loved ones, I went to a village near Tulchin. I wanted to take Iona Reznik's daughter, Fira, from Kilyna, who could barely walk. But an angry neighbour told me that Kilyna had murdered the girl with an axe and now the water in the well was spoiled. She told me that one morning the peasants saw blood in the well. They followed the drops of blood and came to Kilyna, the "Believer." She had cut the five-year-old girl into pieces, put the pieces in a sack and thrown it into the well.

Almost all the members of my extended family perished. My grandfather Azril had lived in Gaisin until 1941, when the Germans entered Ukraine. Both Grandfather and Grandmother were shot. My uncle Naftule was killed in Rostov-on-Don. He was a deeply religious person. He lived on the second floor of a house, sharing a hallway with a Baptist woman. During the bombings, they would go down to the cellar. He gave his valuables to a street sweeper, hoping that he would save him. When the Germans came, Uncle Naftule wouldn't take off his *tallit* and prayed the whole time. After the war, his neighbour said that when the gas wagon drove up to the house, the street sweeper pointed to the old man's room. Uncle Naftule entered the gas wagon wearing his *tallit* and *tefillin* while a German was beating him. The Germans found the street sweeper two days later. He had choked on his own tongue while drunk. My sister, who was a year and a half older than I, died in the Pechora camp. Tsvi-Gersh, Naftule's son, was shot. Tsvi-Gersh's pregnant daughter was stabbed with a bayonet and his son, an eighth grader, was raised up on bayonets for singing the Soviet anthem "The Internationale." The other son of Naftule's, Grisha, was drafted in the Rostov recruitment office. He was captured near Gaisin. He had a good voice, and before the war he used to do vinyl recordings. He was set on fire in a horse shed with other prisoners of war. Grisha managed to escape and, badly burned, reached Gaisin on foot, where a ghetto had also been created. He pretended to be the son of my grandfather Azril, that is to say, a local. Russian neighbours helped him. He started working as a patternmaker at a shoe shop. My uncle Grisha Vaisleib hoped to find his relatives, but this was already after the mass shooting, and not one was left alive. People who had known his relatives helped treat his burns and gave him a change of clothes. He registered a woman named Frida Strizhevsky as his wife and her daughter as a member of his family. Only people with families were allowed to live in the ghetto.

In 1942, through a man named Misha Gerenburg, they went to join the partisans in the forest. Before the liberation, in early March 1944, Grisha, Frida and her daughter were on a mission in Gaisin. As they were walking away from a messenger, Germans noticed them, chased them with dogs, caught them and shot them, along with other partisans. A few days later, Soviet forces liberated Gaisin. Partisans came out of the forest, identified the mutilated Grisha by his yellow leather jacket, and buried him in Gaisin in a city park. The other Grisha, Azril's son who lived in Bershad, was in the army. He was religious and tried to eat only kosher food. Because of malnutrition, he fell ill with night-blindness. He died on the front in Belarus.

I trudged on toward Gaisin. Soviet troops were walking on the road. I got to ride on a tank, sitting next to the gun, for around twenty-five kilometres. A general named Agapov questioned me. To calm me down, he said that my brother was probably alive. When I arrived in Tulchin, I saw that my house on Karl Liebknecht Street had been burned down. My father's printing presses had been taken away. I went to the ghetto. There was nobody left there. I settled in an empty house on 18 Volodarsky Street, living all alone. Bed feathers were flying through cold empty rooms. The owner of the house came back from Bershad. The front was nearby, and there was fighting over Odessa.

I went to Gaisin hoping to find relatives. My grandfather's house was burned down. The house of my aunt, whose last name was Shkolnik, was also gone. I went up the mountain. Among the ruins a man asked me, "What are you looking for?" It was Misha Gerenburg. He had spent the war among the partisans. He took me in. He lived with

Raya Strizhesvky, Frida's sister, near the military quarters. I spent several days there. Raya went to Uman with some peasants who were transporting produce to look for her relatives.

It was still March 1944 when I met a disabled woman and offered to help her with her suitcase. She led me to her home on Sadovaya Street, where she let me spend the night in the kitchen. It was cold; I couldn't sleep. I got up, washed all the dishes, washed the floor. She let me live with her. To earn my living, I washed the windows for a military man whose family had perished. His name was Pyotr Zagrudny. He became the director of a research and training farm. I was training as a dental technician in a dental lab. In the dental clinic, there was a doctor whose last name was Trayan. He had saved the life of a Jewish doctor's daughter by the name of Eva. He had hidden her in his cellar throughout the war.

As I was looking for Jews who returned from evacuation, I ran into an acquaintance, a *ger* (a Russian convert to Judaism). My grandfathers had been engaged in missionary work and many converted to Judaism with their help. During these difficult years, most of them gave their fellow Jewish believers away. But this *ger*, a shoemaker, remained faithful to Judaism. He was disabled, having been beaten up in the market. He asked me, "Girl, why do you follow me around?" I replied, "I know you, you studied under Azril, I am his granddaughter." He invited me to his house, fed me.

After a while I went to Uman and then I left for Kharkov with the help of friends who got me bread ration cards and a train ticket. I knew that my aunt had been evacuated from Kharkov, and I hoped to find her. Maybe she remained alive. Eventually, I found my aunt, Esfir Izrailevna Vaisleib, when she came back from Aktyubinsk. In Kharkov, the governing authorities had assigned her one room. She took in Jewish orphaned children to bring them up, and we all lived in her terribly overcrowded room. My aunt worked sorting cabbage in the Workers' Supply Department. I wanted to study, but my aunt said that I wouldn't be able to get admitted anywhere since I spoke a

476 BEFORE ALL MEMORY IS LOST

terrible mix of languages. This was a result of years spent in the camp among multilingual people. I got upset with my aunt; I took it hard psychologically. I knew that the Institute of Construction Materials was accepting applicants and I tried to take the exams.

In the fall of 1944, I was called in to see Investigator Kapranov in Kharkov. He tried to accuse me of collaboration with the Germans, since I remained alive in an occupied territory. I was laid off from work. The investigator forced me to identify the former Polizei. He shouted that if I didn't identify them, I myself would be shot. The police set up a confrontation: They brought in the handcuffed Polizei, who stood in two rows, unkempt, looking down. It was difficult to identify them, but I did identify Smetansky. Signs that called on people to identify traitors were hung up around the city. Many didn't want to go; they were afraid. I wanted to avenge the dead and punish the perpetrators. These people had done so much evil. It's not only that they betrayed and destroyed Jews; they also betrayed communists. The Polizei traitors got twenty to twenty-five years in prison, but they came back home earlier because of amnesty.[16]

I managed to get a pension of 105 rubles for my brother who perished at the front. I sent Khruschev a letter about my situation, writing that I wanted to study. An officer named Kuklina came to visit me and assigned me one room in a former Jewish apartment; she made a street sweeper share the space. I started visiting the medical clinic to see Doctor Rakuzina, who said that I needed to learn to work. I received twelve metres of gauze. I made curtains out of it, set apart a "closet" for clothes. I made a mattress out of straw and I slept on a bed that had three legs. There was no lock; instead, I put a cobblestone by the door. I sold my bread ration card and bought a lock and a little *kazan* pot. I made a stove for myself to cook beans on.

I improved my dental skills with the dentist Tsilya Iosifovna. Be-

16 On November 27, 1944, at the demand of the head of the unit of Ukrainian Security Services of Vinnitsa region, P.M. Kapranov, Svetlana was a witness at a war tribunal held by the N K V D armed forces of Vinnitsa region.

fore I even mastered the profession properly, I opened a dental office in my room. There was a market nearby, and farmers came to see me. I encouraged the dentist Beletsky and the dental technician Isaac Markovich to help me set up the office, and I sourced all the instruments. I was studying hard to master the dental profession. My aunt brought me a textbook for distance education, and I received a study permit for the dental school as a war veteran.

I soon met my future husband, Hershel Kogan. During the war, he was a partisan. Although he also came from a religious family, he was against a religious marriage, but I insisted. In 1947, we had a secret chuppah in an entranceway of a half-dilapidated house. The communist regime did not allow Jews to observe religious traditions. We celebrated our marriage with Tula gingerbread and one shot of vodka. Hershel gave me a beautiful wedding gift of silk, which I could sew a skirt from. I was happy. My life was such a contrast to the years in the concentration camp and wanderings in the woods and among strangers.

Hershel got an apartment in Kharkov, in a dormitory of the Govorov Academy. Our son, Ilya, was born in 1948. Even before I was released from the maternity hospital, I made an arrangement with an old Hasidic Jew that he would secretly circumcise my son. In Grade 4, my son was beaten for being circumcised, and we had to transfer him to a different school. In 1952, I gave birth to our daughter, Ludmila (Mila).

Over the years, my husband and I often visited the places where our loved ones had perished, where many thousands of Jews had been killed. With the help of local authorities, I succeeded in collecting funds and setting up memorials at mass gravesites. At these memorials I would tell young people about the things we had to live through during the years of the Nazi occupation and about those who were murdered at the hands of Nazi occupants and local traitors.

November 1995, Moscow

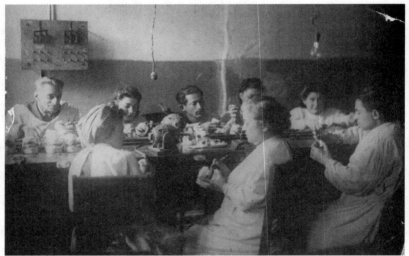

1  Svetlana Kogan-Rabinovich after the war. Kharkov, 1946.
2  Wedding photo of Hershel and Svetlana. Kharkov, August 1948.
3  Svetlana (back row, second from the left) at work in the dental laboratory. Kharkov, 1946.

1 The Kogan family in Odessa, 1956. In back, Svetlana's husband, Hershel Kogan. In front, left to right, Hershel's half-sister, Klara; Svetlana and Hershel's children, Ludmila (Mila) and Ilya; and Svetlana.

2 Svetlana and Hershel. Moscow, 1983.

1 Svetlana (centre) educating a group of students at a mass gravesite. Russia, date unknown.
2 At the memorials in Gaisin, Ukraine.

1 Svetlana and Hershel at the memorial she helped establish in Tulchin, Ukraine.
2 At the opening of the monument to Sholem Aleichem in Moscow. From left to
   right: the sculptor, Yuri Chernov; the Chief Rabbi of Russia, Berel Lazar; Svetlana;
   and the then-ambassador of Israel to Russia.
3 Svetlana on the Congress of World War II Veterans. Moscow, 2003.

1 Three generations of Svetlana's family. Svetlana's granddaughter, Ellie; Svetlana; and Svetlana's daughter, Mila. Toronto, 1999.
2 Svetlana's grandson, David; Mila; and Svetlana. Circa 2005.
3 Svetlana Kogan-Rabinovich, 2013.

# I Have Survived It All
# Gitlia Popovsky

*I wrote this memoir as a legacy for my children, Sofia and Valery, Roman and Raya; my grandchildren, Albinna and Alain, Arthur and Lilia, and Dima; my great-grandchildren, Joshua, Daniel, Jamie and Maya; and for anyone who is interested in reading it. I express my deep appreciation to the Maimonides volunteer program, in particular to Jake Levy, who wrote down my story, administrator Tracey Winter and my daughter Sofia Zatulovsky, who encouraged and helped me in writing this memoir.*

As I was writing my story, I went back in time and relived it. I was born in 1922, the only child of a middle-class family in the shtetl called Skvyra[1] in the Ukraine, close to the capital city, Kiev. In Skvyra, my father owned a textile store and my mother, by herself, ran a restaurant near the train station: she was the cook, the waitress and the manager. The communists called us *Kulaki*[2] because of our business-

---

1  Skvyra is about 101 kilometres south of Kiev. At times, Jews made up half the population of the town; however, the frequent pogroms, particularly in 1917 and 1919, reduced the Jewish population considerably.
2  A term that means "fist" in Russian, representing a category of relatively affluent farmers, landowners, business people or anyone who derived an income from non-labour wealth. *Kulaks*, or *Kulaki*, were designated as class enemies by the Soviets.

es. They arrived when I was four years old and they took everything away from my parents (in accordance with the principle of "equality," which was a cornerstone of communist philosophy). One day we had a house and business, but the next day the communists ensured we had nothing. My family became very poor and we lost all our rights. My father's right to work in Skvyra was revoked, and thus he lost his job, so he went to Kiev in search of new employment and a new life. He soon began working there as a night watchman, where he remained without us, earning money. In 1926, thanks to the money my father had carefully saved for us, the rest of our family was able to go to Kiev to join him.

The Communist Party dominated the former Soviet Union and took away goods from the people. They also took away our right to practise Judaism and brought the notorious pogroms[3] and enforced relocations. Like many others, when we fled to the big city of Kiev, it was for our safety as Jews. And so my family survived the pogroms.

A Jewish education — religious, cultural and didactic — was the standard at the time for Jewish people. When we arrived in Kiev, I spoke only Yiddish, not a word of Russian. My parents sent me to a Jewish school, where I successfully completed seven grades before

---

3   Pogroms have a longer history than the onset of communism in Soviet Russia. "*Pogrom* is a Russian word meaning to 'wreak havoc, to demolish violently.' Historically, the term refers to violent attacks by local non-Jewish populations on Jews in the Russian Empire and in other countries. The first such incident to be labelled a pogrom is believed to be anti-Jewish rioting in Odessa in 1821. As a descriptive term, "pogrom" came into common usage with extensive anti-Jewish riots that swept Ukraine and southern Russia in 1881–1884, following the assassination of Tsar Alexander II. The perpetrators of pogroms organized locally, sometimes with government and police encouragement. They raped and murdered Jews and looted their property. During the civil war that followed the 1917 Bolshevik Revolution, Ukrainian nationalists, Polish officials and Red Army soldiers all engaged in pogrom-like violence in western Belorussia (Belarus) and Poland's Galicia province (now West Ukraine), killing tens of thousands of Jews between 1918 and 1920." See ushmm.org/wlc/en/article.php?ModuleId=10005183.

Stalin closed the Jewish schools. Consequently, I was forced to finish my last three years of high school in the Russian language. After high school, I wanted to find myself a trade. During the daytime, I worked in a shoe factory, and at night, I studied. I endeavored to eventually pursue a career as a secretary and typist. I later worked for the Ministry of Education as a secretary, typing and doing shorthand (which I still remember how to use) until World War II broke out. To graduate from typist school, I had to be able to type 110 words per minute, but when the war erupted and the school was forced to close, I could only type ninety. I was never able to graduate from trade school.

~

I was nineteen in September 1941 when the Germans were battling to occupy Kiev and the effects of the war became clear in the Soviet Union. As Jews, we needed to escape from the Nazis. My parents and I tried to evacuate on one of two boats sailing out of Kiev on the Dnieper River to the city of Tripoli. On the way, we saw soldiers wildly waving flags at us, signalling us to turn back. Luckily, I was in the second boat with my parents; the first boat triggered a mine buried in the river bed and sank, killing all of its passengers. We turned around in a panic to avoid the mines and returned to Kiev.

As the boat pulled into Kiev, I heard the loud reverberations of bombardments. German soldiers were parachuting into the outskirts of the city and others were marching in. As I walked to the main street, I saw wounded and dead soldiers being loaded onto wagons and carried out of the battleground, and other soldiers patrolling on horses: the Nazis were taking over Kiev. We had returned home to the aftermath of a battle.

My uncle, Isaak Budnitsky, came up to us right away and told us not to unpack our things. He was a pharmacist and he said he would try to send us out of the city on a train with the medications he was trying to keep from the Nazis. He wasn't sure exactly when it would happen, but he told us we had to stay home. Three days later he came at night, brought us to a train and hid us in boxes. We left Kiev the night the Nazis completely took over the city, preventing anyone else from leaving.

That night, my uncle, my father's brother, saved my life and the lives of my parents. He stayed in Kiev to run the pharmacy and to provide medicine to the troops, but, when the Nazis took over Kiev, he wasn't as lucky as we were; he was killed in Babi Yar. This notorious massacre of Jewish people took place between September 29 and 30, 1941, when Nazi troops executed 33,771 Jewish civilians in a single operation at the ravine of Babi Yar in Kiev. It was among the largest single mass killings in the history of the Holocaust. Armed with machine guns, the Nazis funneled the Jews, who were under the impression that they were being displaced for the purpose of resettlement, toward a gigantic gravesite that had been dug earlier. One by one, the Jews were forced to remove all their clothes and to lie face down near the edge of the ravine, at which point they were shot in the back of the head. Eventually, the gravesite was layered with corpses, which the Nazis then covered with dirt. Witnesses recalled that the ground at Babi Yar could be heard humming for days afterwards; the sound was the voices of all those whom the Nazis had wounded but not killed, who were actually buried alive. My heroic uncle perished in this genocide. Thanks to his sacrifice, though, my parents and I escaped right before this devastating massacre.

~

The train took us to Kharkov, another city in the Ukraine. Our train was bombarded on the way, but luckily we were unharmed. When we got to Kharkov, the people in charge of evacuation sent us on a train to Kazakhstan. We spent about a year there. It was safe to be evacuated to southern republics because Germans never occupied them. Winters were very cold in Kazakhstan, and we had no fuel with which to heat the houses. Instead, all the refugees were brought to a place with a big pile of cow's manure. We put on rubber boots and stamped on the manure until it became hard bricks, which we then took back to our house and used as fuel to avoid freezing. The smell was overwhelming, but we did what we had to do to survive. My father passed away while we were in Kazakhstan. It took ten days for us to be able to bury him, because the ground was frozen solid.

My mother had a brother who had been evacuated with his family to Uzbekistan, and he sent us papers to go live with him in Namangan, a city in eastern Uzbekistan, after my father's death. There I worked in a factory office, and my mother knit warm clothing for the Russian soldiers. The sanitary conditions we lived in were less than satisfactory. I recall that we lived in a big tent with many Uzbek women, which was typical for southern republics. And so I survived evacuation and the Nazi regime.

My mother and I stayed in Uzbekistan until 1944, returning to Kiev after it had been liberated from the Nazis. I quickly got a job that enabled me to live in the city that had been my home for much of my life. Since Kiev had been destroyed by German bombardments, there was a shortage of living space. My mother's relatives sheltered us and we lived with them in one room, sleeping on the floor.

Meanwhile, World War II persisted, and I met my future husband, Abraham Solomonovitch Popovsky, who had been a soldier in the war. We were introduced through a mutual friend and we liked each other very much. One day in early 1945, Abraham said, "Why don't you and your mother move in with me?" I asked him how this would be possible: changing addresses wasn't so simple in the Soviet Union because the government kept strict records of everyone's assigned address. He suggested we go to the License Bureau to find out how I could change my address, and they told me I'd have to fill out and sign applications, so, being very naive, I did, and the papers turned out to be a marriage licence! I went home and told my mother that I was married. I had been living with my cousin Lisa and ten other people in a very crowded basement room, so I was glad to have the opportunity to move into Abraham's small room with my mother.

In 1945, my son Roman was born in that room. Eight months later, I was pregnant again. We were poor and concerned that we couldn't properly afford our second child. My mother, however, encouraged me by saying I would give birth to a beautiful baby girl, and my daughter Sofia was born in 1947. By this time the war was over and that turbulent chapter of my life had drawn to a close, only to be replaced by a different challenge: raising children.

~

My husband was born into a big family in Warsaw, Poland, in 1910. His mother passed away when he was two months old, and he grew up with a stepmother who hated him. Consequently, he ran away from home at the age of nine. He worked on a collective farm to survive, but ultimately decided he wanted to become a tailor. He returned to Warsaw and completed the special trade school to become a tailor. He worked as a tailor until Germany invaded Poland in 1939.

Abraham escaped the Warsaw ghetto with his wife and daughter and started to flee toward the Soviet Union, as many Polish Jews did at that time. A train he was on with his family stopped in a field and he went to get water; while he was gone, the train was bombarded and his family was killed. He continued alone and managed to get to the Soviet Union. There, he was given two choices: either to go to work in camps east of the Ural Mountains or to join the army. He chose the army; he obtained a passport and worked as a tailor in the city of Saratov from 1939 to 1941, and then fought in the war starting in 1941. He was wounded, received a medal and came to Kiev in 1944 after it had been liberated. He started to work in Kiev as a tailor in a hospital, and the government gave him a little room to live in. This was the room that I later came to share with him.

In 1945, the Soviet government allowed Polish Jews who had lived in the Soviet Union during the war to return to Poland. My husband wanted to go back to find his relatives, but I didn't want to go since my son had just been born. Abraham was not happy living under the Soviet regime since life there was very hard, due in part to the shortage of food. We had to endure long line-ups for bread, sugar, meat and everything else. Living as a Jew was hard because antisemitism was on the rise, especially in the Ukraine, where we were forbidden from practising Judaism. Abraham had supported the Communist Party when he was in Poland; however, he had quickly become disillusioned with the communist ideology after having seen it in action in the Soviet Union, and he decisively re-evaluated his views and left the communists. In the mid-1950s, the government opened the door again for Polish Jews to return to Poland. I still didn't want to go; I didn't want to leave my family. Deciding to stay in Kiev proved to be the biggest mistake of my life.

At this time, my husband worked in a tailor shop that belonged to the government in Kiev. He was a very hard worker, sometimes earning tips, which meant that we could afford some things that other people couldn't. Abraham didn't let me get a job of my own until our children were in high school, since he viewed parenting to be a priority. He was a very good father. I always wanted to get a job, though. I knew I'd need one someday. I spent a lot of time at home while my children were growing up, and then when they were older I finally found work, first as a cashier in a pharmacy across the street from my house and later as a cashier in a fish store.

My husband once told me he was sorry his children had to grow up in Communist Russia under an oppressive and highly antisemitic regime. It was never an easy life for us. Kiev had been destroyed by the Germans and, until it was rebuilt, people were forced to live in communal apartments. First, we lived in a wooden, two-storey building, sharing a kitchen with other families. We had to use an outhouse since there was no indoor plumbing. A few years later, we upgraded to another building with indoor plumbing, a flat that we shared with four other families. We had one common kitchen with three stoves, two burners per family and one toilet for twelve people. Every family had its own toilet seat hanging by the nail on the wall. I remember cutting up newspaper to use as toilet paper, which wasn't available in the Soviet Union until the late 1960s. The country was way behind Europe or America. Each family had a room to themselves;

there were five of us in our room (my mother, my husband, my two children and me), a single room that served as a bedroom, a living room, a dining room and a TV room. That room was our whole life; it was our sanctuary.

In that room, our son, Roman, had his bar mitzvah, which could not be celebrated in the synagogue for there was only one in the whole city and it was to be used only for the elderly. Young people were not allowed inside and were banned from entering by the Russian police. Communist ideology did not allow any kind of religion. So my husband asked the rabbi to come to our room. The rabbi put the *tallis* on Roman's shoulders and the *tefillin* on my son's head and arm and read the part of Torah that my son had to repeat. Of course all of this, as well as our celebratory dinner, was done very quietly so that no one would hear because it was officially forbidden by the government.

In that same room, also quietly, my family celebrated Pesach — we made our own matzot from scratch: my mother made the dough, I rolled it, my children cut it and made the holes with the fork and my mother baked it at night so no one would see — and other Jewish holidays. No one could take away our Jewish souls and our Jewish traditions. On that note, I must say that I am very happy and fortunate that I live in Canada now, a free country, where I can celebrate holidays and follow Judaism.

My mother was the cook for our family. She used to get up at four in the morning and use all three stoves to cook the food for our family for the day before the other families had woken up. One of the other families we lived with had been very rich and famous before Stalin came to power. Their patriarch was a drunk and an antisemite; every night he would threaten to kill our family. He would bang on the door to our room and say, "I'm going to kill all you dirty Jews." My husband wanted to call the police, but I did not allow him to do so as I feared that this man would kill us if we did. We lived there in fear and were forced to endure that intolerance for twenty-five years until we all immigrated to Canada.

There was lots of antisemitism after the war, and the Ukraine, which had the biggest Jewish population in the Soviet Union, was especially bad. The government didn't want any Jews in high positions and government policy rendered it almost impossible for a Jew to get a good job. Most Jews were forced to either not pursue a higher education or to go study elsewhere. The government promised that joining the Communist Party would give people better chances of accessing university, but my family refused.

Furthermore, the former Soviet Union required each of its citizens to carry a passport with them everywhere. People were regularly judged based on their passports, which had to be presented for all manner of social interactions, such as job interviews. These passports included a "fifth paragraph" that listed the individual's ethnicity, referred to then as "nationality." In such an antisemitic environment, the effect of a passport listing each of us as Jewish was devastating.

In 1968, Abraham passed away from a misdiagnosed heart attack. We were one year shy of celebrating our twenty-fifth wedding anniversary. When my husband died, I was devastated. I was only forty-six years old. But at least he had left me two beautiful children. At this time, as I mentioned, antisemitism was rampant in the Soviet Union, and my husband had taken our son, Roman, out of school in the seventh grade and had sent him to a technical college because he was getting beaten up for being a Jew. Roman started working in a garage when he entered technical college. He studied at night and eventually became a car mechanic. He was married in Kiev in 1970 and later gave me two beautiful grandsons, Dima and Arthur.

My daughter, Sofia, finished high school and technical college and then worked in the engineering office of a big aviation plant associated with Antonov Airlines. She became an electromechanical draftswoman. She married in 1967 and, shortly after my husband died, my first grandchild, Albinna, was on the way. Thus life went on without my husband. I continued working, looking after my elderly mother, and I proudly helped raise my granddaughter.

492   BEFORE ALL MEMORY IS LOST

Faced with growing financial troubles and antisemitism, we found the Soviet Union an increasingly impossible place for us to live. Finally, we had no choice but to flee. The effects of the Iron Curtain made it difficult to escape the Soviet regime. However, movements such as "Let My People Go"[4] ultimately pressured the government into finally opening the doors to allow Soviet Jews like us to leave the country of our birth. We saw our chance to find a better and safer life as Jews. At that time, though, the government only allowed Jews to immigrate to Israel. The Israeli government had to send us an invitation, which we then forwarded to the Soviet immigration office, which in turn forced us to renounce our citizenship and give up our Soviet passports. Then the Soviet government gave us an exit visa and a document that would allow us to cross the border out of the Soviet Union. And so we survived the Soviet regime.

Ultimately, I decided I wanted to immigrate to Montreal instead of Israel, because I had six cousins in Montreal who had left Russia as small children in the early twentieth century and I wanted to be reunited with them. Immigrating to Canada proved to be the best decision of my life, both for me and for my family.

~

My daughter Sofia, her husband, Valery, and their daughter, Albinna, went to Canada first; they had previously been labelled *refuseniks*[5], but in 1974 they finally managed to leave. They arrived in Canada in May 1975 and a few months later applied to the Canadian government to sponsor the rest of the family's immigration. My daughter did the required paperwork and, by the government sponsorship re-

---

4  Founded in the 1960s, "Let My People Go" was a grassroots movement organized by the US-based Student Struggle for Soviet Jewry. The group's work led to increased media attention about the plight of Soviet Jewry.

5  The term applied to people, most often Soviet Jews, who were refused permission to emigrate from the Soviet Union because the regime viewed them as traitors and an imagined threat to state security.

quirement, had to show a certain amount of money in her account, which she did not have and had to borrow. Since our family didn't have any money in Russia, my daughter and her husband borrowed money in Canada, which she sent to us so we could pay the Soviet government to let us have our exit visas.

On our way to Canada, we first crossed the border from the Ukraine to Czechoslovakia and then we went to Vienna, the same route as my daughter and her family had taken. In Vienna, we were met by Israeli authorities who gave us permission to go to Italy. We then went to Rome where the Hebrew Immigrant Aid Society set up four embassies for us to choose from — New Zealand, Australia, the United States and Canada. At this point, we were stateless and con- sidered to be political refugees because the Soviet Union had taken away our citizenship and passports when we left. We chose Canada because my daughter was there and we knew Canada was the best country. I travelled with my mother, who was ninety-two at the time, my son and his wife, their two children and my son's mother-in-law.

We left Kiev in 1976 and we arrived in Canada on July 27, 1977. We came with absolutely nothing, but we were happy nonetheless to have four generations reunited in a new, free country. We were met at the Dorval Airport by the Jewish Immigrant Aid Society (JIAS), a Rus- sian rabbi, Israel Sirota, and correspondents from the *Gazette*, which published an article about the reunification of four generations: my mother, myself, my daughter and my granddaughter. In the airport, I was given a pink paper, a status of Landed Immigrant, which gave me the official right to live in Canada. One year after us, my son-in-law's family came to Canada by the same procedure that we had used. All sixteen members of our family had successfully immigrated to Cana- da within three years. It was amazing to finally be in Montreal, a very beautiful city. I was happy to be reunited with my daughter and her family, as well as my six cousins, whom I hadn't seen since we were small children.

Everything was new for me in Canada. I decided I was going to learn to speak English. I knew I'd come here at an age when I was still young enough to learn. I wanted to be independent, which isn't possible in a country if you don't speak its language, and I didn't want to end up stuck listening only to Russian TV. I stayed home and took care of my mother and my granddaughter after school while my daughter worked. At night, I went to courses offered by JIAS, which helped immigrants integrate into Canadian life, find jobs and take language courses. I went at night for many years to study English, my third language after Yiddish and Russian, and, as a result, I can now read, write a little and speak it relatively well.

After three years of living in Canada, I received my Canadian citizenship. Now that I have settled here, I feel that I belong and that I am home. I cherish and value my Canadian citizenship enormously. This is the best country in the world. I remember losing citizenship in the Soviet Union. It means so much to me to live in a free country.

I come from a place where there was a shortage of living space. In Russia, it was standard for three generations to occupy the same apartment. Canada isn't like that. It took me awhile to adjust to the idea that, as a grandmother, I wasn't always going to live with my daughter and help her raise my granddaughter. I rented an apartment for my mother and me and lived there happily. I held different jobs in Canada. I cooked and cleaned for people in need, working for older people as a caregiver and a housekeeper until my health deteriorated and I couldn't work anymore. I spent much time at home looking after my mother. The last two years of her life she stayed in a nursing home far away in the east of Montreal. For those two years, I travelled for an hour and a half each way every single day to stay with my mother and do everything I could possibly do for her to make her life easier. My mother passed away in 1981 at the age of ninety-seven. Up until that point, I had never lived without my mother. I also helped raise my grandchildren as much as possible. I am a real *yiddishe mame*. A *yiddishe mame* would burn in the fire and drown in the water for her children. They are the stars of my life.

After my mother died, I felt quite lonely. My children were very attentive to me and helpful, but they were working hard to build their new lives. At the age of sixty, I was introduced to Nathan Wajsberg, a Polish Jew, and he became another important man in my life. Nathan reminded me very much of my late husband — the way he looked, the way he spoke, his mannerisms — so I felt comfortable with him. He became my companion and friend for the next seventeen years until he passed away in 1999 at the age of ninety. He had no family of his own other than a niece and a nephew in Toronto, so my family became his family.

In 1988, I revisited Kiev, my cousins Sasha, Sonia and Ella, and the site of Babi Yar. It had been long enough; it was time to honour the past. In the 1980s, the Soviet Union had gone through a new chapter called "Perestroika," the more open society. The government had decided to commemorate the Jewish people who were murdered in the mass killing in Kiev. They erected a three-part memorial at the site of Babi Yar. When I left the country years before, it was just an empty field with grass on it. One hundred thousand people, killed by the Nazis between 1941 and 1943, are buried in this mass grave. I was very emotional; standing on the graves of my people, I have never felt so lucky to be alive.

～

My health deteriorated and I was not able to walk because of bad arthritis. With the help of my children, I lived at home as long as I possibly could. Now I live at Maimonides Geriatric Hospital in Montreal, the only place I would want to live outside of home. I felt at home right away when, upon arrival, the administration made me feel welcome by giving me a "blessing for the house" which every Jewish house has. It has been hanging in my room since. Maimonides has everything that the Jewish soul needs: honouring Oneg Shabbat every Friday, celebrating all the Jewish holidays, kosher food, Jewish concerts and Torah studies — things I didn't have the opportunity to pursue while living in the Soviet Union since we were forbidden to practise Judaism. Every year in spring I participate in Yom Hashoah, the Holocaust memorial service, where I, as a Holocaust survivor, light a candle in memory of my uncle and the six million Jews who died in the Holocaust.

My ninetieth birthday was celebrated with both my family and my government. I received letters of congratulation from several government officials: the Member of Parliament Irwin Cotler, the Premier of Quebec Jean Charest, the Governor General of Canada David Johnston and the Prime Minister of Canada Stephen Harper.

At Maimonides, I try to keep busy. I read, I am part of two choirs, I exercise as much as possible and I have recently joined a drama club. My daughter, son, grandchildren and four great-grandchildren come to visit me. But sometimes when it's quiet I think of my uncle who saved my life all those years ago, and I cry.

Gitlia Popovsky at approximately eighteen years old. Kiev, circa 1940.

1  Wedding photo of Gitlia and Abraham. Kiev, January 1945.
2  The Popovsky family, circa 1949. From left to right (in back): Gitlia; her mother,
   Paisa (Pesl); and her husband, Abraham. In front, Gitlia's children, Sofia (left) and
   Roman (right).

1

2

1 The Popovsky family right before Gitlia's daughter and her family left Kiev in 1974. From left to right (back row): Gitlia's daughter, Sofia; her husband, Valery; Gitlia's son, Roman; and his wife, Raye. In the middle row, left to right: Gitlia's granddaughter, Albinna, and her grandsons, Arthur and Dima. In front, Gitlia (left), her mother, Paisa (centre), and Raye's mother (right).

2 Gitlia at part of the Babi Yar Memorial in Kiev, 1988.

1  Gitlia on her ninetieth birthday with her grandchildren, Dima (left), Albinna (centre) and Arthur (right). Montreal, 2012.

2  Celebrating with her great-grandchildren, Joshua and Maya Flora (left), Daniel (in front, right) and Jamie Shmuel (in back, right).

3  Gitlia on her ninetieth birthday with her children, Roman and Sofia.

# A Letter from the Ukraine
# Koine Schachter Rogel

Translated from Yiddish by R. and V. Shaffir (1992)

This all happened in Ciudin[1] in 1941.[2] It was nine o'clock on a Sunday morning when my sister Fraydeh entered my room, completely taken aback: "You are still sleeping and haven't a clue about what's happening outside?"

"Well, what is happening?" I asked.

"There's a war! Germany and Russia. There's bedlam out there on the street. People are running all over the place. The officers are packing up their families and are driving away in their trucks. It's unbelievable. Everyone is in a panic, and you are sleeping."

I sat motionless, not quite able to grasp everything she was saying.

---

1  The author's hometown in Soviet-occupied Bukovina, Ciudin, was originally translated from Yiddish with the spelling "Tshudin." We have chosen a more common spelling of the name — variant spellings of this town include Tshedi, Ciudei, Chudey and Chudin. Ciudin was a town only a few kilometres north of the border between Romania and the Soviet Union, about forty kilometres from the city of Chernowitz (present-day Chernivtsi). Today, Ciudin is known as Chudei and is in Ukraine.

2  The author, born November 11, 1911, was twenty-nine years old when these events took place.

I peeked through the window and saw what Fraydeh described — all kinds of things were happening on the street. I immediately dressed. I wasn't able to eat, and as far as cleaning up was concerned, forget it. Another time, perhaps. For that brief period of time during the beginning of the war when we still remained at home (between one and two weeks, I think), neither the house was cleaned nor the beds made. I simply didn't have the energy or patience for such matters.

We began packing our belongings in knapsacks. If the fighting came to Ciudin, we would be evacuated, or perhaps we might even decide to escape with the Soviets. Whatever happened, we wanted to be ready, and so we filled a number of rather large sacks, too large and heavy to carry, and also prepared four knapsacks with essentials for each of us to carry. These knapsacks contained a pair of underwear, a towel, soap, toothpaste, shoe polish (which seemed essential since I couldn't imagine that we would be left without anything, particularly shoes that would not require polishing), a fine comb, aspirins, cotton, bandages and so on. In case we lost one another and became separated, each of us would be left with these essential items. As the people around us noticed what we were up to, they, too, began making similar preparations.

In the afternoon, we saw the first enemy airplane. A group of us were standing on the street and looking about. Suddenly, we heard gunfire. We were extremely frightened and immediately headed for the fence near the trees. We thought that the firing was simply to disperse us. (Even Morris the dog was frightened. He lowered his tail, gazed at us and barked twice.)

We really didn't know how to proceed — either to take our belongings to gentiles we knew or perhaps even to move in with them ourselves. We were afraid to stay where we were because we lived near a stream, which, it was said, was an area that would surely be bombed.

In the evening, we handed over the duck and chickens to Flora, who used to tidy up our clubhouse. We agreed to meet with Flora again at four o'clock in the morning, both so that I could bring over some linens as well as become acquainted with the exact location of her dwelling in case we actually had to go there.

On Monday morning, at four o'clock, Flora and I headed out toward her place. We both carried the linens. It was quiet outside and there were no people to be seen anywhere. We were in the middle of a field when an airplane appeared and began to fire. We were terrified. There was no fence or tree nearby where we might seek shelter. I had heard that if one were in the middle of a field in this situation, the best thing to do was to fall to the ground. So I yelled at Flora to drop the linens and to dive into the grass. And I did likewise. After the plane flew away, we continued walking. I had a bit of a snack at Flora's place and then, with great fear, headed home. When I arrived home, I could see that Fraydeh was very scared. She regretted that she had allowed me to leave, especially when she heard the gunfire from the plane.

It was late June.[3] The weather was beautiful, and the garden was in full bloom. We lived in a very nice German house on Strashnitzer Street that the Soviets had given us, but we simply couldn't sit still at home. There was a table on the balcony, and we would usually eat outside; however, we had very little appetite. There were endless cannon blasts from early morning until late at night, and the doors and windows shook continually. The front, where the fighting was taking place, was actually very close in Hylboka, Krasnoil's'k and Vikov.[4]

We sat on the balcony and listened to the "music" of the front, which seemed so near. In my mind's eye, I could see Eliku, dear un-

---

3  The Nazis broke the Molotov-Ribbentrop Non-Aggression Pact and initiated Operation Barbarossa, the invasion of the Soviet Union, on June 22, 1941.

4  In the original manuscript translation these town names were rendered as Liboka, Crasna and Vikoff. Hylboka is located approximately forty kilometres from Ciudin; Krasnoil's'k (spelled as Crasna-Ilschi in 1930), approximately five kilometres away; and Vikov (Yiddish), or Vicovul-de-Sus, as it was known by in 1930, is fifteen kilometres from Ciudin.

fortunate Nuteleh, Kopl Shotz and a number of other dear ones, and others that I didn't know so well, all mobilized at the front, and I could only wonder about their predicaments and the dangers that now confronted them. And at that very moment, a plane flew by and began firing.

Our days were spent listening to the news on the radio. Once, a bomb fell near the train station and killed a young child who was playing outdoors. Everyone was dejected and depressed. People would meet and ask, "What have you heard?" or "What do you think is going to happen?" We tried to give each other courage. Surely, Moscow would not allow this to continue, we thought. These thoughts gradually cheered us up a little, although we remained deeply frightened.

One day, I found myself at Yetti Greenberg's, sitting near the radio. The room was filled with people, and all were depressed. The conversation centred around politics. The thunder from the cannons was considerably louder today, and the street was packed with military personnel on their way to the front. It was impossible to stay cooped up indoors with all of the action outside on the street.

Yetti was pressing clothes. She did so precisely, exuding a sense of calmness. I stood and watched her. Surely, I thought to myself, one of us is not normal. Is it me or is it her? Where does she find the patience, I wondered, especially now, to become so absorbed in cleaning and pressing? I could not help wondering what would happen if I lost her as I had the others who had had to leave town. Her attitude was that the wash had to get done. I concluded that she was a very fortunate person for having the capacity to not appear to be as concerned about our predicament as I was. My thinking was that we did not know where we'd find ourselves tomorrow or where the laundry might end up tomorrow.

One morning, a Tuesday, I went to the office to meet Modja. Modja and Kopl were dear friends of Fraydeh and mine. They were Polish refugees who had recently arrived in Ciudin and lived on Strashnitzer Street opposite us. They were two very intelligent people, especially

Modja. She looked much like Fraydeh and was just as affable and in-
timate. That Sunday, when the fighting had erupted, Modja returned
from Hylboka. Kopl, however, was still mobilized there. Modja was
very dejected and felt as though she had parted with him forever. We
welcomed her into our house so that she wouldn't be alone under
such dire circumstances. She ate at our house and slept there just as
though she was part of our family.

When I met Modja in the office she told me a secret: "Come evening, the Red Army will withdraw." Upon hearing this, I froze. In
light of her information, my first thought was to escape from Ciudin.
I didn't know what worried me more: the bombing and the Romanian army[5] that would follow, since we were so close to the border, or
those Ukrainians who might use the turmoil to instigate a pogrom.

I informed Fraydeh of Modja's news and also explained that I
didn't want to remain in town. I wanted to be in Shtrozshnitz[6] until
things calmed down, and from there we might even wind our way to
Chernowitz, if possible. I was sure that Father would listen to my advice. On our way home, we met Kan, the head of the forestry office,
as he was preparing his wagon to return to Shtrozshnitz. He and several others were doing this in great haste. In our estimation, this was
pretty much the last opportunity to leave. We were planning to travel
on foot, but this plan wasn't well thought out. I was able to work up
enough courage to ask him to take my aunt along. Although he wasn't
pleased by the suggestion, he couldn't refuse.

I entered the house. My folks were eating, unaware of our plan or
of the news in general. And so together with Fraydeh, we explained
to them in some detail that we had to escape from here as soon as
possible. We needed to make a decision quickly. We didn't have much
time to waste, as it was already four o'clock.

---

5  Romania, as a German ally, provided a substantial force for Operation Barbarossa, and was the primary invading army of the author's town.
6  Shtrozshnitz is the Yiddish spelling for Storozhynets, which was known as Storo-
   jinet in 1930. Shtrozshnitz is about fifteen kilometres from Ciudin.

"Why are we leaving? Where are we going?" they began to ask. We didn't answer simply because there wasn't enough time. We just presented them with the fact that it was imperative to leave right away. I covered my aunt with a coat, handed her a knapsack, placed her on the wagon and basically said, "Go." I then went into Tiak's house. The Soviets had also provided Tiak with a house on Strashnitzer Street, which had formerly belonged to Germans. He had a broken wagon and a horse that limped. I handed him as much money as he asked for to take our belongings to Shtrozshnitz. We would follow on foot. I had Father go ahead of us slowly, until the wagon was loaded. *Tante*[7] had already left. Tiak's was the last available wagon.

Fraydeh went to the Rosenblatts' to say goodbye, but I didn't have the courage to do so. Everyone was so confused, and I just didn't know how to deal with the situation. People couldn't seem to understand that we were leaving. They thought we were crazy. Wasn't there a war in Shtrozshnitz as well? Wouldn't it just be the same? How was it possible to pick up and leave our house at such a time? And I wondered whether they were right. Where were we running to? Perhaps conditions there would be even worse. And yet something pushed me to leave.[8]

Fraydeh returned from the Rosenblatts'. Mrs. Rosenblatt, she said, was in a deep state of despair. She was prepared to leave for Chernow-

---

7  *Tante*, also referred to as "aunt," is the author's stepmother.

8  Ciudin was invaded by the Romanian 16th Infantry Battalion on Thursday, July 3, 1941, as part of Operation Barbarossa. According to Simon Geissbühler, when the Romanian army was invading in 1941, "nearly all of Ciudei's Jews ignored these warnings, and those who did not flee in time experienced occupation by Romanian troops. At first the Jews believed they were safe, but armed bands of locals soon began to plunder the area" (433). For a more detailed history of the pogroms that followed the invasion, see Simon Geissbühler, "'He spoke Yiddish like a Jew': Neighbors' Contribution to the Mass Killing of Jews in Northern Bukovina and Bessarabia, July 1941," *Holocaust and Genocide Studies* 28, no. 3 (2014): 430–449.

itz but couldn't bring herself to abandon everything. Her husband had said that if she wanted to leave, she must go with the children. Quite understandably, they weren't prepared to do this — to leave each other at such a difficult moment. "Yidl," she said, referring to her husband, "is my angel of death."

We loaded the wagon to the brim. Fraydeh was determined to fill it completely and added as much as possible. I rushed her. I couldn't quite grasp why it was necessary to take everything. Did she even know where we were going or where we would end up? What couldn't fit in the wagon had to be left behind. We took the cat and the kittens onto the balcony and left them with a plate of milk and some bread. We shut the gate to our yard. Morris, the dog, wanted to follow us. Why should he be left behind, in charge? Modja and I were forced to throw stones at him to send him back. He simply could not understand why we, of all people, were pelting him with stones. Finally, he sat down and sadly watched us leave.

I gave Chaikeleh Greenberg the key to our house. She ran after me in despair. She was afraid to remain in charge in case the place was robbed. "What should I do with this key?" she asked.

"Throw it away," I answered and I left because my folks were already some distance ahead.

"Where are you going?" she yelled after us.

"I really don't know," I answered without pausing. She gazed at us for as long as possible. Occasionally I'd turn to look at her and did so until she finally disappeared. Had I known that this was the last time I would see her, I would have treated her more warmly. After all, she was one of my dearest friends.

As I turned around one last time, the town looked deserted. Although it was still light outside, almost no one was in the streets. Anyone I did see looked absolutely hopeless. Modja, Fraydeh and I walked quickly away from the town until we finally caught up to Father and the wagon.

A number of people followed us, but there was no longer any

means of transportation. The next day, they returned to their houses. Shikeleh returned from Budenets. He was homesick. Sheah Mozes and Pepi Holinger, along with their child, had almost reached Shtrozshnitz when Sheah was shot and the child was wounded. Pepi tried escaping by hiding under a bridge.

We had thought that conditions would be better in Shtrozshnitz — no such luck! When we arrived we saw that people were scurrying about with packages and belongings of various shapes and sizes. Everyone was in a state of panic. We were heading for Zisman's place, in the town's centre at the head of Chernowitz Street, and my aunt was already there. However, an order was issued to evacuate Chernowitz Street, exactly where we were staying. By now it was dark, so Fraydeh, Modja and I placed our bedding on the floor for the night. I wasn't able to sleep. We were close to a street and could hear the hustle and bustle of the deserting military. I kept thinking about how this was only the beginning of our wanderings.

On Wednesday, my folks decided that Fraydeh and Modja should go back to Ciudin. Everything there had been left in a state of disarray. The chickens had to be fed, and Fraydeh's satchel with her outfits was left there. *Tante* badly missed her dress, which was left hanging in the closet, and asked that it, too, be brought.

I was very opposed to this plan, but no one listened to me. I couldn't convince them, so I fought with myself instead, arguing that I'd be happy if I could survive this confused state of affairs, even if I was left with only the clothes on my back. I don't know why I was more frightened than everyone else. Probably because I have always been a bit timid.

Fraydeh and Modja left amid considerable panic — everyone was running frantically here and there. I was standing with Zisman in the yard. Suddenly I heard a bang — an incredibly loud explosion that lasted, it seemed to me, for several moments. We were standing at one end of the courtyard, but then we suddenly found ourselves at the other end, still holding on to each other after being thrown the length of the courtyard by the force of the explosion. Electrical lines opposite Zisman's place were uprooted. All of the windows were blown out of the surrounding houses. Some buildings were completely demolished. The noise and the confusion were horrible. There were rumours that the bridge would be blown up, and Fraydeh and Modja were on their way to Ciudin. How would they cross back over the water? I was especially worried because it had been decided that Fraydeh and Modja would spend the night there and return the following morning since it was too far to make the round trip in one day. You can't imagine my despair.

By the afternoon, there they were! They had turned back! They had gone as far as Budenets, four kilometres from Ciudin. They had spoken with an officer there who was sitting in a trench, listening to the telephone, and had asked him if there was enough time for them to reach Ciudin and to return. The officer thought they could manage to get there but that they might not get there in time to be able to return safely. So they turned back before even reaching Ciudin, tired and broken. They had punished their feet for twenty-four kilometres and all in vain.

As we were sitting in the house, an airplane suddenly passed overhead. Some Soviet officers came into Zisman's place. One of them asked what we were doing there. We live here, we answered. Then he said, "You are still young, and if you want to stay alive, leave, because things are going to get very bad here." We already thought that the situation was bitter, but now we knew for sure.

Zisman threw his fortune (so to speak) into his cellar, and we also threw in our belongings. We left with our essentials and got as far along Chernowitz Street as Aryeh Vatelmacher's. Zisman had already left, having loaded a wagon on Wednesday morning, headed for the city of Chernowitz. He had wanted to take us along as well, but Father, not wanting to go any farther, wouldn't hear of it. I was pleased enough that Father had come as far as Shtrozshnitz.

Aryeh had given us the key to his dwelling. When we got there, we made ourselves as comfortable as possible. He lived at the home of a very nice elderly couple named Shmeltzer. We had no food or drink and waited in fear. We managed to sleep through the night. All was quiet. Meanwhile, the Soviet military was retreating. In the morning, two young boys we knew came by with a wagon. They were en route to Chernowitz and asked us to join them. I was willing, but Father still wouldn't consider it. He said he wanted to wait another day and then return home. The boys left without us.

Flames were already visible in the town's centre, which had been on fire since Wednesday evening. Firebombs had landed on the beautiful large buildings. It was horrifying and impossible to go onto the street. The smoke was so thick it caused us to choke. Fraydeh wanted to retrieve our bags from Zisman's cellar, but that wasn't possible because the house, too, was on fire. At night, once again, a terrible panic descended. People were running in all directions with no particular destination in mind. I was in favour of heading toward Chernowitz and finally everyone agreed with me that it was time to go. We prepared our knapsacks and set out. We slowly made our way there. It was hot, and the knapsacks were quite heavy. Father and *Tante* were already resting. Hundreds of people were dragging themselves in both directions, since no one was sure where to go to be safe. However, since night was approaching, we returned to the Shmeltzers'.

This is when my story really starts — the fighting we had been hearing from afar had finally reached us. I will not forget that night in the basement for as long as I live. There was an incredible amount of gunfire, which sounded as though it were hailing. It felt like we were right in the middle of it. Not far from us, on the hill, were the Soviets with their dug-in machine guns to stop the Romanian military. The Romanians were in Shtrozshnitz just before the bridge. The Romanians fired in one direction and the Soviets returned fire from the other direction. All of this took place right above us.

This situation seemed to continue forever. The sound of gunfire didn't let up for five minutes, let alone for even one minute. As soon as the thundering finally ceased, we could then hear the whistling and the terrible thunder of a bomb exploding. The walls actually shook, and the lamp was extinguished. We were extremely fearful. And this lasted the entire night. It is impossible to adequately describe our fear. We sat huddled and bunched up together on the sacks — Fraydeh, Modja and I — and we trembled. Father cautioned us to move away from the door and suggested that we sit near him, over to the side.

I was worried that the house would soon simply collapse and cover us, with a mighty battle taking place around us. I began to lose hope. The walls continued to shake, and we were all sitting in the dark, and I was thinking about my dear family in America and about my brother Mattias. They wouldn't ever know where our remains were located. These thoughts were painful, but there was nothing to be done.

Father wondered why he had allowed himself to be persuaded to flee his home; in Ciudin, he said, we would have been spared. He was certain we wouldn't have had to run away if we had stayed. Perhaps he was right, I thought to myself, but we didn't know the situation in Ciudin.

Father told a story about the Baal Shem Tov.[9] It is traditional, he said, to relate stories of our saintly ancestors when in danger. When he finished the story, Fraydeh asked him to continue. For a moment we forgot where we were, despite the fact that the gunfire and bombing continued. The time dragged on. It was midnight, then one o'clock, and then three o'clock, and we found it increasingly difficult to lie on those sacks. The night was interminably long. There was no possibility of sleep. At around five o'clock, the gunfire waned and then it was completely silent.

When daytime finally came we slowly left the basement. Father

---

[9]  Baal Shem Tov, or Rabbi Yisroel ben Eliezer, is known as the founder of Hasidic Judaism.

went upstairs to pray. The older Shmeltzer also went outside to the gate. The first Romanian military detachments began to arrive.[10] The old man, not knowing better, welcomed the soldiers in a friendly manner. As they came closer, he tipped his cap and greeted them by saying, "Welcome." One of the soldiers yelled back at him, "Get lost, old timer, get back into your house!"

And so he returned to the basement, frightened. He said, "Until today, I wasn't afraid, but now I'm terribly frightened." Old lady Shmeltzer was inside preparing for the Sabbath, since it was Friday morning. Fraydeh helped Father pray. We suddenly heard a knock at the door. A soldier broke the door down, and those of us on the top floor hurriedly escaped to the basement.

We could already hear the soldiers being greeted with cheers outside, and could also hear the beginnings of robbing and plundering. We could even hear people moving around upstairs in the house. Suddenly we heard firing on the street. We heard lamentable yelling and screaming. We gazed at one another, becoming increasingly pale, terrified of what was happening. We sat here for the entire day, although it felt that the wait lasted an entire year. There was no food. In any case, we didn't have an appetite.

We heard gunfire outside and other Jews yelling. Soldiers were firing into basements and onto roofs to chase out anyone who was hiding. Gentiles were using the chaos and violence to rob houses. We heard these people running through nearby yards trying to catch hens and drive out cows. We were sure the soldiers would soon see our basement and would find us. The woman next to me simply didn't want to stay put, and she jumped at every possible moment. She wanted to see what was happening upstairs. Grabbing her skirt, I said, "You need to stay down here. You might be able to save your

---

10 Romanian troops occupied Shtrozshnitz on July 4, 1941.

life. Forget about the things upstairs. Where exactly do you want to go under such dangerous circumstances?"

She seemed prepared to agree with me, but only for a few moments, and then she got up again to head for the door. Again, I had to restrain her. This scenario repeated itself throughout the day. The old man also said to her, "Please don't go. For the first time in your life, why not listen to someone younger than yourself?"

She surprisingly listened to me for the entire day, until just before evening. Suddenly, she jumped up once again, and, before I could even turn around, she was on her way upstairs and wouldn't allow herself to be held back. The old man hurried after her, and they both went outside. They were immediately captured, and we heard them pleading for their lives. The sounds became increasingly faint. Suddenly, there was a terrible cry followed by a shot. It was already quite dark in the basement — there hadn't been any light during the entire day. That couple never returned.

I was scared out of my mind. We held our breath from sheer fear. To this day, I can still hear that terrible cry. Father said that it wasn't them. They were, he said, led down the street. I agreed with him but thought that perhaps he was simply trying to comfort us. We waited. I expected the soldiers to return for us, having seen the cellar door. What were they waiting for?

It was now Friday evening. Father prayed to himself quietly. There was nothing to eat. We were hungry, tired and broken, and it felt as though we were living in hell. It seemed like we'd been in this cellar forever and that we would never leave. I searched everywhere for something to eat and finally found a piece of *mămăligă*, cornmeal cakes, and half a glass of jam. I broke off tiny pieces of the cakes, which I dipped in the jam and distributed to each person. We hovered together, sitting on the sacks and packages next to one another. We had not changed our clothes since the previous Tuesday. It was very quiet during the night, but from time to time we could still hear gunfire.

Early Saturday morning, a neighbour who we hardly knew arrived and said, "Escape however you can. There's no point in sitting in this basement while everyone is being shot. They'll come to plunder and they'll catch you."[11]

We went upstairs into the yard and headed toward the street. We couldn't see a living soul. It is impossible to describe the scene adequately. Occasionally we caught glimpses of people who were scurrying to find safety. Opposite the field was a piece of the church that had been struck by a bomb the previous night. We entered a house but no one was there. Everywhere windows were shattered and houses were empty. Where were the people? Even beyond the town, there wasn't anyone to be seen. We thought that if we moved closer toward the centre of town, we might find someone there. We decided to try reaching the home of the local *shochet*, the ritual slaughterer, who was Father's dear friend.

We didn't all leave together. First we sent Father and then *Tante*. If either of them saw someone in the distance, they were to hide in a yard immediately. A few minutes later, Fraydeh, Modja and I, each carrying a few packages, followed. We were silent. The houses were empty and ransacked. A woman lay on the sidewalk in a pool of blood. I recognized the body — it was Mrs. Shmeltzer. We stepped around her and continued. There was still quite a distance to go. And because we were so afraid, the distance seemed much greater. As we were walking in this manner, I saw that far away, on the right-hand side of the field, a soldier was marching with two young boys who were carrying packages. They were approaching us and we didn't know what to do, since it was impossible to retreat. The soldier had already seen us, and we could only hope for a miracle to escape.

How would all of this end, I wondered? The soldier and boys were

---

11  Romanian troops murdered two hundred Jews in the first two days of the occupation. See Radu Ioanid, *The Holocaust in Romania: The Destruction of Jews and Gypsies Under the Antonescu Regime, 1940–1944* (Chicago: Ivan R. Dee, 2000), 97.

now on the same sidewalk as us, just a bit ahead. We started walking slowly so that we wouldn't overtake them. The boys saw that we were Jews and kept looking back. One of them stopped for a second and called, "Where are you going?"

I stopped walking and pretended as though I didn't understand, but Fraydeh didn't clue into what was happening and went up to them, asking, "What did you say?"

I grabbed her by the sleeve, held her back, and without moving my lips said, "Shut up."

The soldier also looked at us, and then he entered the yard not far from the *shochet*'s house, where we were headed. We had to move along and didn't even turn our heads to look back. We heard two shots ring out.

To this day, I still can't explain how we managed to stay alive. Perhaps the soldier was mixed up and thought that we were Christians carrying bundles of plundered goods. If he had arrived a few minutes earlier and seen Father and *Tante*, he would have never mistaken us as Christians.

We arrived at the *shochet*'s. He had already left, and his house was in shambles. Father and our aunt were there — that, for me, was most important because I had wondered whether they would even manage to get there. The homeowner, a non-Jewish woman, told us we had to keep moving. We begged her to hide us somewhere, in the attic or anywhere, but she didn't want to hear any of this. As it turned out, the soldiers had already rounded up a few Jews — she didn't know where they had been taken and she had been warned that if Jews were found at her place she, too, would be shot. Our pleading didn't help, and we were chased away.

Her daughter came running up to us and told us to run away immediately. Two soldiers were on their way. She motioned to us to escape to her garden. Five of us together in one place made it very difficult to hide. And the soldiers were already in the courtyard. I didn't quite realize what I was doing, but before I knew it I found myself standing in a young tree, a short one and not very thick (I must have climbed up it like a cat). I was now separated from the others. I only knew the direction they had run in.

I was standing on a branch where there was space for only one foot and I had to hold on with both hands, as though I were crucified. I stood one foot on top of the other and had to keep changing feet. Sure enough, a soldier entered the garden with the homeowner's daughter. Did he notice us? Had they told him where we were?

"Where are they?" I heard him asking her, as they stood near the tree I was in. She answered by pointing in the direction where the others had run. I closed my eyes so that I wouldn't attract them with my glance. "How many?" he asked her. "One zid [Jew] and four women," she answered. The soldier proceeded farther into the garden, in the direction she had pointed. The jig is up now, I thought to myself. It's too late for them. I shut my eyes and wanted to block my ears (but I had to use my hands to hold on), so that I would neither see nor hear what was surely about to happen. But the soldier soon returned empty-handed, stood near the girl, looked around with regret and said that he would soon start to shoot. Then he left.

I didn't realize where I had ended up. As it happened, the soldiers had settled in this gentile's place. They kept entering and leaving and just sitting around the yard. The garden served as a thoroughfare to the other gardens and houses. I knew that I must not budge from my spot.

After standing in the tree for a few minutes, I noticed that Fraydeh had returned and was approaching the garden. She obviously wasn't aware that I was standing in the tree or that the soldiers were in the courtyard. She must have thought that I was still in the house and wanted to call for me.

I was petrified — she was on her way to the fire without realizing it. She wasn't standing too far from me, so I called quietly to her, "Fraydeh, Fraydeh, go back!" She seemed to hear me, but couldn't ascertain the direction of the voice and turned back. I could only see where she was heading, but not where everyone was hiding.

Ten minutes later Fraydeh returned again. I felt as though I was about to explode. I began to yell again (it is possible to yell quietly),

"Fraydeh, get out of here!" She still didn't know that soldiers were in the yard. She couldn't understand why I was chasing her away, but she obviously appreciated the importance of turning back. And yet only two minutes passed and again Fraydeh returned. I again began yelling quietly to draw her attention. She noticed me in the tree and beckoned me to follow her. Apparently she and my father had secured a good hiding place. I whispered to her, "Come back during the night to get me then. There are soldiers in the yard now. Get out of here!"

However, Fraydeh returned again, took just a few steps, and I could hear the soldiers yell to her, "Hello!" I was convinced that it was all over now. Fraydeh turned around and stood there looking extremely pale. I almost could not control myself. A soldier had noticed her from a distance and merely asked, "Is there a drinking fountain nearby?"

The soldier thought she was a Christian who lived in the neighbourhood. Fraydeh maintained her cool and answered, "There," pointing toward a house. She turned around and departed quickly, and as she was getting a bit farther away he called again about the direction of the fountain. But Fraydeh was no longer present, and this upset him. It didn't take long before I heard gunfire very close to where I was. I heard a second soldier yell out, "Who is firing there?" The first soldier explained about Fraydeh, telling the second soldier that a Jewish person had disappeared and so he had fired several shots into the garden toward her. I now began considering the possibility that a bullet might strike me. Meanwhile, the second soldier told the first to leave the gun. "It's my weapon," he said. The first soldier stopped shooting. I felt incredibly lucky at this point, like my grandfathers had been watching over me.

Saturday afternoon and almost dinner time. My mouth was so dry, and although I was not thinking about food, I badly craved some water. How long would I have to stand here with my hands held in the air? It was a very long summer's day. I had to change the position of my foot slowly so that the branch wouldn't move and I wouldn't be heard. My arms were beginning to ache, but there was little I could do. That one day standing in the tree felt like an entire year.

I heard the soldiers returning to eat. A tall soldier who looked like an officer — I'm not familiar with the insignia on uniforms — entered the yard. He took off his jacket and sat down to rest by my tree. I held my breath and turned my head. I shut my eyes and thought, Now, whatever will be, will be. Opening my eyes, I gazed in a different direction and noticed a leather jacket lying on the ground. Looking at it more carefully, I realized it belonged to Modja who, I saw, was lying on the grass not far from where I stood. I hadn't realized how close she was to me. I, of course, had thought that she was with Fraydeh. I feared that she would soon be spotted by the soldier, who was so close to her, but he sat there for a while longer and then left.

I was now so thirsty that my throat was parched. I noticed that there were onions and carrots planted nearby, and I made a simple plan: as soon as it turned dark, and before Fraydeh returned, I would climb down and pick a few carrots for myself and for Modja. There was also a small hole with some filthy water — I planned to have one or two sips.

I was incredibly tired, still standing on one foot. My eyes were shutting by themselves. If only it were night and Fraydeh would arrive. What I wouldn't give for an opportunity to lie down and forget my fear. Meanwhile, a light summer rain was falling. Beads of water had accumulated on the leaves. I attempted to reach a leaf to lick it and quench my thirst even a little, ignoring the dirt on the leaf, which also filled my mouth. But the sun once again began to shine, and the leaves quickly dried. I felt as though I were about to pass out.

Suddenly a soldier jumped over the fence near Modja and noticed her. Modja began to stand up, and the soldier, unexpectedly, asked whether she had been asleep. She didn't understand Romanian, and I didn't hear her answer. Then he looked in my direction, and I was sure that our eyes met. I was now convinced that the end was in sight. Instead, he passed by me in the yard and quickly returned with another person. They both spoke to Modja rather quietly. At one point, I overheard them asking if she had any money.

Evidently, they hadn't seen me, and I suppose that it was out of sheer fear that I was convinced that he had been looking straight at me. As it happened, he was looking toward the fence to make sure that nobody was approaching. The second person left quite suddenly, and the first remained with Modja. I leave it to your imagination to guess what horrible act transpired, but the soldier who stayed with Modja didn't shoot her. I closed my eyes and shuddered.

I can barely record what I have lived through. The fear and pain will remain forever. My dear friend Modja! Even though the soldier left her to live, Modja was so devastated that she was never able to recover and be the same person that I knew.

When I heard him leave, I noticed that Modja was now standing, leaning against a small tree. She was no longer hiding. It was now irrelevant to her whether or not she was seen. She stood in this manner for some time, and then she approached me and stood absolutely silent. It was still light outside. It was as though the sun exposed Jewish tragedies. I said to her quietly, "Go, Modja, return to your hiding place, so that no one will see you. I'll come down when it is dark and Fraydeh will come for us."

Again, I told her to hide. She no longer cared what happened to her, she answered, but she did listen to me and hid nearby. There were no trees that she could climb. There were several young trees but none tall or sturdy enough for climbing.

In the evening, I heard some terrible yelling and shooting from the direction of my family's hiding place. I heard the same sounds coming from the street — people were yelling and cannons fired. I then heard an excruciating yell from a woman, "Father is dead!"

I did not know what was happening to my parents. If Fraydeh failed to appear this evening, I would have to conclude that there probably wasn't anyone left to come for me. Standing in the little tree, I decided not to surrender. I started to understand what was happening around me. To give myself up meant certain death, and so I was determined to hide in this tree for as long as I could last. Perhaps the pogrom would subside, and then I'd try making my way through the forest outside of Ciudin to peasants we knew. However, I had no clue about what had happened in Ciudin. I just knew that I would never give myself up willingly!

It was now dark outside. I was surrounded by silence as I descended from the tree. My throat was extremely parched from days of neither eating nor drinking. I was able to pull out two carrots from the garden; I had no way to wash them, so I just brushed off some dirt.

A cloudy moon showed its face every so often. Modja and I sat under the tree huddled together — and waited. We didn't speak of what had happened nor of what could happen to us later. We simply sat and waited. It was very late. We were exhausted and very sleepy. Silence surrounded us.

Fraydeh was still unaccounted for. She wouldn't be returning, I thought. I then wondered whether anyone I knew was even left alive, judging by last night's violence. I quickly tried to erase that thought from my mind. But I was worried, since Fraydeh had come three times during the day and now that it was quiet she had not come by. Modja suggested that we move farther into the garden, where there were empty houses. Perhaps we would find the others there. At least, there we'd be able to sleep a little and rest.

We began to creep quietly through the gardens, but it was difficult to see. It was extremely dark. Suddenly, a dog barked and a shot rang out. We could hear Romanian spoken in a house. We turned back to sit against our tree again, and waited.

No sign of Fraydeh. It was very late. We were so tired that we could barely keep our eyes open. I simply couldn't understand why Fraydeh didn't arrive. If she were alive, she would surely come. Once again we set out in the same direction. Modja called out quietly, "Fraydeh!" No reply. We crawled quietly and passed a bush. Modja said that this would be a fine hiding spot, that we should lie here since no one would even think of coming here during the day. She then asked how it had been possible for me to stand in that tree for so long.

However, I didn't like the plan to hide near that bush, so we returned to the tree. There we sat down and held each other because it was chilly. We tried to make each other more comfortable. I'll never forget that night with Modja as long as I live. We repeatedly asked each other: "You're not cold? Are you lying comfortably?" We covered each other as much as possible with the coat. Modja wanted to take off her leather coat to cover me so that we'd be comfortable and warm, and I wanted to do the same for her with my coat — as if we both sensed that we were spending our last night together. And in that way we both dozed off. As soon as I fell asleep, I dreamt of a pail of water that I was drinking from continuously. I had never realized how exhausting thirst could be.

It was just beginning to get light outside when we were awakened by the sound of a gun in the distance and the howling of a dog. I climbed back into the tree while Modja remained on the ground. I was so tired that I was barely able to keep my eyes open. Somewhere in the distance, I heard a lamenting cry, a pleading call from a woman that tore at my heart. And meanwhile Fraydeh had still not returned, probably because no one had survived.

Within a short time, two mean-looking soldiers returned. They were sporting moustaches and their eyes were filled with hatred. I was terrified that I was about to fall. They passed right by where we were hiding yesterday and checked the bush where Modja had suggested we hide. Not finding anyone there, they turned around. I thought that the danger had now passed. They hadn't seen us — but in the last second they caught a glimpse of Modja. They started yelling at her. She sat up and approached them with her head bowed. They yelled at her to move along more quickly. They took her.

When I saw this, I immediately abandoned my plan to go to the forest outside Ciudin. I was just going to give myself up; there was no point continuing without Modja. I was absolutely convinced that everyone had perished and that Modja was the only person I had left.

As soon as they left the garden, I climbed down from the tree and went into the yard that belonged to the Christians. I was already quite hoarse, my throat tight from thirst. The woman was surprised to see me. I asked her for a bit of water. Instead she poured me a cup of coffee. I thought to myself that if I were to be shot, then at least I will have had something to drink. I headed toward the street, because, she informed me, all of the Jews who had survived had been assembled in the Jewish school.

Not a soul could be seen on the street. Neither military nor civilian people were around. I couldn't spot a trace of Modja anywhere. As I approached the town centre, I saw a group of military people in the distance. They looked at me in amazement as I approached them nonchalantly and greeted them with, "Good morning." Among them was a young officer who asked where I was heading. I motioned in the direction where I believed the Jews were. "You are Jewish?" he asked. "Where have you been until now?" I replied, "I've been with the Jews that were rounded up but somehow I was left behind."

He asked the others for the whereabouts of the Jews and was informed that they were at the Jewish school. I indicated that I knew its location. We walked together. I was barely able to decipher where I was in light of the surrounding devastation. As we walked, I asked about the purpose of rounding up the Jews. Was it to shoot us or to send us to a camp? "To a camp," he answered. That answer pleased me. My reasoning was that if we weren't to be shot, I would soon be reunited with Modja. And I was convinced that she would be overjoyed to see me as well.

At the school, a police officer searched new arrivals before they were brought in. I carried on my person some Soviet money, a watch, a ring, a nice wallet and some other small articles. The officer let me in without taking these things. Inside the school, there was another sentry. Again the same search was repeated, and the officer allowed me to pass through with my belongings. When I reached the interior of the school with the young officer who had walked me here, we took leave of each other; we shook hands, and he wished me the best. If he had sent me with one of his soldiers, I might have been led elsewhere and probably would have been robbed of my possessions.

Inside the school there was virtually no room to move. It was packed with women. I was stunned that there were so many people still alive, and I began running to the various classrooms searching for Modja. Since the corridors were so congested, I was forced to push my way through to get from one classroom to another. I met Chaya Tresser, Schneider and Lenger. I asked about Modja, but they hadn't seen her. Nor would they permit me to continue on my way as they began questioning me about the whereabouts of my folks. I ran away from them. I was certain that Modja was there somewhere.

I began pushing my way through the masses of people. I carefully examined each face. Perhaps I would be lucky. People were upset by my pushing, but I ignored them. However, I was still unable to locate Modja. I was rushing all over the place, upstairs and downstairs. I couldn't understand what had happened. After all, if they had not shot her, then surely Modja would have been brought here. I returned to the classroom where the few people left from Ciudin were gathered to ask if in the meantime Modja had appeared. She hadn't.

Slowly I began to understand what must have happened to her. And I must admit that until that moment I hadn't truly let myself believe the worst. I lay down on the floor, face down, and began crying uncontrollably. It was as though my experiences of the past few days were released by this crying. Evidently, I concluded, I had lost Modja along with the rest of my family.

And that was how that Sunday passed. Those who had been rounded up earlier had survived since Friday without any food. I checked my pockets and found some onions that I had picked that night when I climbed down from the tree. I also had a piece of bread that the Christian woman had given me. The women around me begged me for this food for their children.

The women were assembled in this high school, while the men were in two synagogues. In addition, of course, there were the several hundred Jews who had been shot — these people, injured and bloodied, were continually brought in. There was a young girl with a bullet in her foot and another with one in her back whose body was burning up with fever.

Nighttime approached. I still couldn't find a place to lie down. I had never experienced such hunger and exhaustion in my life. There were a few school benches, but they were taken. There was only one empty bench, which was not even a bench for sitting on but a narrow one for stacking books. Not only was it extremely narrow, but it was also slanted. I placed my coat under my head and lay down on my side, as the bench was too narrow for me to lie on my back. I was sure that I'd fall off when I finally fell asleep.

After nightfall, everyone lay down like slaughtered lambs. There was nothing to eat. It was dark and no one even had a match. The place was scattered with bodies. The air was sickeningly thick, but we were afraid to open a window because the guards outside kept shooting into the air. Every once in a while a shriek came from one of the classrooms. And when the shrieking began in one room, people in other rooms, not knowing exactly why, also began to shriek.

Soldiers with flashlights came by. They lit everything up, and if they saw a ring or a watch or earrings they pulled it off. The soldiers forced themselves on any young girl who appealed to them. There was much panic in the dark. Shots were regularly fired outside to help ensure quiet on the inside.

At dawn, people began to rise. The uncomfortable beds we were perched on were not conducive to sleeping any longer. People began to count those they had lost and to share with others the number of sacrifices they had endured in their families, bemoaning their fate. I didn't do any such counting, but was convinced that none of my family was left.

I wanted to go into the yard to breathe some fresh air, to wash my face and to enjoy a bit of water, but the door was locked. On the other side stood an eighteen-year-old *shegetz*, a young non-Jew, who was guarding us. At around nine o'clock, he would do us a great favour and let us out for a few minutes. An older woman who knew him begged him to let her have a bit of water and tried passing by without his permission. He beat her with a stick and chased her back inside.

The conditions were horrible. The washroom sewers were blocked up, and the dirty water began to overflow into the corridors where people were sitting on their belongings. Going to the washroom required walking through this sewage. All of the rooms and corridors were filled with a stifling air. The women were panicking and were screaming, fighting and crying all day.

It was now Monday and there still hadn't been any food since Friday. Women who had a bracelet, ring or earrings would offer these to the soldiers for a bit of cornmeal or a few beans from their already plundered homes. The women were able to cook in the yard on two bricks, which served as a stove. We were gradually allowed into the yard, and peasant women occasionally came to the fence offering food. Unfortunately, they demanded only Romanian currency as payment for this food and would not accept the Soviet equivalent. Very few among us possessed such currency.

Two soldiers drove in during the day. They spoke with us and offered some comfort and asked where we were from. One soldier remarked, "What I saw in Ciudin, I never want to see again for as long as I live. I walked in blood up to here," and he pointed to his knees. He spoke about a beautiful girl with golden hair and how she cried and pleaded for them to shoot her, even in front of her father, instead of forcing her to submit to their violation of her. I knew that the girl was Erna Hassner.

I could only imagine what was happening in our town. My God, how is it possible to put up with all of this? The excuse used by the Romanians was that Jews had fired on the Romanian army from the rooftops. That was the excuse. The Romanians claimed that since the Jews had shot, they were forced to arm themselves and respond accordingly — and weren't to blame for their actions.

Although I experienced other kinds of pain, the one I didn't feel any longer was hunger. I sat on a bench and felt dejected all day. I hadn't seen Fraydeh, Father or my aunt since early Saturday morning. I believed that the very worst had befallen them. Strangely enough, having reached this conclusion, I felt a little better. My eyes welled with tears. I lay down with my arms outstretched and allowed myself to cry. Suddenly I felt someone tapping my shoulder. I looked up. A woman handed me a piece of bread with some butter. I thanked her, but I wasn't crying from hunger; I had more legitimate reasons for my tears.

Even while crying, I ate that piece of bread with butter, since it had been two-to-three days since I had last eaten. The soldiers seemed to take pity on us in the afternoon, and a bag of hard dry bread was thrown into each classroom. The bread was as hard as rocks, proba- bly left here since the time of the Soviet army. It might have been pos- sible to eat this bread with some tea, but where was tea to be found? Instead, we dipped our bread in water to make it edible. People went mad when they saw the bread, as though they had never seen bread before. There was yelling, screaming and pushing, and it was impos- sible to get people settled down.

Someone reached a decision to designate a special area in each classroom for the distribution of food, along with a person in charge. A list of names of those present was drawn up to determine the re- quired portions of bread for everyone. It didn't seem to take very long before I was chosen. I really didn't have the patience for this and would have preferred to be left alone. On the other hand, I couldn't turn them down and so I accepted the responsibility of allo- cating the portions of bread.

By Tuesday morning, we were surrounded by tremendous dirt and filth. We had no clean clothes to change into and couldn't wash or even rinse our hands and faces. And even if we could have washed, there were no towels. I concluded that we would all become very ill. In fact, there were already sick people on the top floor.

It was raining. People were pushing to get closer to the window, but

I couldn't understand why. What was the problem? Then I heard that people were being chased toward the school we were in, among them people from Ciudin. I immediately headed for the door. There were indeed people being chased in. Some were injured. They were from Banyliv, Krasna and other places. And among them were some from Ciudin, including Dr. Wald and his wife, who was seven months pregnant. She was bruised and injured. There was Azuh Moses with a bandaged head, Dr. Mentshl and Mr. Gutman, the teacher, with his son and daughter, who had been hiding. As soon as she saw me, she ran over, embraced me and began crying. "Where's your mother?" I asked. "She was shot," she replied. "All of Ciudin was shot!" She burst out crying and ran to keep up with the rest. I was shocked to hear this. Was this even possible? Had this really happened?[12]

I went to the second floor, hoping to find a familiar face. I ran into someone from Shtrozshnitz, a niece of the Kent family. Upon seeing me, she ran over and started crying, listing the people she had lost. She used to have such a large family in Ciudin, and I assumed that she was now crying over their demise. However, she then enumerated the material possessions that she had lost: a golden chain and a lot of jewellery. I turned to her and said, "To hell with your jewellery! Why are you crying over that? Others are crying over loved ones that they've lost, parents and children! And you're crying because of some jewellery?"

Suddenly there was panic. A high-ranking officer appeared and issued an order that eleven of us were to go outside into the courtyard as we were, without any packages. There was bedlam. We were all frightened and wondering whether we would be shot. Some people were screaming. We were quickly pushed out into the courtyard. I was standing near the front of the group. There was a young woman nearby with a

---

12 On July 4, 1941, the Romanian army killed approximately 450 Jews in Ciudin; on July 6, most of the remaining Jews were shot. See "Ciudei" in *The Encyclopedia of Jewish Life Before and During the Holocaust*, eds. Shmuel Spector and Geoffrey Wigoder (New York University Press, 2001), Vol. 1, 262.

compress on her head who placed her arms around another person and began to dance and sing. Evidently, she had had a nervous breakdown. Another woman, standing in a corner, sighed lamentably, "Where are my children?"

While standing amid the pushing, I noticed a woman who kept staring at me. She asked if I happened to be the daughter of the *shochet* from Ciudin. "Yes," I replied, "I am his daughter. But how do you know me?"

"Well, you look much like your sister. Do you know that your father, sister and aunt are still alive? They're at my house."

Can you even imagine how I felt upon receiving this news? I asked how she knew they were alive, since she was here. She explained that they had been at her place for several days. "As for myself," she said, "I'm here only since this morning. I left my house to check up on the chickens. They saw me and brought me here. If your folks only knew that the shooting had ceased, they too would venture outdoors, plead and probably be brought here. But they're so frightened. However, they needn't be, because no one will find them where they are. Much of the house was destroyed by a bomb. And as for you, I am sure they don't believe that you are still alive."

Upon receiving this news, I decided that I would bring my family here, especially since I had heard that anyone found in hiding would be shot immediately. When I asked the woman where she lived, she drew a diagram leading to some out-of-the-way place, and I had no idea if I would even be able to find it. How could I reach my folks to bring them here? It wasn't possible to do it alone, so I would have to ask a soldier to accompany me. I was worried because I had heard that soldiers were in the habit of taking people to where they wanted, but that they felt no obligation to return them safely to the school. How could I be certain that I wouldn't meet up with a soldier who was escorting me simply to rob me? I imagined the following: we would reach our destination and he would see that my folks were hiding, among them an elderly Jew with a beard. Then, he would shoot them. No! I couldn't trust a soldier when the situation was so uncertain, with the town destroyed and with the complete absence of people on the streets.

I decided to wait. There was a very pleasant watchman at the gate, an elderly gentleman with whom I had spoken several times. I decided to explain the situation to him and to ask him to accompany me. It was Tuesday night, and now when I needed him, he wasn't around.

Darkness fell quickly and the sky was covered with very dark and ominous-looking clouds. There was a terrible storm with violent winds and rain coming down in sheets. It had been raining this way, on and off, since Sunday. It stormed each night. There was thunder and lightning. Rain of this magnitude hadn't been seen for some time. It poured all night without any interruption.

More people were brought to the school that night, people who had been rounded up in the neighbouring villages. They were soaked, naked and without shoes. These new arrivals recounted horrible tales. I also heard that there had been a flood in Ciudin, and the crops were lost. According to the farmers, the rain was symbolic: the famine was caused by the killing of all of the Jews. Those were the kinds of stories that were circulating.

I couldn't sleep. When I woke on Wednesday at dawn, the older watchman was still not there, nor did he arrive later in the day. I was beside myself, because I knew that my family was in danger as long as they remained in hiding. Later, I heard a commotion in the yard. Some people ran to inform me that Fraydeh and my aunt were here. I ran out to the yard; my aunt was crying bitterly. Fraydeh looked ill, her face shades of green and yellow. (I wasn't aware of how I looked.) We embraced and kissed — I felt like the dead had arisen. A watchman was checking their packages and baskets. They told me that Father was already at the synagogue with the other men. They brought some food that they had found at the Jewish woman's house and also had two satchels with some of our belongings.

At this point, my only wish was to see Father or to somehow let him know that I was alive. But how? Some people were going from one synagogue to another but no one ventured out alone. We were now allowed to sit in the yard to our hearts' content. Shtrozshnitzers had brought some provisions and were cooking outside on two bricks. A woman boiled a kettle of water and treated us to a cup. The three of us were shaking as we each took a sip, as though we were drinking the most delicious cocoa. We hadn't tasted a drop of anything warm for three-to-four days. I wished I could bring Father a little boiled water just so that he could enjoy this small pleasure.

Two days passed. I begged the people who arrived from the men's camp to inform Father that I was here, but I wasn't sure if any of them did. One morning, I asked the well-intentioned guard at the gate to accompany me to where the men were stationed because I wanted to see my father. We would return immediately, I promised. He agreed to accompany me as soon as another guard was available to take over for half an hour. And so it was. Fraydeh joined us because she, too, wanted to see Father. I took some bread along. Upon arriving there, we quickly found Father and we all embraced.

The men's quarters were much quieter than the women's. But the men seemed much more beaten down. We didn't spend very long there and quickly returned. When we reached the gate, I handed my watch to the soldier who had escorted us. He was so decent a person that he actually couldn't believe that I was giving it to him to keep. In fact, I could have gotten away without giving him anything at all. What I didn't realize was that our situation was only the beginning of the years of hardships to follow, and that watch I gave away would have been of use on many different occasions, either to sell or to exchange for bread. At the time I thought that we would soon be free and that I would simply buy myself another watch.

We stayed in that school for a period of ten days with very little food. We were exhausted from lying on those uncomfortable beds and weary from both the confusion and the dirt. Suddenly an order was issued that everyone who was from this area must gather outside, from where they would be led to two streets that had become a ghetto. The rest of us were all being taken to Vizhnitz and Vashkovitz.[13] Confusion and noise reigned. For the Shtrozshnitzers this was significant news. We were told to get our belongings and to head for the yard. Our belongings were loaded onto several wagons along with a few sick people who were unable to walk. The rest of us followed on foot.

The streets were teeming with action. I ran quickly to the men's area to fetch Father so that we could head together for somewhere else in the city. Fraydeh questioned my plan and asked, "What will we do here in this burned-out city where there's already a famine? We'll be better off in Vashkovitz."

When I arrived at the men's quarters the same confusion greeted me. I searched for Father everywhere, in every corner, but I couldn't find him. I asked around to no avail. We had probably crossed paths if he had gone to the school looking for us and so he was probably waiting for us there. I ran back breathlessly. It was already late afternoon, and I heard that one transport had already left. I returned and Fraydeh and *Tante* were waiting. "Where's Father?" they asked me.

I had been so certain that he would already be with them. We were unable to make any sense of this predicament and so Fraydeh and I both ran back to the men's area. We took different routes — I along one street and Fraydeh along another — so that we wouldn't miss him. We again arrived to the same confusion. And again, Father wasn't there. I asked everyone about the Ciudiner *shochet*. Had anyone seen him? No one knew his whereabouts. Finally, an acquaintance blurted, "Your father? He left with the first transport. I saw him myself."

We ran back to our camp. *Tante* was waiting. Where was Father? We were beside ourselves. We couldn't afford to wait any longer, since the last transport was leaving and couldn't be delayed. We were terribly

---

13  Vizhnitz (Yiddish), known as Vyzhnytsya, is fifty-five kilometres from Shtrozshnitz; Vashkovitz (Yiddish), known as Vashkivtsi, is forty-two kilometres from Shtrozshnitz.

confused. A Jew all alone! How would he be able to survive? Who knew where his transport would end up? We felt like sheep being herded in any which way. This was how so many families were being separated, often never able to reunite.

Reluctantly, we left on the very last transport. Our guard had a sour disposition. We were forced to walk quickly. He beat many of us with his stick. We tried to remain in the centre of the group, because he walked by the sides and the back. We helped *Tante* by bracing her on either side so that she would be able to keep up. The journey was terrible for the elderly and the weak who could not maintain the pace. The wagons were mainly loaded with baggage and our few packages, with little room for people who needed help.

We could not stop wondering about Father. What kind of guard did he have to contend with and was he able to keep up? Perhaps he had been shoved or even beaten. If only we were together, we would have been able to look after him. We would have sacrificed anything for him.

We travelled until nighttime. Suddenly a woman from Cheresh started to give birth, which meant that her wagon stopped at the last house. This was near an open field. As it happened, a midwife lived there, so that was where the driver dropped off the woman who was giving birth. Some two days later, both she and her child were sent back to the group.

We continued moving as the sky filled with dark clouds. There was a storm starting, and twigs and branches broken by the wind were all around us. It started pouring rain, and there was no place to hide or to even seek shelter. We plodded along in the rain until we saw, in the distance, a large barn. We had to reach that point for that was where we would sleep and then continue in the morning.

I heard that a previous transport had also stopped there, and in my absolute wildest imagination, I considered the possibility that my father might be there as well. We were driven into the yard, to the barn, absolutely soaking wet, and what do you think I saw? Father, walking in our direction. We were overjoyed to see him. What were the very first words he uttered? You'll never guess. "Do you, perhaps, have a radish? I'll be able to wash it and make the appropriate blessing." He was as calm as if he were at home, having washed and about to sit at the table.

Father didn't appear confused at all. It seemed natural to him that we were there. Were it not for the storm, we might not have even stopped, and his transport would have ended up elsewhere, and we would never have been reunited. Well, this was his nature under all circumstances — very calm, just as I was the opposite. He seemed oblivious of our frightful circumstances.

During that very first moment when he asked for a radish, I actually felt like laughing. Unfortunately, I had passed the point of being able to laugh, and I was a little resentful. I said to him, "Perhaps you'll hold off on the radish until we find some shelter? Is a radish the most important thing on your mind?"

We entered the barn. Father had saved us a little room; people were pushing all over the place. We spread our packages and rested. I still remember distinctly what I said: "Let me tell you, Father, if with God's help we survive these troubled times, I will write to the family in America at the very first opportunity. I'll describe what happened and how you just approached us as though nothing unusual had occurred, and that you asked for a radish. I want to warn you that I plan to do this, providing that we escape. How is it possible for someone, under such terrible circumstances, to separate from his own family, to leave in another transport, when he could have waited or come to us, as others did with their own families so they could remain together? Had we not arrived, what would you have done all alone in these difficult circumstances?" There were, in fact, many situations where elderly persons were forever separated from their families. These were terrible tragedies.

Later, when I asked Fraydeh why she did not return that evening when I was perched in the tree, she answered that she had been too terrified of the soldiers she saw during the day. She also said that they had assumed that I had hid elsewhere, given the gunfire and yelling they had heard. They believed that if I were not hiding elsewhere, then I was likely dead, in which case I was actually envied because at least my ordeal had ended.

~

We were taken to Vashkovitz. It was incredibly hot, so hot that people were dying from sheer thirst and hunger. I had at this point lost the use of my right hand from my time standing for hours in the tree. I was sure that I'd be left permanently disabled, especially since there was no physician or hospital where I might go for help. I did, however, gradually regain the use of that hand.

We didn't remain long in Vashkovitz, where we slept in empty houses in which other families were already hiding. From Vashkovitz we were chased to the region of Bessarabia, to Yedinetz, where there was a camp.[14] The journey was horrible. When I turned around, it was impossible to see the end of the long succession of transports. We were marched through fields to avoid the villages. When we did occasionally pass through a village, all we could see were empty Jewish houses with gates and doors wide open. Occasionally, written in Yiddish on the side of a house was, "The site of a mass grave." If we passed a well, those who were first in line were able to drink. There was such a push to reach the pail that more water was often spilled than remained for drinking. Before we knew it, we would be forced to start moving again without having had any water at all.

We were stopped on a mountain without any trees or leaves for shade. There was no well here. We were left with blisters both on our lips and on our feet. We didn't meet a single soul from our town,

---

14 The Jewish population of Yedinetz (Edineț) had been evacuated in July and August 1941. The author would have arrived to a transit camp, which eventually held 23,000 Jews in stables and sheds, under horrific conditions. In November 1941 the camp was closed and the Jews were forced to Markolesht (Mărculeşti), Ataki and Mogilev. See "Edineti" in *The Encyclopedia of Jewish Life Before and During the Holocaust*, eds. Shmuel Spector and Geoffrey Wigoder (New York University Press, 2001), Vol. 1, 354; and "Edinets" at http://www.jewishgen.org/Yizkor/pinkas_romania/rom2_00323.html.

because there simply wasn't anyone left to meet — aside from Mrs. Venger and her two young boys and Malvi Knoier and her mother. Her father and brother had both been shot in Ciudin, and Malvi and Mrs. Venger had been in hiding.

As we were chased through forests, I noticed a young blond girl lying naked in the woods. If only the forest could speak! A soldier arrived each evening and took Malvi with him. She would return in the morning with some bread for her mother.

We continued to be forced to move along. It was extremely hot, and we were even more thirsty than we were hungry. When I spotted a muddied stream, I immediately ran over to drink, but Fraydeh tried to stop me. Nonetheless, I just had to take a few sips. There had been a well in the Yedinitzer camp that was poisoned. People became ill and children died from drinking the water. We were so thirsty that when it rained it was as though the water were sent by God, and I would drink as much of that rainwater as possible.

The march continued. It was now autumn. There was a cold rain with a bit of a wind and the snow began to slowly fall. We continued to walk for entire days in the muddy fields of Bessarabia. Unable to keep up, people would fall to the ground. At one point, I saw a house in the distance that belonged to a gentile, and I heard the barking of a dog. I said to Fraydeh, "If only I could transform into a dog. How lucky that dog is, as he's lying under the balcony. He is neither wet nor afraid of anyone. And he is at least being fed."

Years later, when we eventually returned home again from the Ukraine, the very first thing I did was run to that tree where I had hid to save my life — the tree had already grown so much taller.

~

For some time, the above pages were lost. They were originally written in 1941 and intended as a letter to family in America, which never got sent, to let them know what we had gone through. I found them and began writing again in 1989, filling the blanks with as much as I could recall. Mattias always urged me to record the entire set of experiences (especially since what I had written in pencil was, by now, barely visible) and to deposit the work at Yad Vashem. There was a dearth of material from Transnistria.[15]

This, then, is the story of how we left our home for the Ukraine. A completely different chapter of this larger story relates to the years that we actually spent there. Unfortunately, I lack the energy to recall those experiences.

---

15 During the especially severe winter of 1941–1942, the Romanian army chased tens of thousands of starving Jewish deportees from Bukovina, Bessarabia and Dorohoi to the north and east with no plans for their resettlement, resulting in the deaths of tens of thousands. Transnistria was a 16,000-square-mile region between the Dniester and Bug rivers that originally had been part of Ukraine. After German and Romanian forces conquered Ukraine in the summer of 1941, Romania administered this territory and deported hundreds of thousands of Romanian and Ukrainian Jews there, where between 150,000 and 250,000 were killed or died of illness and starvation. See "The Final Report of the International Commission on the Holocaust in Romania" at https://www.ushmm.org/m/pdfs/20080226-romania-commission-holocaust-history.pdf and Diana Dumitru, *The State, Antisemitism, and Collaboration in the Holocaust: The Borderlands of Romania and the Soviet Union* (New York: Cambridge University Press, 2016).

Koine and family before the war. Back row, left to right: Koine's brother Moishe; her sister Fraydeh; and Koine. In front, left to right; Koine's sister Faige (Fanny); her mother, Miriam; her father, Chaim; and her brother Mattias. Ciudin, Bukovina, circa 1920s.

1 & 2 Koine before the war. Romania, date unknown.

1

2

1 With family in Canada. Back row, left to right: Koine's brother Gedalia and her brother-in-law Avrumtche. In front, left to right; her niece Beulah; Koine; her sister Faige; and Koine's husband, Yossel (Josef). Circa 1950s.

2 Koine and family in Montreal, circa 1970s. Back row, left to right; Koine's brother Avrum; her brother Gedalia; her husband, Josef; Koine; and her sisters-in-law Munia and Rose. In front: her niece Beulah and Beulah's sons.

Koine and her brother Gedalia in the late 1980s or early 1990s. Montreal.

# Glossary

**Aktion** (German; pl. *Aktionen*) The brutal roundup of Jews for forced labour, forcible resettlement into ghettos, mass murder by shooting or deportation to death camps.

**aliyah** (Hebrew; pl. *aliyot*, literally, ascent) A term used by Jews and modern Israelis to refer to Jewish immigration to Israel; the term is also used to refer to "going up" to the altar in a synagogue to read from the Torah.

**Allied Zones of Germany and Austria** The four zones that Germany and Austria were divided into after their defeat in World War 11, each administered by one of the four major Allied powers — the United States, Britain, France and the Soviet Union. These administrative zones existed in Germany between 1945 and 1949. In Austria, Vienna was divided into the four sectors and also held an International Sector. Austria regained its independence in 1955.

**American Jewish Joint Distribution Committee (JDC)** Also known colloquially as the "Joint." A charitable organization founded in 1914 to provide humanitarian assistance and relief to Jews all over the world in times of crisis. It provided material support for persecuted Jews in Germany and other Nazi-occupied territories and facilitated their immigration to neutral countries such as Portugal, Turkey and China. Between 1939 and 1944, JDC officials helped close to 81,000 European Jews find asylum in various parts

544 BEFORE ALL MEMORY IS LOST

of the world. Between 1944 and 1947, the J D C assisted more than 100,000 refugees living in DP camps by offering retraining programs, cultural activities and financial assistance for emigration.

**American zone.** *See* Allied Zones of Germany and Austria.

**antisemitism** Prejudice, discrimination, persecution and/or hatred against Jewish people, institutions, culture and symbols.

*Appell* (also *Zählappell*) (German) Roll call.

*Appellplatz* (German; the place for roll call) The area in Nazi camps where inmates had to assemble to be counted. Roll calls were part of a series of daily humiliations for prisoners, who were often made to stand completely still for hours, regardless of the weather conditions.

**Armia Krajowa** (Polish; Home Army) Also known as AK. Formed in February 1942, the Armia Krajowa was the largest Polish resistance movement in German-occupied Poland during World War II, best known for orchestrating the 1944 Warsaw Uprising. Although the organization has been criticized for antisemitism and some factions were even guilty of killing Jews, it is also true that the AK established a Section for Jewish Affairs that collected information about what was happening to Jews in Poland, centralized contacts between Polish and Jewish military organizations, and supported the Relief Council for Jews in Poland. Members of the AK also assisted the Jewish revolt during the Warsaw Ghetto Uprising in 1943, both outside the ghetto walls and by joining Jewish fighters inside the ghetto. Between 1942 and 1945, hundreds of Jews joined the AK. *See also* Warsaw Uprising.

**Armia Ludowa** (Polish; People's Army) a communist partisan force established by the Polish Workers' Party that supported Soviet military action against the Nazis; the Party also supported a future communist-led government in Poland.

**"Aryan"** A nineteenth-century anthropological term originally used to refer to the Indo-European family of languages and, by extension, the peoples who spoke them. It became a synonym for people of Nordic or Germanic descent in the theories that inspired Nazi racial ideology. "Aryan" was an official classification in Nazi racial laws to denote someone of pure Germanic blood, as opposed to "non-Aryans," such as Slavs, Jews, part-Jews, Roma and Sinti, and others of supposedly inferior racial stock.

**Auschwitz** (German; in Polish, Oświęcim) A town in southern Poland approximately forty kilometres from Krakow, it is also the name of the largest complex of Nazi concentration camps that were built nearby. The Auschwitz complex contained three main camps: Auschwitz I, a slave labour camp built in May 1940; Auschwitz II-Birkenau, a death camp built in early 1942; and Auschwitz-Monowitz, a slave labour camp built in October 1942. In 1941, Auschwitz I was a testing site for usage of the lethal gas Zyklon B as a method of mass killing, which then went into wide usage. Between 1942 and 1944, transports arrived at Auschwitz-Birkenau from almost every country in Europe — hundreds of thousands from both Poland and Hungary — between May 15 and July 8, 1944, approximately 435,000 Hungarian Jews were deported to Auschwitz — and thousands from France, the Netherlands, Greece, Slovakia, Bohemia and Moravia, Yugoslavia, Belgium, Italy and Norway. As well, more than 30,000 people were deported there from other concentration camps. It is estimated that 1.1 million people were murdered in Auschwitz; approximately 950,000 were Jewish; 74,000 Polish; 21,000 Roma; 15,000 Soviet prisoners of war; and 10,000–15,000 other nationalities. The Auschwitz complex was liberated by the Soviet army in January 1945.

**Austro-Hungarian Empire** Also known as the Dual Monarchy of Austria and Hungary, ruled by the royal Habsburg family. It was successor to the Austrian Empire (1804–1867) and functioned as a dual-union state in Central Europe from 1867 to 1918. A multinational empire, the Dual Monarchy was notable for the constant political and ethnic disputes among its eleven principal national groups. The Austro-Hungarian Empire dissolved at the end

546   BEFORE ALL MEMORY IS LOST

of World War I and divided into the separate and independent
countries of Austria, Hungary and Czechoslovakia.

**bar/bat mitzvah** (Hebrew; plural b'nai mitzvah/b'not mitzvah; literally, son/daughter of the commandment) In Jewish tradition, the
time when children become religiously and morally responsible
for their actions and are considered adults for the purpose of synagogue and other rituals. Traditionally this occurs at age thirteen
for boys and twelve for girls. A bar/bat mitzvah is also the synagogue ceremony and family celebration that mark the attainment
of this status, during which the boy/girl is called upon to read a
portion of the Torah and recite the prescribed prayers in a public
prayer service.

*Blockälteste* (German; literally, block elder) Prisoner appointed by
the German authorities as barracks supervisor, charged with
maintaining order and accorded certain privileges.

**British Mandate Palestine** The area of the Middle East under British
rule from 1923 to 1948, as established by the League of Nations after World War I. During that time, the United Kingdom severely
restricted Jewish immigration. The Mandate area encompassed
present-day Israel, Jordan, the West Bank and the Gaza Strip.

**Canadian Jewish Congress (CJC)** An advocacy organization and
lobbying group for the Canadian Jewish community established
in 1919. The CJC was restructured in 2007 and its functions sub-
sumed under the Centre for Israel and Jewish Affairs (CIJA) in
2011.

**cheder** (Hebrew; literally, room) An Orthodox Jewish elementary
school that teaches the fundamentals of Jewish religious observance and textual study, as well as the Hebrew language.

**chuppah** (Hebrew; literally, covering) The canopy used in traditional Jewish weddings that is usually made of a cloth (sometimes a
prayer shawl) stretched or supported over four poles. It is meant
to symbolize the home the couple will build together.

*cohen* (Hebrew; pl. cohanim) In biblical times, the word for priest. In the post-biblical era, a *cohen* refers to a male Jew who can trace his ancestry to the family of Judaism's first priest, Aaron, the brother of Moses. *Cohanim* occupy a special ritual status in Judaism, such as reciting certain blessings in synagogues.

**Displaced Persons (DP) camps** Facilities set up by the Allied authorities and the United Nations Relief and Rehabilitation Administration (UNRRA) in October 1945 to resolve the refugee crisis that arose at the end of World War II. The camps provided temporary shelter and assistance to the millions of people — not only Jews — who had been displaced from their home countries as a result of the war and helped them prepare for resettlement. *See also* United Nations Relief and Rehabilitation Administration (UNRRA).

**Einsatzgruppen** (German) Mobile death squads responsible for the rounding up and murder of Jews in mass shooting operations. They were a key component in the implementation of the Nazis' so-called Final Solution in eastern Europe. *See also* Final Solution.

**Final Solution** (in German: *Die Endlösung der Judenfrage*) Euphemistic term referring to the "Final Solution to the Jewish Question," the Nazi plan for the systematic murder of Europe's Jewish population between 1941 and 1945.

**gendarmes** Members of a military or paramilitary force.

**Generalgouvernement** The territory in central Poland that was conquered by the Germans in September 1939 but not annexed to the Third Reich. Made up of the districts of Warsaw, Krakow, Radom and Lublin, it was deemed a special administrative area and was used for the Nazis to carry out their racial plans of murdering Jews. From 1939 onward, Jews from all over German-occupied territories were transferred to this region, as were Poles who had been expelled from their homes in the annexed Polish territories further west.

**Gestapo** (German; abbreviation of Geheime Staatspolizei, the Secret State Police of Nazi Germany) The Gestapo were the brutal force that dealt with the perceived enemies of the Nazi regime and were

responsible for rounding up European Jews for deportation to
the death camps. They operated with very few legal constraints
and were also responsible for issuing exit visas to the residents of
German-occupied areas.

**ghetto** A confined residential area for Jews. The term originated
in Venice, Italy, in 1516 with a law requiring all Jews to live on
a segregated, gated island known as Ghetto Nuovo. Throughout
the Middle Ages in Europe, Jews were often forcibly confined to
gated Jewish neighbourhoods. During the Holocaust, the Nazis
forced Jews to live in crowded and unsanitary conditions in rundown districts of cities and towns. Most ghettos in Poland were
enclosed by brick walls or wooden fences with barbed wire. The
Warsaw ghetto was the largest in Poland, with more than 400,000
crowded into an area of just over 300 hectares; the Lodz ghetto,
with more than 160,000, was the second-largest.

*Gymnasium* (German) A word used throughout central and eastern
Europe to mean high school.

**Hasidic Judaism** (from the Hebrew word *hasid*; literally, piety) An
Orthodox Jewish spiritual movement founded by Rabbi Israel ben
Eliezer in eighteenth-century Poland; characterized by philoso-
phies of mysticism and focusing on joyful prayer. This movement
resulted in a new kind of leader who attracted disciples as opposed to the traditional rabbis who focused on the intellectual
study of Jewish law.

**Hebrew Immigrant Aid Society (HIAS)** An organization founded
in New York in 1881 that continues to provide aid, counsel, support and general assistance to Jewish immigrants all over the
world. Since the early 1970s, HIAS has been especially active in
providing assistance to Jews emigrating from the USSR.

**Hitler Youth** (in German, Hitlerjugend, or HJ) An organization
founded in 1926; in 1939, HJ membership was made compulsory
for youths over seventeen, after which membership comprised 90
per cent of German youth. The focus of the paramilitary organiza-

tion was to create soldiers for the Third Reich who were properly indoctrinated in Nazi ideology.

**"Internationale"** A well-known and widely sung left-wing anthem. Adopted by the socialist movement in the late nineteenth century, it was the de facto national anthem of the Soviet Union until 1944 and is still sung by left-wing groups to this day.

**Jewish Brigade** A battalion that was formed in September 1944 under the command of the British Eighth Army. The Jewish Brigade included more than 5,000 volunteers from Palestine. After the war, the Brigade was essential in helping Jewish refugees and organizing their entry into Palestine. It was disbanded by the British in 1946.

**Jewish Committee (post-war)** Also called the Central Committee of Polish Jews (in Polish: Centralny Komitet Żydów w Polsce, or CKZP). An organization established in 1944 and officially recognized as the highest administrative body of Polish Jewry, the Jewish Committee sought to reconstruct post-war Jewish life in Poland. It set up various departments to help survivors search for their families and document their testimonies. The organization also provided legal assistance, social services and health care, established orphanages, and disseminated reports and newsletters on the state of Jewish life in post-war Poland.

**Jewish ghetto police** (in German, Ordnungsdienst; literally, Order Service) The force established by the Jewish Councils, under Nazi order, that was armed with clubs and carried out various tasks in the ghettos, such as traffic control and guarding the ghetto gates. Eventually, some policemen also participated in rounding up Jews for forced labour and transportation to the death camps and carried out the orders of the Nazis. There has been much debate and controversy surrounding the role of both the Jewish Councils and the Jewish police. Even though the Jewish police exercised considerable power within the ghetto, to the Nazis these policemen were still Jews and subject to the same fate as other Jews. *See also* Judenrat (Jewish Council).

**Jewish Immigrant Aid Society (JIAS)** An organization that has provided a variety of services to Jewish immigrants to Canada from 1919 to the present. Its origins trace back to the first assembly of the Canadian Jewish Congress in 1919 when it was faced with a Jewish refugee crisis in Canada after World War I. In 1955 the organization changed its name to Jewish Immigrant Aid Services of Canada.

**Judenrat** (German; pl. *Judenräte*) Jewish Council. A group of Jewish leaders appointed by the Germans to administer and provide services to the local Jewish population under occupation and carry out Nazi orders. The *Judenräte*, which appeared to be self-governing entities but were actually under complete Nazi control, faced difficult and complex moral decisions under brutal conditions and remain a contentious subject. The chairmen had to decide whether to comply or refuse to comply with Nazi demands. Some were killed by the Nazis for refusing, while others committed suicide. Jewish officials who advocated compliance thought that cooperation might save at least some of the population. Some who denounced resistance efforts did so because they believed that armed resistance would bring death to the entire community.

**kapo** (German) A concentration camp prisoner appointed by the SS to oversee other prisoners as slave labourers.

***Kennkarte*** (German, pl. *Kennkarten*) Official identity documents used by the Germans during World War II. *Kennkarten* were issued to various groups and distinguished by colour: grey for Poles, yellow for Jews and Romas, and blue for Russians and other non-Polish Slavic peoples.

**Lager** (German) Camp.

***Lagerälteste*** (German; literally, camp elder) A camp inmate in charge of the prisoner population who reported to the SS *Rapportführerin* (Report Leader).

***landsmanshaftn*** (Yiddish; in English, hometown societies) Groups of Jewish immigrants from the same towns, cities or regions in eastern and central Europe. In North America, Jewish immigrants often joined these organizations for support and a social network. A *landsleit* (landsman) is a member of a group who comes from the same town.

**Luftwaffe** The German air force.

**matzo** (Hebrew; also matzah, matzoh, matzot, matsah; in Yiddish, matze) Crisp flatbread made of plain white flour and water that is not allowed to rise before or during baking. Matzo is the substitute for bread during the Jewish holiday of Passover, when eating bread and leavened products is forbidden. *See also* Passover.

**Mengele, Josef** (1911–1979) The most notorious of about thirty SS garrison physicians in Auschwitz. Mengele was stationed at the camp from May 1943 to January 1945; from May 1943 to August 1944, he was the medical officer of the Birkenau "Gypsy Camp"; from August 1944 until Auschwitz was evacuated in January 1945, he became Chief Medical Officer of the main infirmary camp in Birkenau. One of the camp doctors responsible for deciding which prisoners were fit for slave labour and which were to be immediately sent to the gas chambers, Mengele was also known for conducting sadistic experiments on Jewish and Roma prisoners, especially twins.

**Molotov-Ribbentrop Pact** Also known as the Treaty of Non-Aggression between Germany and the USSR. The treaty that was signed on August 24, 1939, after signatories Soviet foreign minister Vyacheslav Molotov and German foreign minister Joachim von Ribbentrop. The main provisions of the pact stipulated that the two countries would not go to war with each other and that they would both remain neutral if either one was attacked by a third party. One of the key components of the treaty was the division of various independent countries — including Poland — into Nazi and Soviet spheres of influence and areas of occupation. The Nazis breached the pact by launching a major offensive against the Soviet Union on June 22, 1941. *See also* Operation Barbarossa.

*Muselmann* (German; Muslim) A slang term used by camp prisoners to describe prisoners who were near death and seemed to have lost the will to live. Some scholars attribute the use of the word Muslim to the fact that the prostrate and dying prisoners were reminiscent of devout Muslims at prayer.

**Nazi camps** The Nazis established roughly 20,000 prison camps between 1933 and 1945. Although the term concentration camp is often used to refer generally to all these facilities, the various camps in fact served a wide variety of functions. They included concentration camps; forced labour camps; prisoner-of-war (POW) camps; transit camps; and death camps. Concentration camps were detention facilities first built in 1933 to imprison "enemies of the state," while forced labour camps held prisoners who had to do hard physical labour under brutal working conditions. POW camps were designated for captured prisoners of war and transit camps operated as holding facilities for Jews who were to be transported to main camps — often death camps in Poland. The death camps — Auschwitz-Birkenau, Bełżec, Chelmno, Sobibor and Treblinka — were killing centres where designated groups of people were murdered on a highly organized, mass scale. Some camps, such as Majdanek and Mauthausen, combined several of these functions into a huge complex of camps.

**New Economic Policy (NEP)** The Soviet policy change from a socialist ideology to one of private ownership of small industry and nationalized, state-controlled large industry. The NEP was in practice between 1921 and 1928.

**Nuremberg Laws** The September 1935 laws that stripped Jews of their civil rights as German citizens and separated them from Germans legally, socially and politically. They were first announced at the Nazi party rally in the city of Nuremberg in 1933. Under "The Law for the Protection of German Blood and Honour," Jews were defined as a separate race rather than a religious group; whether a person was racially Jewish was determined by ancestry.

**Nuremberg Trials** A series of war crimes trials held in the city of Nuremberg between November 1945 and October 1946 that tried twenty-four key leaders of the Holocaust. A subsequent twelve trials, the Trials of War Criminals before the Nuremberg Military Tribunals, was held for lesser war criminals between December 1946 and April 1949.

*Oberscharführer* (German; senior squad leader; pl. *Oberscharfürerin*) A Nazi SS party rank between 1932 and 1945. *See also* SS.

**Operation Barbarossa** The code name for Germany's attack on the Soviet Union during World War II. On June 22, 1941, more than 4 million Axis troops crossed the Soviet front and invaded Soviet territory in the largest military operation in history. Both sides suffered severe losses, with Soviet military casualties numbering more than 2 million and Axis military casualties approximating 800,000. Germany, though initially gaining control of much of the western Soviet Union, eventually failed in its ultimate bid to capture Moscow in the long and bitter battle.

**Orthodox Judaism** The set of beliefs and practices of Jews for whom the observance of Jewish law is closely connected to faith; it is characterized by strict religious observance of Jewish dietary laws, restrictions on work on the Sabbath and holidays, and a code of modesty in dress.

**partisans** Members of irregular military forces or resistance movements formed to oppose armies of occupation. During World War II there were a number of different partisan groups that opposed both the Nazis and their collaborators in several countries. The term partisan could include highly organized, almost paramilitary groups such as the Red Army partisans; ad hoc groups bent more on survival than resistance; and roving groups of bandits who plundered what they could from all sides during the war. In Poland, the partisans were collectively known as the Polish Underground State and the primary armed partisan group developed into the Armia Krajowa, the Polish Home Army. *See also* Armia Krajowa.

**Pesach (Passover)** One of the major festivals of the Jewish calendar, Passover takes place over eight days in the spring. The festival begins with a lavish ritual meal called a seder, during which the story of Exodus is retold through the reading of a Jewish religious text called the Haggadah. The name of the holiday refers to the fact that God "passed over" the houses of the Jews when he set about slaying the firstborn sons of Egypt as the last of the ten plagues aimed at convincing Pharaoh to free the Jews.

**pogrom** (Russian; to wreak havoc, to demolish) A violent attack on a distinct ethnic group. The term most commonly refers to nineteenth- and twentieth-century attacks on Jews in the Russian Empire.

**Righteous Among the Nations** A title bestowed by Yad Vashem, the Holocaust Martyrs' and Heroes' Remembrance Authority in Jerusalem, to honour non-Jews who risked their lives to help save Jews during the Holocaust. A commission was established in 1963 to award the title. If a person fits certain criteria and the story is carefully corroborated, the honouree is awarded with a medal and certificate and commemorated on the Wall of Honour at the Garden of the Righteous in Jerusalem.

**Shoah Foundation.** *See* Survivors of the Shoah Visual History Foundation.

*shochet* (Hebrew; in Yiddish, *shoyket*) Ritual slaughterer. A man conversant with the religious teaching of *kashruth*, trained to slaughter animals painlessly and to check that the product meets the various criteria of kosher slaughter.

**SS** (abbreviation of Schutzstaffel; Defence Corps). The SS was established in 1925 as Adolf Hitler's elite corps of personal bodyguards. Under the direction of Heinrich Himmler, its membership grew from 280 in 1929 to 50,000 when the Nazis came to power in 1933, and to nearly a quarter of a million on the eve of World War II. The SS was comprised of the Allgemeine-SS (General SS) and the Waffen-SS (Armed, or Combat SS). The General SS dealt with policing and the enforcement of Nazi racial policies in Germany and the Nazi-occupied countries. An important unit within the SS was the Reichssicherheitshauptamt (RSHA, the Central Office of Reich Security), whose responsibility included the Gestapo (Geheime Staatspolizei). The SS ran the concentration and death camps, with all their associated economic enterprises, and also fielded its own Waffen-SS military divisions, including some recruited from the occupied countries. *See also* Gestapo.

**Stalin, Joseph** (1878–1953) The leader of the Soviet Union from 1924 until his death in 1953. Born Joseph Vissarionovich Dzhugashvili, he changed his name to Stalin (literally: man of steel) in 1903. Very soon after acquiring leadership of the Communist Party, Stalin ousted rivals, killed opponents in purges and effectively established himself as a dictator. During the late 1930s, Stalin commenced "The Great Purge," during which he targeted and disposed of elements within the Communist Party that he deemed to be a threat to the stability of the Soviet Union. These purges extended to both military and civilian society, and millions of people were incarcerated or exiled to harsh labour camps. During the war and in the immediate post-war period, many Jews in Poland viewed Stalin as the leader of the country that liberated them and saved them from death at the hands of the Nazis. At the time, many people were unaware of the extent of Stalin's own murderous policies. After World War II, Stalin set up Communist governments controlled by Moscow in many Eastern European states bordering and close to the USSR, and instituted antisemitic campaigns and purges.

**Star of David** (in Hebrew, *Magen David*) The six-pointed star that is the ancient and most recognizable symbol of Judaism. During World War II, Jews in Nazi-occupied areas were frequently forced to wear a badge or armband with the Star of David on it as an identifying mark of their lesser status and to single them out as targets for persecution.

*Stubendienst* (German; room orderly) A prisoner in charge of maintaining the cleanliness of the block, next in command to the *Blockälteste* (barracks head). *See also* Blockälteste.

**Survivors of the Shoah Visual History Foundation** A project founded by Steven Spielberg in 1994 as a result of his experience making the film *Schindler's List*. Its mission is to record and preserve the testimonies of Holocaust survivors in a video archive and to promote Holocaust education. In 2006, after recording almost 50,000 international testimonies, the foundation partnered with the University of Southern California and became the USC Shoah Foundation Institute for Visual History and Education.

*tallis* (Yiddish; in Hebrew, *tallit*) Prayer shawl. A four-cornered ritual garment traditionally worn by adult Jewish men during morning prayers and on the Day of Atonement (Yom Kippur). One usually wears the *tallis* over one's shoulders but some choose to place it over their heads to express awe in the presence of God.

*tefillin* (Hebrew) Phylacteries. A pair of black leather boxes containing scrolls of parchment inscribed with Bible verses and worn by Jews on the arm and forehead at prescribed times of prayer as a symbol of the covenantal relationship with God.

**United Nations Relief and Rehabilitation Administration (UNRRA)** An international relief agency created at a 44-nation conference in Washington, DC, on November 9, 1943, to provide economic assistance and basic necessities to war refugees. It was especially active in repatriating and assisting refugees in the formerly Nazi-occupied European nations immediately after World War II.

*Volksdeutsche* The term used for ethnic Germans who lived outside Germany in Central and Eastern Europe; also refers to the ethnic German colonists who were resettled in Polish villages as part of far-reaching Nazi plans to Germanize Nazi-occupied territories in the East. After the collapse of Nazi Germany most *Volksdeutsche* were persecuted by the post-war authorities in their home countries.

**Waldsee** In the summer of 1944, Hungarian deportees were forced to write to their relatives and friends back home that all was well — they were working and healthy. The Nazis attempted to deceive the remaining Hungarian population in Budapest by stamping the word "Waldsee" (meaning "forest lake") on the postcards, which was the actual name of towns in Austria and Switzerland, to convey the feeling of calm and tranquility. Although the Nazis checked and censored the postcards, prisoners often managed to use coded language to warn their family members.

**Warsaw Ghetto Uprising** The largest rebellion by Jews during the Holocaust, the Warsaw Ghetto Uprising developed in response to the *Gross-Aktion* — the Nazis' deportation of more than 275,000 ghetto inhabitants to slave-labour and death camps and the murder of another 30,000 of them between July and September 1942. When the Nazis initiated the dissolution of the ghetto on April 19, 1943, aiming to deport all those remaining to the Treblinka death camp, about 750 organized ghetto fighters launched an insurrection. Despite some support from Jewish and Polish resistance organizations outside the ghetto, the resistance fighters were defeated on May 16, 1943. More than 56,000 Jews were captured; about 7,000 were shot and the remainder were deported to death camps and concentration camps.

**Warsaw Uprising** An uprising organized by the Polish Home Army (AK) to liberate Warsaw from German occupation and initiate the establishment of an independent Poland in the post-war period. In August 1944, as the Soviet Red Army neared Praga, a suburb of Warsaw situated on the east bank of the Vistula River, the uprising began. The AK, however, had only 2,500 weapons for its 40,000 troops and the Soviets, under Joseph Stalin's orders, did not give support to the uprising. By October 2, 1944, the attempt at liberation had been crushed and the results were devastating — more than 150,000 civilians had been killed, and more than 25 per cent of Warsaw had been destroyed.

**Wehrmacht** (German) The German army during the Third Reich.

**Yad Vashem** The Holocaust Martyrs' and Heroes' Remembrance Authority, established in 1953 to commemorate, educate the public about, research and document the Holocaust.

**Yellow star.** *See* Star of David.

**Yiddish** A language derived from Middle High German with elements of Hebrew, Aramaic, Romance and Slavic languages, and written in Hebrew characters. Spoken by Jews in east-central Europe for roughly a thousand years from the tenth century to the mid-twentieth century, it was still the most common language among European Jews until the outbreak of World War II. There are similarities between Yiddish and contemporary German.

**Yom Kippur** (Hebrew; literally, day of atonement) A solemn day of fasting and repentance that comes eight days after Rosh Hashanah, the Jewish New Year, and marks the end of the high holidays.

# Author Biographies

**Ifa Demon**, née Szyfra Zytler (1923–2015), married under the name Szyfra Dmiszewicki, was a woman of valour, distinction and spunk. She was born in Baranowicze, Poland. During the war, to escape the Nazis, she worked for the railroad as a bookkeeper on a collective farm in Kazakhstan. Ifa married Morris Demon in 1945 and they immigrated to Toronto in 1949 with their two-year-old son, Marvin; their son Brian was born in 1956. Through Ifa's innate business acumen, sheer determination and hard work, she and Morris built up a successful real-estate portfolio. Ifa was fluent in nine languages; wrote numerous well-received Jewish poems; and was a regular guest on the Toronto Sunday Jewish Hour for a number of years, reading her poetry. She also wrote a number of articles on Israel, world affairs and Jewish life. Ifa was an ardent Zionist who devoted her life to many charitable Jewish causes, including Friends of Pioneering Israel, the Lithuanian Society and Baycrest, and she was an active member of the UJA Endowment Committee. Ifa Demon was blessed to have two sons, two daughters-in-law, seven grandchildren and six great-grandchildren. She left an indelible and memorable legacy, and will always be remembered with love, respect and devotion.

**Ida Dimant** (née Ita Urbach) (1918–1988) was born in Lodz, Poland. Before the war, Ida loved poetry, plays, music, dance and education.

She married Abram Toter in the Lodz ghetto just weeks prior to their deportation in 1944 to Auschwitz-Birkenau. After the war, she found her brother, Nathan, in Lodz and learned that her husband and her entire family had not survived. Ida was staying in a home where some men were sleeping in the hall and she literally tripped over Abraham Dimant. They married two weeks later and went to Bergen-Belsen, from where he had been liberated. Their first daughter, Sharon, was born there in 1947. In 1948 they immigrated to Canada and two more daughters arrived: Lorraine in 1949 and Sylvia in 1952. Tragically, Sharon passed away in Toronto at the young age of thirteen. Ida loved music and she had a sweet singing voice; she often could be found singing to her only grandchild, Nicole. When ESL classes were offered in Ida's apartment building, she was delighted at the chance to have formal English lessons and joined the class for two years. This gave her the confidence to write her memoirs, which the family found when they were sitting shiva for her.

**Fela Zylberstajn Grachnik** (1924–1997) was born in Lodz, Poland, where she had a loving relationship with her parents and extended family. During the war she was interned in the Lodz ghetto, Auschwitz and the Gross-Rosen concentration camp. Fela is the sole survivor of a family of eighty people. In 1946 she married Moishe Grachnik in the Displaced Persons camp in Schwandorf, Bavaria. Their daughter, Myra, was born a year later. In 1949, they immigrated to Israel, where their son Issie was born. In 1953, the family immigrated to Montreal and rebuilt their lives. Education was important to Fela and she took English classes so she could teach her children to speak the language. Their son Allan was born in 1960. She and her husband joined the Lodzer Society, where Fela eventually became President of the Ladies' Auxiliary. Under her leadership the organization participated in numerous local and Israeli projects. She was a beloved leader, respected by all who knew her. Fela died on September 8, 1997, at age seventy-three. She leaves a memorable legacy and is remembered with love, respect and devotion by her three children, five grandchildren and nine great-grandchildren.

**Svetlana Kogan-Rabinovich** and her family moved to Moscow in 1975, where she worked as a dentist in her own spacious office near the Oktyabrskoye Pole metro station. Svetlana was active in commemorating Holocaust victims and survivors, and was successful in establishing memorials for Holocaust victims in Tulchin and Gaisin. She led groups to mass gravesites, educating students and the public about the atrocities during the war, and also fought to have Jews specifically recognized as victims, as Soviet memorials listed only "Soviet peoples" as victims. In 2000, her efforts were successful and the plaques on the memorials were changed. In 1985, after a serious illness, her husband, Hershel, passed away. He was buried at a Jewish cemetery in Malakhovka, Moscow. In 1989, Svetlana moved to Canada with her daughter and her daughter's two children. In 1995 in Toronto, she founded and led an organization for Holocaust survivors from the Soviet Union called the Club for Former Prisoners of Concentration Camps and War Veterans. That same year, she flew to Moscow to establish contacts with Russian societies of prisoners and war veterans. Svetlana was sixty-eight years old when she wrote her memoirs in memory of the dead and the Nazis' evil deeds in Ukraine, in the hopes that none of this would ever happen again. Svetlana Kogan-Rabinovich lives in Toronto.

**Bianka Kraszewski** was born in Warsaw on November 28, 1929. After the war, she remained in Poland until November 1946, at which point she immigrated to Scotland with her cousin Gabrys to join their uncle Leon, who had left Poland in 1939 as the Germans were taking over the country. In Glasgow, Bianka went to high school and then university, where she earned her master's degree in French and German and completed all the courses for her PhD in both languages. She met her future husband, Ludek, who was a pilot during the war in the Royal Air Force's famous No. 303 Fighter Squadron. They immigrated to Canada, where Bianka's uncle Leon had moved, in July 1951. Bianka and Ludek married on September 4, 1951. Ludek worked as an engineer and they lived in Oakville, Hamilton and Toronto before resettling in Oakville, where they raised their two daughters, Renata and Tamara. Bianka took night classes in Spanish at the University of Toronto, earned her master's in Spanish and completed the courses for her PhD. She taught Spanish to adults in Oakville and also worked as a court interpreter in Polish and Spanish across Ontario as well as for the Immigration and Refugee Board in Toronto. Bianka belonged to Toronto's child survivors' group for hidden children and spoke at schools to educate students about the Holocaust for many years. Bianka Kraszewski lives in Oakville.

**Barbara Kuper** (1920–2016) was born in Częstochowa, Poland. Out of five siblings, she and one brother survived the war. The rest of her family was murdered at Treblinka. After the war, Barbara returned to her studies, earning an MSc in physical chemistry (with distinction) from the Jagiellonian University in Krakow. In 1947 she married Anthony (Abram) Kuper and along with his young daughter, Eva, they immigrated to Canada in 1949. Her career in industry was complemented by post-graduate courses at McGill University in nuclear-magnetic resonance spectroscopy. In her leisure she pursued her lifelong interest in art and progressed from figure drawing and painting to her most-loved medium when she began to sculpt in black-and-white marble and bronze. Barbara's works have found a home in many international and Canadian collections and museums and she has had six solo exhibits at the prestigious Dominion Gallery in Montreal. Legendary gallery owner Dr. Max Stern stated, "Simplicity and symbol, these two principles form the goals and guidelines of Barbara Kuper's work." Her sculptures are marked with the concern for exactness and clarity that one expects to find in someone with a penchant for science. If all art speaks to the heart and the feelings, Barbara insisted in addressing the intellect as well. Barbara died on September 22, 2016, in her ninety-seventh year, surrounded by her family.

**Eva Kuper** was born at the start of World War II in Warsaw, Poland. Eva survived the war by a series of miraculous events involving luck, coincidence and the courage and faith of several individuals, both family members and virtual strangers, especially the incredible Sister Klara Jaroszyńska. In 1949, Eva and her family immigrated to Canada, where she grew up "practically Canadian" with the history of the Holocaust always in the background. She was educated at Sir George Williams University and Concordia, spending the major part of her work life in education and educational administration. Eva has taught and directed programs and workshops for children and adults in a variety of settings including early childhood development centres, elementary schools, Vanier College and Concordia University. She was Principal of Jewish Peoples' Schools and Peretz Schools. Eva retired in 2005 and has made Holocaust education an important mission in her life. She sits on the board of the Montreal Holocaust Memorial Centre and is an active volunteer at the Jewish General Hospital, Child Psychiatry Department; the Cummings Jewish Centre for Seniors; and Temple Emanu-El Beth Sholom. Her free time is spent with family, friends, and pursuing her many interests such as reading, hiking, skiing and cultural activities such as cinema, theatre and concerts.

**Helen Mahut** (1920–2010) was born as Walentyna Dudekzak in Kiev, Russia. She passed as a Catholic girl during the war, joined the Polish resistance in Warsaw and administered refugee camps after the war. Helen immigrated to Canada in 1949, joining her husband, Stefan Mahut. She earned a doctorate in 1955 at McGill University in physiological and comparative psychology. An accomplished researcher specializing in behavioural and cognitive neuroscience, she taught in the psychology department at Northeastern University in Boston for twenty-three years. Helen passed away on March 7, 2010, at age ninety.

**Catherine Matyas** (née Grunfeld) was born in Debrecen, Hungary, on July 11, 1928. In 1942, Catherine's father, Ignatz, was drafted into the Hungarian forced labour service and disappeared on the Soviet front. In the spring of 1944, she and her mother, Esther, her younger brother, Tibor, and her maternal grandparents, Aron and Gizi, were sent to the Debrecen ghetto. They were deported from the ghetto to a transit point in Strasshof, then to Lobau, a suburb of Vienna, and later to a labour camp in a school in Vienna, working as forced labourers. In early 1945 in Vienna, her brother, Tibor, who was disabled, was taken away; they never saw him again. The rest of the family was sent to a holding area on Hackengasse in Vienna, and in early March 1945 they were deported to the Terezín (Theresienstadt) concentration camp/ghetto. Although the family starved, they managed to survive until liberation in May 1945. After the war, Catherine finished school in Debrecen and in 1948 she left for Paris, where one year later she met and married her husband, Herman. Their daughter Yvette was born in 1951, and the family, unable to receive French citizenship, immigrated to Montreal in 1955. There, Catherine and Herman set up a business and had their second daughter, Hedy, in 1959. Catherine Matyas lives in Montreal.

**Dyna Perelmuter** (1921–2010) wrote her memoir in Polish in 1999 and titled it *Mewa* (seagull), after her nickname as a child — *mewa* was a term of endearment for someone lively and gregarious. After the war, Dyna reunited with her brother Shimshon and her sister Ruza (who had left Palestine in the 1950s) in Montreal and travelled to Israel to reunite with her brother Benjamin and her sister Rifka. Dyna had a lifelong interest in art, politics and world affairs, and after her retirement, she enrolled in painting classes at Concordia University and took courses on current events at McGill University's

School of Continuing Studies. Dyna's daughters, Sophia and Wendy, describe their mother as incredibly resilient, generously loving and fabulously mischievous.

**Irena Peritz** and her family left Poland in 1949 to rebuild their lives in Montreal. Her first years in the city brought their share of challenges, but Irena established the foundation of a rewarding new life. She found work as a filing clerk at a pharmaceutical firm, which helped her to learn English. She met her husband, Simon, in a choir and gave birth to their first child, Nina, in 1954. A son, Paul, followed in 1957 and a second daughter, Ingrid, in 1959. Irena devoted herself to the family. When the children had grown up, she joined a jogging group at the local Y W H A. Hiking mountains across North America became her passion and spending summers at a lakefront camp in Maine, her favourite pastime. Irena appreciates the wonder and beauty that each day brings, marveling at the inner strength she didn't know she had. She feels blessed to have survived the war with her late sister and parents and grateful for the time she is able to spend with her three children and four grandchildren. Irena is eighty-eight and lives in Montreal.

**Gitlia Popovsky** was born in 1922 in the shtetl of Skvyra, Ukraine. In 1926, six years after the notorious pogroms, she and her parents moved to Kiev. In 1941, during the Nazi occupation, she escaped right before Babi Yar, the massacre of Jews in Kiev, and was evacuated to Uzbekistan; she lived there with her parents, under terrible conditions, until she returned to Kiev in the summer of 1944. In 1945, Gitlia married her husband, Abraham, and they had two children, Roman and Sofia. Abraham passed away in 1968, when Gitlia was forty-six years old. In 1977, Gitlia immigrated to Canada, settling in Montreal. By doing so, she reunited four generations of her family — her mother, Paisa Budnitsky, herself, her daughter, Sofia Zatulovsky, and her granddaughter, Albinna Abitan. Later on, her family grew with the fifth generation, her great-grandchildren, Joshua, Daniel, Jamie (Shmuel), Maya (Flora) and, most recently, Leah. Gitlia is proud to be the matriarch of such a large family. She has lived the best years of her life in Canada and currently resides at Maimonides Geriatric Centre in Montreal.

**Suzanne (Katz) Reich** (1930–1994) was born in Kisvárda, Hungary. She wrote *Sometimes I Can Dream Again* in 1982 as a testimony to the power of resilience — her resilience of surviving Auschwitz as a young girl. Suzanne's parents were murdered at Auschwitz; her sister, Mary, survived and she and Suzanne were reunited after the war. Suzanne immigrated to Canada in 1949 and married Peter Reich on June 18, 1950. They went on to parent two daughters, Edwina and Sandra, and had a happy marriage until her death in 1994. Suzanne had an incredible passion for art, culture, cooking and life in general. She believed strongly in the power of conviction and never turning your back on people being persecuted. She fought passionately in the civil rights movement and against discrimination of any kind. Her story of "dreaming again" exemplifies the power of the human spirit and the choices we make when faced with terrible adversities.

**Koine Schachter Rogel** (1911–2002) was born in Ciudin, Bukovina. She was the youngest of eight children; two of her brothers, Abraham and Itzik, had immigrated to Detroit before the war; her brother Mattias studied medicine in the states and in Italy; and two other brothers, Gedalia and Moishe, as well as a sister, Fanny, lived in Montreal. Koine grew up with her father, Chaim, the town *shochet* and cantor, her mother, Miriam, and her sister Fraydeh. Her mother passed away in 1930 and her father remarried. Koine spent the war years in Transnistria and managed to survive the ordeal together with her family. After the war, Koine met and married Josef Rogel and, together with the rest of Koine's family, they immigrated to Montreal in 1949. Unfortunately, Koine's father, Chaim, did not survive the trip. Koine and

Josef eventually earned a good living by selling lunches in an industrial area that housed many clothing factories. Josef later wrote poetry, and his poems were translated and published in both English and German. Josef passed away in 1989; although Koine was widowed for many years and had no children of her own, she had long-standing relationships with her nieces and nephews, who visited regularly and enjoyed her wry sense of humour. Koine passed away in Montreal on July 6, 2002.

**Magda Sebestian** was born in Sečovce, Slovakia, in 1928. After surviving the war with her immediate family, she continued her schooling in Košice. She graduated in 1948 and enrolled in the Faculty of Medicine of the University in Brno, completing her studies in 1953. Magda met her husband, Ady, in 1945 and they married in 1949. In 1954, their son, Ivan, was born. Tania, their daughter, was born in 1962. Magda worked in pediatric cardiology until 1968, at which point she and her family fled to Vienna after the Soviet army invaded Czechoslovakia to quash the liberation movement for democratic freedom. In October 1968, they immigrated to Toronto. There, Magda worked to obtain her medical credentials, passing her licencing examination in 1971. She worked at Women's College Hospital where she became acting chief of the Department of Neonatology for two years. She opened a private practice in 1975. Magda retired in 1999 and enjoys spending time with her family, especially her two grandchildren, Matthew and Jessica.

**Rebekah (Relli) Schmerler-Katz** (1923–2005) emigrated from Czechoslovakia to Duparquet, Quebec, where her uncle lived, in 1948. Before the war, her uncle had tried, in vain, to sponsor her family to emigrate and escape the looming dangers for Jews in Europe. Yet it was only after the immigration policy for Jews changed that she could come to Canada along with her sole surviving relatives — her mother and sister. Relli then sponsored her fiancé, Sam Katz, whom she had met in Czechoslovakia soon after the war. Sam had survived a labour camp but had lost almost his entire family. They married in 1949 and tried to normalize as much as possible under difficult circumstances, choosing to maintain their values of caring for others and working hard. They had one daughter, Shirley. They were fiercely dedicated parents, in-laws and grandparents to Shirley's three children, Stephanie, Robert and Caroline. Relli had an incredible sense of commitment to others, and agreed to write her memoirs at the urging of her son-in-law in the hope that by describing these true events, future generations would understand what can happen when a seemingly normal world gets taken over by irrationality, cruelty and unaccountability. Relli and Sam led successful, ethical lives. Their resilience was always evident but especially so when they provided their dedicated support during the chronic illness and loss of their first grandchild, Stephanie, who passed away at age eight.

**Babey Widutschinsky Trepman** (1924–2009) was born in Šiaulai, Lithuania. She survived the war alongside her sister, Dora. The sisters were held in the Šiaulai ghetto, Stutthof and Bergen-Belsen, from which they were liberated on April 15, 1945. In the Displaced Persons (DP) camp at Belsen, Babey was the musical accompanist for the Kazet Theatre. With her husband, Paul Trepman, whom she met in Belsen, she immigrated to Montreal, where they started a new life together. She taught hundreds of kindergarteners at the Solomon Schechter Academy for more than four decades, and was a devoted bubby to her six grandchildren. Babey was passionate about living life to the fullest. She was an avid gym-goer, folk dancer and reader, and loved to attend concerts, theatre and lectures. Her schedule was always full and she never let physical or health issues impact her life. She travelled the world, visiting many countries, including South Africa, Cuba, New Zealand, Peru and Thailand. On her last major trip, she was able to visit her sister, Dora, who had moved to Hawaii to be near her children and grandchildren. Babey Trepman died on June 7, 2009.

**Fela Yoskovitz-Ross** (née Pacanowska) was born in 1921 in Lodz, Poland. She endured the Lodz ghetto — where she worked in factories making the upper parts of shoes and the military emblems on uniforms — with her parents and two brothers until the ghetto was liquidated. In August 1944, Fela and her family were deported to Auschwitz. Fela was later transferred to a forced labour camp in Hamburg, Germany, a subcamp of the Neuengamme concentration camp. In September 1944 she was transferred to another subcamp in the Hamburg suburb of Poppenbüttel, where she removed rubble after the frequent bombardments. In early April, the camp was evacuated and Fela was deported to Bergen-Belsen; she was liberated by the British army on April 15, 1945. Fela met her husband, Jacob, in Bergen-Belsen and they immigrated to Canada, settling in Montreal, in 1948. As Fela raised her two children, Mike and Allen, she became the person in the neighbourhood that everyone went to for advice, whether it was on hairdos, makeup or medicinal cures. In the late 1960s and 70s, Fela was president of Hadassah. Fela lives at the Maimonides Geriatric Centre in Montreal.

**Chana-Mindla Wolkowicz** (née Mina Herzlikowicz) (1920–2003) was born in Piotrków Trybunalski, Poland. When the war broke out, she was in the Soviet Union with her husband, Herman Geisler. They were convicted as spies and sent to the Gulag. Their daughter, Lily, was born on December 22, 1943, after Mina and Herman had managed to reunite; he later died on the frontlines. After the war, Mina met and married Pinchas Wolkowicz in Lodz; their son Henry was born in 1948. The Wolkowicz family immigrated to Canada in 1949 and lived in Montreal. Mina worked as a furrier to help support their new family of three — her son Nathan was born in 1950. Mina was also a writer and many of her articles were published in the *Jewish Forward*. In 1960, Mina's husband, Pinchas, suffered a severe heart attack and Mina had to fully support the family. Pinchas passed away in 1976. When Mina retired from work, she and took up sculpture and painting. She was extremely successful and had several shows.

Mina was also involved in helping Russian immigrants in Canada. In the 1990s, Mina moved to Cambridge, Ontario, to be closer to family. Her son Henry lives in Cambridge. Her daughter, Lily, and son Nathan both developed multiple sclerosis and passed away, in 2008 and 2011, respectively.

**Irene Zoberman** (1914–1982) was born in Sandomierz, a town on the Vistula River in Poland. She was the second-eldest of four daughters in her family. Twenty-five years old when World War II began, Irene spent much of the war years in Warsaw. Having obtained false documents establishing a Christian identity for herself to be safe there, she became an active member of the anti-German underground. She located false papers to help her family members find safety in Poland and raised money to fund her parents', sisters' and other Jews' escapes from labour camps. Irene found places for them to hide in Warsaw and acquired equipment to manufacture false papers to save many Jews. After the war, Irene spent time in Canada, Israel and Poland. She was married twice relatively late in life and lived between Toronto, Canada, and Miami, Florida. Although she did not have children of her own, she was close to her sisters and loved and adored by their children. Irene would tell her nieces and nephews that, "You are my children too." Irene was responsible for saving many lives during the war and those in the generations to come.

# Index

The Azrieli Foundation was established in 1989 to realize and extend the philanthropic vision of David J. Azrieli, C.M., C.Q., M.Arch. The Foundation's mission is to support a wide spectrum of initiatives in education and research. The Azrieli Foundation is an active supporter of programs in the fields of Education, the education of architects, scientific and medical research, and the arts. The Azrieli Foundation's many initiatives include: the Holocaust Survivor Memoirs Program, which collects, preserves, publishes and distributes the written memoirs of survivors in Canada; the Azrieli Institute for Educational Empowerment, an innovative program successfully working to keep at-risk youth in school; the Azrieli Fellows Program, which promotes academic excellence and leadership on the graduate level at Israeli universities; the Azrieli Music Project, which celebrates and fosters the creation of high-quality new Jewish orchestral music; and the Azrieli Neurodevelopmental Research Program, which supports advanced research on neurodevelopmental disorders, particularly Fragile X and Autism Spectrum Disorders.